The Confederate Battle Flag

America's Most Embattled Emblem

JOHN M. COSKI

THE BELKNAP PRESS OF
HARVARD UNIVERSITY PRESS
Cambridge, Massachusetts, and London, England

Printed in the United States of America

First Harvard University Press paperback edition, 2006

Library of Congress Cataloging-in-Publication Data
Coski, John M.
    The Confederate battle flag : America's most embattled emblem /
John M. Coski.
        p.   cm.
    Includes bibliographical references and index.
    ISBN 0-674-01722-6 (cloth: alk. paper)
    ISBN 0-674-01983-0 (pbk.)
    1. Flags—Confederate States of America.   2. United States—History—Civil War,
1861–1865—Flags.   3. Symbolism in politics—Southern States.   4. Symbolism in
politics—United States.   I. Title.

CR113.5.C67 2005
929.9'2'0975—dc22   2004055407

To the memory of Christopher Dean Fullerton,
a serious student of southern history who could
make us laugh at anything—even southern history.

Preface

On July 12, 1993, the public debate over the Confederate flag found its way onto the floor of the United States Senate. "The fact of the matter is the emblems of the Confederacy have meaning to Americans even 100 years after the end of the Civil War," observed Illinois Senator Carol Moseley-Braun, the Senate's only African-American member. "Everybody knows what the Confederacy stands for . . . Now, in this time, in 1993, when we see the Confederate symbols hauled out, everybody knows what that means." Senator Moseley-Braun certainly knew what Confederate symbols meant to her—virulent racism—and her speech was powerful enough to persuade her colleagues not to renew a special congressional patent for the insignia of the United Daughters of the Confederacy. Others, outraged by her speech and its impact, were equally certain what Confederate symbols meant to them: a proud heritage and the honor of their ancestors.[1] Moseley-Braun's widely publicized speech and the reaction to it highlighted the essential point at issue in the debates over the Confederate flag. Certainly, in 1993, or in 2005, a lot of people who see Confederate symbols "hauled out" have very strong opinions about what those symbols mean to them. But they hardly agree on the meaning of Confederate symbols—on what the Confederacy stood for or what it means when its symbols are hauled out today.

Ten years after Moseley-Braun's Senate speech, Democratic presidential candidate Howard Dean raised a firestorm when he told a reporter, "I still want to be the candidate for guys with Confederate flags in their pick-up trucks. We can't beat George Bush unless we appeal to a broad cross section of Democrats." Rivals for the Democratic presidential nomination pilloried Dean for embracing "one of the most divisive, hurtful symbols in American history" and denied that the party needed to court people who fly Confederate flags. Political commentators observed that Dean's appeal to a stereotype managed to offend African Americans and insult white rural southerners at the same time.[2] Howard Dean metaphorically hauled out the Confederate flag to invite white southerners into the Democratic Party tent. His detractors chose to interpret his remark as an invitation to racism. Once again, a high-profile discussion of the Confederate flag on the national political stage revealed divergent understandings of its meaning.

The Confederate Battle Flag explores the history behind the continuing conflict over the St. Andrew's cross battle flag—the most familiar, potent, and embattled of all Confederate emblems. The book traces the origins of the flag, the evolution of its diverse use and meanings, the reactions to the flag over the course of its history, and how these uses, meanings, and reactions have been played out in the controversies of recent decades. It rests on the simple proposition that a symbol's use determines its meanings and affects the way people perceive it. Commonsensical as this approach is, it is dismissed by those who believe that the meaning of the flag (or of any symbol) is fixed and absolute—that there is one true or legitimate meaning and that others are deliberate or ignorant distortions. In contrast, this book is explicitly relativist. Rather than judging the various readings of the flag as right or wrong, correct or incorrect, it seeks to help readers understand how those meanings originated and why people believe them. In response to the flaw identified and exemplified by Senator Moseley-Braun and by her critics, it seeks to distinguish between what Confederate symbols mean to one person and what they mean in general.[3]

This book began in 1992 with research for an exhibition at The Museum of the Confederacy in Richmond, Virginia. "Embattled Emblem: The Army of Northern Virginia Pattern Battle Flag, 1861 to the Present" presented the full history of the battle flag, in order to explore the historical reasons for different perspectives on the flag. To the consternation of partisans on all sides, the exhibit did not attempt to vindicate any viewpoint or lead viewers to a conclusion. Instead, the exhibit objectively presented the history of the flag's use and literally gave voice to a variety of different viewpoints in the form of audiotape comments from spokesmen representing organizations involved in the flag debates. The guiding question in creating "Embattled Emblem" was: What does the viewer need to know in order to understand the modern debate over the battle flag? The guiding question of this book is the same as that of the exhibit.

The years spent on this book have been eventful ones in the history of the battle flag. When "Embattled Emblem" opened, the new governor of Alabama had just declared that he would not challenge a court order ending the display of the battle flag over the state capitol. After a bruising political battle, Georgia Governor Zell Miller had conceded defeat in his effort to remove the battle flag motif from the Georgia state flag; his effort provoked the formation of powerful pro-flag lobbying groups. In 2004 Georgians voted overwhelmingly in favor of a new flag that closely resembles the one for which Miller had lobbied unsuccessfully in 1993. Mississippi also held a popular referendum in which two-thirds of its citizens decided to retain a state flag featuring the battle flag motif. In the years between, South Carolina went through three distinct rounds of extremely divisive conflict over the battle flag that had flown over the state capitol since 1962. Hundreds of controversies occurred over battle flags in public schools and universities and government buildings. In Tennessee, an African-American teenager fatally shot a young white man apparently because he flew a Confederate battle flag in the back of his pick-up truck.

Researching a subject very much in the news occasionally seduced me into believing that this book could be a work of contemporary reporting. It became clear that I did not have the wherewithal to follow breaking stories and interview all the people involved and interested in modern flag controversies. In the end, this is a work of history—history that informs and is informed by current events.

Even so delineated, the topic is limitless and fraught with potential pitfalls. Nearly every southern community (and many northern ones) has a historical or contemporary story to tell about the battle flag: as the scene of a Confederate veterans reunion or a public event celebrating southern identity, or as home to a high school with a Confederate mascot, or as a front-page story about a bitter interracial controversy surrounding that event or mascot. Nearly every public library or museum has materials that could provide more details and possibly new perspectives on the history of the flag. For that reason, this study cannot claim to be comprehensive. It is based on an examination of diverse published and unpublished sources which have yielded clear patterns that subsequent research has confirmed and validated. The study is also subject to the vagaries of the evidence. Determining whether or not the battle flag was used in any situation depends upon eyewitnesses mentioning it or capturing it on film. Is the absence of references to the flag an indication of the flag's absence or, on the contrary, an indication that it was so commonplace as to not warrant notice?

Most people who follow the debates over the Confederate flag are emotionally or ideologically engaged with the issue. I do not share that emotional or ideological engagement. My reaction to the debates is amazement at others' strongly held and strongly expressed opinions. I do not share the reverence for the Confederate heritage (as opposed to an interest in Confederate history) that blinds so many people to truths that seem painfully clear to others. Similarly, I cannot share the hurt and the offense that African Americans feel toward the flag. I do not believe that anyone's hurt feelings or people's desire to feel good about themselves should be the basis of how we perceive history or decide public policy. After considerable *angst,* I have concluded that this detachment from the emotions surrounding the issue is a virtue.

Debates over the Confederate battle flag have inflamed passions and garnered headlines but are still portrayed as sideshows, distractions from truly important public policy issues. Not surprisingly, I have come to the opposite conclusion. The battle over the battle flag represents one of the most intensive and extensive ongoing public dialogues about U.S. history. The debate over the proper place of the Confederate battle flag in American life is an important means by which citizens engage with the meaning of the Civil War and its legacies. More specifically, the flag debates offer a barometer of modern popular perceptions of the Confederate States of America. The Confederacy was the most important organized and armed dissent in American history since the Revolution. The conflicting attitudes toward it reflect accurately the divergent views on constitutional and racial issues that have persisted from the nineteenth century to our own day, despite the Civil War and despite the civil rights movement. A careful exploration of the history of the Confederate battle flag reveals the fundamental disagreements among Americans about our past, our present, and our future.

Contents

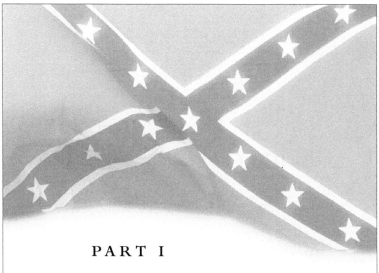

PART I

Confederate Flag

The familiar red flag with a star-studded blue diagonal cross was never the national flag of the Confederate States of America—it never flew over government buildings or other facilities. By the middle of the Civil War, however, it was the most visible Confederate battle flag pattern and had become the most important symbol of the fledgling nation. The blue St. Andrew's cross (or, more correctly, the saltire) on the red flag became in effect what it never technically was: *the* Confederate flag. The chapters in Part I explore the origins of the flag, its wartime use, and the subsequent decades during which the Confederate generation of southerners made it the primary Confederate symbol. The era from the Civil War through World War II was a relatively coherent period of the flag's history, especially in contrast to the subsequent half-century. For those 85 years, the Confederate battle flag was the object of virtually uncontested public reverence in the South and increasing acceptance from the rest of the nation. Few people abused the flag, and few people complained openly about its public presence. Not coincidentally, African Americans were virtually excluded from the South's public life during most of those years.

Chapter 1

"Emblem of a Separate and
Independent Nation"

The search for symbols of an independent Confederate nation began before the formation of the Confederacy itself. The leaders of the states that seceded from the Union in 1860 and 1861 believed that they were legitimately repossessing the sovereignty that their states had delegated conditionally upon joining the Union. When they formed the Confederate States of America in February 1861, southern statesmen made the conditional nature of union explicit in their new Constitution. The trappings of sovereignty were especially important to men who staked so much on constitutional theory, so it was not surprising that the states of the new Confederacy adopted seals and flags expressing their identities as sovereign entities.[1]

The most popular symbols in the heady first months of secession were the palmetto tree—a symbol of secessionist pioneer South Carolina—and the so-called Bonnie Blue Flag. Immortalized in southern lore by a song composed in early 1861 by Harry Macarthy, the Bonnie Blue Flag was simply a blue flag bearing a single white star. In early 1861, several southern states incorporated the Bonnie Blue into their new state flags, and a few military units adopted it as their battle flag.[2] The flag most symbolic of southern separatism and martial spirit in early 1861, the Bonnie Blue, however, never achieved prominence as a symbol of the Confederate nation.

Among its first acts, the Provisional Congress of the new Confederacy on February 9, 1861, appointed a Committee on the Flag and Seal chaired by William Porcher Miles of South Carolina. The committee solicited ideas from citizens and officials alike and received hundreds of design suggestions. Many of them the committee dismissed as "elaborate, complicated, or fantastical." Many others, much to the dismay of William Miles, urged the adoption of a flag that preserved "the principal features" of the Stars and Stripes. The committee was "overwhelmed with memorials not to abandon the 'old flag,'" Miles complained to a sympathetic correspondent. One Confederate sympathizer living in Washington, D.C., urged Miles to "Let the Yankees keep their ridiculous tune of 'Yankee Doodle,' but by all that is sacred, do not let them monopolize the stars and stripes." A woman in Savannah, Georgia, submitted a design along with some unsolicited advice. "Although I have not much more veneration than you for the stars & stripes, there are many who have, whose feelings, or fancies have a right to be respected," wrote M. E. Huger. "Besides, it is a flag well known & respected, & does not represent to the world our oppressions & wrongs—but—the independance [sic] & prosperity of a great country."[3]

Miles scorned such thinking. He told the committee that he had always regarded the Stars and Stripes as a flag of "tyranny" and was, he later claimed, "terribly abused for doing so." In his March 4, 1861, committee report, Miles explained his opposition to the Stars and Stripes, but, in deference to the majority, struck a conciliatory pose:

> Whatever attachment may be felt, from association, for the "Stars and Stripes" (an attachment which your committee may be permitted to say they do not all share), it is manifest that in inaugurating a new government we can

not with any propriety, or without encountering very obvious practical difficulties, retain the flag of the Government from which we have withdrawn. There is no propriety in retaining the ensign of a government which, in the
opinion of the States composing this Confederacy, had become so oppressive and injurious to their interests as to require their separation from it. It is idle to talk of "keeping"
the flag of the United States when we have voluntarily seceded from them.

"It must be admitted, however," Miles added, "that something was conceded by the committee to what seemed so strong and earnest a desire to
retain at least a suggestion of the old 'Stars and Stripes.'"[4]

Indeed, the design recommended by the committee and approved by
the Provisional Congress became known as the Stars and Bars and was
ultimately renounced for resembling too closely the Stars and Stripes.
The new flag consisted of three horizontal stripes, alternating red and
white, with a union (or canton) of blue emblazoned with a circle of
white stars corresponding to the number of states in the Confederacy.
Red, white, and blue—the colors of the Stars and Stripes—were, Miles
wrote, "the true republican colors," representing in heraldry the virtues
of valor, purity, and truth, respectively.[5]

While the Stars and Bars later proved unpopular with many opinion
makers in the South and impractical on the battlefield, the flag was the
object of popular enthusiasm in the months following its adoption. As
the new nation's first official standard, the Stars and Bars was celebrated
in song and poetry. Harry Macarthy, author of the "Bonnie Blue Flag,"
also published "Our Flag and Its Origins," also known as "Origin of the
Stars and Bars." Echoing the sentiments of those citizens who implored
William Miles to adopt the Stars and Bars, Macarthy's lyrics lamented
the abandonment of the old Union and its symbols:

> But alas! For the flag of my youth
> I have sighed and dropped my last tear
> For the North has forgotten her truth,

And would tread on the rights we hold dear;
They envied the South her bright stars,
Her glory, her honor, her fame,
So we unfurl'd the Stars and Bars
and the CONFEDERATE FLAG is its name.[6]

William Miles's disappointment with the Stars and Bars went beyond his strong ideological objections to the Stars and Stripes. He had hoped that the Confederacy would adopt his own design for a national flag—the pattern that later generations mistakenly and ironically insisted on calling the Stars and Bars. The design that Miles championed was apparently inspired by one of the flags used at the South Carolina secession convention in December 1860. That flag featured a blue St. George's (or upright) cross on a red field. Emblazoned on the cross were fifteen white stars representing the slaveholding states, and on the red field were two symbols of South Carolina: the palmetto tree and the crescent. Charles Moise, a self-described "southerner of Jewish persuasion," wrote Miles and other members of the South Carolina delegation asking that "the symbol of a particular religion" not be made the symbol of the nation.[7]

In adapting his flag to take these criticisms into account, Miles removed the palmetto tree and crescent and substituted a diagonal cross for the St. George's cross. Recalling (and sketching) his proposal a few months later, Miles explained that the diagonal cross was preferable because "it avoided the *religious* objection about the cross (from the Jews & many Protestant sects), because it did not stand out so *conspicuously* as if the cross had been placed upright thus." The diagonal cross was, Miles argued, "more *Heraldric* [sic] than *Ecclesiastical,* it being the 'saltire' of Heraldry, and significant of *strength* and *progress* (from the Latin *salto,* to leap)."[8]

Although Miles diplomatically described the cross as the saltire, a heraldic device (and an act of the Confederate Congress later described it as a "saltier"), his contemporaries and subsequent generations have tended to identify it as a cross, specifically as a St. Andrew's cross—a familiar symbol in Western culture. The X-shaped cross derived its name from the first-century Christian martyr who did not believe himself worthy to die on the same kind of cross as Jesus Christ. Crucified in 69 A.D., Andrew's remains were transported to the Scottish coast in the fourth century. He later became the patron saint of Scotland and his cross the symbol of Scotland. The St. Andrew's cross was incorporated into the new British flag in 1606 when King James VI of Scotland became King James I of England.[9]

While medieval tournaments, the novels of Sir Walter Scott, and other expressions of romanticized Scottish culture permeated the antebellum South, the St. Andrew's cross enjoyed no special place in southern iconography. If Miles had not been eager to conciliate southern Jews, the traditional Latin (or St. George's), cross would have adorned his flag. Whatever Miles's concern for avoiding "conspicuous" religious symbolism, the Confederacy was an overtly religious state with appeals to God in the Preamble of its Constitution and a penchant for Christian symbols in its flags. Despite serving as committee chairman, Miles was unable to impose his pet design upon the committee. His critics supposedly scoffed that the diagonal cross looked "like a pair of suspenders." Miles's faith in this motif was eventually vindicated, of course, but vindication came via the circuitous route of the Confederate army.[10]

When the secession of the Deep South states precipitated war between the United States and the Confederate States at Fort Sumter, South Carolina, in April 1861, the Confederacy's survival became dependent on its military forces. Not surprisingly, the symbols of the Confederate army and navy became important to the nation as a whole, especially when approximately three-quarters of the South's white males between 17 and 45 served in those forces. In addition to adopting a new national standard, Confederates demonstrated their patriotism with battle flags presented to their military units.

In the years before the outbreak of war in 1861, local volunteer and militia companies were formed in preparation for what seemed the inevitable conflict. Those units often received from the ladies of their communities silk flags, usually bearing the state seal and a company motto. When the local companies mustered into Confederate service in the spring and summer of 1861, these home-made silk flags entered the service with them.[11] A few were carried throughout the war, but most were packed away and sent home early. Consistent with military tradition, Confederate regiments carried standard-issue battle flags. Regimental flags marked the positions of forces on the battlefield and assisted officers in maneuvering their troops. The flags also served as sources of unit pride and morale. On the battlefield and in the memory of the war, battle flags became the focus of a unit's *esprit de corps*. Although the practice was not regulated by law or military order, many of the regiments that entered the armies of the Confederacy in the spring of 1861 carried the Stars and Bars as their battle flag.

The outbreak of war and Lincoln's call for 75,000 volunteers to crush the "rebellion" prompted Virginia, Arkansas, Tennessee, and North Carolina to secede, shifting the military frontiers northward. In Virginia, Brigadier General Pierre Gustav Toutant Beauregard, the Louisiana native who had led Confederate troops opposing Fort Sumter, commanded the troops concentrated at the important railroad junction at Manassas, 25 miles south of Washington, D.C. Beauregard called his nascent force the Army of the Potomac. Further to the west, Brigadier General Joseph Eggleston Johnston commanded a force (the Army of the Shenandoah Valley) at Winchester, facing a Federal garrison at Harpers Ferry. Beauregard, formerly the superintendent of the U.S. Military Academy at West Point, and Johnston, formerly U.S. Army quartermaster general, were two of the five highest-ranking generals in the Confederate army. They were also the men most instrumental in adopting and diffusing the St. Andrew's cross battle flag.

The first major engagement of the Civil War occurred on July 21, 1861, at Manassas (Bull Run) when the Federal army under General Irwin McDowell confronted Beauregard's Army of the Potomac. McDowell's plan to turn Beauregard's left flank went awry. Johnston's army slipped away unnoticed from Winchester, arrived at Manassas early on the 21st, and turned the tide against the Federals. The inexperience of the troops on both sides, combined with complex maneuvering, made Manassas a very confusing battle for soldiers and commanders.

Adding a further complication was the similarity of uniforms and battle flags. At least one Confederate regiment fired on another Confederate regiment, possibly because it was unable to distinguish between battle flags. Beauregard recalled dramatically that late in the afternoon of the battle, when "victory was already within our grasp," he spied an unidentified force on his left flank. Fearing that it might be Federal reinforcements arriving on the field, he stared at a flag among the troops but could not tell whether it was Confederate or Federal. The force turned out to be Brigadier General Jubal Early's Confederate brigade, and the flag was the Stars and Bars of the 7th Louisiana Infantry.[12]

After the battle, Beauregard "resolved then to have [our flag] changed if possible, or to adopt for my command a 'Battle flag,' which would be Entirely different from any State or Federal flag." For assistance Beauregard turned to the man who had served as his aide during the summer of 1861: William Porcher Miles. In late August, when Miles was back in Richmond for the last days of the legislative session, he described to Beauregard his "favorite" pattern which he had unsuccessfully urged upon the Congress.[13] Miles told the Committee on the Flag and Seal of the general's complaints and recommended that the flag be changed. As expected, the committee rejected the proposal by a 4–1 vote. General Beauregard proposed to his commander, General Johnston, that the army try something different.

> I wrote to [Miles] that we should have *two* flags—a *peace* or parade flag, and a *war* flag to be used only on the field of battle—but congress having adjourned no action will be taken on the matter—How would it do for us to address the War Dept. on the subject for a supply of Regimental or badge flags made of red with two blue bars crossing each other diagonally on which shall be introduced the stars, the edge of the flag to be trimmed all around with white, yellow or gold fringe? We would then on the field of battle know our friends from our Enemies.[14]

The high command of the Virginia army met at Fairfax Court House in September to adopt a new battle flag. Beauregard later remembered that James B. Walton, colonel of the elite Washington Artillery of New Orleans, had submitted a design nearly identical to Miles's, but with a Latin cross instead of the St. Andrew's cross. Beauregard, like Miles, preferred the St. Andrew's cross, since it "removed the objection that many of our soldier[s] might have to fight under the former symbol." Walton subsequently claimed that Edward M. Hancock of New Orleans designed the Confederate battle flag at Walton's request in April 1861. Miles took umbrage at this claim and wrote an indignant letter to his old friend Beauregard reminding him of his sponsorship of the battle flag as the national flag in February 1861.[15]

In any case, a blue cross with white or gold stars emblazoned on a red field was the clear choice as the battle flag of the Confederate army in Virginia. The designs considered to that point all had been rectangular or, in the parlance of the day, "oblong." General Johnston suggested that the battle flag should be perfectly square and thus better proportioned and that they be standard sizes varying according to service branch: forty-eight inches square for infantry regiments, thirty-six inches for artillery batteries, and thirty inches for cavalry regiments. Beauregard and the other officers agreed.[16]

The army's quartermaster, General William L. Cabell, also present at the Fairfax Court House meeting, was ordered to arrange for prototypes to be made. He delegated the task to another officer, Captain Colin M. Selph, who asked Mary Lyons (Jones), an Alabama woman living in Richmond, to create a model. Selph then gave this model to Constance Cary and her cousins, Hetty and Jennie Cary, to produce prototypes for the army's consideration. The Cary flags assumed legendary proportions in Confederate history. "It is generally stated by historians that these flags were constructed from our own dresses," wrote Constance Cary, "but it is certain we possessed no wearing apparel in the flamboyant hues of poppy red and vivid dark blue required." Each girl presented her flag to a Confederate general: Jennie to Beauregard, Hetty to Johnston, and Constance to Earl Van Dorn who, for a brief time, commanded a division in Beauregard's army. Selph purchased large quantities of silk from at least one Richmond dry goods merchant, and consigned the task of making 120 silk regimental flags to 75 women in four Richmond churches. Some units received flags of the new pattern at the end of October. Beauregard issued orders on November 24th that "in the event of an action with the enemy, the new battle flag recently issued to the regiments of this army corps will alone be carried on the field. Meantime regimental commanders will accustom their men to the flag, so that they may be thoroughly acquainted with it."[17]

On the afternoon of November 28, 1861, the army (still at that point known as the Army of the Potomac) was assembled on the heights overlooking Centreville, Virginia, to formally receive the new battle flags. "The day for our division went off admirably," wrote staff officer G. Moxley Sorrel. "It was brilliant weather, and all were in their best outfits, and on their best mounts. The troops looked well as the colonels successively received their colors to defend." General Beauregard issued a general order that officers read to the troops:

> A new banner is intrusted to-day, as a battle-flag, to the safe keeping of the Army of the Potomac. Soldiers: Your mothers, your wives, and your sisters have made it. Consecrated by their hands, it must lead you to substantial victory, and the complete triumph of our cause. It can never be surrendered, save to your unspeakable dishonor, and with its consequences fraught with immeasurable evil. Under its untarnished folds beat back the invader, and find nationality, everlasting immunity from an atrocious despotism, and honor and renown for yourselves—or death.[18]

The ceremony was, according to a soldier in the 4th South Carolina Infantry, "the grandest time we have ever had. We were told that the flags were made and sent to us by our wives, mothers, and sisters, with an order to defend them. We will most assuredly obey that order. We were drawn up in a hollow square and several speeches were made . . . I have never heard or seen such a time before. The noise of the men was deafening. I felt at the time that I could whip a whole brigade of the enemy myself, but after due reflection I concluded I couldn't." "We received another beautiful flag a few days ago," wrote Sam Payne, of the 19th Virginia Infantry, to his cousin. "It is called a battle flag and to be used only in an engagement. I think it much the prettiest one we have. It is beautiful read [sic] silk with a deep blue cross on it and a stare [sic] representing each state in the cross."[19]

The elaborate ceremony and the importance of the event made the distribution of the new flags a memorable event, recounted in many letters and diaries. Familiar with the confusion that had occurred on the Manassas battlefield, soldiers and officers alike were happy to receive a distinctive "war banner" or "fighting colors," and some soldiers described or sketched the new emblem for their families. "You know it was difficult at times during the battle of Manassas to distinguish between the flags of the enemy and our own," Alabama soldier William J. Reese confided to his fiancé. "Our generals are determined that it shall not occur again if it can be avoided."[20]

Battle flags subsequently issued to the army were made not of silk but of wool bunting and differed slightly from the original issue and from one another in such detail as color and width of the border. The distance between stars decreased as the number of states accepted into the Confederacy increased (reaching thirteen when the secessionist factions of Missouri and Kentucky joined in late 1861).[21] The flags were not made by the mothers, wives, and sisters of Confederate soldiers but by women and men employed by Confederate army quartermaster depots around the South. While the name and *élan* of the Army of Northern Virginia awaited the command of Robert E. Lee in June 1862, by the end of 1861 the Confederate army in Virginia had the flag under which it would fight its greatest battles.

The St. Andrew's cross battle flag was often dubbed the "Beauregard flag." Although the name does injustice to its patron, William Porcher Miles, it certainly credits the man who did much to promote its diffusion throughout the Confederate army. P. G. T. Beauregard never reclaimed the fame of Fort Sumter or First Manassas, but he did hold a series of important, geographically disparate commands. In February 1862 he left Virginia for Mississippi, where he became second-in-command to General Albert Sidney Johnston. Under Beauregard's immediate command were several forces that were soon to coalesce into the Army of Mississippi, later renamed the Army of Tennessee.

Beauregard found that commanders in the West had adopted their own unique battle flag designs. General Leonidas Polk, a West Point graduate who was also an Episcopal bishop, adopted a flag featuring a red St. George's cross on a blue field, while General William J. Hardee adopted a blue flag with a white disc. The Hardee pattern did not have any red on it, making it easily distinguishable from all other battle flags. Major General Earl Van Dorn, the officer to whom Constance Cary had given her battle flag prototype, introduced his own battle flag—an exotic red flag with thirteen white stars, a white crescent moon, and a gold border—in the Confederacy's Army of the West late in 1861. A few of the Missouri units carrying flags with the Van Dorn design subsequently transferred east of the Mississippi River, further confounding Beauregard's push for uniformity. Beauregard gave orders to have these other flags "replaced as soon as practicable by the Battle Flag of the Army of the Potomac." He arranged with Confederate authorities in New Orleans to have St. Andrew's cross battle flags manufactured and delivered to his troops. The new flags arrived in March, and Beauregard apparently distributed them to Braxton Bragg's division.[22]

The efforts of Beauregard and his equally well-traveled comrade, Joseph Johnston, to impose battle flag uniformity on the western army were doomed to failure. Many units in the Army of Tennessee willfully continued to use the flags they carried before Beauregard came west, including many variations on the Stars and Bars. Then, too, the St. Andrew's cross flags that Beauregard arranged to have made in New Orleans differed in details from the flags used in Virginia (most notably by featuring six-pointed stars), and subsequent issues differed from the first. Far from being perfectly square (as in Virginia) or nearly square (as in the first issue from New Orleans), the second issue from New Orleans measured about forty-two inches on the hoist, or staff, edge and more than six feet on the fly edge.[23]

Beauregard's crusade for battle flag uniformity continued when he was transferred again. "In September 1862," Beauregard recounted, "when I returned to Charleston, I substituted the same banner for the state flags then used in the Department of South Carolina, Georgia & Florida; it became thus in our Armies the Emblem of southern valor & patriotism."[24]

Further pressure toward flag uniformity in the Army of Tennessee mounted in December 1863 when General Joseph E. Johnston replaced the unpopular General Braxton Bragg as commander of the Army of Tennessee. Johnston, who had acted with Beauregard in adopting the St. Andrew's cross battle flag in 1861, redoubled Beauregard's standardization efforts. He declared that "the battle flag of the Virginia army" would henceforth be used to mark his headquarters. Another veteran of the Army of Northern Virginia, General John Bell Hood, became one of the Army of Tennessee's corps commanders in February 1864 and imposed the Virginia design on his corps. "To avoid dangerous confusion in action," Hood's order read, "each regiment will be required to bear the Confederate battle flag," later specified as "the Virginia battle flag." Anticipating resistance to the order, Hood wrote that he could "well understand the pride many regiments of the corps feel in other flags which they have gloriously borne in battle, but the interests of the service are imperative. He would suggest that such standards be kept for safe-keeping to the capitol of the States to which the troops belong, as it will be found inconvenient to have more than one flag in a regiment."[25]

The Johnston–Hood orders succeeded in diffusing the St. Andrew's cross more widely throughout the western army, but the flag was not the same one found in Virginia. Instead, the Army of Tennessee's flag was rectangular without a border, similar in appearance to the most popular twentieth-century reproduction flags. Ironically, the man who in 1861 suggested the square St. Andrew's cross design in Virginia was responsible for introducing to the western army the rectangular version.

Nevertheless, units in the western theater resisted standardization of the battle flag. Few of the Polk or Van Dorn banners remained long in the army. But the troops of Hardee's division were loath to surrender the flags under which they had fought so long. The regiments in Hardee's original division, commanded by Major General Patrick R. Cleburne, apparently received permission in 1864 to continue using their square blue flags with the white disc. At least one regiment brought its Hardee flag when it transferred to the Army of Northern Virginia; the flag was captured by the Federals near Petersburg, Virginia, in June 1864.[26]

Throughout the South, Confederate units used and revered state flags, various national designs, particularly the Stars and Bars, and other battle flags; but the St. Andrew's cross was, as Beauregard boasted, clearly the most prolific and popular choice. It predominated not only among the Confederacy's field armies but also at sea. In 1863 the Confederate navy adopted as the navy jack (the flag flown from the ship's bow) a rectangular St. Andrew's cross pattern.[27]

Further evidence of the St. Andrew's cross's primacy came in 1863 when Congress referred to it matter-of-factly as "the battle flag" and incorporated it into a new national flag. By 1863 the St. Andrew's cross had been consecrated on the battlefield. For a nation that survived only as long as its armies survived, the flag of the soldier understandably became the flag of the nation. Robert E. Lee's Army of Northern Virginia, not the government of President Jefferson Davis, was the entity in which southern civilians placed their confidence and their hopes for victory. In the Confederate South, nationalism sprang from the relationship of the populace with its most accomplished army.[28] The exalted status of the battle flag associated most closely with Lee's Army of Northern Virginia suggests that the Confederate battle flag was not only a soldier's flag but a bona fide national symbol.

Before the Confederacy and the war were a year old, influential voices spoke out against the Stars and Bars and, significantly, for a cross pattern national flag. Frustrated in his advocacy of a distinct flag in 1861, William Miles must have taken perverse pleasure in the growing contempt for the Stars and Bars. The Richmond *Dispatch* complained in November 1861 that the national flag of the Confederacy "looks too much like the old concern for the emblem of a separate and independent nation." A month later, the *New Orleans Delta* denounced it as "the hybrid bunting" that was useful "during our transition state from attempted to confirmed independence." The renowned naval scientist Commander Matthew Fontaine Maury began lobbying as early as April 1861 to dump the flag he denounced as a "servile imitation" of the Stars and Stripes, which he once served loyally but which now symbolized "tyranny, cruelty, & oppression." Instead of the Stars and Bars, he suggested a blue flag emblazoned with eleven white stars forming the "southern cross." Maury petitioned Congress to adopt his flag and organized a Fredericksburg, Virginia, ladies club to create a prototype. Maury's fellow Virginian, editor and humorist George W. Bagby, similarly lobbied beginning in 1861 for the southern cross as a new national flag. Referring to the (upright) cross constellation visible only in the southern hemisphere, the southern cross provided a unique geographical motif for a distinctive Confederate flag.[29]

The growing disenchantment with the old flag carried over into official circles. The Confederate Congress, elected anew in November 1861 and seated as the first permanent Congress in February 1862, continued to receive suggestions for national flags, and House and Senate committees considered them. The Richmond *Examiner* reported on March 28, 1862, that the only clear consensus among the committee members was "that the Flag should be as unlike as possible the Stars and Stripes of the United States." On April 19, 1862, the committees on flag and seal presented a joint resolution for a new national flag. The design was elaborate and brightly colored: a red field emblazoned with a white "saltire" cross which, in turn, had over the cross an amber sunburst on an azure (blue) shield. The joint resolution insisted that the pattern was simple, distinct in color, symbolically significant of "a free and prosperous people" (obviously referring to the Confederacy's eight million white people, not its nearly four million enslaved blacks), and consistent with the rules of heraldry.[30]

The foremost consideration influencing the committee was that the new flag not resemble that of any other nation. The report further stated that "nearly all the designs submitted to the committee contained a combination of stars. This heraldic emblem, however, has been discarded as a manifestation of our absolute severance from the 'United States' and the complete separation of every sentiment indicating the faintest hope of reconstruction." Miles, then serving as a representative from South Carolina, told the House that he was "glad that a flag had been [recommended] so dissimilar to the old." Neither the House nor the Senate was moved, and the sunburst flag was never considered or adopted. It was clear, however, that sentiment was shifting toward a rejection of the old flag and that a saltire, or St. Andrew's cross, would be part of a new national flag. As early as January 1862, the Charleston *Mercury* predicted that "the Battle Flag will become *the* southern Flag by popular acclaim."[31]

Congress again took up the flag question in April 1863. All of the patterns considered what members called alternatively a saltire or St. Andrew's cross. The Senate committee recommended a design that featured the cross as the canton on a field of white with a horizontal blue stripe filling the middle third of the white field. In a widely published letter of April 24, General Beauregard voiced his support of making the battle flag the national flag. "Why change our battle flag, consecrated on so many battlefields?" Beauregard asked a Louisiana congressman. "A good design for the national flag would be the present battle flag as Union Jack, and the rest all white or blue." The *Southern Illustrated News* went further and urged that the battle flag alone replace the Stars and Bars, which, it opined, "is suggestive of the detested Federal Government and its oppressions." "We repeat that the baptism of blood and fire has made the battleflag of General Johnston our national emblem. It is associated with our severest trials and our proudest achievements."[32]

On May 1 the Confederate House favored eliminating the blue stripe but debated whether to emblazon the battle flag on a white field with or without a border on the outer edge of the entire flag. Committee Chairman Alexander Boteler explained the need for an outer border: "True, the battle flag was endeared to every Confederate heart," he conceded, "but what meant the white field? If any border were adopted, let it be red, symbolizing the blood shed on our frontiers."[33]

William Miles disdained both the border and the blue stripes, and delivered a plea for the pattern that finally won congressional approval. Making the most of his opportunity for self-vindication, Miles recounted his sponsorship of the design as a national flag and subsequently as a battle flag. "The country was aware of how it had been received in the army—it had been consecrated," Miles's speech was reported in the Charleston *Mercury*. "The battle flag should be used then with simplicity, but to the demand that it should be taken alone, he would reply that it was necessary to emblazon it. The battle flag, on a pure white field, he thought was the best they could find."[34] The House bill was sent back to the Senate, which approved it with little debate. President Jefferson Davis signed the bill into law the same afternoon, on May 1, 1863.

The flag act specified that the new flag was to be a white field "with the union (now used as the battle flag) to be a square of two-thirds the width of the flag, having the ground red; thereon a broad saltier of blue, bordered with white, and emblazoned with mullets or five-pointed stars, corresponding in number to that of the Confederate States." The adoption of that flag, which soon became known as the "Stainless Banner" for its pure white field, was the first official government recognition of the Confederate battle flag. A large Stainless Banner was produced in time to drape the casket of Lieutenant General Thomas J. "Stonewall" Jackson as it lay in state in the Virginia capitol on May 12.[35]

Reaction to the new flag was favorable. As did the Stars and Bars, the Stainless Banner inspired popular songs. "Hail symbol of the Sunny South! / Bright Banner of the free!" began E. V. Sharp's "Flag of the Sunny South." The chorus proclaimed: "Flag of the Sunny South still wave. / Where first from gloom the stars arose / Thy dazzling lustre ne'er shall pale / Where freedom's martyr'd sons repose." "The new flag, which was displayed from the Capitol on Thursday [May 14, 1863], it is gratifying to say, gives universal satisfaction," commented the Richmond *Daily Dispatch*. "Almost any sort of a flag, to take the place of the detested parody of the Stars and Stripes for so long the lawful emblem of the Confederacy, would have been hailed with pleasure." The new flag was all the more satisfactory because "in it is preserved that immortal banner—the battle flag—which has been consecrated on so many battle fields." The Columbia *Daily South Carolinian* observed that with the battle flag emblazoned on a flag of truce, there was a danger of sending a mixed message. "The flag is very simple, but it is—very white." Sentiment would eventually consecrate the flag, but "till then, it looks—very white."[36]

According to the editors of the Savannah *Daily Morning News,* the flag's whiteness carried another symbolic significance. "As a people, we are fighting to maintain the Heaven ordained supremacy of the white man over the inferior or colored race," the paper reasoned. "A white flag would thus be emblematical of our cause." The editors subsequently dubbed the second national flag the "white man's flag." This was a rare, perhaps unique, overt wartime linkage of the flag to white supremacy.[37] In heraldry, white is symbolic of purity, and purity certainly can imply racial purity; but that issue—explicitly or implicitly—did not otherwise figure into the discussion over the second national flag.

The second national flag was occasionally issued to units of the Confederate army as battle flags. More often, national flags in camps of the Confederate army were displayed at the headquarters of commanding officers. Evidence suggests that soldiers sometimes transformed the Stainless Banner into a battle flag by cutting out the square canton and discarding the white field.[38]

Although William Miles argued that the pure white field had precedent as the "French Bourbon flag" and would "not be taken as a flag of truce," it became apparent by late 1864 that the flag was indeed too white. Major Arthur L. Rogers offered the ironic observation that the Stainless Banner was "very easily soiled from its excessive whiteness." Rogers, a former staff officer wounded in the same volley that mortally wounded Stonewall Jackson at the battle of Chancellorsville, proposed modifying the flag by adding a vertical red stripe to the outer edge. Rogers argued that the pure white field was easily mistaken as a flag of truce, especially when flown on naval vessels.

With written support from an impressive array of naval and army officers, Rogers lobbied successfully to have his design introduced in the Senate in December 1864. Reiterating the familiar argument that this battle flag was appropriately distinct from the old United States flag, Rogers wrote the Senate Military Affairs Committee chairman: "I am opposed to all stripes, many or few, red or blue. Instead of the 'stars and stripes,' let us have the stars and bars [sic]. The colors of the new flag would be chiefly white and red, with as little as possible of the Yankee blue." The design further symbolized the primary origins of the southern people: the cross of Britain and the red bar from the flag of France. Congress adopted it as the third national flag in March 1865.[39] A month later, Robert E. Lee surrendered his army to Ulysses S. Grant. By May 10, 1865, all but one of the Confederacy's military departments had surrendered, and Federal forces had captured President Jefferson Davis. Few third national flags were issued or flown on Confederate government buildings or facilities.

A general overview of Confederate flag history necessarily oversimplifies the details about the wartime production, distribution, and use of Confederate flags.[40] But an overview reveals clearly the symbolic triumph of flags—of whatever shapes, sizes, and details—bearing the blue St. Andrew's cross on a red field. By the war's end, the saltire/St. Andrew's cross had become in effect *the* Confederate flag. The flag was incorporated into the national flag, consecrated on battlefields in every theater of war, and flown over Confederate naval vessels. When seeking a convenient Confederate equivalent to the Stars and Stripes, modern Americans habitually choose the St. Andrew's cross flag, and then they compound the identity problem by calling it the Stars and Bars. This identity confusion is especially ironic because Confederates embraced the St. Andrew's cross flag as the practical and symbolic antithesis of the Stars and Bars. The Confederate government decided to replace the Stars and Bars in order to give the Confederacy an appropriate symbol for "a separate and independent nation." In the language of the *New Orleans Delta,* if the Stars and Bars was useful for "the transition state from attempted to confirmed independence," the St. Andrew's cross symbolized the Confederacy's putative "confirmed independence."

The triumph of the St. Andrew's cross as a symbol of Confederate nationalism carries profound implications for subsequent discussions of its meaning and place in American life. In the decades immediately after the war and in the century since, former Confederates and their partisans have insisted that the battle flag is an apolitical symbol, distinct from the Confederacy's national flags, and therefore not objectionable to a reunited America. Carlton McCarthy, a veteran of the Confederate artillery, insisted in his 1882 *Detailed Minutiae of Soldier Life in the Army of Northern Virginia* that the battle flag "was not the flag of the Confederacy, but simply the banner . . . of the Confederate soldier. As such it should not share in the condemnation which our *cause* received, or suffer from its downfall. The whole world can unite in a chorus of praise to the gallantry of the men who followed where this banner led."[41]

The rhetoric was forceful, and the logic commanded the allegiance of many Americans, South and North. But is it valid? At the same time that Confederate veterans and their descendants demanded respect for the brave Confederate soldier and for his flag, they also sought to vindicate the cause for which that soldier had fought. Carlton McCarthy certainly did not suggest that the cause for which the national flags of the Confederacy stood *should* be condemned. General Beauregard's order distributing the first silk St. Andrew's cross to the army in November 1861 told the soldiers that the flag "must lead you to substantial victory, and the complete triumph of our cause."

Just what was the Confederate "cause"? This question underlies the debates among people who look to the 1860s to find the true meaning of the Confederate flag. The crux of the debate is the relative importance of slavery in the birth and life of the Confederacy. There was little explicit discussion during the war about the Confederate flag as a symbol of slavery or racism; the 1863 editorials in the Savannah *Daily Morning News* were rare exceptions. Based on this evidence, one modern scholar concluded that the battle flag in its Civil War context was not a "racist symbol" because it did not have an explicit racist referent. Men did not create or carry it as a statement of racism or as a symbol of an unequivocally racist objective.[42]

But since men carrying the battle flag preserved and perpetuated the Confederate cause and their flag became the symbol of Confederate nationalism, linking the flag to slavery and racism requires only linking the cause to slavery. Understanding and evaluating the battle flag's historical meaning requires opening the ultimate Pandora's box of Civil War history and examining the role of slavery in the origin and *raison d'être* of the Confederacy. A brief dip into the evidence reveals countless contemporary statements that support conflicting interpretations about slavery and the origins of the Confederacy.

Defenders of the flag have insisted vehemently that the Confederacy did not exist to defend or preserve slavery, and they impugn the motives and intelligence of those who argue that it did. Although slavery was, by 1860, confined to the southern and border states, racism was not. Racism and segregation prevailed in the North, and the states that went to war to prevent the secession of the South denied fundamental rights to free blacks and even prohibited them from living there. Among southern whites themselves, slave ownership was limited (often claimed today to have been as low as five percent). More passionately, flag defenders argue that the Confederate soldier, for whom the battle flag is a symbol, did not own slaves or fight for slavery. James McPherson's study of soldier motivations suggested that most Confederate soldiers did not fight consciously for the preservation of slave property. Confederate soldiers believed they were fighting, above all, to defend their states, their country, and their homes from invasion and to preserve the individual and constitutional liberty that Americans won in 1776.[43]

Although hundreds of thousands of white southerners remained loyal to the Union and dissented from Confederate orthodoxy, most white southerners believed that secession was a constitutional right and that Abraham Lincoln's use of federal power to "preserve the Union" was in fact unconstitutional coercion. Regardless of what prompted southern states to secede or who fired the first shots, the subsequent war of secession cast southern armies in the role of defending their states against military invasion by Federal forces—forces that inflicted incalculable damage on people and property. The soldiers' battle flag thus symbolized defense of home and resistance to invasion.

Historians and partisans in the flag debates can disagree legitimately with the logic of their argument, but they cannot deny the reality of the perceptions of those who suffered the consequences of invasion. If we wish to understand why many people perceive the Confederate flag as a symbol not of slavery but of liberty, we must understand that a war which "somehow" was caused by slavery (as Lincoln said in his second inaugural address) also necessarily entailed the destruction of an exercise in self-determination. It is specious to assert that people got what was coming to them because they held to constitutional and moral beliefs that were wodely accepted in their own time.

Modern neo-Confederate orthodoxy not only denies that slavery was the cause of the war but posits that the Confederacy's reason for being was the defense of constitutional liberty against Big Government. Furthermore, according to this reasoning, the growth of an intrusive federal government in modern times can be traced directly to the defeat of the Confederacy. Anti-government ideology has combined with historical analysis and ancestor veneration to give the Confederacy and its symbols exalted status as icons of freedom.[44]

While generations since 1865 have embellished this orthodoxy, it originated in the rhetoric of Confederate leaders seeking to justify secession and win support for their new nation. Confederate President Jefferson Davis in 1861 passionately proclaimed that the true issue at stake was the consolidation of the national government at the expense of the states. "Consolidation would be the destruction of the Union, and far more fatal to popular liberty than the separation of the States." Far from undermining the principles on which the United States was founded, secession and the creation of a new confederation would perpetuate those principles.[45]

Davis's most bitter internal critic, South Carolina editor and politician Robert Barnwell Rhett, echoed Davis in the address that he penned to explain his state's secession to the people of the other slaveholding states. "The Southern States now stand exactly in the same position towards the Northern States that the Colonies did towards Great Britain," Rhett wrote. "The Government of the United States, is no longer the Government of Confederated Republics, but of a consolidated Democracy. It is no longer a free Government, but a Despotism." The "great object" of the American Revolution was "a limited free Government." The northern states had undermined that ideal, and the southern states must leave the Union to recover the "great object."[46] Rhett's words resonate for modern Americans who blame an omnipotent federal government for America's political, social, and cultural evils. Undeniably, distrust, in principle, of a powerful central government is a strong and consistent motif in American history and was an intellectual foundation for the Confederacy.

Equally undeniable is the fact that the South's theoretical distrust of a powerful central government was related directly to its real fear of what that would mean for the institution of slavery. For proof, it is not necessary to look any further than the speech by Jefferson Davis and the address by Robert Barnwell Rhett. In his farewell speech to the U.S. Senate, Davis blamed the crisis on the Republican Party's refusal "to recognize our domestic institutions [an acknowledged euphemism for slavery] which pre-existed the formation of the Union or property which was guarded by the Constitution." Following his plea for "limited free Government" and condemnation of the North for using the federal government to impose oppressive taxes on the South, Rhett made it clear that conflict over slavery was the paramount reason for secession. "The agitations on the subject of slavery, are the natural results of the consolidation of the Government."

Republican Party support for anti-slavery "fanaticism" made the South's position in the Union untenable, according to Rhett. "The Union of the Constitution, was a union of slaveholding states. It rests on slavery, by prescribing a Representation in Congress, for three-fifths of our slaves." In the decades following the Constitutional Convention, the divergence of their "institutions and industrial pursuits" had made southerners and northerners "totally different peoples." "We but imitate the policy of our fathers in dissolving a union with non-slaveholding confederates, and seeking a confederation with slaveholding States." For the people of the other slaveholding states, Rhett painted the ambitious picture of "a great Slaveholding Confederacy, stretching its arms over a territory larger than any power in Europe possesses." In the subsequent convention to form the Confederacy, Rhett advocated—and the delegations of South Carolina and Florida voted for—the reopening of the transatlantic slave trade.[47]

The statesmen who led the secession movement were unashamed to explicitly cite the defense of slavery as their prime motive. South Carolina's December 1860 declaration justifying secession dwelled on the victory in the 1860 presidential election of a party explicitly hostile to "the rights of property established in fifteen of the States and recognized by the Constitution" and friendly to groups dedicated to abolition of slavery. Mississippi's state convention declared that the people of northern states had defied constitutional provisions regarding slavery and were seeking to achieve a two-thirds majority in both houses so that they could amend the Constitution to abolish slavery in the states. The commissioners sent by the seceded states to lobby the governments of the non-seceded slave states not only emphasized the threat of a Republican-dominated central government but also exploited lurid fears of "social equality" and racial amalgamation.[48]

In his widely quoted February 1861 "Cornerstone Address," Confederate Vice President Alexander H. Stephens declared that the new government's "foundations are laid, its cornerstone rests, upon the great truth that the negro is not equal to the white man; that slavery, subordination to the superior race, is his natural and moral condition." Confederate apologists have long dismissed Stephens's speech as an unauthorized, careless, atypical, and misquoted statement that in no way reflected the true purposes of the government. The opposite is true. Stephens's speech was very consistent with private and public statements by southern leaders in 1860 and 1861. Stephens's own clarification did not deny the accuracy of the quote but merely emphasized that he believed his observations to be consistent with the intentions of the founding fathers.[49]

The determination of the Confederacy's founders to preserve and protect slavery was evident not only in their rhetoric but in the substance of their work. The Confederate Constitution of March 1861 guaranteed the institution of slavery where it existed and in any newly acquired territories; it also restated provisions in the U.S. Constitution requiring the return of fugitive slaves.

The numbers that pro-flag partisans cite as proof that slavery was peripheral to the Confederacy simply do not hold up under scrutiny. While only 5.6 percent of whites in the southern and border states in 1860 were slaveholders, this number (384,000) represented more than 25 percent of the 1.5 million heads of household and suggests that one-quarter of white southerners lived in slave-owning families. James D. B.

De Bow, the Deep South editor and economist and superintendent of the 1850 U.S. census, found in the census evidence that slavery was not the exclusive province of the elite. Slaveholders, he observed, "make up an aggregate, greater in relative proportion than the holders of any other species of property whatever, in any part of the world; and that of no other property can it be said, with equal truthfulness, that it is an interest of the whole community."[50]

Whether or not they owned slaves, white southerners had a stake in slavery as a system of racial control and a source of identity. As Jefferson Davis explained to Mississippi voters in 1851, "The institution of negro slavery, as it now exists among us, is necessary to the *equality* of the *white* race."[51] Southern whites defined their "liberty" in terms of their rights to own slaves, take them into the western territories, and reclaim them if they ran away to the free states. Even if the vast majority of Confederate soldiers were not slave owners, their service helped establish and perpetuate a nation founded to protect slavery from a hostile federal government.

This "Confederately correct" orthodoxy that the South fought for independence, not slavery, rankled a few southern realists, including the editors of the Richmond-based *Southern Punch* in 1864:

> "The people of the South," says a contemporary, "are not fighting for slavery, but for independence." Let us look into this matter. It is an easy task, we think, to show up this new-fangled heresy—a heresy calculated to do us no good, for it cannot deceive foreign statesmen nor peoples, nor mislead any one here nor in Yankeeland . . . Our doctrine is this: WE ARE FIGHTING FOR INDEPENDENCE THAT OUR GREAT AND NECESSARY DOMESTIC IN-STITUTION OF SLAVERY SHALL BE PRESERVED, and for the preservation of other institutions of which slavery is the groundwork.[52]

After the war, a few ex-Confederates expressed similar disgust with the insistence that defense of slavery had not been the cause of the war.

Confederate veteran Ed Baxter unashamedly told a reunion in 1889: "In a word, the South determined to fight for her property right in slaves; and in order to do so, it was necessary for her to resist the change which the Abolitionists proposed to make under the Constitution of the United States as construed by them . . . Upon this issue the South went to war, I repeat that the people of the South had a right to fight for their property. It was best for them, and best for the Government, that the South should have made the fight."[53]

A chapter of the United Daughters of the Confederacy in 1904 published a "catechism" for children. Consistent with the evolving Confederate orthodoxy, the catechism emphasized that the North, not the South, started the "War between the States" by disregarding southern rights. "What were these rights?" asked the catechism. "The right to regulate their own affairs and to hold slaves as property" was the answer. Famed Confederate partisan leader Colonel John S. Mosby was equally forthright. "I've always understood that we went to war on account of the thing we quarreled with the North about," he wrote a former comrade in 1894. "I've never heard of any other cause than slavery."[54]

Mosby, Rhett, Davis, Stephens, and other Confederates had no difficulty conceding what their descendants go to enormous lengths to deny: that the *raison d'être* of the Confederacy was the defense of slavery. It follows that, as the paramount symbol of the Confederate nation and as the flag of the armies that kept that nation alive, the St. Andrew's cross is inherently associated with slavery. This conclusion is valid whether or not secession was constitutional. It is valid whether or not most southern soldiers consciously fought to preserve slavery. It is valid even though racism and segregation prevailed among nineteenth-century white northerners.

Modern Americans looking for this kind of definitive judgment go wrong, however, in concluding further that the St. Andrew's cross was *only* a symbol of slavery. Historians emphasize that defense of African-American slavery was inextricably intertwined with white southerners' defense of their own constitutional liberties and with nearly every other facet of southern life. Descendants of Confederates are not wrong to believe that the flag symbolized defense of constitutional liberties and resistance to invasion by military forces determined to crush an experiment in nationhood. But they are wrong to believe that this interpretation of the flag's meaning can be separated from the defense of slavery. They need only read the words of their Confederate ancestors to find abundant and irrefutable evidence.

The modern debate over the flag is inherently flawed and unproductive because opposing sides create false dichotomies—arguing that the war was or was not about slavery and that the flag is or is not a symbol of slavery. Both sides distort the historical record and try to impose simplicity on an ambiguous past. Acknowledging the centrality of slavery to the Confederacy does not assign moral superiority to the North and guilt to the South. The war was fundamentally about slavery, but it is erroneous to reduce it to a simple moral equation defined in sectional terms. Acknowledging the centrality of slavery to the Confederacy is essential for understanding the subsequent uses and perceptions of the Confederate battle flag. Understanding that the Confederacy could rest on a "cornerstone" of white supremacy but also embody liberty (obviously only for southern whites) and national self-preservation is equally essential for understanding attitudes toward the Confederacy and its preeminent symbol.

Southerners justifiably believed that interference with slavery was a violation of a constitutional and customary understanding upon which the nation was founded. The flags of the Confederacy were, therefore, symbols of resistance to this violation. As a battle flag, the St. Andrew's cross battle flag accumulated additional layers of meaning related to duty, soldierly valor, ancestry, heritage, and tradition. This accumulation of meanings has taken on a life of its own—a life that we must understand and appreciate in the quest to understand attitudes toward the battle flag. If we are to understand why people today defend the battle flag and why they resent the categorical denunciation of it as only a symbol of slavery and racism, we must be able to understand how a flag so closely associated with the defense of slavery could also be, for many people past and present, a symbol of liberty, courage, and commitment.

Chapter 2

"The War-Torn Cross"

In her 1902 novel, *The Battle-Ground,* Ellen Glasgow chronicled the last days of Robert E. Lee's Army of Northern Virginia through the experiences of her protagonist, Dan Lightfoot. On the road west from Petersburg to Appomattox Court House, the army fought its last major engagement at Sailor's Creek. Dan Lightfoot's unit prepared for the enemy assault.

> Near him the colour bearer of the regiment was fighting with his flagstaff as a weapon, and out in the meadow a member of the glee club, crouching behind a clump of sassafras as he loaded, was singing in a cracked voice: "Rally around the flag, boys, rally once again!" Then a bullet went with a soft thud into the singer's breast, and the cracked voice was choked out behind the bushes.
>
> Gripped by a sudden pity for the helpless flag he had loved and followed for four years, Dan made an impetuous dash from out of the pines and, tearing the colors from the pole, tossed them over his arm as he retreated rapidly to

cover. At that instant he held his life as nothing beside the faded strip of silk. The cause for which he had fought, the great captain he had followed, the devotion to a single end that had kept him struggling in the ranks, the daily sacrifice, the very poverty and cold and hunger, all these were bound up and made one with the tattered flag upon his arm.

Three days later, upon learning that the army had been surrendered to the Federal forces under General Ulysses S. Grant, Dan decided to deny the flag to the enemy: "Taking out his jack-knife, Dan unfastened the flag from the hickory pole on which he had placed it, and began cutting it into little pieces, which he passed to each man who had fought beneath the folds. The last bit he put into his own pocket."[1]

The character and the incidents were fictional, but they were based on actual events. Confederate soldiers did rush to catch their fallen flags and did destroy their flags rather than surrender them. Ellen Glasgow, a southern writer who prided herself on the realism of her work, confessed that "one cannot approach the Confederacy without touching the very heart of romantic tradition." "It is," she wrote, "the single occasion in American history, and one of the rare occasions in the history of the world, when the conflict of actualities was profoundly romantic."[2] Romantic stories surrounding battle flags proliferated more widely in the postwar decades than during the war itself, and soldiers' memories embroidered the telling of their wartime experiences, but flags undeniably occupied a vital place in the culture of the Confederate soldier.

Although it served very important practical functions on the Civil War battlefield, the battle flag became imbued with all the values of honor, courage, patriotism, and camaraderie that motivated most soldiers of the era. The emotions that Dan Lightfoot felt toward his flag were those that defined the meaning of the flag for Confederate soldiers (and, for that matter, of U.S. flags for Federal soldiers). Accustomed as Americans today are to viewing the Confederate battle flag as a controversial symbol, they have difficulty appreciating the practical and symbolic meanings of the original flags to the men who followed them.

For millennia, military units have carried battle flags primarily for very practical purposes of identification and alignment. Battle flags allowed commanders to determine the size and composition of their own —and their enemy's—troops and follow their progress on the battlefield. During the Civil War, individual regiments carried battle flags. Federal regiments generally carried both a regimental flag and a national flag that was marked with the regiment's designation. Confederate regiments carried a single battle flag. Individual companies (ten of which comprised a regiment) were often presented by the civilians of their communities with elaborate silk flags, but those were not customarily used on the battlefield. Although no copy of it has survived, the Confederate army adjutant general apparently issued an order in the spring of 1862 forbidding units from carrying any flag but the regimental battle flag.[3]

Regulation of battle-flag use was necessary because of the flag's importance to the discipline and effectiveness of the regiment. The flag was visible not only to commanders directing troops from afar but to the men and noncommissioned officers directing the troops from the ranks. Tied to wooden flagstaffs typically measuring between eight and ten feet, flags were visible above the thick clouds of white smoke that covered the Civil War battlefield. The sergeants and lieutenants responsible for ensuring orderly lines of battle sighted the flags to align and realign their men.[4]

The responsibility of carrying the colors was obviously not merely ceremonial. Mid-nineteenth-century American military manuals detailed the position, composition, and character of color guards. Following prewar precedents, William Gilham's 1861 *Manual of Instruction for the Volunteers and Militia of the Confederate States* prescribed a color guard of eight men—seven corporals and one sergeant (the color bearer)—chosen from among the companies of the regiment. The guard was to be "posted on the left of the right centre company," thus as close as possible to the middle of each regiment. The color sergeant, selected by the regiment's colonel, was the only man in the line who marched unarmed, carrying only the flag. The seven corporals marched beside and behind the color bearer, ready to drop their weapons and pick up the flag if necessary. The regiment's colonel marched behind the color guard, a position that allowed him to best view and maneuver his troops. The color guard of a seasoned Confederate regiment consisted typically of four or five men, not the prescribed eight.[5]

According to William Hardee's 1855 *Rifle and Light Infantry Tactics,* the color corporals should be "selected from those most distinguished for regularity and precision, as well as in their positions under arms as in their marching."[6] Though the Civil War was a romantic war, the obvious valor of the color bearer won the admiration, but not the mercy, of the enemy. Fully aware of the flag's practical and symbolic importance, troops consciously targeted the enemy color bearers. At Pickett's Charge on the third day of the battle of Gettysburg, an anonymous Confederate color bearer leaped over the stone wall crowning Cemetery Ridge, holding aloft his colors and cheering on his own troops. Conscious of the impossible odds, he turned and, in the words of an admiring comrade, "walked off the field, still displaying his colors and *drawing the fire of the whole line.*" By walking off the field with his colors, the anonymous color bearer (probably that of the 38th Virginia Infantry) was the exception to the rule at that battle. The color guards of other regiments in all three divisions in the assault were decimated.[7]

Private Lyman Via, a Virginia boy who had run off at age thirteen to join the army, talked his way into becoming color bearer for the Charlottesville Artillery. During the battle of the Bloody Angle at Spotsylvania (May 12, 1864), Via planted the unit's colors on the breastworks. When an enemy shell knocked the colors down, Via climbed the works to replace them and was killed. His unit was effectively destroyed during the battle.[8] An 1864 song celebrated the foolish bravery of "The Standard Bearer":

> "Dost see the foe outnumbers us?"
> A veteran calmly said;
> The youthful soldier laughed aloud,
> And gaily shook his head.

Then onward rode him to the fray,
Before the cannon's mouth,
Waving aloft exultingly
The banner of the South!
The morn gazed bright and peacefully
Upon the mighty slain;
The gallant boy lay on the field,
Ne'er more to fight again.
A ray of light was in his eye,
A smile upon his mouth,
While to his death-chilled breast he clasped,
The banner of the South![9]

As an incentive and a reward for color bearers, the Confederate Congress in February 1864 authorized the appointment of one new officer in each infantry regiment to be known as an ensign. The man appointed exercised no command authority but held the rank and received the pay and allowances of a first lieutenant. Sergeant William Samuel Woods of the 20th Alabama Infantry received the honor in his regiment. It was, he wrote his mother, customary "to Appoint the Bravest & Most Meritorious to that Position. I don't no whether they think that I was the Bravest or not any how I got the appointment." The job, Woods noted, was easy. "As Long as I carry the colors I Hav nothing to Doo only to carry them No duty to Doo." He hoped the promotion would bring him a much-anticipated ninety-day furlough. Instead, Ensign Woods was killed in battle at Marietta, Georgia, on June 22, 1864. The wife of another man who apparently intended to become a color bearer had a more realistic appraisal of the job. She warned him that "if you go in to battle every thing will aim right at you so dont you have nothing to do with it if you dont you will be shot down soon as you go in to battle."[10]

In the Confederate army, as in most nineteenth-century armies, the battle flag embodied the unit's *esprit de corps*. Defending the flag was tantamount to defending home and hearth, honor and principle. The symbolic value of battle flags for soldiers transcended design. One Confederate veteran later remarked that the battle flag of the Army of Northern Virginia was "the only flag that we veterans venerate." While the St. Andrew's cross was most emblematic of Confederate nationalism and most revered by veterans, it did not have a monopoly on the Confederate soldier's affection. More Confederate soldiers marched and fought under some version of the St. Andrew's cross than any other single design, but soldiers formed an emotional attachment to whatever pattern their battle flag displayed. A Georgia soldier wrote his mother in April 1862 (before his unit went into battle with the new flag) asking her to make him two small Confederate banners, "either stars and bars or battle flags which ever you think will be the prettiest. I would rather have the stars and bars if you think it will be as pretty as the other."[11]

The 43rd Battalion, Virginia Cavalry—Colonel John S. Mosby's legendary rangers—was among the many units that carried the Stars and Bars throughout the war and, in fact, adopted this as its flag more than a year after the St. Andrew's cross made its debut in Virginia. The many stories surrounding the dedication, defense, and surrender of battle flags rarely distinguished among the different designs. The most famous color bearers in South Carolina history—honored with a plaque placed in the state house—died carrying their state's palmetto flag in battle at Gaines's Mill during the Seven Days' Battles near Richmond in June 1862.[12]

Sent home after the first year of war, those state flags and unique company banners retained immense sentimental value, but they were eventually eclipsed in symbolic importance by the flags that actually accompanied men onto the battlefield. The presentation of the first silk St. Andrew's cross flags to the army in Virginia on November 28, 1861, dramatized how the ritual and rhetoric of company flags were transferred to the new regimental flags. After the first issue of St. Andrew's cross flags, the receipt of government-issue regimental battle flags did not occasion symbolic ritual. By some accounts, the Confederate quartermaster system became so efficient that units on the march or in the field could obtain new flags from supply wagons. Efficiency did not mean insignificance, however. Being carried in battle consecrated a flag. Bullet holes and the blood of color bearers created a bond between the flag and the soldiers who followed it. The horrific, yet exhilarating, sights of comrades falling in battle while carrying the flag made for vivid memories that became the stuff of postwar reminiscences.

By the end of 1861, Confederate units marked their flags with their unit designations and with "battle honors"—the names of the engagements in which the unit had fought. General Beauregard in May 1862 told his Army of the Mississippi that units "whose gallantry and bravery shall have been most conspicuous" to inscribe the name of the battle on their flags. Suggesting how important flags were to morale, Beauregard warned in the same message that units "misbehaving in action will be deprived of their colors until they have shown themselves worthy of defending them." A War Department order of July 23, 1862, authorized commanders of the various armies "to cause to be entered in some conspicuous place on the standards the names of the several battles in which their regiments, battalions, and separate squadrons have been actually engaged."[13] This practice—the precursor of modern army practice of carrying "battle streamers" on the staffs of regimental flags—proved popular with the troops. The red fields of many surviving battle flags are nearly filled with the names of their units' engagements. Lieutenant Whitfield G. Kisling, of the 10th Virginia Infantry, wrote to his cousin on August 26, 1863:

> We have received a new flag for the Regiment it is emblazoned with the names of nearly all the principal Battles that have occurred in this department since the war beginning with Manassas 1st and ending with Gettysburg fourteen in number in all of which I have been engaged myself except the first—does not this show that we are veterans indeed—fourteen regular pitched Battles beside numerous skirmishes—it is wonderful that so many of us are alive, but the old Regiment is now as able to do as efficient service as ever—Our old flag will be sent back to Buckingham where it will be preserved as a mimento [sic] of valor of the glorious old 10th it has some ten or twelve

bullet holes in it beside several large [rents?] made by
pieces of shell, the staff has also been struck several
times.[14]

The history of the flag of the 26th Tennessee Infantry reveals the ways
in which flags were endowed with symbolic meaning. In July 1861 two
ladies from the home town of Company I made a battle flag (presumably
the Confederacy's first national design) to be presented to the regiment
in which the company was eventually incorporated. At a dress parade,
the flag was proffered in the name of the two ladies and was accepted by
the regiment's colonel. In early 1864 the regiment procured an Army of
Tennessee flag and applied to it a piece of cloth cut from the old flag and
bearing the unit designation. "This flag was regarded merely as the old
flag repaired," a veteran later remarked at a regimental reunion. To reinforce this continuity, the men stenciled the flag with the names of the engagements in which the unit had fought under the old flag.[15]

On both the practical and symbolic levels, battle flags embodied the
welfare and morale of Confederate military units. Irish-born General
Patrick R. Cleburne tried in 1863 to create a fraternity of patriotic Confederate soldiers dedicated to assisting wounded veterans, widows, and
orphans as well as to reinforcing the army's morale and fighting spirit.
Significantly, Cleburne called his organization Comrades of the Southern Cross. As one soldier pointed out, it was ironic that the men of
Cleburne's division fought under the Hardee flag, not a southern cross
battle flag. That Cleburne was the founder of the Comrades of the Southern Cross testified to the symbolic prominence of the St. Andrew's cross
motif.[16]

Because flags were so important practically and symbolically to troops
of both sides, the capture of flags was considered among the greatest acts
of battlefield heroism and the loss of flags the greatest of disasters. The
United States government recognized the act of capturing enemy flags
with the Medal of Honor. Created by Congress in 1862, the medal was
to be issued to soldiers and noncommissioned officers who "shall most
distinguish themselves by their gallantry in action, and other soldier-like

qualities." The U.S. army adjutant general in late 1864 listed the names of 106 men who had won the medal "for taking colors from the enemy in battle, and for other acts of distinguished bravery." More than half of the 2,100 Medals of Honor awarded during the Civil War were for the capture of enemy colors. The medal not only recognized bravery but also offered soldiers an incentive for turning over captured flags to the War Department instead of keeping them as trophies. Nevertheless, countless Confederate flags did become private trophies. A general in the Federal Army of the Ohio reported after the November 30, 1864, battle of Franklin, Tennessee, that he could not forward all the flags he claimed his division captured because "some were sent home by their captors." Another general similarly explained that "the men have a passion for tearing them into bits to send home as relics, and in spite of orders have thus destroyed nine."[17]

Confederate soldiers who captured enemy flags received no medals but were sometimes rewarded with promotion.[18] Sam Watkins of the 1st Tennessee Infantry, the irrepressible author of the memoir Co. Aytch, offered a characteristically unromantic account of his experience as a flag-capturing hero. Asked by a fellow named Sloan where he got the two yellow stripes on his sleeve, Watkins replied:

> "Why sir, I have been promoted for gallantry on the battlefield, by picking up an orphan flag, that had been run over by a thousand fellows, and when I picked it up I did so because I thought it was pretty, and I wanted to have me a shirt made out of it."
>
> "I could have picked up forty, had I known that," said Sloan.
>
> "So could I, but I knew that the stragglers would pick them up."
>
> I felt sorter cheap when complimented for gallantry, and this high honor of fourth corporal was conferred on me . . . And had I only known that picking up flags entitled me to promotion and that every flag picked up would raise

me one notch higher, I would have quit fighting and gone picking up flags, and that means I would have soon been President of the Confederate States of America.[19]

If the capture of flags were a reason for reward and promotion, the loss of flags occasioned grief and embarrassment. The commander of the 1st Texas Infantry reported with "mortification" and "deep regret" that the regiment had lost its colors at the battle of Sharpsburg (Antietam), Maryland, in September 1862. The regiment suffered appalling losses in the fight; no one noticed until it was too late that the last color bearer never made it back to friendly lines.[20]

The battle of Franklin was one of the most disastrous of the war for the Confederacy and resulted in an enormous loss of flags. General John Bell Hood, commander of the Confederate Army of Tennessee, bristled at Federal reports of capturing thirty-one rebel flags. "We lost thirteen, capturing nearly the same number," Hood wrote the secretary of war. "The men who bore ours were killed on and within the enemy's interior line of works." To refute what he believed to be inflated claims, Hood had requested a count of battle flags lost at Franklin. Confederate generals who submitted their reports did so with explanations of the extreme circumstances in which the colors were lost. Three regiments in General W. S. Featherston's Mississippi brigade lost their colors. Featherston explained that two flags were lost when the color bearers "planted their colors on the enemy's works, and were wounded and captured with their colors." The third flag was lost when the color bearer was killed while planting it on the works and fell forward with the flag into the enemy trench.[21]

As Featherston's report suggested, the loss of a battle flag, though traumatic, was not necessarily dishonorable, especially when it occurred during an assault against enemy positions. Thus, in the many postwar accounts of Pickett's Charge at Gettysburg, the loss of flags provided evidence of soldierly valor in desperate fights. Ten men carried the colors of the 53rd Virginia to the stone wall crowning Cemetery Ridge. The last of the ten, Lieutenant H. L. Carter, found himself the lone unwounded man of the regiment inside enemy lines; he surrendered himself and the flag despite threats from a wounded comrade. Massachusetts soldier Benjamin Falls reached for what he believed to be the abandoned battle flag of the 19th Virginia Infantry at the stone wall, only to discover that it was still in the grasp of a wounded Confederate soldier. Falls pointed his bayonet at the soldier, forcing him to surrender the flag. A New York soldier encountered no resistance at all in "capturing" the flag of the 7th Virginia Infantry; he found it among the regiment's dead and wounded.[22]

The most celebrated story of courage and sacrifice by flag bearers at Gettysburg is that of the 26th North Carolina Infantry. On the first day of battle, the entire color guard and a total of fourteen (some accounts say fifteen) men fell carrying the colors during the regiment's successful but costly assault against McPherson's Ridge. After twelve other men had been killed or wounded bearing the flag, the unit's "boy colonel," Henry King Burgwyn, seized the flag, gave the order to "dress on the colors," and handed the flag to Private Franklin L. Honeycutt, who asked to carry it. Moments later, a burst of enemy fire struck Honeycutt in the head, killing him, and mortally wounded Burgwyn. Picking up the flag from where it lay by Honeycutt's body, the regiment's lieutenant colonel declared, "No one can take these colors and live." Raising the flag, he was shot through the neck and mouth.

Despite its horrific casualties on the first day of Gettysburg, the 26th was thrown into action on the third day as part of Pickett's Charge. The color guard was decimated again. As the remnants of the regiment approached the stone wall on Cemetery Ridge, two impromptu flag bearers advanced ahead and were captured along with the colors by men of the 12th New Jersey Infantry. The 26th North Carolina lost more than eighty percent of its men at the battle of Gettysburg.[23]

While sometimes the result of misfortune, carelessness, and even cowardice, the loss of battle flags usually indicated a hard fight and high casualties, and the capture of flags a smashing success. Major General John Schofield wrote U.S. Army Adjutant General Lorenzo Thomas that his XXIII Corps captured twenty flags at the battle of Franklin and that those flags "afford at the same time evidence of the strength of the enemy's column of attack, and of its disastrous repulse."[24]

In the postwar spirit of reconciliation between North and South, soldiers of both sides paid tribute to their opponents' battle flags as symbols of bravery that transcended principle. During the war, while enemy flags commanded soldierly respect, they also symbolized the enemy's will— the will that prolonged a bloody conflict. Many Federal soldiers never abandoned the belief that "Rebel" battle flags were symbols of treason that warranted nothing but contempt. In the aftermath of Pickett's Charge at Gettysburg, the commander of one of the Federal divisions that repulsed the attack, Brigadier General Alexander Hays, along with several members of his staff, tied captured Confederate battle flags to their horses' tails. Hays and his compatriots reportedly "rode down in front of his command, and in the rear, trailing the Rebel colors in the dust, and amid the deafening shouts and cheers of the men who for a moment forgot the terrible battle and thought only of the glory of their victory."[25] The sheaves of captured flags—so many that officers joked that there were enough flags for everyone—were the tangible symbols of the northern victory and Confederate defeat.

Carried heroically against the enemy's position in the face of certain death, the battle flag was also defended heroically—often to the death. On the evening before the battle of Cold Harbor, Virginia (June 3, 1864), Captain Thomas Colgate Morton encountered Color Sergeant Allen Woodram of the 26th Battalion, Virginia Infantry: "The brave fellow had picked up somewhere a stout brass spear, which he had rubbed until it shone like gold, and fastened it securely on the end of his flagstaff. I remarked that it was very pretty. He replied: 'It is not only pretty; but if anybody tries to get these colors, I'll run this through him.'" During the brief but intense battle, the battalion's position was overrun temporarily. A Federal officer confronted Woodram and demanded "'Surrender that flag, sir.'" According to Morton, Woodram replied:

> "This is the way I surrender, d–n you," and charged him
> with his flagstaff, running him clear through the body with
> the spear. The officer threw up his hands and fell dead. The
> two men with him fired into Wood[ram], and he fell with
> two bullets through his body, still holding on to his staff

with a death grip. Then there was a rush for the flag by the men of both sides, and a fierce scramble was had over both bodies. But the Confederates pressed the Union men back; Wood[ram], opening his eyes, saw that his precious flag was still safe, and with one last superhuman effort pulled himself forward and, reaching over, tore the colors from the staff, threw them behind him, and fell back a corpse.[26]

Even when defeat or surrender was inevitable, Confederate soldiers were still loath to see their colors fall into enemy hands. Men of the 7th Louisiana Infantry captured at the battle of Rappahannock Station, Virginia, in November 1863 kept their flag hidden and burned it in a campfire at the first opportunity. On the retreat from Richmond to Appomattox, the 19th Virginia Infantry was cut off by Federal cavalry. The southerners rallied around the flag but had no cartridges left. A member of the 19th later recounted the unit's last moments:

> The color bearer's name was L—, and as he stood there hatless, coatless, with passion blazing in his eyes, he clung to his flag. The Yankees flourished their sabers, brandished pistols, and called, "Give up that old rag, you d—d rebel! or we'll blow your brains out."
>
> "Touch it if you dare and I'll punch your d—d Yankee head off!" rejoined L—.
>
> The colonel of the 19th urged the soldier to spare his own life: "L— surrender the flag; it's all over with us."
>
> And thus the battle-flag of the Nineteenth was surrendered . . . L— is a successful tobacco planter, is a quiet man and an honest citizen. He says very little now about the war, but his eyes fill with tears whenever he speaks of the battle-flag of the old Nineteenth Virginia.[27]

When it became apparent that Lee's entire army was surrendered at Appomattox, Captain Napoleon Bonaparte Bowyer and two comrades of the 10th Virginia Cavalry decided that they would not surrender. "Not wanting the old Flag to fall into [Yankee] hands," the cavalrymen asked an Appomattox woman "to take it and keep it until called for." The soldiers cut three stars from the flag—one for each of them—then made their escape across the Appomattox River. Before surrendering the flag of the 4th Georgia Infantry at Appomattox, Private John Gay cut out the part of the fabric bearing the unit designation, symbolically saving the flag from capture.[28] Like Ellen Glasgow's fictional Dan Lightfoot, other soldiers cut up their battle flags and divided them among the surviving members of their units.

Two months after Appomattox and a thousand miles to the west, several hundred survivors of Brigadier General Joseph O. Shelby's Missouri cavalry division fled to Mexico rather than surrender. On July 4, 1865, they symbolically buried their battle flag in the Rio Grande. Shortly afterward, a colonel in the division penned a poem, "The Burial of Shelby's Flag":

> They buried then that flag and plume
> In the river's rushing tide,
> Ere that gallant few
> Of the tried and true
> Had been scattered far and wide.
> And that group of Missouri's valiant throng,
> Who had fought for the weak against the strong—
> Who had charged and bled
> Where Shelby led,
> Were the last who held above the wave
> The glorious flag of the vanquished brave,
> No more to rise from its watery grave![29]

So wrenching was the prospect of Confederate soldiers surrendering their battle flags that a January 1864 editorial used it as a metaphor for subjugation. Surrender meant that "some maimed and battle-worn Confederate" would watch as his flag was "formally lowered, officially torn, trampled and abolished forever." The southern cross had been symbolic of the soldier's "love and devotion," and its triumphs had been associated with "a secure and peaceful home and an honorable future for his country." Laying down the flags spelled the disarming of the Confederacy—tragic not only because it meant the death of the new nation but also because it dashed the hopes and wasted the heroic efforts of the Confederate soldiers.[30]

However lamentable, surrender to the Yankees was the fate of hundreds of flags of the Army of Northern Virginia, the Army of Tennessee, the Department of Alabama and Northern Mississippi, and the Department of the Trans-Mississippi in April and May 1865. An estimated seventy-one regiments in the Army of Northern Virginia surrendered their colors at Appomattox in April 1865. Federal General Joshua Lawrence Chamberlain, the hero of Little Round Top at Gettysburg, described the surrender of the Confederate forces at Appomattox on April 12th. The "worn and half starved" Confederates fixed bayonets, stacked arms, and laid down their cartridge boxes.

> Lastly, reluctantly, with agony of expression, they tenderly fold their flags, battle-worn and torn, blood-stained, heart-holding colors, and lay them down; some frenziedly rushing from the ranks, kneeling over them, clinging to them, pressing them to their lips with burning tears. Twenty-seven thousand men surrendered what Chamberlain estimated to be one hundred battle flags. And many a bare staff was there laid down, from which the ensign had been torn in the passion and struggle of emotions, and divided piece by piece; a blurred or shrunken star, a rag of smoke-stained blue from the war-torn cross, a shred of deepened dye from the rent field of red, to be treasured for precious keepsakes of manhood's test and heirlooms for their children.

Echoing the reconciliationist sentiment that filled many Federal veterans after the war, Chamberlain concluded: "We could not look into those brave, bronzed faces, and those battered flags we had met on so many fields where glorious manhood lent a glory to the earth that bore it, and think of personal hate and mean revenge. Whoever had misled these men, we had not."[31]

Three weeks later, near Greensboro, North Carolina, the other major Confederate field army, the Army of Tennessee, surrendered to the army of Major General William T. Sherman. Among the regiments folding their colors that day were the 1st and 26th Tennessee Infantry regiments. The usually sardonic Sam Watkins described in reverential tones how the 1st Tennessee, consisting of "a mere squad" of men, "gathered around the tattered flag that they had followed in every battle through that long war. It was so bullet-riddled and torn that it was but a few blue and red shreds that hung drooping while it, too, was stacked with our guns forever."[32]

The flag of the 26th Tennessee, adorned with the unit designation from the regiment's original flag and battle honors dating back to 1861, was left upon the field. Somehow, instead of going into the War Department collection of captured flags, the 26th's banner fell into the hands of the son of the governor of Massachusetts. Thirty-two years later, H. H. Andrew returned the trophy to the survivors of the regiment.[33] Carried in battles from Fort Donelson to Chickamauga to Atlanta to Bentonville, the old flag (and its predecessor) embodied the very identity of the 26th Tennessee Infantry.

Whether hidden or torn up to avoid capture, or captured and turned over to the U.S. War Department, hundreds of Confederate battle flags survived the war and ultimately were deposited in public collections.[34] Those that remain in private hands are among the most prized of all Civil War collectibles—pieces of wool and cotton that were defended to the death on the battlefield and consecrated with the blood of soldiers. Taken literally, it is those flags *only* that have association with the Confederate soldier and command respect as symbols of the soldier. But in the decades after the war, facsimiles of the St. Andrew's cross battle flag would play a prominent role in the memory and veneration of the Confederate soldier and the vindication of the Confederate cause. Flags were omnipresent at Memorial Day services, monument dedications, and other events, and they continue to be displayed at such events in the twenty-first century. Occasionally those events featured the actual flags used by Confederate soldiers during the war, but most of the flags used in the postwar era were reproductions of the original design. Clearly, it was not just the actual Confederate battle flags that became the objects of veneration but the pattern itself.

Chapter 3

"Unfurl the Old Flag"

Shortly after the surrender of the Confederate armies in April and May of 1865, Father Abram J. Ryan wrote a requiem for the Confederacy entitled "The Conquered Banner." Its closing lines urged southerners to

> Furl that banner, softly, slowly,
> Treat it gently—it is holy—
> For it droops above the dead;
> Touch it not, unfold it never,
> Let it droop there, *furled* forever,
> For its people's *hopes* are dead.[1]

In Ryan's popular and widely published poem, the Confederate flag—specifically the St. Andrew's cross—was a metaphor for resignation to defeat. Furling the "conquered banner" did not mean dishonoring or forgetting it (for it will "live in song and story") but merely accepting that the armies which carried it were no more.

Father Ryan's advice did not meet with universal approval and in fact elicited poetic rebuttal. Upon reading Ryan's poem, Sir Henry Houghton, an English friend of the Confederacy, wrote "A Reply to the Conquered Banner":

> Gallant nation, foiled by numbers!
> Say not that your hopes are fled;
> Keep that glorious flag which slumbers,
> One day to avenge your dead.
> Keep it widowed, sonless mothers!
> Keep it, sisters, mourning brothers!
> Furl it now but keep it still—
> Furl that banner, sadly, slowly,
> Treat it gently, for 'tis holy;
> Till that day—yes furl it sadly;
> Then once more unfurl it gladly—
> Conquered banner! keep it still![2]

Subsequent decades brought a flood of poems replying to Ryan and respectfully beseeching southerners to "furl it not" and proclaiming that the battle flag deserved the respect of the reunited nation. Without Houghton's belligerence ("One day to avenge your dead"), the latter-day poets celebrated the flag as a symbol of "the right of a cause that has never been lost!"[3] As it turned out, history favored Henry Houghton over Father Ryan. White southerners soon unfurled their battle flags and in the process elevated the flag to an even more lofty importance than it had enjoyed during the war.

The years immediately following the war were not exactly friendly to the unfurled banner. Modern Confederate partisans have written that, "as a vindictive measure, Reconstruction despots forbade postwar display of the Confederate flag." A North Carolina woman remembered that Confederate flags (along with other relics such as locks of General Lee's hair and pictures of President Davis) were treated as "contraband articles" during Reconstruction. Orders in several U.S. military departments prohibited the wearing of gray uniforms and Confederate military insignia (including buttons), and heavy-handed enforcement of these regulations provoked much resentment. General Daniel Sickles issued a special order in Charleston, South Carolina, prohibiting rumored ceremonies "tending to revive feelings against the government of the United States." Research fails to reveal explicit orders regarding Confederate flags. Southern civilians presumably understood—or were made to understand—that flags associated with their late nation were forbidden in public.[4]

The implied prohibition of flags was demonstrated in an incident that occurred in Rome, Georgia, in early 1867. On January 25, federal troops arrested four young men—former Confederate soldiers—in the town and confined them for three weeks in an Atlanta jail. Their offense was participating a few weeks earlier in a tableau depicting "an officer's funeral." The young men wore Confederate uniforms and briefly hung a Confederate battle flag over the casket. A federal official of the Freedmen's Bureau walked out during this display, eliciting hisses and jeers from the audience. The official, Captain C. A. de la Mesa, had reported in December "a public exhibition of the Confederate Flag in this place where it was received with the honor and applause due to the United States Flag, which I have never seen here." After the January 3 tableau, he requested permission to issue an order "prohibiting all such displays, as they are unnecessary and only serve to excite feelings which are detrimental to the good order of this place."[5]

Not surprisingly, the citizens of Rome had a completely different perception of the incident. Rome city officials and newspaper editors hastened to explain that the tableau was a fundraiser for the war-damaged church. Organizers of the tableau intended no disrespect toward the United States and believed that using the flag was not a problem because the same flag had been used in December as part of an entertainment at the Episcopal Church while the choir performed the new musical version of Father Ryan's "The Conquered Banner." On both occasions the flag used was an actual battle flag that a Georgia unit carried in the war. Indignant newspaper editors throughout the state criticized and ridiculed the arrests, echoing the protest that no orders forbade such innocent flag displays. A Macon, Georgia, newspaper concluded that "no relics of the dead Confederacy" were permissible at public occasions. "Therefore, let all the flags, buttons, boots, sashes, swords, grey uniforms, and so on, of the late Confederacy, slumber in the dust of our garrets, or our young men and maidens may find themselves unexpectedly in some U.S. dungeons."[6]

General William D. Whipple, adjutant to the department commander, scoffed at these explanations and chastised the citizens of Rome and elsewhere for their insistence on characterizing themselves as "Confederates" and not as the traitors and rebels that the U.S. deemed them to be. "It is pretended by certain newspapers that because no order had been issued from these headquarters, that the 'flag of the Confederacy' was not to see the light, the citizens were not warned that it would be a treasonable act," Whipple wrote in reply. The very name and emblems of the Confederacy were "hateful to the people of the United States," and anyone who would parade with them must be "obtuse."[7]

The Rome incident revealed several things about the Confederate flag in the South during Reconstruction. Federal officials were obviously hostile toward it, but white southerners soon unfurled it, at least on seemingly appropriate memorial occasions. The correspondence and published accounts of the incident suggest that even by early 1867, southerners and northerners alike used "Confederate flag" and "rebel flag" to mean the St. Andrew's cross battle flag.

In the wake of the Rome incident, a reporter complained in early 1867 that recently the "Rebel flag" was being displayed in the South more than the Stars and Stripes. While the *Times'* complaint may have been hyperbole, other testimony suggested that some southerners were not shy with their flags. The U.S. Congress 1866 Joint Committee on Reconstruction, which laid the groundwork for so-called Radical Reconstruction policy initiated in 1867, noted that unrepentant white southerners "openly insulted" the Stars and Stripes, but the committee seemed not to care whether southerners still clung to their Confederate colors. One witness, Dr. James M. Turner, former editor of the *Nashville Gazette,* testified that "Secesh [secessionist] flags are peddled publicly on the streets" in New Orleans. U.S. Army Sergeant Mathew Woodruff, in

Mobile, Alabama, related an incident in which a black woman repri-
manded three white girls for waving a rebel flag. The girls' mother "appeared with a saucy rebuke & insults to all *Yanks,* saying 'they' [the South]
was not whip[p]ed & if they got a chance would rise again." Woodruff believed these "to be the prevailing sentiments throughout the South."[8]

Former Confederates resisted federal Reconstruction policy, especially the enfranchisement and empowerment of freed blacks, with terrorist and paramilitary activity, but nearly all did so without unfurling
their wartime flags. The most famous resistance group, of course, was
the Ku Klux Klan, which was born in a Pulaski, Tennessee, law office in
the winter of 1865–66 and had strong Confederate roots. Nevertheless,
the original KKK did not use Confederate flags in its rituals or in its terrorist acts. The KKK's use of the Confederate flag awaited its second re-
incarnation in the 1940s.

In contrast to the Klan, the Carolina Rifle Club of Charleston, South
Carolina, fulfilled its mission of providing "the only organized defence of
the white race against negro aggression" under the same battle flag carried by Confederate troops a decade earlier. Founded in 1869, the club's
moment came during the 1876 gubernatorial campaign when members
patrolled the streets to prevent rumored Negro rioting. Former Confederate General Wade Hampton won the election, and South Carolina was
"redeemed" from Reconstruction rule. The club's official banner was a
state flag with the letter "C" superimposed over the palmetto tree. In
1874 the club was presented with a "valued relic": an old Secession Flag
that had flown on a prominent corner in wartime Charleston. A year
later, members of the club donated the stars that had been torn from two
battle flags in 1865 just before the flags were burned to prevent their
capture. Then, in June 1875, the club's new president, C. Irvine Walker,
presented to the club the original battle flag carried during the war by his
unit, the 10th South Carolina (Infantry) Volunteers. The men of the club
carried the flag through the streets of Charleston shortly afterward.
Walker, who subsequently became a commander-in-chief of the United
Confederate Veterans, later boasted that "the Carolina Rifle Club had the

honor of being the first military body of white men which paraded in the streets of the city or the State, bearing arms and the first to march under the Confederate Banner, since the struggles of the War had ceased."[9]

Even before the final struggle to redeem South Carolina and end Reconstruction in the South, the Confederate battle flag began to appear in what became its most familiar postwar role—as a memorial and ceremonial symbol. Reconstruction ended in most southern states by 1870, and Confederate flags began appearing in memorial observances almost immediately. A flag was used to drape the cornerstone of a monument in an Atlanta cemetery during its unveiling in October 1870. In Richmond, the former Confederate capital, flags appeared in observances as early as 1872. Coffins containing the remains of Confederate soldiers transferred to Hollywood Cemetery from the Gettysburg battlefield were covered with flowers and Confederate flags. Also at Hollywood Cemetery, a battle flag made of flowers was displayed during the funeral service for Major General George E. Pickett in 1875.[10]

The ritual celebration of the Confederacy and its heroes—what historians call the Confederate memorial period—flourished from the mid-1880s into the 1920s. Local women's and veterans' organizations were formed immediately after the war to honor the war dead and care for the survivors. In the 1890s, as the Civil War generation reached the apogee of its political and social influence, those local organizations blossomed into national umbrella groups that were as dedicated to vindicating the "Lost Cause" as to assisting veterans and their families. Throughout the era, Confederate veterans and their descendants staged celebrations, erected monuments, and built equally enduring edifices of historical interpretation.[11]

The earliest memorial organizations were often direct outgrowths of wartime ladies' aid societies in the South. Their postwar purposes were to assist veterans and their families and to maintain Confederate cemeteries. Among the accomplishments of those organizations were the establishment of Memorial Day and the erection of the first Confederate monuments in the late 1860s. Monuments to Confederate heroes, such as General Thomas J. "Stonewall" Jackson in Richmond and to General

Robert E. Lee in New Orleans, were dedicated as early as 1875 and 1884, respectively, but the frenzy of Confederate monument building awaited the late 1880s and 1890s. The veterans themselves began organizing immediately after the war, usually in benevolent associations intended to help soldiers adjust to civilian life. Sometimes the associations consisted of men from a few prestigious military units. The veterans of Memphis and Charleston, South Carolina, formed citywide associations in 1866; South Carolina formed the first statewide survivors association in 1869.[12]

Not until 1889 did southern veterans form a national organization to mirror the Grand Army of the Republic (GAR), the Federal veterans organization formed in 1866. Veterans met in June 1889 in New Orleans and called upon all local and state associations to send delegates to a convention in Chattanooga in 1890. With the 1889 meeting was born the United Confederate Veterans. The UCV, with its monthly magazine, *Confederate Veteran* (published 1893–1932), became the voice of virtually all organized Confederate veterans. At its peak in 1903, the UCV had 47,000 active and 35,000 inactive members in 1,523 camps. Encouraged by veterans (especially in Virginia) afraid that Confederate ideals would die with them, sons of veterans in 1896 formed the United Sons of Confederate Veterans, or simply the Sons of Confederate Veterans. As the veterans aged, the SCV assumed a larger role in reunions, eventually taking over the symbols and ideology of the UCV and perpetuating the ideals and the rituals of the memorial period into our own time.

The United Daughters of the Confederacy, conceived originally as an auxiliary to the UCV, was created in 1894 at a meeting in Nashville, Tennessee. The UDC derived its name from the nickname "Daughter of the Confederacy" that General John B. Gordon bestowed upon Varina Anne "Winnie" Davis, the daughter of President Jefferson Davis. Statewide women's organizations in Missouri and Tennessee and countless local organizations had adopted the name by the time of the Nashville meeting. Under the auspices of the UDC, an extensive network of state divisions and local chapters was formed throughout the South and beyond. The UDC created its own auxiliary group, the Children of the Confederacy, but this organization never achieved significant size or influence. By 1900 a formal structure of Confederate memorial organizations was in place: Veterans, Sons, Daughters, and Children.

Common to all of these groups was a reverence for Confederate flags, especially the St. Andrew's cross battle flag. They frequently used reproduction and even original wartime battle flags in their rituals. The earliest and most persistent Confederate celebrations were Memorial Day observances. Memorial Day began as "decoration day." Throughout the late nineteenth century, it was customary for ladies to "lay their tributes of flowers and praise" upon graves. Not until the early twentieth century did it become common to place small flags—usually battle flags—by the headstones of Confederate soldiers (as it became customary to put U.S. flags on the graves of northern soldiers in the 1890s). Women from Virginia to Arkansas decorated soldiers' graves with flags as well as flowers and evergreens. In 1916 the UDC incorporated flags into the official Memorial Day program. Chairmen and organizers were instructed to "urge every child to have a Confederate flag to place on some soldier's grave that day." As early as 1880, citizens in Columbus, Georgia (the home of the first "official" Confederate Memorial Day), insisted on their right to display Confederate flags. If it were considered disloyal to display the Confederate flag on Memorial Day, "we are going to do something terribly outrageous," someone wrote to the *Columbus Enquirer.*[13]

At Richmond's Hollywood Cemetery, the final resting place of 18,000 Confederate dead, the lady caretakers were sensitive to the particular importance of the battle flag. Each year a private benefactor donated "a large bundle of our beloved battle flags, which enable us to place one at each grave." The chairman of the Hollywood Association's decorating committee suggested in 1910 that the association "procure a few *bunting, Battle* flags. With the exception of two, all our bunting flags are the flags of the Confederacy, just right in its place, but not so suitable for the soldiers in the field as the Battle-flag under which they fought."[14]

In the earliest monument dedications, Confederate battle flags were few in number but great in their power to inspire. Apparently the only battle flags present at the October 1875 dedication of a statue of Stonewall Jackson in Richmond's Capitol Square were actual wartime flags, not postwar reproductions. Veterans of Jackson's original command, the Stonewall Brigade, carried a "battle-torn" flag which, according to the *Daily Dispatch,* "excited hurrahs that were hearty and loud, but not rebellious."[15]

Original battle flags proliferated at one of the largest Confederate celebrations ever held: the dedication of Anton Mercier's monumental statue of Robert E. Lee in Richmond in May 1890. "Confederate colors were omnipresent," waved from windows and front porches as Confederate veterans passed by on parade. The veterans themselves carried battle flags, many of them originals from the war. According to one account, "The wonder was where they all came from, but one on the inside would soon hear touching stories of how some brave color bearer concealed his colors on his person when he found the surrender must come, and has sacredly guarded them all these years to bring them forth to honor their loved old chief."[16]

Seventeen years later, when the veterans gathered again in Richmond to dedicate statues to J. E. B. Stuart and Jefferson Davis, flags were "omnipresent" along the parade route as well as in Hollywood Cemetery. One of the highlights of the ceremonies was the creation of a "human battle flag" on a grandstand near the Lee statue.[17] The pageant was reprised at the UCV reunion in Richmond in 1915.

Carrying original battle flags was apparently part of the ritual during early reunion parades as well. The survivors of the 6th Virginia Cavalry carried their flag in their first reunion, where it "was looked upon with deep emotion by many a battle-scarred veteran." Six months later, they donated the flag to the Confederate Museum (now The Museum of the Confederacy), requesting the privilege to borrow it "for regimental reunions and public occasions." The wife and daughters of Brigadier General John R. Cooke made a battle flag for the veterans of the 46th North Carolina Infantry (a regiment in Cooke's brigade) to use at the 1897 reunion in Nashville. Although the flag was new, it still held great sentimental value, for the center star had been cut and saved from the regiment's original flag surrendered at Appomattox.[18]

It became customary for cities hosting the annual reunion of the

United Confederate Veterans to deck out the streets and buildings with flags, both American and Confederate. "'The Conquered Banner,' which our poet, Father Ryan, bade us furl lo, so many years ago, multiplied a thousand fold to-day, floats gayly and proudly on every side, each flutter a triumphant wave of pride," intoned a speaker at the 1903 UCV reunion in New Orleans.[19]

"From one end of the city to the other the battle flag of the Confederacy is waving in the breeze," observed the New Orleans *Picayune* during the 1906 reunion. The Richmond *Times-Dispatch* described the site of the 1907 UCV reunion: "Confederate flags, battle-flags, red, white and blue bunting, hung from every rafter, and it was not considered at all disloyal that the Stars and Stripes was conspicuous by their absence." Katharine Du Pre Lumpkin, a southern liberal, recalled an early-century veterans reunion in Columbia, South Carolina: "Confederate flags. They were everywhere, by the thousands, of every size. People thronging Main Street carried flags. A few might also have South Carolina's banner—a palmetto tree and a crescent against a field of blue—but all would have a Confederate flag."[20]

Such ceremonies and rituals were part of the rhythm of public life in the South well into the twentieth century. In contrast to the diminished scale and marginalization of Confederate memorial ceremonies held in the late twentieth and early twenty-first centuries, the celebration of important dates on the Confederate calendar—Robert E. Lee's birthday, Confederate Memorial Day, and Jefferson Davis's birthday—were mainstream events before World War II. It was, of course, in this long era that Confederate veterans and their immediate descendants controlled public culture in the South and, not coincidentally, when African Americans in the South were excluded from mainstream public life. The widespread ceremonial use of Confederate flags in this era was the norm—a norm that came under challenge in the late twentieth century.

As it was during the war itself, the St. Andrew's cross was the most meaningful flag for white southerners. Confederate memorial groups by no means ignored or disdained the other flags. Each of the major memorial groups adopted one of the four major Confederate flags: the

UDC adopted the first national flag; the SCV the third national flag; the Children of the Confederacy the second national flag; and the UCV the Confederate battle flag. By 1927 the SCV took over the battle flag as its own. Even before the creation of the UCV, the Louisiana Division of the Association of the Army of Tennessee adopted as its seal and badge a rectangular battle flag bearing a pelican motif over the center star. Veterans agreed with the writer of a 1904 article who insisted that the battle flag was the "real" Confederate flag and worried that the Stars and Bars—the first national pattern—would go down in history as "the Confederate flag."[21] Thanks to the concerted efforts of Confederate veterans, his prophecy proved far from accurate.

Instead of being eclipsed by the Stars and Bars, the battle flag was the primary beneficiary of a campaign to define and enshrine Confederate flags. This campaign coincided with the birth of a Stars and Stripes "cult" among northern patriotic organizations. Beginning in 1889, the New York GAR lobbied for placing U.S. flags in every public school in the state, for passing legislation to protect the flag from desecration and commercial exploitation, and for designating an annual flag day. While some northern veterans questioned "these mysterious flag gesticulations," the flag cult gathered steam nationally. It culminated in the creation of a national flag code and Flag Day in the 1920s.[22]

The UCV and other memorial organizations sought to preserve for posterity official histories and specifications of the Confederate flags and especially to define the correct shape of the Confederate battle flag. The question arose in the 1890s as reproduction flags proliferated and became fixtures at reunions, Memorial Day ceremonies, and other Confederate celebrations. At the beginning of the twentieth century—as in the early twenty-first—most battle flags produced for sale were rectangular. While those dimensions were commonly used for flags in the Army of Tennessee (especially after 1864) and were adopted for the naval jack, they did not conform to the specifications of the flags carried by the Army of Northern Virginia. "I venture to say that not a veteran of the Army of Northern Virginia recognizes this oblong thing that we parade under at our reunions as the flag we fought under," wrote R. A. Owen of

Mississippi to the *Confederate Veteran* in 1903. "As we are making history for the sake of our children and children's children, let us transmit our flag to them in its proper shape." Particularly worrisome to Confederate veterans was the depiction of oblong battle flags in the atlas accompanying the *Official Records* and other "great works of reference and the school histories."[23] Clarifying the proper shape of the flag was of "historical importance" and had to be settled "by the veterans now living." Furthermore, until the veterans authenticated the proper shape of the flag, it would be impossible to obtain "correct" flags from commercial manufacturers except through special order.[24]

In November 1903 the UCV created a committee to investigate the proper shape of the battle flag. Chaired by Dr. Samuel E. Lewis of Washington, D.C., the committee inspected the largest collection of flags: the captured battle flags housed at the U.S. War Department. The committee also received voluminous correspondence from fellow veterans, many of whom agreed with Owen that they never saw oblong flags during their service. The committee reported to the 1904 UCV reunion and annual meeting in Nashville, and, in accordance with the report, the veterans passed a resolution declaring officially that the Confederate battle flag was a square.[25]

In making its case, the committee imposed a uniformity on the history of Confederate battle flags that did not exist during the life of the Confederacy. Ironically for an organization based in Nashville, the UCV committee paid scant attention to the diversity of battle flag patterns that had existed especially in the western armies. John H. Hill, a veteran who had been a courier in Lieutenant General William Hardee's Corps, Army of Tennessee, described to Lewis the Hardee battle flag (blue with a "white Globe in Centre") that was in use as late as the battle of Resaca in May 1864. "Possibly you belonged to the Army of Northern Virginia[;] you should have on your committee Some one familiar with the army of Tennessee," Hill suggested. Lewis's report maintained—erroneously—that the Hardee, Polk, and other patterns were replaced in the spring of 1862. The committee could not ignore the oblong St. Andrew's cross flags that it found in its investigation, but it did minimize their significance. The flag of the 10th South Carolina Infantry, which C. Irvine Walker had resurrected for use by the Carolina Rifle Men in 1875, was oblong. It was, Walker assured Lewis, "most notably exceptional." In correcting a UDC officer about flags, Lewis conceded: "It is true that there were some oblong battle-flags carried but they were of domestic make."[26]

On June 3, 1906, a general order promulgated the resolution and requested all members of the UCV, SCV, UDC, and other memorial associations "to exert their utmost influence in support of the Resolution and the Abridged Report, as above given, to the end that manufacturers of flags, designers, engravers, and others, may hereafter be required to conform therewith in all respects." General Clement A. Evans, chairman of the UCV's Historical Committee, praised the flag report, linking the shape of the battle flags with the larger effort to vindicate the Confederate cause. "The shape and features of that flag belong to history," Evans said. "It is the revered symbol of our martial life in the Confederacy, and a token of our everlasting comradeship. It is too dear to us to be furled, for it proclaims a Cause that was never lost."[27]

Proclaiming the square flag the correct flag did not, however, make it the most available flag. Although all of the UDC's approved suppliers of Confederate flags were based in northern cities, the reluctance to produce correct flags stemmed not from sectional petulance but from the alchemy of Yankee business sense and southern demand. Northern firms began making and marketing Confederate flags even before the Spanish-American War. By 1924 Annin & Co., a New York City firm that designated its address "Old Glory Corner," advertised an impressive array of flags and such related products as shields, paper plumes, and paper festooning. (Echoing the 1863 Savannah *Daily Morning News,* Annin's 1924 catalog labeled its replica of the second national flag the "White Man's Flag.") In reply to a complaint about the "ridiculous" sizes and shapes of flags on the market, Annin officials explained that the firm had made square battle flags—according to "regulation" size—since 1914. "It is only occasional that we have orders for these regulation size Confederate Battle Flags," Annin explained. "The demand seems to be for the Confederate Battle flag in a size that will harmonize with the other confederate flags, the first and the second National flags and stars and bars." Annin had "had difficulty in disposing of a few gross" of the regulation flags. After years of intermittent negotiation with the UDC, Annin agreed to produce square miniature battle flags if guaranteed an exclusive contract and a minimum order of 150 gross. The UDC appointed a Committee to Arrange for Manufacture and Distribution of the Correctly Designed Battle Flag of the Confederacy, and it urged members to buy them.[28]

The long struggle to obtain correct square flags revealed how the St. Andrews cross had become in effect *the* Confederate flag. As a Norfolk, Virginia, manufacturer explained to the UDC in 1926, "There will always be a greater demand for the oblong sizes that compare with the U.S. Flags in use for they are used together so often."[29] Because the battle flag was (as it was conceived to be) a distinctive pattern, it was the preferred Confederate counterpart to the Stars and Stripes. Yet in its historically revised role, it was commonly given a shape that was officially incorrect as a battle flag but correct as a national flag. It was also saddled with an incorrect nickname—the Stars and Bars—that properly belonged to the first national flag but which was adopted because it was alliterative with the Stars and Stripes. The interrelated problems of status, shape, and name still exist today.

To its postwar devotees, the battle flag was, as Clement Evans declared in 1904, a symbol of the Confederate cause as well as of the Confederacy's martial life. The battle flag's meaning in the memorial era was tied inextricably to a body of thought and feeling known then and since as the "Lost Cause." Even as Abram Ryan counseled southerners to furl their banners of war, other influential voices advised southerners how to win the peace. Edward A. Pollard, editor of the Richmond *Examiner,* borrowed the term "Lost Cause" from the lore of the Scottish Jacobites, who had been defeated by the English in 1745. In doing so, Pollard gave the vanquished Confederacy a new name and new identity. The South had been overcome by superior force, not by a superior civilization. Pollard appealed to southerners not to surrender their ideas and their ideals along with their armies and their banners. "It would be immeasurably the worst consequence of defeat in this war," Pollard wrote in *The Lost Cause*

(1866) "that the South should lose its moral and intellectual distinctive-ness as a people, and cease to assert its well-known superiourity in civili-zation, in political scholarship, and in all the standards of individual char-acter over the people of the North." The South, Pollard wrote,

> must submit fairly and truthfully to *what the war has properly decided*. But the war properly decided only what was put in issue: the restoration of the Union and the excision of slav-ery; and to these two conditions the South submits. But the war did not decide negro equality; it did not decide negro suffrage; it did not decide State Rights, although it might have exploded their abuse; it did not decide the or-thodoxy of the Democratic party; it did not decide the right of a people to show dignity in misfortune, and to maintain self-respect in the face of adversity. And these things, which the war did not decide, the southern people will still cling to, still claim, and still assert them in their rights and views. [30]

Postwar southerners heeded Pollard's rallying cry. The sense of the su-periority of their civilization and character became an article of south-ern faith. The South's traditional institutional religion reinforced a new "civil religion" that sanctified the Confederacy and deified Confederate heroes. [31] The Lost Cause pervaded southern literature in the late nine-teenth century and much of southern historical writing well into the twentieth century. Pollard's argument that the war compelled the South to accept only emancipation and reunion—narrowly defined—similarly inspired the South's postwar political and social life.

The Confederate memorial organizations born in the 1890s embraced and embellished the Lost Cause ideology. They conducted "historical" and "educational" work which promoted an explicitly southern view of the Civil War and countered what they believed to be the pro-northern bias of prevailing histories. As Confederate organizations embarked on this corrective mission, the Grand Army of the Republic complained that history texts were too forgiving of the South and even-handed in their treatment of the causes of the war. The work of southern organizations helped preserve valuable documents and artifacts associated with the Confederacy and produced a body of literature—"revisionist" in the purely objective sense of the term—which is part of the historical dialogue today.

The UDC created a History Committee which reported matter-of-factly in 1898 that in any acceptable school history "we must insist on declaring our own principles, that we knew we were right, and that those who fought and died in that struggle were neither traitors nor rebels." Among the means devised to achieve this end was the publication in 1904 of the *U.D.C. Catechism for Children*. This small pamphlet consisted of a series of questions and answers designed to foster reverence for the Confederacy and its heroes. The history of the Confederacy's national and battle flag and their adoption by latter-day "Confederate organizations" occupied one page of the 10-page catechism. The UDC also spearheaded the enormously successful educational effort to make "War between the States" the quasi-official southern name for the war.[32]

At its 1892 convention the UCV appointed a Historical Committee, charged "to formulate a plan to secure a true and reliable history of the late civil war, and to select a proper and truthful history of the United States to recommend for use in the public and private schools of the South." "What is needed," the Historical Committee reported in 1895, "is history equally fitted for use of North and South, divested of all passion and prejudice incident to the war period."[33]

The committee in 1907 posed questions about the war that could "be discussed dispassionately, without engendering sectional bad feeling." The questions and the answers provided to them revealed, however, that underlying the UCV's conciliatory rhetoric was an insistence that history show simply that the South was right. The committee asked: Which side was responsible for the underlying causes of conflict? If slavery was *a* cause (but not *the* cause), who was responsible for slavery? Which side provoked the conflict? "Which side had the legal right to do what was done?" and "Which side conducted itself the better and according to the rules of civilized warfare pending the conflict?" Predictably, Committee

Chairman Judge George L. Christian answered all the questions in favor of the Confederacy. Accepting this historical interpretation effectively asked northern veterans to admit that their cause was unjust and illegal and their behavior uncivilized.[34]

In the years following World War I, Confederate veterans believed that events had vindicated their cause. Echoing a refrain heard often in the wake of President Woodrow Wilson's 1918 call for the "self-determination" of nations, the UCV in 1924 declared that "the principles for which we fought have risen triumphant over the whole world . . . Our sublime Confederate efforts have not been in vain." A southern woman expressed the conviction poetically:

> The cause of Lee and Jackson, though 'twas trampled in the dust
> By overwhelming odds, has risen, commanding world-wide
>   trust;
> 'Tis now the cause of Pershing and our brave boys o'er the sea
> The cause upheld by Dixie's knights with Jackson and with Lee.
> Yes, Dixie's cause triumphant is the South's "lost cause" no more;
> Speak not of it as "lost," for it gleams out as ne'er before.[35]

While denying vehemently that Confederates fought for slavery, southern partisans of the era did not hesitate to boast that Confederates fought for "white supremacy." The Sons of Confederate Veterans sought to recruit members in the early 1920s by appealing to the need to preserve the "high ideals and principles" for which their forefathers had fought. Having "strategically won the victory in arms," the Confederates succumbed to overwhelming odds only to fight during Reconstruction "another great battle for white supremacy and southern ideals, and won again."[36] UCV Commander-in-Chief R. A. Sneed in 1930 elaborated on the South's "Superb Victory in Defeat":

> Great in war, you were even greater in Peace, for by the
> exercise of wise patience and statesmanship, by the display
> of the same gallantry that characterized you at Manassas,
> Shilo [sic], Gettysburg, and the wilderness, you wrested

Dixieland from the "Tragic Era" of Reconstruction Rule, with its reign of ignorance, mongrelism, and depravity, and established once and all [sic] on southern soil the incontrovertible doctrine of White Supremacy. History records no parallel to your illustrious achievements, both in War and Peace. There is no other instance where brave armies worn out by four years of arduous and unequal contest, witnessed as an aftermath to their defeat, the triumph of the principles for which they fought, the re-establishment of the principles of local self-government, sanctioned by the Declaration of Independence, and safeguarded in the Constitution of the United States of America.[37]

Building upon Sneed's tribute to the Confederate veteran's postwar victory for "the supremacy of the white race," George H. Armistead, of the Nashville *Banner,* told veterans two years later that "in saving the South to Anglo-Saxon civilization, we can now see that, in large measure, [the Confederate soldier] saved the nation; and that service will be history's greatest monument to him."[38] Such rhetoric was consistent with the so-called scientific racism that enjoyed a vogue among American elites early in the twentieth century, in the North as well as in the South.

During the memorial period, Confederate flags were used not merely to honor the veterans who fought under them but also as symbolic manifestations of "correct" history. Metaphorical references to flags, latter-day representations of flags, and especially the ceremonial use of actual wartime battle flags symbolized not just the character and accomplishments of Confederate soldiers but the societal ideals for which they fought. Just as the battle flag became during the war the most important emblem of Confederate nationalism, so did it become during the memorial period the symbolic embodiment of the Lost Cause ideology. UCV Commander-in-Chief Irvine Walker reflected on the meaning of the battle flag in a 1912 letter to Samuel Lewis. The Stars and Bars (referring now to the first national flag), Walker noted, was simply a change of the U.S. flag, enough to make a change for distinguishment—We were attached to the old flag & did not care to abandon it. I think some of our statesmen were more apt to have made this change for political or sentimental objects & not for artistic effect. As the war went on, our feelings changed, our Battle flag had won a place in the hearts. So at a later period, the Confederate people were ready to [receive] the flag of 1863. The Stars & Bars first, the Stars & Stripes with a very slight difference, then in 1863 that Confederate flag clearly reflects the Sentiment as it progressed.[39]

In his "explanatory notes" to his 1904 report, Lewis waxed poetic on the meaning of Confederate flags, especially the Stars and Bars "and the glorious Battle Flag": "These flags in history will be as the Memorial Tablets of a great and good people, and a holy cause they endeavored to maintain."[40]

White southern reverence for the battle flag was related clearly to reverence for the Confederate cause—for the memory of the Confederacy and its martyrs and sacrifices and for the principles of states' rights and white supremacy. Rhetorical efforts, then and now, to demote the battle flag's historical importance in order to make it more universally acceptable run afoul of overwhelming evidence that the battle flag was a powerful symbol of the Confederate cause and the entire Confederate experience.

A more accurate defense of the battle flag was the argument that the flag, the veterans who carried it, and the cause for which they fought did not pose a threat to the reunited nation. The flag no longer flew as a symbol of a powerful army or of a people seeking separation from the Union. The flag was the symbol of a cause which was lost but, in memory and in idle principle, not forsaken. Former Confederates argued that they could revere their cause and their old flag and yet still be good Americans. The viewpoint was articulated best by the Reverend Randolph H. McKim, a former Confederate staff officer, in a lengthy oration at a UCV reunion in Nashville, Tennessee, on June 14, 1904. For the veterans assembled, McKim pledged "our love and sacred honor" to the defense of the flag of the United States. "And yet," he asserted

> to-day, while that banner of the Union floats over us, we bring the offering of love and loyalty to the memory of the flag of the Southern Confederacy! Strange as it may seem to one who does not understand our people; inconsistent and incomprehensible as it may appear; we salute yonder flag—the banner of the Stars and Stripes—as the symbol of our reunited country, at the same moment that we come together to do homage to the memory of the Stars and Bars [sic; the following passage suggests that he alluded to the battle flag]. There is in our hearts a double loyalty to-day; a loyalty to the present, and a loyalty to the dear, dead past. We still love our old battle flag with the Southern Cross upon its fiery folds! We have wrapped it round our hearts! We have enshrined it in the sacred ark of our love; and we will honor it and cherish it evermore,— not now as a political symbol, but as the consecrated emblem of an heroic epoch; as the sacred memento of a day that is dead; as the embodiment of memories that will be tender and holy as long as life shall last.[41]

Significantly, McKim's widely published address was delivered on Flag Day, and his message fell upon receptive ears. By 1904 much of white America was willing to concede the Confederate veteran and his flag a place of honor.

From the 1870s through the 1930s, discussion of the Confederate battle flag's meaning occurred, for the most part, within larger discussions over the South's dual loyalty. At rituals of sectional reconciliation, southerners declared their fealty to the Stars and Stripes. Although genuine, this fealty amounted also to a kind of *quid pro quo* which earned respect for Confederate flags, especially the battle flag. The demand by Confederate veterans and their descendants that U.S. citizens respect the southern battle flag was the symbolic equivalent of the demand that they respect the valor of southern soldiers and the righteousness of the Confederate cause.

Those demands for respect succeeded to a remarkable degree. As David Blight has shown, between 1865 and 1915 the United States chose sectional healing over racial justice. "The kind of 'peace among whites' that [Frederick] Douglass had so feared in 1875 had left the country with a kind of southern victory in the long struggle over Civil War memory," Blight concluded.[42] Similarly, within a generation of a war that cost more than 600,000 lives, the Confederate battle flag had shed its negative image with much of the white American public. By the 1930s the passage of time, along with the demonstration of southern patriotism in two foreign wars, the romanticizing of the Old South and the Confederacy in literature and film, and the national acceptance of the South's system of racial segregation made it possible for members of Confederate organizations to maintain a dual loyalty.

With the lessons of defeat and Reconstruction still vivid, postwar southerners were careful to exhibit their loyalty to the Union. The Stars and Stripes was a fixture at all Confederate celebrations. At the 1875 Jackson statue dedication in Richmond, when the crowds gave loud— but "not rebellious"—hurrahs to the battle flag, the predominant flags were those of the United States and Great Britain (an Englishman donated the statue). While former Confederate General Daniel Harvey Hill denounced in a newspaper editorial the "new, bright" U.S. flags as "the flags of the conqueror," the crowds reportedly welcomed them. At the 1890 Lee statue dedication in Richmond, "the confederate flag was everywhere conspicuously displayed," observed the New York–based *Harper's Weekly*. Yet even more conspicuous was the Stars and Stripes— outnumbering Confederate flags fifty to one, according to one eyewitness. "The paradox is explainable only by the fact that the Confederate flag no longer meant disunion," the *Harper's* reporter wrote. "It stood, rather, for past trials and heroism in adversity looked back upon from the standpoint of changed views and unforseen prosperity." The Stars and Stripes and the Confederate flag similarly shared the spotlight at the 1905 dedication of the statue of Tennessee's hero, Nathan Bedford Forrest, in Memphis and during the 1907 UCV reunion in Richmond. "Everywhere is seen the American flag side by side with the Confederate," observed a Richmond newspaper, "and it is this spirit which prevails among the Veterans and which pervades the reunions."[43]

Not everyone was so generous in their interpretation of Confederate flag-waving. "Rebel flags were everywhere displayed" during the Lee monument dedication, agreed John Mitchell, the crusading African-American editor of the *Richmond Planet*. To him, those "emblems of the 'Lost Cause'" testified that Confederate veterans "still cling to the theories which were presumably to be buried for all eternity." The South's celebration of the Confederacy "serves to retard its progress in the country and forges heavier chains with which to be bound." Patriotic and fraternal gestures went only so far in earning the respect of northern veterans and the northern public. The GAR in 1896 adopted a resolution which declared that "those who wore one uniform and fought under one flag, fought for their country and were right, while those who wore the other uniform and fought under the other banner, fought against their country and were wrong, and no sentimental nor commercial efforts to efface those radical differences should be encouraged by any true patriot."[44]

This uncompromising view of the morality of the war was reflected in a lingering hostility to Confederate flags. Despite the Confederate veterans' appeal for respect for their battle flags as symbols of apolitical soldierly valor, many of their old foes never surrendered their conviction that the flags were symbols of treason. In October 1887 Georgia Governor John Gordon, a former Confederate General, faced severe criticism when he traveled to Ohio months after he and former Confederate President Jefferson Davis reportedly paraded in Macon, Georgia, with Confederate battle flags. Gordon, soon to become the first commander-in-chief of the United Confederate Veterans, pointed out that there had been only a dozen Confederate flags in Macon among some 50,000 U.S. flags. He appealed to Ohioans to understand the motives for displaying Confederate flags. "I should have no hope for liberty in America if those men had not loved those flags and cheered them . . . Was there any disloyalty in our cheers to our battle-flags?"[45]

GAR members decried the "rebellious spirit" shown at the 1890 dedication of the Lee monument. GAR Commander-in-Chief John A. Palmer issued an order in 1891 which stated: "A Comrade wearing the badge or uniform of the Order and participates in any demonstration where the 'Rebel' Flag is displayed, violates his obligation 'to maintain true allegiance to the United States of America' . . . and brings disgrace upon the order of which he is a member." Palmer argued that "there still lurks in the hearts of a few a desire, by the display of the flag, to fire the hearts of the young generation of the south to rebellion." The GAR national encampment subsequently endorsed the order. Palmer reiterated his order two years later when members of an Atlanta GAR post marched in a parade in which Confederate flags were carried. "A rebel officer . . . has as much right to bear the traitor's flag through the streets of a loyal city as he has to wear the traitor's garb. It is against the terms of surrender, and is an act of hostility against the government of the United States."[46]

A decade earlier, the GAR's newspaper, the Washington *National Tribune,* articulated an attitude toward Confederate battle flags that eventually became the foundation for an understanding between North and South: "As ensigns of an unholy cause the Confederate flags are, and of right ought to be, odious to the eyes of loyalty; but as the exponents of manly daring, fortitude, and devotion to an idea (although a wrong one) they are entitled to the respect of all men and well worthy the reverence of those who upheld them so bravely on the field of martial strife."[47]

But in 1887, before this distinction could engender an acceptance of the Confederate battle flag, a bitter display of hostility toward it occurred among Union veterans. More than 550 flags captured from Confederate units during the war (along with flags captured from other "enemies" of the United States since 1812) were stored in the War Department building. U.S. Army Adjutant General R. C. Drum proposed to return the battle flags to the southern states. "Over twenty years have elapsed since the termination of the late civil war," Drum wrote to the secretary of war in April 1887. "Many of the prominent leaders, civil and military, of the late Confederate States are now honored representatives of the people in the national councils." Why, Drum asked, should the United States not return the captured flags? Drum's argument swayed

President Grover Cleveland, who authorized the adjutant general to contact southern state governors to arrange the return of the flags. Cleveland soon reconsidered his authorization, but not before letters were sent to the governors.[48]

Upon learning of this correspondence, Cleveland's Republican opponents smelled a rat, as well as an election year opportunity. They decried the danger of Cleveland "turning the country over to the southern rebels." The House of Representatives passed a resolution requesting the secretary of war to report whether any flags had been removed from their storage places, whether anyone in the government had proposed surrendering flags to officials of states "lately involved in the rebellion," and why "such propositions to surrender these sacred trophies of the valor of the nation's defenders were made." A contrite Cleveland responded with a complete report and with the explanation that he had given Drum authorization before he realized that congressional approval was necessary to return captured flags.[49]

The response of Federal veterans was as withering as a volley of musket fire. President Cleveland received letters calling him a "viper," "traitor," "contemptible politician," "skulker" (a reference to his having hired a substitute to fight in his place during the war), and "the oppressor of the widow and fatherless." An Iowa GAR post passed resolutions (written on "blood red" paper) which evinced hostility not only toward Cleveland but toward former Confederates as well. The post protested "the surrender of the rebel flags to the men who bore them in their mad attempt to destroy the country, either by the president of the United States or by Congress." "These flags," the Iowans wrote in the uncompromising language which so angered Confederate veterans, "can now have no other meaning than a representation of treason."[50]

Though out of public view in the U.S. War Department, the battle flags were still capable of arousing public sentiment. But not all voices were so impassioned. At its June 1887 meeting, the Association of the Army of the Potomac, a Federal veterans organization, resolved that "the battle banners wrested by the valor of our comrades, living and dead, from the hands of a gallant foe" remain forever under the protection of the government. In stark contrast to the language of the letters sent to

Cleveland, the resolutions urged preservation of the flags "in order that generations yet to come may gaze upon them, not in humiliation or exultation, but to the end that such contemplation may produce reflections upon the awful sacrifice through which we have reached our high plane of national existence, and give them firm resolve that through all their lives this generation will stand solidly for Union, for Peace and for Fraternity." The editor of the New York *Nation* observed that "the day will surely come when Americans will cease to treasure memorials of the humiliation and defeat of a large body of their own countrymen . . . But we fear the day has not come yet."[51]

Confederate veterans resented this lingering hostility toward their flags and attempted to defuse it. An 1895 editorial in *Confederate Veteran* explained to northerners that "there is nothing in this world that could induce the southern people to surrender their affection for [the Confederate battle flag]." While professing loyalty to the Union and the Stars and Stripes, the editorial admitted that respect for the Union and its symbols could never be as great as it was before the war. Praising Cleveland's aborted gesture, the editorial argued that the North should view the South's continued devotion to the Confederacy as a source of American strength: "Veterans of the United States army, who are proud of being Americans, can well afford to want the CONFEDERATE FLAG [sketches of battle flags accompanied the editorial] as emblematic of the strongest patriotism and highest type of chivalry that the human race has ever known."[52] In response to northern veterans who protested the cheering of Confederate battle flags at the 1896 UCV reunion, a Confederate veteran from South Carolina penned a poem, "The Southern Battle Flag."

> Now, Southern men, take off your hats, and ho! ye, all the
>   world,
> Stand up and with uncovered heads salute those flags unfurled!

He admonished his former foes:

> You are the victors. Brave you were, you boys who wore the
>   blue . . .

The fight is o'er. Our wounds are healed. We clasp your hands
  again;
But while we hold it fast and fair, remember we're but men
Who cannot quite forget the flag for which our brave ones fell.
And so whene'er we see its folds, we feel our bosoms swell.
Then grudge us not, brave boys in blue, that once or so a year
We meet our comrades of lang syne and give the flag a cheer.
Do it dishonor? That battle flag? Look on it with disdain.
No: never while our pulses beat our honor will we stain:
Yet we will touch our elbows close to yours, if comes the need
That we for our united land be called upon to bleed.
The North and South as friends again shall be to each so true
That both can march to "Dixie's Land" and "Yankee Doodle," too;
But never ask that we shall be so false unto our dead
That we can turn our backs upon the flag for which they bled.[53]

The long-awaited official gesture of respect for the Confederate battle flag came in 1905, when the U.S. Congress passed an act to return the captured battle flags to the states of the units that carried them. A second act was passed a year later, turning over to the Confederate Museum in Richmond, Virginia, all the remaining unidentified Confederate battle flags.[54] In the ensuing years and decades, northern state governments and individuals possessing captured Confederate flags followed suit and returned the trophies to southern states.

Several factors made possible and even desirable in 1905 what was objectionable in 1887. After Reconstruction, northerners relaxed their pressure on the South to guarantee political and economic rights to blacks. They acceded to southerners' request to deal with the "Negro problem" in their own way. Whether this change occurred because of growing racism in the North or simply the exhaustion of northern politicians with the race issue, the result was the same: by the first decade of the twentieth century, most southern blacks were denied the vote, and southern states lived under the new "social custom" of legalized segregation.[55] Most notably, the U.S. Supreme Court ruled in *Plessy v. Ferguson* in 1896 that "separate but equal" schools and facilities did not violate the "equal protection" guarantees in the Fourteenth Amendment to the Constitution. As the cause of racial justice—never the strongest motivation for the individual northern soldier—faded from the North's political agenda, symbols of a cause once popularly associated with treason and with slavery no longer seemed so threatening.

A more palpable factor in the changed attitude toward the return of captured battle flags was the South's enthusiastic participation in the war against Spain in 1898. Southern and northern boys rubbed elbows and bled for their united land. In addition to the young southern men who swelled the ranks of volunteers to fight against Spain, several former Confederate leaders held high-profile positions in the American command. Fitzhugh Lee, Confederate cavalry leader and nephew of R. E. Lee, was American consul to Cuba at the outbreak of war. Several other former Confederate cavalry leaders, including Matthew C. Butler and Thomas L. Rosser, were also in American service during the war.[56]

President William McKinley appointed as major general of volunteers Joseph Wheeler, an Alabama congressman who had commanded the Confederate cavalry contesting William Sherman's 1864 "march to the sea." Commander of the U.S. cavalry in Cuba, Wheeler personified the reunion of North and South. The nation smiled at the tale of Wheeler ordering his troops in Cuba, "Boys, give the 'damn' Yankees h——." Asked about this story at a Confederate reunion, Wheeler denied that he said "damn," but confessed that he did say "Yankees." "Yes, I said it several times. I could not help it. Things did not look so different from what they did during the War between the States, and I forgot where I was."[57]

The United Confederate Veterans, meeting in Atlanta in July 1898, sent to President William McKinley a "patriotic resolution" pledging support in the war. McKinley, who had commanded an Ohio infantry company during the Civil War, returned the gesture with a letter to the Confederate veterans reunion. "The present war," McKinley wrote, "has certainly served one useful purpose in completely obliterating the sectional lines drawn in the last one."[58]

Union veterans, led by Captain Theodore Allen of Cincinnati, hastened to assert that the obliterating of sectional lines should prompt the federal government to return the captured battle flags to the southern states. In an open letter to Federal veterans, Allen wrote: "The present war for humanity having demonstrated that the ex-Confederate soldiers and their sons and the ex-Union soldiers and their sons are one in devotion to our united country, and that we are all good Americans now, fighting under one flag—is not this the right time to wipe out the last trace of ill feeling engendered in the 'argument' of 1861–1865, and return to the survivors of the southern regiments the battle-flags which have been held for the last thirty years or more as war trophies at state capitals of the North and at the War Department in Washington?" General James H. Wilson, then a compatriot of Wheeler's in Cuba but who in 1865 had raided through the Deep South, burning property and breaking the backbone of remaining resistance, seconded Allen. "As to the flags," Wilson wrote, "send them back. The men who fought under them are as loyal to the stars and stripes now as if they had never thought of any other standard. They know as well as we do that their flags represent nothing to-day, but they are dear to them because of associations connected with painful memories."[59]

The sentiment was not universal. Even after the Spanish-American War, the Confederate flag continued to arouse the wrath of some northerners, especially Federal veterans, and never lost its connotation as the symbol of the Confederate cause. But Senator Weldon B. Heyburn of Idaho learned about the shift in attitude toward the flag in 1910, when he protested a joint resolution authorizing the UCV to use U.S. army tents for its annual reunion. "Mr. President," Heyburn appealed, "if there are any Senators here now or when this vote shall be taken who think it is appropriate that the rebel flag should wave over property of the United States, by recognition of Congress, they can vote for the joint resolution and answer for it. If they believe that the rebel flag was furled forever at Appomattox, they had better look to their vote." The Senate approved the resolution by a vote of 61 to 1, with 30 abstentions.[60]

The fiftieth anniversary celebration of Gettysburg in July 1913 was a watershed in the symbolic reconciliation of North and South. The event's sponsors, officials of the state of Pennsylvania, were anxious over the prospect of reawakened sectional passions and over the relative prominence of Federal and Confederate symbols. Reunion organizers held a conference in Philadelphia in January 1913 to discuss "vital questions" such as whether to permit the wearing of blue and gray uniforms and the display of both the Federal and Confederate flags. After some discussion, the issue was finally decided by Pennsylvania Governor John K. Tener in favor of inclusion of both sets of symbols.[61]

The highlight of the reunion occurred on the afternoon of July 3rd at the "angle," the point of furthest penetration of George E. Pickett's Virginia troops. The survivors of the Philadelphia Brigade, which defended the angle, presented a silk United States flag to the survivors of Pickett's Division. Pennsylvania Congressman J. Hampton Moore, a Philadelphia Brigade veteran, addressed the former enemies about the history of the Stars and Stripes:

> It was your flag and our flag in the closing days of the Revolution . . . It was your flag and our flag when we marched upon the Mexican capitol . . . It was our flag when you raised the "Stars and Bars," but we continued to hold and to cherish it, not alone for ourselves, but for you. Then came the war with Spain. Again it was your flag and our flag, the flag of Dewey and the flag of Wheeler, fighting together as patriots and countrymen. And now, when we boast of a reunited country, more rich and powerful in men and wealth than any nation on the face of the globe, it is still your flag, as it is still our flag—the glorious emblem of a peaceful and a prosperous people. This, veterans of the Gray survivors of Pickett's charge against "the Bloody Angle," is the token that your quondam adversaries of the Seventy-First Pennsylvania desire me to present to you. It is their expression of loyalty, friendship and good will.

As Moore spoke, color bearers holding flags of each association met and crossed staffs. As Moore finished, a third color bearer, holding the silk presentation flag, ran forward, unfurled his flag, and held it aloft over the two others. With the Confederate battle flag subordinated symbolically to Old Glory, a representative of Pickett's Division read an acceptance speech.[62]

While they were willing to participate in this reconciliation ritual, which acknowledged the supremacy of U.S. flags, Confederate veterans were concerned lest the gesture be misconstrued. Contributors to *Confederate Veteran* denied that the Gettysburg reunion was a confession of "the folly of secession." If that were the interpretation, wrote a Nashville minister, "not a corporal's guard would have attended." The South, he wrote, accepted the Stars and Stripes as its national flag and "conceded the honesty and integrity" of those who fought against the Confederacy, but reunions were not confessions of error or approval of the "barbarities" inflicted upon the South. "We still believe that our cause was right, that we were justified in defending it to the last extremity, and that the victory of the federal government was the triumph of might over right. To us the Stars and Bars [sic: battle flag] will ever be cherished in memory as the flag that our armies followed in defense of constitutional liberty and the right of self-government."[63]

America's entry into World War I provided another opportunity for Confederate veterans to prove their loyalty to the reunited nation and in return earn respect for their battle flag. At the suggestion of a Federal veteran, the UCV was invited to hold its 1917 annual reunion in Washington, D.C., the city of Lincoln. The reunion became all the more important symbolically when, two months before, the United States declared war on Germany. Woodrow Wilson, the first southern-born president since 1869, addressed the reunion and saluted the parade of veterans up Pennsylvania Avenue in the footsteps of the triumphant Federal veterans in May 1865.

As in the ceremonies at Gettysburg four years earlier, the Washington reunion of the UCV featured a presentation of a United States flag to the Confederate veterans. Colonel Andrew Cowan, the artillery officer who won immortality by ordering "Double canister, twenty feet!" against Pickett's charging Virginians at Gettysburg, and who suggested the Washington reunion, asked the commander of the UCV to accept the flag "to be carried here, side by side, with the southern flag at the head of the Confederate parade." "We saw your southern battle flag on a hundred battle fields," Cowan told UCV Commander George P. Harrison: "It was borne with honor through the war; it was furled with honor at the end. As long as red blood flows in your veins you will cherish its noble and tender memories in your hearts. We honor you more for that. American valor, proved on the battle fields of the Civil War, is the glorious heritage of our sons and our country's pride."[64]

Harrison accepted the Stars and Stripes amid "loud and continuous cheering" from the veterans. Much to the delight of the American public, the reunion was marked by speeches, presentations, and parades at which the Stars and Stripes and the Confederate battle flag (not, significantly, the Confederate national flags) flew side by side.[65]

But unlike the 1913 Gettysburg reunion, the Washington reunion was a Confederate show. *Confederate Veteran* urged men traveling to the national capital to "wear their war-time uniforms or to carry historic battle flags or other relics of the war."[66] Genuinely willing to accept the place of the Stars and Stripes and committed to the cause of the reunited nation, the Confederate veterans did not, however, feel compelled to mute their enthusiasm for their old symbols.

Major E. W. Ewing, commander of the Washington Camp, Sons of Confederate Veterans, was particularly pointed in reminding the veterans of their southern and Confederate loyalties. Expressing resentment at the implication that southerners had to prove their Americanism, Ewing emphasized that the best of Americanism was southern. And while Federal soldiers had reason to be proud of their accomplishments and symbols, southerners had more reason to be proud. Ewing similarly compared the significance for southerners of their respective state flags, the United States flag, and the Confederate flag (unspecified). "Few in the South do not love the flag of the late Confederate States of America," intoned Ewing, evidently unconcerned with the feelings of black southerners. "So far as that confederacy is concerned, the flag represents only a memory . . . We love that old banner because it stood for the struggle of our people to maintain domestic peace and tranquility, the most basal of the principles upon which organized society rests. We love that standard because it represents a sane and wholesome demand for real constitutional government. We venerate that emblem because it is the symbol of self-government by consent of the governed. Oh, yes, these are but a few of the grounds upon which southern love for the flag of the Confederacy rests."[67] Even as the South pledged its loyalty to the United States as it entered a bloody foreign war, some southerners felt compelled to remind their fellow Americans that the wrong side and the wrong principles had won the bloody domestic war a half-century before.

Flags were still a point of contention in the 1930s when the boys in blue and gray met together for the last time. UCV officials in 1930 recommended against participating in a proposed "Blue and Grey" fraternal meeting because the Grand Army of the Republic had "asserted that our Confederate Flag must be put away in museums before we can be allowed to parade in the so called meeting of the Blue and Grey." Commander-in-Chief R. A. Sneed personally favored a joint reunion, "but not unless the Confederate Flag were allowed in the parade and given as much prominence as the American Flag."[68]

Similar disharmony arose in preparation for the 75th anniversary of the battle of Gettysburg in 1938. Between 1933 and 1936 several GAR officials and posts stated publicly that they would not allow Confederate flags in the joint reunion parade. A Massachusetts veteran declared that he would "rather pass out than go down there and be a member of that gang and have them bring in that rebel flag. I, for one, won't stand for it." The SCV commander-in-chief later boasted that in response to the GAR resolution, he "introduced a resolution telling them to go to hell." Pennsylvania officials, fearful of losing the reunion to the flag dispute, played peacemakers. The secretary of the Pennsylvania State Commission for the Blue & Gray told the participants at the 1935 UCV reunion: "If you do vote to come to Gettysburg to a joint Reunion, I want you to know this: that you can fly the Confederate Flag and give it all honor when and where you desire."[69]

A year after the 75th anniversary of Gettysburg, the editor and Pulitzer prize–winning historian Douglas Southall Freeman commented on trends in the writing of Confederate history. "I never quite swallowed the story of the Connecticut lady of abolitionist stock who was alleged to have exclaimed, 'Those damn Yankees!' as she read Miss Mitchell's description of Sherman's march to the sea," he quipped; "but I began to wonder if the children of the Confederates who lost the war in the field were, in the realm of letters, winning the peace."[70]

How the Confederacy captured the national imagination (with the assistance of such influential children of Confederates as Douglas Southall Freeman) and effectively "won the peace" is an often-overlooked chapter in American history between the Civil War and World War II. One facet of this story is the widespread national acceptance of the Confederacy's most visible symbol. America in 1865 faced the vexing question of how to regard people who tried unsuccessfully to divide the nation. Banishing forever the heroes, symbols, and memories of the failed Confederacy was one possible answer to the question. Immediately after the war, the United States government seemed determined to do just that. A half century later, former Confederates were wearing their old uniforms and bringing their old battle flags to a reunion in the nation's capital.

For most of the era between the Civil War and World War II, Americans indulged white southerners in their celebration of their heroes and their cause. "Let no old passions men betray, For *both* were right and true," wrote a Spanish-American War veteran in a poetic tribute to the Confederate flag.[71] Within a remarkably short time, the country accepted the white South's profession of a "dual loyalty" and agreed to honor Confederate veterans and their battle flag. One of the many poetic tributes to the Confederacy urged southerners to "unfurl the old banner":

> Unfurl the old flag that our children may know
> It once waved in pride midst the scorn of a foe,
> And fierce in a conflict for right it was tossed —
> The right of a cause that has never been lost![72]

The unfurled "conquered banner" was a metaphor for the era. The widespread respect accorded to the flag and to the Confederacy became the status quo of the mid-twentieth century. It was a status quo never entirely without dissent and was destined to encounter challenge and compelled to change.

Chapter 4

"A Harmless and Rather Amusing Gesture"

The back cover of the March 9, 1907, *Collier's Weekly* carried a color advertisement by the Olds Motor Works of Detroit promoting the prowess of its new Model A, which had recently completed a 1,400-mile trip from New York to Daytona Beach, Florida. Displayed prominently on the car's hood were the Stars and Stripes and a rectangular Confederate battle flag. This was, noted *Confederate Veteran* magazine approvingly, the "first illustration . . . of any northern concern giving prominence to the Confederate flag. Let it not be the last." The flag, the *Veteran* declared, "should be the pride of every American, and the tendencies are that way."[1] The *Veteran* might have noted as well that the *Collier's* cover was a rare example of the Confederate flag being used in advertising or in popular culture divorced from formal Confederate memorial activities. It would certainly not be the last instance, but decades would pass before it became commonplace.

From the perspective of the early twenty-first century, it is remarkable how limited was the use of the Confederate flag from the end of the Civil

War through World War II. The widespread visibility that the flag has enjoyed—and from which it has suffered—in modern times simply did not occur until its association with the States' Rights (Dixiecrat) Party campaign of 1948, a "flag fad" in the early 1950s, and the battle against racial integration.

The marketing gurus at Olds hinted at the shape of things to come. Displayed alongside the Stars and Stripes, the Confederate battle flag represented "the South." Future generations of advertisers, publishers, and film and television producers would find the battle flag an effective symbolic shorthand for the region. It is significant that Olds and others chose the battle flag, not one of the Confederate national flags—further evidence that by 1907 the battle flag had become the symbolic counterpart to the Stars and Stripes in the North as well as in the South. The appearance of the advertisement in a popular northern metropolitan magazine also revealed that the Confederate battle flag had become at least a neutral symbol in a region whose people had regarded it as a banner of treason forty years earlier.

Harbingers can be found for other uses that the battle flag acquired after 1948. Some were related to the continuing effort to remember and honor the Confederate soldier, but others deliberately or effectively imbued the flag with meanings divorced from the Confederacy. Those who promoted the flag in the pre–World War II era shared the *Veteran*'s belief that the flag deserved respect and visibility even after the Confederate veteran generation had passed on. Subsequent generations would confront the unintended consequences of that increased visibility.

The Confederate veteran generation insured the survival of the battle flag as an official symbol of several southern states. The legislatures of Alabama and Florida in the 1890s adopted new state flags featuring a plain red St. Andrew's cross on a white field. The red cross on the white field was (and still is) the whole Alabama state flag. The governor of Florida (a Confederate veteran) recommended adding a red St. Andrew's cross to Florida's flag, which bore only the state seal in the middle of a white field. Voters approved that change in November 1900.[2]

The legislative records offer no clue whether the new flags were intended as references to the Confederate battle flag. In the 1910s an officer in the Alabama Division of the United Daughters of the Confederacy explained that the legislature did intend "to preserve in permanent form some of the more distinctive features of the Confederate battle flag, particularly the St. Andrew's cross." As a result, she contended, "the Alabama flag should be square, and in all of its lines and measurements conform to the well known battle-flag of the Confederacy." In fact, the Alabama flag conformed to the more customary rectangular shape of state flags.[3] Late twentieth-century Confederate heritage activists claimed that the Alabama legislature settled with the vague suggestion of the battle flag because it did not want to risk retribution from the federal government. This reasoning seems weak, however, given the explicit use of the battle flag in neighboring Mississippi in 1894.

With no apparent provocation and with little evident public attention, Mississippi in 1894 adopted a state flag that featured the Confederate battle emblem in the canton of a flag that also included three horizontal bars (red, white, and blue instead of the red, white, and red of the Stars and Bars). Confederate veterans organizations did not pressure the state government to adopt the flag, nor did they lavish praise or attention of any kind when the change was made. When the state's press reported the change at all, it did so without commentary.[4]

The flag changes in Mississippi, Alabama, and Florida coincided with the passage of formal Jim Crow segregation laws throughout the South. Four years before Mississippi incorporated a Confederate battle flag into its state flag, its constitutional convention passed pioneering provisions to "reform" politics by effectively disenfranchising most African Americans. According to the white conservatives (including many Confederate veterans) who controlled the convention, "hucksters and their ignorant negro dupes" had been allowed to "pull down civilization" since the introduction of Negro suffrage. The so-called Mississippi Plan required a literacy test and poll tax for all voters; but those who had enjoyed the right to vote prior to 1866 or 1867, or their lineal descendants, could register to vote without paying the tax or taking the test. Since former slaves had not been granted the franchise until the Reconstruction Acts of 1867, these "grandfather clauses" prevented blacks from voting while awarding the vote to many impoverished and illiterate whites. Despite later suspicions, there were no tangible links connecting the two acts aside from the chronological coincidence.[5]

During a wave of patriotism in the first decades of the twentieth century, most states in the country adopted nearly identical laws prohibiting and punishing "desecration" of the United States flag. Some states passed laws to protect their state flags. One state—Mississippi—extended its law to protect the Confederate flag. Mississippi's law preceded by more than four decades similar actions by five other southern states. Unlike the later laws, which were passed in reaction to publicized cases of Confederate flag "desecration," Mississippi's followed no apparent provocation. The law apparently originated because the legislature balked at affording protection to the U.S. flag without giving the same protection to the state flag and Confederate flag.

The original bill to protect the Stars and Stripes from desecration in Mississippi was introduced at the request of the state division of the Daughters of the American Revolution (DAR) as part of a nationwide lobbying effort to protect the Stars and Stripes. When the bill came up in the state House of Representatives, several members spoke passionately for it, but others ridiculed it. "The House took the bill as a joke," reported the *Jackson Daily News*. Representative Fred B. Smith wanted to amend the bill to include the Confederate flag. This amendment and one also including the state flag passed, and the bill was signed into law. Following almost verbatim the model legislation passed in other states, Mississippi's law declared it a misdemeanor to "place or cause to be placed any word, figure, mark, picture, design, drawing, or any advertisement of any nature" upon the U.S. flag, Mississippi state flag, or Confederate flag, or to "publicly mutilate, deface, defile, or defy, trample upon or cast contempt, either by word or act, upon any such flag" or representation of such flag.[6]

No other southern state officially promoted or protected the Confederate flag until 1938, when the South Carolina House of Representatives voted to place the Confederate flag (a rectangular St. Andrew's cross pattern) inside its chamber. This was done at the behest of Representative John D. Long of Union County. Son of the man who led Union County's Ku Klux Klan in the 1870s, Long was both a Civil War historian and a staunch segregationist. He later won election to the state Senate; and, not coincidentally, the Confederate flag graduated with him. Several years before the Confederate flag began its controversial career over the South Carolina state house, the flag was present inside both chambers. Alabama in 1939 formally adopted a coat of arms (designed sixteen years earlier) that featured the emblems of the five governments that have had sovereignty over Alabama; among those emblems is the St. Andrew's cross representing the Confederacy. It is still the state's coat of arms today.[7]

Incorporation into state symbolism did not translate into political exploitation of the flag. Campaign literature and ephemera and accounts of campaign rallies reveal almost no use of the Confederate flag in electioneering. Modern Americans expecting to trace a racist lineage for the Confederate flag find barren ground in the politics of an era infamous for its racism and barbarism. Fierce race-baiters such as James K. Vardaman of Mississippi, "Pitchfork Ben" Tillman, and "Cotton Ed" Smith, both of South Carolina, spoke at rallies to the strains of "Dixie" but apparently did not share the platform with Confederate flags.[8]

The candidates who did use the battle flag had some legitimate claim to it. Francis T. Nicholls, in his successful bid for the governorship of Louisiana in 1876, used broadsides featuring his face flanked by the U.S. flag and Confederate battle flag. The broadside symbolized the "dual loyalty" theme that was and is so evident in the Confederate heritage tradition, but it was also a reminder to voters that Francis Nicholls was a Confederate hero. He was a brigadier general in the Confederate army; his opponent, radical Republican Stephen B. Packard, was a northern-born "carpetbagger." John Purifoy, a veteran of Alabama's Jeff Davis Artillery and a veteran officeholder in subsequent decades, ran successfully for state treasurer in 1909. His campaign literature included a poster showing pictures of Purifoy in 1909 and as a Confederate soldier in 1861; the latter was emblazoned in the center of a Confederate battle flag.[9]

Why did so few candidates and officeholders exploit the flag for political advantage? During the era in which Confederate veterans could most profit by wrapping themselves in the flag, they could not do so without making room for a lot of company. Large percentages of officeholders throughout the South were Confederate veterans—understandable considering that approximately three-quarters of military-age white southern males in the 1860s were in the Confederate service. Claiming Confederate heritage in an era of Confederate veteran ascendancy (1870s–1910) was less a distinction than a prerequisite.

Because of the reverence white southerners accorded veterans and their flags, political use of the flag by a subsequent generation of non-veteran candidates may have been taboo. A hint of this attitude came during the 1940 presidential campaign between Franklin D. Roosevelt and Republican Wendell Willkie. Sally Archer Anderson, president of the Confederate Museum in Richmond, sent an indignant letter to the Willkie Club Committee of Richmond protesting "the impropriety of using that poster with the Confederate flag with the senseless slogan under it." Appealing to the memory of the recipient's mother (a founder of the museum and wife of a Confederate veteran), Anderson wrote: "Were your dear Mother here she would point out to those in charge of this political propaganda that the Confederate Flag is a sacred emblem in a large section of this country, and cannot be permitted to be desecrated as your poster did. As President of the Confederate Museum for more than 25 years I cannot sit idle but must try to present such things as this, & warn you that there are many Confederate organizations which will back me up should anything come of this post[er]."[10]

Perhaps the indignation at the poster was greater because it was for a Republican candidate in the still solidly Democratic South, but the opposition of Confederate heritage groups to political use of the flag transcended party. Eight years later, the United Daughters of the Confederacy chided states' rights Democrats for using the flag and later protested the incorporation of the battle flag into Georgia's new state flag. On at least one occasion, a daughter of the Confederacy—a grandniece of the states' rights patron saint John C. Calhoun—used the flag to make a political statement. Nina Pinckard, president-general of the Southern

Women's League for the Rejection of the Susan B. Anthony Amendment, posed with an actual Confederate battle flag (and with several Stars and Stripes) to dramatize her widely shared belief that women's suffrage threatened the Confederate principles of states' rights and white supremacy.[11]

A few postwar southerners employed the battle flag as the logo of their businesses. The Lee Photograph Gallery of Richmond, Virginia, whose proprietors were friends of the Jefferson Davis family and other Confederate notables, produced photographs with back marks featuring a battle flag motif and the business name and address emblazoned on a shield. Wholesale dealer and merchandise broker J. W. Reed of Chester, South Carolina, was an unreconstructed Confederate veteran who gave his address as Rebel Hall. His early twentieth-century business card included a square Confederate battle flag and his business envelope the motto "For me, but two Flags: Stars and Bars and Flag of South Carolina."[12]

Perhaps it was the flag's "sacredness" that prevented or at least severely limited its use in connection with racist violence before World War II. Late twentieth-century flag critics claimed that the Confederate flag accompanied mobs during the half-century of lynching that occurred in the South and Midwest from the 1880s to the 1930s. Accounts of lynchings do not support these claims, however. When civil rights activist James Forman visited Little Rock, Arkansas, in the late 1950s, a local resident recounted that when a mob of whites lynched twenty-two-year-old John Carter in May 1927 and then mutilated his body, "they took the American flag down and ran up a Confederate flag." Contemporary news accounts of the brutal lynching were silent on the subject of flags.[13]

Similarly, the Ku Klux Klan did not use the Confederate flag with any visibility until the 1940s. Much to the dismay and outrage of Confederate heritage groups today, no organization has had a greater role in shaping the media's perception and presentation of the Confederate flag than the KKK. The anti-flag camp in modern debates often claims that the Ku Klux Klan adopted the flag early in its history and has been using it consistently in the 135 years since. Evidence suggests that, to the contrary, the KKK did not embrace the Confederate flag until the mid-twentieth century.

The Ku Klux Klan was born in a law office in Pulaski, Tennessee, in December 1865. Its defenders describe the original Klan as a "social club" but do not deny that it existed primarily to intimidate newly freed African Americans and their "carpetbagger" allies and that the social club employed violence in its effort to keep freedmen in their place. By the spring of 1867, the KKK had been transformed into a terrorist organization whose members believed that intimidation was necessary to curb growing African-American political power. The belief that the original KKK was an unfortunate but necessary response to political events—a portrayal dramatized in D. W. Griffith's influential 1915 film *Birth of a Nation*—was the orthodox view, especially in the South in the early twentieth century, and still commands a wide following today.[14] The original Klan aroused a response from the federal government in the form of the 1871 Force Bill and a full-scale investigation of its activities. The Klan dissolved itself formally that same year, though many local organizations continued to exist long afterward.

The original Ku Klux Klan certainly had a strong Confederate flavor. The thirteen men who met in the Pulaski law office were Confederate veterans. Former Confederate General George Gordon, grand dragon of the Realm of Tennessee, chose as the Klan's first grand wizard the Confederate hero (and antebellum slave trader) Nathan Bedford Forrest. Other Confederate leaders, including Generals John B. Gordon (later the first commander of the United Confederate Veterans), Zebulon Vance (North Carolina's war governor), and Albert Pike (a Confederate general) agreed to hold figurehead posts in the organization. Victims and opponents of the Klan told congressional investigators that the KKK was in effect a resurrected Confederacy continuing the war by another, underground means.[15]

With such Confederate credentials, the first Klan members seem likely candidates to have used the Confederate flag in their rituals, but no evidence exists that the first KKK used the flag at all. The organization's official symbol was a triangular pennant with a flying dragon and a Latin motto *Quod Semper, Quod Ubique, Quod Ab Omnibus,* or "What always, what everywhere, what by all, is held to be true."[16] Klan founders may have declined to use the battle flag because of respect for it or because they feared the consequences of using the emblem of a recently vanquished nation so soon after the end of the war, while federal troops still occupied southern soil. There is evidence, however, that the Klan founders and their admirers revered and identified with the flag. *Confederate Veteran* magazine carried an obituary of one of the founders, John B. Kennedy, featuring a later-in-life photograph in which he posed in Confederate uniform with the battle flag of his wartime unit, the 3rd Tennessee Infantry. Three of the Klan's six founding members were veterans of this unit. The same flag draped Kennedy's casket. Similarly, in 1917 an organization of Confederate women dedicated a plaque marking the Pulaski law office in which the Klan was organized. "The office was beautifully decorated with red and white bunting and Confederate and United States flags," wrote one of the organizers. Draping the plaque during the unveiling ceremony was a Confederate battle flag.[17] These were the closest evidence of association between the first Klan and the battle flag.

Interest in the long-dormant Klan grew following the popularity of *Birth of a Nation*. A highly publicized cross burning in 1915 on Stone Mountain—an enormous granite rock near Atlanta—signaled the birth of a new Klan. Owing to the charismatic leadership of William J. Simmons and an elaborate structure and ritual based on fraternal organizations, the new Klan grew quickly, especially in the South and the Midwest. By 1921 KKK rolls exceeded 100,000 men, and its members wielded considerable political influence, particularly in Oklahoma and Indiana. But internal dissent and legal troubles wracked the organization, and its membership and influence faded quickly. The new Klan was a superpatriotic, 100 percent Americanism organization, whose primary targets were foreigners and Catholics, not blacks. Confederate heritage organizations did not embrace the new Klan and, in fact, bitterly denounced it as a blasphemy on the original Klan. Even "Joe" Simmons emphasized that his Klan was not comparable to the original.[18]

The second KKK was not without Confederate connections. Stone Mountain, which was then emerging as the site of a Confederate monument, became a favorite Klan ceremonial spot. Stone Mountain's owner, Samuel Venable, was a Klan leader, and many people associated with the monument project, including the memorial's first sculptor, Gutzom Borglum, signed on as members.[19] Some of the local organizations, or klaverns, bore the names of Confederate generals and original KKK figurehead leaders, such as John B. Gordon and Nathan Bedford Forrest.

Not surprisingly, however, the primary symbol of the new Klan was the Stars and Stripes. Garbed in white sheets and hoods, Klansmen paraded through the streets of American towns and cities, including a massive 1924 march in Washington, D.C., carrying the U.S. standard. The Klan ritual included a "devotional ceremony" with a U.S. flag unfurled next to a vessel of water ("dedicating fluid") and an unsheathed sword symbolizing the ability of American citizens "to strike in defense of the flag." Klansmen also took a pledge of allegiance "to no flag but the Star Spangled Banner." Confederate flags do not appear in accounts of parades or rituals of the second Klan. Even a quasi-Klan women's group, the Dixie Women's League, whose members paraded in Atlanta in 1922 dressed in white robes and masks, carried U.S. flags.[20]

The earliest documented use of Confederate symbols by the Ku Klux Klan was in its third incarnation in the late 1930s and 1940s. The second Klan never died out entirely, though local organizations primarily in the South lay dormant for some years. On April 26, 1939, a hooded Klan honor guard carrying rifles, the Stars and Stripes, and a Confederate naval jack paraded through Atlanta during a large (but not uncommon) Confederate Memorial Day parade. The streets were "colorfully alive with flags of the embattled southland of the sixties," and the parade had a distinctly "martial character." Some of the few remaining Confederate veterans were the stars of the parade, but they were followed by a variety of other organizations, including—as the *Atlanta Constitution*'s editor Ralph McGill remarked—"even the masked Klan, alien to most things American, marching in ridiculous sheets and hoods, in the line of march."[21] Although the Klan's identification with the Confederacy was significant, the parade was a Confederate memorial event, not a Klan event, and the flag was not a symbol of the Klan.

Within a few years, however, Stetson Kennedy, a Florida-born labor organizer and KKK investigator, uncovered use of the Confederate flag in the symbolism and ritual of several home-grown fascist groups. A small tract published in 1938 by the Florida-based White Front pictured the U.S. and Confederate flags on a page inviting membership in the White Front and its sponsoring military order, the White Guard. The United Sons of Dixie, a group incorporated in December 1943 in Chattanooga, Tennessee, used an initiation ritual requiring candidates to give the right answer to a battery of questions about segregation and making the United States "a white man's country," then to take an oath on the Bible and the Confederate flag.[22]

In 1946, Kennedy decided to go undercover and investigate the Nathan Bedford Forrest Klavern No. 1 in Atlanta. His first exposure to the klavern's ritual noted the presence on the altar of a U.S. flag and neon cross. Members saluted the U.S. flag in military style and then the Confederate army with their palms extended outward. Later, as he was being initiated, Kennedy noted that the altar "was draped as usual with the Confederate flag, with a cavalry sword lying diagonally across it and a ceremonial bowl in the centre." The spoken ritual interpreted the flag as a representation of "illustrious forbears." Offering graphic evidence of Kennedy's account, the May 27, 1946, issue of *Life* magazine published a photo sequence showing a KKK altar spread with the Confederate flag, the Bible, and a sword, and flanked by the Stars and Stripes and a Christian cross.[23]

Kennedy interrupted his infiltration of the Atlanta Klan to investigate a group he dubbed the "Juvenile Delinquents of the KKK." What attracted his attention to the group was an enormous Confederate battle flag hung from the second story of an Atlanta office building. Across the center of the flag were a thunderbolt and the legend "Columbian Workers Movement / Race, Nation, Faith." The explicitly fascist organization offered a blend of Nazi and Confederate symbolism that included not only the flag and the thunderbolt but Robert E. Lee and Hitler's *Mein Kampf.*[24] Such marriages of Confederate and fascist icons became commonplace beginning in the late 1950s, but Kennedy's description of it in 1946 represented a new and sinister use of Confederate symbolism.

At about the same time, the Confederate flag enjoyed a short burst of popularity in a role that would become familiar after 1948—as a pop culture symbol of the Old South and the Civil War. As they would be for so many post–World War II cultural developments, college students were the pioneers. As early as 1904, boys at the all-male South Carolina State Agricultural College (later renamed Clemson University) made headlines when they ceremoniously raised a Confederate flag on a newly erected flag pole. The school's commandant ordered the flag lowered, inciting a small riot. According to newspaper reports in Washington, D.C., the students raised the flag again the following day. The commandant led three cheers for the southern Confederacy but told the boys that "the South proved that there was only one [flag] in 1898." He had the band play "Dixie" while the students raised the Stars and Stripes on the pole. Concerned that the incident made their school appear disloyal, administrators insisted that the reports were exaggerated and denied that the students had lowered the Stars and Stripes before raising the Confederate flag. "A few" students, "in a spirit of mischief," did raise the Confederate flag, but the president dismissed this as "a boyish prank to do the unusual thing and with the sole purpose of trying to worry the authorities." More than a half-century later, in 1959, the former students claimed that published reports had understated the extent of the "insurrection."[25]

A southern college fraternity, the Kappa Alpha Order, may have been responsible for the widening presence of the Confederate battle flag on college campuses. KA was founded in December 1865 at Washington College in Lexington, Virginia, a school of which the recently retired general, Robert E. Lee, was president. In essence it was a kind of Confederate memorial organization, whose "essential teaching," according to an early history, was "that members should cherish the southern ideal of character—that of the chivalrous warrior of Christ, the Knight who loves God and country, honors and protects pure womanhood, practices courtesy and magnanimity of spirit and prefers self-respect to ill-gotten wealth." Self-consciously endeavoring to preserve the ideals of a civilization that lay in ruins in 1865, the order also preserved the genteel and chivalrous trappings of an idealized Old South. As the decades and generations passed and the Old South faded into obscure memory, KA's connections with its Confederate roots assumed the characteristics of modern "retro" fads. By the 1920s, KA chapters around the South began holding Dixie Dances—soon dubbed Old South Balls—replete with Confederate uniforms, 1860s dresses, mint juleps, and, at some schools, Confederate flags. One KA source speculated that the University of Oklahoma chapter may have begun the flag tradition in 1920 when it imported magnolia buds and moss to decorate its hall in a Dixie motif.[26]

Anticipating by a decade what became commonplace by the 1950s, the KA chapter at the University of Florida began using a full panoply of symbols and rituals in the early 1940s. Upon their chapter's founding in 1940, the Floridians began holding Plantation Weekend, which included an Old South Ball. By 1942 the University of Florida yearbook included photographs of what the 1947 yearbook described as a "gala affair" at which "hoop-skirted southern Belles danced beneath fluttering Confederate flags and were toasted by uniformed Colonels, while (non-alcoholic) mint juleps were served on the veranda." The Old South Ball came to define Kappa Alpha, and the ritual of Old South week became very elaborate and very Confederate. The KA chapter at the University of Georgia used a large battle flag (the naval jack) as a backdrop for its more staid formal banquet as early as 1946.[27]

The Old South Ball tradition may have owed its success to the wild popularity of the film *Gone with the Wind* in 1939. Margaret Mitchell's 1936 novel and the film based on it inaugurated a brief but intense Old South chic that influenced ideas and popular culture beyond the world of southern universities. When the film made its debut in Atlanta on December 15, 1939, the city pulled out all the stops, welcoming the movie stars with a parade that brought out more than 300,000 people. Official ceremonies included raising a Confederate battle flag when the parade ended. United Daughters of the Confederacy chapters in Richmond, Virginia, sponsored a Gone with the Wind Ball in February 1940. "The ballroom and stage will be decorated with Confederate flags, rope laurel and Spanish moss and a large landscape of southern plantation life will be placed on the stage behind the orchestra," announced the society pages. Photographs of the event showed not only Confederate flags but children in black face.[28]

The United States' entry into World War II interrupted this wave of Confederate chic but did not halt the emergence of the Confederate flag as a wider symbol of popular culture. On the contrary, the war reinvigorated a sense of regional identity and the flag's association with a southern martial tradition. This association had been evident to a much lesser extent during the First World War. Soldiers at Camp Lee, near Petersburg, Virginia, displayed Confederate battle flags in the post's YMCA Service Club in 1917. A Tennessee soldier reportedly carried a Confederate flag as a "talisman" in France during World War I—the same flag that his father had carried in the Civil War and that his nephew took into France in 1944.[29]

On May 30, 1945—Memorial Day—Captain Julian D. Dusenbury, of Florence, South Carolina, led Company A of the 5th Marine Regiment into the ruins of Shuri Castle, Okinawa, killed the last Japanese defenders, and captured that long-contested strong point. Someone in the self-styled "Rebel Company" then raised a Confederate battle flag over the ruins—as Dusenbury had done months earlier on Peleliu Island. "'Just to show that the South is now willing to do its bit for the Union,'" the soldiers quipped about their flag. Visible for miles, the battle flag apparently rankled senior officers, who had their own plans for a ceremonial flag-raising over the castle. Captain Dusenbury denied raising the flag or even having his own flag with him, but witnesses credited him for the much-publicized act. According to his men, only Dusenbury was allowed to carry or raise the flag he dubbed "the spirit of the company." Chicago sociologist William F. Ogburn, upon hearing of the incident, observed: "I am inclined to think that it was the tradition of the valor of the Confederates which gave him the courage and daring to do the wonderful feats he did do in the South Pacific." A few weeks after the capture of Shuri Castle, Captain Dusenbury was seriously wounded and paralyzed for the rest of his life. His family is convinced that he was denied the Medal of Honor because of the fallout from the battle flag-raising incident.[30]

Dusenbury was hardly alone in carrying a Confederate battle flag along with him during his wartime service. Dusenbury himself gave a 4″ × 6″ battle flag to a fellow South Carolinian who served in the European theater and flew the flag from the antenna of his jeep. A marine photographer snapped a picture of navy surgeon Lieutenant Thomas M. Davis, of Columbia, South Carolina, tying a small battle flag to a crude pole on the beachhead at Okinawa two months before Dusenbury's flag went up over the ruins of Shuri castle. A Richmond, Virginia, store fulfilled several hundred orders of flags for servicemen all over the world. The store owner described his customers as "servicemen proud of their southern origins and with a yen for doing things up brown, their prevailing spirit seems to be one of pride rather than any bitter antinorthern idea."[31]

"What is the explanation for this display of these flags of the Confederacy?" asked the *Baltimore Evening Sun*. "Offhand, one might dismiss it as youthful high jinks, the natural ebullience of certain southerners in the army," the editors mused, but then argued that the reason was deeper. Southerners had a martial tradition steeped in stories of Confederate heroism, along with a paucity of career opportunities that made the military more attractive. "And so, just to emphasize and particularize their own region, they hoist a Confederate flag. It seems a harmless and rather amusing gesture, though it probably puzzles not a few of the inhabitants of the countries in which our men are fighting."[32]

"Harmless and amusing" was certainly the spin that the press put on CONFORSOLS—the Confederate Forces in the Solomon Islands. CONFORSOLS originated when a Richmond, Virginia, native, Lieutenant Joseph Bryan III, received a small Confederate flag from Douglas Southall Freeman, a family friend and historian of the Confederacy, with instructions to "claim and colonize in the name of Jefferson Davis." Lieutenant Bryan tacked the flag to a dowel and put it in a jelly jar, which he kept in a tunnel at the Munda airfield on the island of New Georgia, where he served in an air combat intelligence unit. The flag became the source of good-natured jesting between northern and southern servicemen over regional accents, stereotypes, and, of course, the Civil War.

The southern contingent encouraged Marine Colonel William O. Brice, of Winnsboro, South Carolina, to form and command a special force. Brice dashed off General Order Number 1 on November 17, 1943: "Effective at once, the following enemy priorities are assigned: Yankees fust, Japs second," and signed it "W. O. Brice, Colonel, C.S.A." CONFORSOLS issued reports in southern dialect, recited stanzas from its "national anthem" ("I'm a good old rebel"), and celebrated holidays such as "Secession Day" (the anniversary of South Carolina's secession on December 20) and Robert E. Lee's birthday. In imitation of the American "Jap-baffling" passwords, CONFORSOLS devised a code of words that southerners pronounced differently: guitar, dispatch, and direct.

CONFORSOLS disbanded in February 1944 after a war correspondent got hold of the story—and of General Order Number 1—and made it headlines in the United States. Accused in some American papers of "fomenting ugly partisan passions," the men of CONFORSOLS knew their fun was over. In a solemn ceremony, they struck the colors (that is, removed the flag from the dowel) and dissolved the unit.[33]

The CONFORSOLS episode fit a clear pattern that carried over from World War II into the Korean War. The men who displayed Confederate flags did so in the spirit of competitive sectionalism, having become more aware of their southernness as a result of contact with northerners. The men acquired their flags from individuals or groups steeped in Confederate history. Chapters of the United Daughters of the Confederacy often answered appeals for flags from American servicemen. A UDC leader in Florence, South Carolina, provided the flag to Julian Dusenbury. A group of southern-born marines fighting in the Pacific who dubbed themselves The Professional Rebels, Inc., turned to the UDC in Richmond, Virginia. "I do not have to tell you that the Fifth Marine Division covered itself with glory on Iwo Jima and without a doubt will be in many more operations," wrote the Professional Rebels' leader. "If we could have [a] replica of the Confederate battle flag to carry along with us, I feel strongly that it would be of immeasurable benefit from a morale standpoint."[34]

CONFORSOLS also typified the outcomes of most wartime Confederate flag episodes. However humorous and harmless the intent, the display of unofficial, non-American flags ruffled official feathers, even if it did not violate specific regulations. Men from the South and the North serving on the aircraft carrier USS *(New) Yorktown* kept up a constant good-natured war of words over the Civil War. The ship's lieutenant commander, a New Jerseyan, ribbed the southern-born pilots, prompting an imaginative response from Lieutenant Joseph Tucker, an Alabamian. Using fragments from a parachute, Tucker made a little St. Andrew's cross flag and substituted it for the checkered flag used by the landing control officer. Asked for an explanation by the ship's commander, Lieutenant Tucker replied, "Why, Captain, it's only the state flag of Alabama." In another reported example, the U.S. War Department forbade soldiers at Camp Lee, Petersburg, Virginia, to use the "stars and bars" [sic] as the background for a quartermaster insignia.[35]

On the eve of World War II and especially in the years immediately following the war, college students merged the flag with another facet of the southern martial tradition—football. Civic boosters in Montgomery, Alabama, inaugurated the "Blue-Gray" football game in January 1939, pitting players selected from northern and southern colleges against each other in "a football contest between the rollicking, robust descendants of the men who wore the Blue and the Gray a long time ago." Appropriately, the motif for the game was a stand of crossed U.S. and Confederate (battle) flags. The game's boosters distributed flags as promotional souvenirs, while the state governor gave one to each member of the legislature.[36]

At that time, football was still primarily an Ivy League sport. Southern teams had not fared well in intersectional competition until the University of Alabama upset the University of Washington in the 1926 Rose Bowl. Jubilant fans reportedly decorated lampposts in Tuscaloosa with Confederate (as well as U.S. and state) flags to welcome home their heroes.[37] In subsequent decades, contests against northern schools heightened the sense of southern identity—and brought out more Confederate flags.

Schools in the Deep South were associated most closely with the Confederate battle flag. By 1948 the University of Mississippi adopted the flag as an all-but-official school symbol. The school's use of Old South and Confederate imagery had evolved over the preceding half-century. The nickname "Ole Miss" (slave dialect for the mistress of the house) had been adopted in the late 1890s. The student body chose Colonel Rebel as the school symbol in 1936, and the sports teams soon became known as the Rebels. Significantly, two of the other top-five nickname choices were Confederates and Stonewalls. Despite the obvious connection, Colonel Rebel's reign as mascot did not bring out the Confederate flags for at least a decade. "But some smart Ole Miss students merged the Confederate Flag, the large black hat and the black string tie in 1946," noted a 1951 alumni association article, "and Johnny Reb undergrads, [World] War II veterans included, Rebel-yelled in their rush to wear and wave the regalia." Photographs from 1947 captured at least two uses of the battle flag at Ole Miss. A group of professors was shown seated at a table with a battle flag visible on the wall behind them. And the newly elected "Football Sweetheart" of the Sigma Chi fraternity for November 1947 posed before crossed Confederate flags.[38]

It was not Ole Miss or other Deep South schools, however, that first brought the collegiate use of the flag to public attention. As early as the 1940 season, football fans at the University of Virginia in Charlottesville began waving Confederate flags to cheer on their team when it played against northern schools. University of North Carolina fans later claimed that they had begun using Confederate flags years before their southern neighbors to the north.[39] The practice attracted national headlines in October 1947 when Harvard came to Charlottesville for Homecoming. Among the Harvard players was an African-American tackle named Chester Pierce, the first black to play football in Charlottesville. *Time* magazine noted that "many in the crowd of 24,000 southerners waved flags of the Confederacy," implying that this was a gesture of intimidation directed toward Pierce. The *Washington Post,* in contrast, congratulated the players for their "unimpeachable sportsmanship" and the university for "setting at rest the silly notion that Virginians could not be counted upon to behave as Americans."[40]

Perhaps with this negative publicity in mind, the Virginia Club in Philadelphia asked UVA students not to bring their flags when the team traveled north to play the University of Pennsylvania in early November. The previous season UVA students had brought flags with them to Philadel-phia and to Princeton, where inebriated flag-waving Virginia students had torn down the goal posts after their team upset their hosts on the field. "Not only would the appearance of the Confederate flag cause row-dyism in the crowd," commented a UVA newspaper, "but damnyankee disrespect to the great flag as well." Predictably, this request provoked a rush on Confederate flags in Charlottesville-area stores and facetious plans for a "Confederate color guard" ceremony at the game. Flag wavers at pep rallies and at the bus station launched an invasion that the college newspaper declared "the largest concentration of southerners in Pennsyl-vania since Gettysburg, but this time there lives in every Cavalier heart the fond hope that history won't repeat itself." The Cavaliers lost the game but were cheered on by fans waving the Confederate flag.[41]

The University of Virginia Wahoos marched off to Pennsylvania in the fall of 1947, but a higher tide for the Confederate flag occurred the fol-lowing year when other schools and groups embraced the emblem and made it their own. The unfounded suspicion that UVA fans used the flag to taunt a black athlete foreshadowed a politicized Confederate flag. It would be simplistic to portray the invasion of Pennsylvania in 1947 as the end of the Confederate flag's innocence, since innocent flag use contin-ued for decades to come. It is not too simple, however, to suggest that even a year later the apparently innocent use of a Confederate flag was more ambiguous and dubious than it had been in the fall of 1947.

PART II

Rebel Flag

"It's history. It can't be changed or denied." This is a familiar refrain from those who defend the place of the Confederate battle flag in modern American life. The history in question is that of the Confederate States of America and the experiences of Confederate soldiers.[1] But the history of the flag did not end in 1865. More people have carried Confederate flags in memorial parades and ceremonies, displayed them in houses or yards, worn them on T-shirts and hats, or waved them at football games, stock car races, and segregationist rallies since World War II than fought under them during the Civil War. Those latter-day uses of the flag are also history and cannot be changed, denied, or ignored. Proliferation of the flag's use between World War II and the early 1970s generated the diversity of meanings and perceptions that underlay subsequent controversies about its place in American life. The flag ceased being a virtually exclusive symbol of Confederate heritage and became also a widely and carelessly used symbol of many things, including the South as a distinctive region, individual rebelliousness, a self-conscious "redneck" culture, and segregation and racism.

Chapter 5

"The Shadow of States' Rights"

At 10:18 A.M. on July 17, 1948, in the Birmingham City Auditorium, students from several southern colleges and universities serving as delegates to the States' Rights Party convention carried the Confederate battle flag into the convention hall as the other delegates stood silently with hats over their hearts.[1] The moment announced the marriage between the flag's emerging pop-culture status and its ideological roots. Once again, in the 1940s as in the 1860s, the Confederate battle flag was the chosen symbol of people dedicated to defending states' rights as a means to preserve a social order founded upon white supremacy. In the 1860s white supremacy meant slavery; in 1948 it meant legalized segregation.

The battle flag was not the official symbol of the National States' Rights Democratic Party—which the headline writers dubbed the "Dixiecrat Party." In fact, party leaders shunned symbols that implied a strictly regional identity.[2] Significantly, it was party supporters, primarily young men, who most often waved the flag for the Dixiecrats. The same young people who made the flag more visible as a symbol of collegiate high jinks and regional pride were the ones who thrust it into an increasingly ideological political arena. This coincidence inevitably tainted the ostensibly innocent uses of the flag and established a well-defined pattern for subsequent decades.

Southern white disaffection from the Democratic Party had been building for more than a decade, as Franklin D. Roosevelt and then Harry Truman tilted toward the party's liberal wing at the expense of the conservative South. The African-American vote in northern cities was becoming increasingly important to the national Democratic Party, and Truman responded by supporting the civil rights movement. In 1947 he appointed a Civil Rights Commission, and early in 1948 he endorsed the recommendations embodied in the commission's report, "To Secure These Rights." Further confirming that he did not want or count on the support of southern conservatives, Truman in late July 1948 issued Executive Order 9981, which mandated equal treatment within the U.S. armed forces and anticipated their integration.

At the July 1948 Democratic National Convention in Philadelphia, liberal delegates introduced a platform plank committing the party to continue efforts "to eradicate all racial, religious, and economic discrimination." The convention approved a milder plank commending the president's civil rights program and calling upon Congress to support Truman in guaranteeing civil rights, including "the right of full and equal political participation." Minneapolis Mayor Hubert H. Humphrey exhorted his fellow Democrats that "the time has arrived for the Democratic party to get out of the shadow of states' rights and walk forthrightly into the bright sunshine of human rights." In response to this obvious challenge, the Mississippi delegation and part of the Alabama delegation walked out of the convention hall. According to some reports, the Alabama delegates carried Confederate flags.[3]

Even after the dissenters left the building, the convention was contentious. The nominating roll call began with Alabama. Speaking for the remaining delegates, Senator Lister Hill paraphrased William Jennings Bryan's powerful 1896 "Cross of Gold" speech, warning his fellow Democrats from the North, West, and East not to "crucify the South on the cross of civil rights. You cannot elect a Democratic President without the votes of the South." He then nominated Georgia Senator Richard B. Russell. Pandemonium broke out in the convention hall. "There are yells and the rebel flag is working overtime," wrote a *Christian Science Monitor* reporter. "Cowbells ring. Waved back at them are the Truman placards of other states." A band struck up "Dixie."[4]

Spearheaded by the Mississippi and Alabama delegations, the bolt from the Democratic convention was scripted during many months of preparation, and plans for the climactic moment included the symbolic use of Confederate flags. In Jackson, four thousand white Mississippians had gathered on February 12—Lincoln's birthday—to sing "Dixie," wave Confederate flags, and adopt resolutions denouncing Truman's recent civil rights proposals. Even the newly elected governor, Fielding Wright, held a small battle flag as he entered the auditorium. The self-declared States' Rights Democrats condemned the federal government's civil rights proposals and urged "all true white Democrats" to convene in Jackson to plot a course of resistance.[5]

This conference occurred in early May. On the day it opened, the streets of Mississippi's capital city reportedly were "bedecked" with Confederate flags. The day before, Governor Wright gave a radio address in which he told the state's blacks: "If any of you have become so deluded as to want to enter our white schools, patronize our hotels, and cafes, enjoy social equality with the whites, then kindness and true sympathy requires me to advise you to make your home in some other state than Mississippi." South Carolina Governor Strom Thurmond delivered a keynote address that anticipated the one he would give in Birmingham two months later, warning the federal government not to force integration on the South. The Jackson meeting also resolved that if the Democratic National Convention nominated Truman or any other unacceptable candidate, the meeting would reconvene in Birmingham.[6]

The Democratic rebels gambled that they could capture the party apparatus in several southern states and, by denying both major parties sufficient electoral votes, throw the presidential election to the House of Representatives. Gathering in Birmingham on July 16, the Dixiecrats adopted a platform that answered Hubert Humphrey's challenge with a strong reaffirmation of states' rights as embodied in the Tenth Amendment to the U.S. Constitution. The platform appealed for resistance to the civil rights agenda on the basis that it was a form of "totalitarianism" that threatened "the integrity of the states and the basic rights of the citizens." The Dixiecrats were not reluctant to state bluntly, however, that "we stand for the segregation of the races and the racial integrity of each race," and "we oppose the elimination of segregated employment by federal bureaucrats called for by the misnamed civil rights program."[7]

The Birmingham convention nominated Strom Thurmond for president and Fielding Wright for vice president. Thurmond reportedly strode to the dais to deliver his acceptance speech escorted by the Stars and Stripes and by a Confederate battle flag. "No true southerner could fail to answer the call of his people," Thurmond told the overflowing, enthusiastic convention. He then delivered his infamous warning that "there's not enough troops in the army to force the southern people to break down segregation and admit the negro race into our theaters, our swimming pools, into our homes, and into our churches."[8]

The state delegations that came to Birmingham consisted of some southern Democrat regulars, but also many college students who supported the Dixiecrat rebellion. According to one report, convention delegates included students from Alabama College, Alabama Polytechnic, Birmingham-Southern College, Cumberland University, Georgia Tech, Howard College, Loyola of The South, Mississippi State University, the University of Alabama, the University of Georgia, the University of Tennessee, and the University of Virginia. The Anniston, Alabama, *Star* commented that the gathering was "more like a Roman holiday than a convention." It provided "irreconcilables a chance to blow off steam and afforded the college boys and girls an opportunity to get out of Summer School and join in the high jinks that characterized the parade."[9]

The largest delegation was from the University of Mississippi, and it was these students whom reports credited with bringing the Confederate flag into the convention hall. Certainly, the university community was proud to send off fifty-five delegates to Birmingham after a mass meeting of states' rights enthusiasts. The student-delegates posed for photographs in the Birmingham hotel lobby, standing in front of a battle flag and wearing their Colonel Rebel black hats. However, the students denied vehemently that they brought the flag or the hats with them to the convention hall. Quoting extensively from newspaper reports linking them to the flag, the students responded that they did not bring the flags to the Birmingham City Auditorium. They admitted that they did yell "To Hell with Truman" and "States' Rights, by damn." Instead, it may have been students from Birmingham-Southern who paraded the flag in front of the cameras on July 17, 1948.[10]

Regardless of just which students waved the Confederate flags on that day, there was a clear connection between the battle flags that appeared on college campuses and the flags associated with the Dixiecrat Party. It is tempting to conclude that the Dixiecrats' association with the flag was devoid of ideological content because the flag wavers were primarily college students who had become accustomed to waving the flag at football games and fraternity parties. The testimony of the student-delegates— and the use of the flag during the May meeting in Jackson—contradicted this explanation. The Ole Miss students told a Birmingham newspaper that they were in Birmingham on "serious business" and not "as college students on a lark." A University of Alabama student-delegate told a reporter, "We're just here to protest. Every fraternity at Tuscaloosa is flying a Confederate flag from the roof today."[11]

The Confederate flag became a central motif for the subsequent analysis and discussion of the Birmingham convention. Reports in African-American newspapers invariably noted the presence of the flag and other Confederate and Old South symbols in the states' rights rebellion. "Screaming, frenzied, frightened and comical, Dixie ran up the Confederate flag again here Saturday, eighty-three years after Lee hauled it down and handed it over to Grant at Appomattox . . . and those frantic Democrats bellowed their resistance to civil rights and their allegiance to the principles of the KKK," wrote the *Pittsburgh Courier*. Decrying the Dixiecrats' "half-truth distortions" of civil rights, the *Birmingham World* reported that "the 'secessionists' sported Confederate flags, pictures of Robert E. Lee, and various state standards as they paraded almost incessantly in the pandamonious[sic]-flooded auditorium." The venerable

Chicago Defender chose an obvious historical analogy for the Dixiecrats' retreat from the Democratic convention in Philadelphia: "The Rebels got as far as 'Gettysburg.' The Confederate banner waved as again and again States' Rights stormed the battlements. But Human Rights threw them back, beat them down to their knees, and when last seen they were slinking back to Mississippi and Alabama."[12]

Conservative and liberal southern white journalists debated the appropriateness of the Confederate flag and a Confederate mentality in the presidential campaign. William D. Workman, columnist for the Charleston *News & Record,* praised the appearance of the flag. "The Confederate spirit was resurgent today," he wrote from Birmingham. "The Stars and Bars [sic] were much in evidence, not the tiny colors which appeared infrequently in Philadelphia, but big bold battle flags of the Confederacy." Observing the same scene, Virginius Dabney of the *Richmond Times-Dispatch,* whose editorials against the Dixiecrats earned him a Pulitzer Prize, denounced "the Confederate flag waving and futile posturing in Alabama." The Dixiecrats, he warned, represented the "worst caricatures of southern politicians."[13]

John Temple Graves of the *Birmingham Post* and Ralph McGill of the *Atlanta Constitution* fought a war of words over the flag and the Dixiecrats. Mocking McGill's "charge" that "Dixie" was sung and Confederate flags were waved at the convention, Graves argued that southernness did not preclude Americanism. "This is a time for a proud Dixie-singing, Confederate flag-waving South that will stand up for all that's best of its own, and do it in the spirit of no lost cause or secession but of a new place to be won in our land of the free and home of the brave. So, begging your cosmopolitan pardon, Ralph, I say three cheers for the Red, White and Blue and in Dixieland I'll take my stand. With emotion." McGill responded by not only reiterating his emphasis on an "American" political solution but also condemning the political use of Confederate symbols. "Then ask yourself if those who are trying to make us take the Confederate Flag, with all its glory and honor, and warp [sic] our minds and our politics and our political planning in those glorious folds, are being honest with the South and loyal to it." We must, he concluded, "despise those who prostitute the Confederate Flag and the song 'Dixie' to their own uses."[14]

The Dixiecrat leadership shared McGill's concern for the "provincialism" that the Confederate flag implied and shunned the flag as an official symbol. Instead, the party's campaign materials featured bust portraits of candidates Thurmond and Wright with the legend "states' rights." One fund-raising brochure carried an image of the Statue of Liberty with the slogans: "States' Rights / Shield of Your Liberty" and "Support These Courageous Men / Get in the Fight for States' Rights." A party informational handbook depicted "additional symbols of states' rights Democrats" as an outline of the United States with legends "States' Rights" and "States' Rights Democrats." Thurmond told a Virginia audience that he was not campaigning as a southerner. "We are fighting this cause as Americans and not as southerners, and the principle concerns every American as well as every southerner."[15]

Leaders of Alabama's dedicated Dixiecrats did not share this reluctance to embrace the flag; nor did they find it necessary to subordinate the party's segregationist *raison d'être* to a more nationally appealing constitutional principle. The Alabama Democratic States' Rights Committee issued "an Appeal to the People of Alabama to help in the Fight to Preserve Our Way of Life" featuring as a logo crossed U.S. and Confederate battle flags. The paid advertisement urged Alabama voters to vote "under the Rooster" for the slate committed to Thurmond and Wright. The "Rooster" referred to the symbol of the state Democratic Party—a crowing rooster with the legends "White Supremacy" and "For the Right." Shortly after the fall elections, state party chairman and Dixiecrat stalwart Gessner T. McCorvey urged that the motto be strengthened to read "For White Supremacy" and "For States' Rights." He was confident that this change would "meet with the approval of an overwhelming majority of the rank and file of the real Democrats of the State."[16]

Thanks to the strong images from the convention, the Dixiecrats were unable to escape identification with the battle flag. Keynote speaker and former Alabama governor Frank Dixon received a letter (addressed simply to "Dixiecrats / Birmingham, / Ala.") from a woman in Fort Lauderdale asking where she could purchase "a Bars and Stars Flag" because she had not been able to find one at home. Thurmond not infrequently found himself in the company of Confederate flags along the campaign trail. In August, when the Dixiecrats gathered in Houston for the formal launch of the campaign, supporters decorated the hotel with U.S., state, and Confederate flags. Repeating the spectacle in Birmingham, supporters filled the Sam Houston Coliseum, waving flags and playing "Dixie." A group of young men waved Confederate flags and displayed a sign mocking the three other candidates in the presidential race: "Harry, Henry, Dewey, Phooey!" Speakers urged voters "to preserve the American way of life" from the "proposed federal police state." A few weeks later, four fifteen-year-old boys raised a Confederate flag on the pole at Houston City Hall after the Dixiecrats carried a county referendum for president.[17]

Even when the candidates left the Deep South, they found themselves among flag-waving supporters. Thurmond spoke at a Richmond, Virginia, hotel in October. The crowd of five hundred gave the rebel yell. "The room itself was draped in the immortal Stars and Bars [sic]." The publisher of the paper that printed this account was himself an enthusiastic flag-waving Thurmond supporter. According to the Richmond *News-Leader,* he was at the time flying a Confederate flag from the front of his building.[18]

The campaign brought a surge of popularity to the Confederate flag, reflected in sales figures at flag stores and novelty shops. Flag stores in Richmond, Virginia, in May 1948 reported sales of Confederate flags equaling or surpassing the sale of U.S. flags. By August, after the Dixiecrat Convention, a Dallas store reported a three thousand percent increase in Confederate flag sales and a Richmond store a ten thousand percent increase. Some Deep South dealers attributed the explosion to "the Dixiecrat movement against Truman," but these and other dealers noted that sales peaked during football season as well as before Memorial Day and other Confederate holidays. Dealers in Richmond, the old Confederate capital, denied any local Dixiecrat boom, despite the unprecedented sales.[19]

Organizations of descendants of Confederate veterans diverged in their opinions about the Dixiecrats and the Confederate flag-waving accompanying the campaign. The Sons of Confederate Veterans (SCV) at a national convention in Montgomery in October 1948 passed resolutions supporting the States' Rights Party: "We stand within the very shadow of our Confederate ancestors in affirming our stand." In contrast, the United Daughters of the Confederacy (UDC) in November 1948 passed and sent to the southern states model "Legislation to Protect the Confederate Flag from Misuse." In its preface to the legislation, the drafting committee explained its rationale:

> The attention of members of our organization has been called to the fact that in certain demonstrations of college groups and some political groups at times the Confederate Flag or insignia has been displayed with seeming disregard of its significance. Perhaps this was done purely in the exuberance of youth with no intent of disrespect, but, so that the flag and insignia of the Confederacy may be protected as the United States and other insignias are protected, this Convention deems this bill appropriate and needed at this time.[20]

The push for legislation came to naught in 1948, but the UDC maintained its wariness of flag "misuse" and gathered support as flag use spread in the 1950s.

The November election brought defeat for the States' Rights Party. The Dixiecrats won in Alabama, Mississippi, Louisiana, and South Carolina—states in which they had captured control of the electoral apparatus—but their thirty-six electoral votes played no decisive role in the election's outcome.[21] Many conservatives, such as Georgia's Richard Russell and Herman Talmadge, believed that a third party marginalized the South in national politics and refused to support the Dixiecrats. The party did not die immediately after the election, but it did not mount another serious campaign for the presidency or play a role in national politics.

While the Dixiecrat Party passed from the headlines, the Confederate flag did not. In fact, the campaign intensified the popularity that had been growing before 1948 and made the flag a fixture in places where it had been only a novelty before. Nowhere was this more true and dramatic than at the University of Mississippi. Despite the strong modern association between the flag and the university, the flag appeared only sparingly in photographs or accounts of school activities before 1948. The battle flag and the full panoply of Old South/Confederate symbols did not become institutions on the Ole Miss campus until the fall of 1948. The school's home economics department sewed and painted a huge Confederate battle flag that the band carried onto the football field at half-time. The flag made its debut in October 1948, and the band presented it to Governor Fielding Wright in a half-time ceremony a month later. It was a football game tradition until 1962, when the flag began to fall apart.[22] The oversized flag apparently had more to do with the school's centennial than it did with the Dixiecrats.

In 1861, thirteen years after its chartering, the school essentially closed when the student body enlisted in the Confederate army as Company A of the 11th Mississippi Infantry, known as the "University Greys." In October 1948 the school's ROTC commemorated the centennial and the services of the University Greys by dressing in Confederate uniforms and black hats and carrying Confederate battle flags.[23] These developments did not occur until months after Ole Miss students showed their colors in the rebellion against Harry Truman and his civil rights reform proposals.

Ole Miss's embrace of southern symbolism was deliberate, with distinctly political undertones. Rarely has a tradition taken root faster than the Confederate battle flag did at Ole Miss. The student handbook of 1948 observed that "many Ole Miss customs are fairly new; they lack only the savoring which time brings. Still these actions are future traditions and mean as much as our established ones. Ole Miss has adopted the Confederate flag as a symbol of the Mississippi spirit. Each football game finds the scarlet flag frantically waving to the rhythm of the Rebel band."[24]

A few short years vindicated the handbook's prediction. The yearbook for 1949 advised students that they would need to know "Dixie" as well as the alma mater and explained: "We are proud southerners and want people to know it . . . This doesn't mean that we are not citizens of the Union; it simply means that we don't want anybody to run over us— anywhere, anytime." By 1951 the college yearbook waxed poetical on "Colonel Rebel, blind Jim, Confederate flags. / Symbols of our Southern heritage. / All these are our Ole Miss."[25]

The flag became a part of campus life at the University of Alabama as a direct result of the 1948 campaign. In July 1948, when University of Alabama students were in Alabama serving as convention delegates, their fellow students back home in Tuscaloosa were also raising the flag. According to a story in the university newspaper, University of Alabama fraternities "brought Confederate and Alabama state flags out of moth balls" to fly on the fraternity houses. The university's chapter of Kappa Alpha passed a resolution which read:

> Due to the recent encroachment by the antagonistic North
> upon Southern culture and ideals, the ends of government
> as laid down by our great defenders of States' Rights is
> upon the rocks of destruction and decay. No longer can
> the brothers of Alpha Beta chapter sit idly by and watch
> the destruction of the noble doctrine of States' Rights . . .
> In view of these facts, let it be known, from this day on the
> Confederate flag shall fly from the hights [sic] of the Kappa
> Alpha mansion amidst the sweet aroma of magnolias and
> the tinkling of mint juleps.

"Rise up, ye men of Lee!" declared the Kappa Alphans. "Don your colors and put asunder this menace which threatens our age-old tradition." Another fraternity member declared that the flag would fly "until the North calls its wolves away from attempting to devour Southern culture." Alabama's KAs did not have a magnolia and mint juleps tradition. The first Old South Ball, replete with Confederate flags, the singing of "Dixie," hoop skirts, and a secession ceremony, was held in April 1949, the year after flags flew from the fraternity houses to symbolize support for states' rights. Even at the venerable and quiet College of William and Mary in Virginia, the events of 1948 invited interest in the Confederate battle flag. In October a representative of the college's Kappa Alpha chapter wrote to the Confederate Museum in Richmond to ask about obtaining a large flag to hang in the front yard of the new lodge.[26]

Even more than in 1939, with its "Gone with the Wind" Old South chic, the battle flag after 1948 became an almost obligatory element in southern symbolism. Perhaps it was only coincidental that the would-be football classic, the Dixie Bowl, played in Birmingham, began using crossed Confederate and U.S. flags on its official stationery between February and October 1948.[27] Insignificant as this change was, it exemplified the discovery of the Confederate flag that occurred during the Dixiecrat year. The early 1950s brought a nationwide explosion in the use of the Confederate flag—a phenomenon that echoed both the ideological message of the Dixiecrats and the playful regional pugnacity of pre-1948 collegiate flag wavers. The 1950s fad completed the flag's transformation into a symbol with a myriad of contemporary associations.

Chapter 6

"Keep Your Eyes on Those
Confederate Flags"

Sometime after midnight on May 30, 1950, a prankster hoisted a rebel flag over a holy shrine of Yankeedom—the Massachusetts State House in Boston. Discovered at 3:00 A.M., the flag still flew at dawn and was not removed by state maintenance workers until 7:00 A.M. A year later, vendors hawked small Confederate flags in Washington, D.C., during the parade for General Douglas MacArthur down Pennsylvania Avenue. So common had the rebel flag become in the nation's capital that police at the Capitol building were busy enforcing regulations against the display of unauthorized flags. In previous years, enforcement meant telling southern school students to leave their rebel flags on the bus, but in recent months police had encountered countless cars from Ohio, New Jersey, Wisconsin, and other northern states sporting the Confederate flag and visitors who preferred to drive away rather than park without their flags flying high. Confederate flags were for sale in the Barbara Frietchie House in Frederick, Maryland, where poem and patriotic legend celebrated the woman who dared the invading rebels to tear down the Stars and Stripes. The *Montgomery Advertiser* took puckish glee in reporting that a boy scout in Springfield, Illinois, contacted the Montgomery Chamber of Commerce requesting a Confederate flag for his "Rebel Patrol."[1] Such incidents were common fare between 1950 and 1952 during the height of what the headline writers dubbed the "flag fad."

"Eighty-five years after Appomattox, the Old South has suddenly gone flag-happy," reported *Business Week* in November 1950. "The Stars and Bars [sic] are waving in a flurry the like of which Dixie has never seen before, not even in the days of the War between the States." *Business Week* missed the real story, evidenced by the headlines from Boston, Washington, D.C., and the "Land of Lincoln." The significance of the flag fad was not the flag's popularity in the South but the enormous, seemingly inexplicable, popularity of the flag in the North. Continuing the trend begun in 1948, Confederate flags outsold U.S. flags in stores all over America, and southern flag dealers received many of their orders from the North and the West coast. Legerton Company of Charleston, South Carolina, was busy filling orders from Michigan, California, and New York. A Washington, D.C., novelty store sold three times as many Confederate flags as U.S. flags and another sold ten thousand rebel flags in a short span. The largest maker of Confederate flags, Annin & Co., based in Verona, New Jersey, was turning out 100,000 a week. Annin sold a total of 1.6 million small Confederate flags in 1951, a two thousand percent increase from 1949. The regent of Richmond's Confederate Museum reported a "noticeable increase for the demand for Confederate flags, small and large . . . from every section of the country and Canada."[2]

National media reported the fad with amazement and amusement. "The fad that began slowly last year reached mammoth proportions in the July 4th parade at Daytona Beach, Fla.," reported *Newsweek* in September 1951. "Rebel flags were flown from planes at the air races in Detroit, carried by Shriners in their New York jamboree, and flaunted at the Atlantic City Beauty pageant." "Everywhere along the Atlantic seaboard from New York to Miami and westward to the Mississippi watershed pert little banners wave in the breeze from car antennae, souvenir stands, bicycles or in the hands of youngsters, teenagers and grownups," observed John Long in the *New York Times Magazine* a month later.[3]

While the causes and meanings of the fad occasioned discussion, most observers chalked it up as another product of a youth-driven culture. Most investigators traced the fad to the Kappa Alpha fraternity's Old South celebrations and the flag's continuing popularity as a totem for southern football fans. A New Orleans newspaper editor speculated that the fad owed its strength somehow to the use of the flag and other Old South paraphernalia at the Natchez, Mississippi, "pilgrimages" that began in 1932. "Why fly it now," nearly a century after the death of the Confederacy? John Long mused. "Why do cars of the northern states which defeated the Confederacy display it? Is there some deep underlying significance or political undertone or sectional significance to the movement? The answer, of course, is Certainly not. Although it may be difficult to explain to an outsider, America has a word for it: *fad*."[4]

Other commentators agreed. The historian E. Merton Coulter observed that the flag was more visible in the South than it had been during the Confederacy and that it had a currency in the North that it had never enjoyed before. It was, however, "merely one of those fads, which the American people eagerly like to grab up and promote and then drop as quickly . . . When the football fans tire of flying it and its commercial promoters see their markets drying up, the Confederate flag will recede to the respectability of historical significance." Even a contributor to the NAACP's magazine *The Crisis* concluded "that the waving of the Confederate battle flag is just a fad like carrying foxtails on cars, or the increasing use of skull and cross-bones on flags, T-shirts, caps, and cuff links." A merchant in Birmingham capitalizing on the flag fad declined to pinpoint a cause for the craze: "Don't ask me why. Sometimes it's little green lizards, sometimes it's birds-on-a-stick. Now it is Confederate Flags."[5] Nationwide fads became commonplace after World War II as improvements in communications, transportation, and business practices further homogenized American culture. The Confederate battle flag became part of that culture in the early 1950s, and no one has been able to get the genie back in the bottle since.

Perhaps the most remarkable aspect of the 1950–1952 flag fad was the popularity of the flag among American servicemen at home and abroad. Although this theoretically could have been a reaction to the first steps toward racial integration in the armed services, it carried on the well-publicized trend evident in World War II. So familiar was the scenario of a southern serviceman carrying his beloved Confederate battle flag that it became fodder for Hollywood. Made in the midst of the early 1950s fad, *Operation Pacific,* starring John Wayne and Patricia Neal, was about the crew of a World War II submarine. When a crewman on the submarine died, his mates discovered among his belongings a battle flag, which they brought respectfully to Commander Wayne.[6]

The presence of the Confederate flag within the army became apparent during one of the U.S. Army's largest ever military maneuvers, Operation Southern Pines, in the summer of 1951. The operation concentrated enough forces—and flags—to raise eyebrows around the nation. Thousands of jeeps and armored vehicles in the army's 28th Division (National Guard) drove from Camp Atterbury, Indiana, to Fort Bragg, North Carolina, many of them with small Confederate battle flags flapping on their antennas. A photographer in Asheville, North Carolina, estimated that fifty percent of the vehicles boasted the flag.[7]

Even before Southern Pines, veterans and servicemen embraced the battle flag as a regional symbol. One hundred soldiers from Camp Lee near Petersburg, Virginia, visited Richmond's Confederate Museum in July 1949. "Twenty-one of them bought Confederate flags," reported the museum's administrator. "When they finally left one wondered if they might not be a detachment from the Confederate Army come to life from the display of the Confederate Battle Flag."[8]

Someone walking into Fort Jackson, South Carolina, in 1951 had particular reason to wonder whether he had stumbled across a forgotten outpost of the Confederate Army. For much of 1951, Fort Jackson was home to the U.S. Army's 31st Infantry Division, nicknamed the Dixie Division. Organized in 1917 as a National Guard division consisting of units from Alabama, Mississippi, Louisiana, and Florida, the Dixie Division saw action in the Pacific in 1944–1945. The division's official insignia was a red and white double D, and the soldiers in the division were not especially noted for use of Confederate symbolism during World War II. This changed in January 1951 when the division (by this time consisting of National Guard units from Alabama and Mississippi) was reactivated for the Korean War and reported to Fort Jackson. According to the U.S. Army's Institute of Heraldry, the division's official insignia remained the double D, but its 1951 official yearbook revealed that the St. Andrews cross was hands down its *de facto* symbol. Officers wore battle flag insignia on their shoulders, and the men wore them on their helmets. Battle flags adorned reviewing stands and offices and served as decorations for dances. The honor guard of the 167th Infantry, based in Birmingham, carried the battle flag (naval jack) along with the Stars and Stripes and the state flags of Alabama and Mississippi. The division's band wore mock Confederate uniforms and music pouches emblazoned with the battle flag; the flag was emblazoned on the skin of the band's drum. The division's mascot, a small spaniel named Dixie, wore a cape-like battle flag (decorated with the double D) when the division traveled to Texas for maneuvers in 1952.[9] Deactivated again after the Korean War, the division retained vestiges of its flag symbolism, which again drew nationwide attention in the 1960s when the Alabama National Guard found itself uncomfortably in the middle of the civil rights struggle.

Such blatant official use of the Confederate flag seemed to violate U.S. Army regulations governing the display of flags. A new set of flag regulations approved on October 25, 1944, forbade the use of flags, pennants, banners, streamers, and so on, "other than those required for marking or identification purposes." But the regulations qualified this prohibition: "This restricts the displaying for official purposes of any unofficial flag . . . that may be purchased or received as donations or gifts from any person or organization." The regulations did "not restrict the display of official, obsolete colors, standards, flags, guidons, etc., for decorative or historical purposes, nor the display of flags of cities, States, friendly foreign nations, or officials thereof for official or special occasions." Subsequent regulations omitted the prohibition but explicitly allowed "the display of official or obsolete colors . . . for decorative or historic purposes."[10] These regulations apparently allowed enough latitude for units to employ Confederate flags for historical or decorative purposes. In effect, the use of the Confederate flag and other insignia by U.S. Army units depended on the discretion of the unit or post commander and upon pressures brought to bear from other sources.

Far from censuring the use of Confederate symbols, the U.S. Congress recognized and rewarded Confederate heritage. In March 1948 Congress passed and President Truman signed a law that allowed National Guard units that traced their lineage to state organizations to display battle streamers—narrow ribbons attached to the tops of flag poles bearing the names of battles in which ancestral units participated. Battle streamers were reserved previously for units that had a history of federal service. "The effect," admitted the secretary of war, was "to authorize the use of battle streamers which were carried by Confederate regiments and permit such streamers to be carried with regimental colors." Introduced in 1943 and endorsed by the War Department in 1944, this act was a World War II era gesture of respect for the South's martial contribution to the war effort. The result was that many modern units added to their flag poles blue and gray striped streamers with the names of Civil War battles stenciled in golden yellow.[11] The act did not authorize units to carry Confederate flags.

Several flag-waving U.S. military units probed and found the outer limits of official tolerance of Confederate flags. The 1602nd Air Transport Wing and other units stationed in Wiesbaden, Germany, flew the Confederate flag at the base. The Defense Department reminded the 1602nd of Regulation 260–10. Southerners at the base posed for a photo lowering the flag from an office wall. The photo caption read: "The solemn occasion being enacted took place around many military installations recently when directives were issued banning the display of the Confederate flag."[12]

A similar incident occurred later on the high seas. Four ships of the 122nd Destroyer Division, dubbed the Dixie Division because all four commanders hailed from the South, raised small Confederate battle flags from their signal halyards when they left Hong Kong. A complaint to the navy secretary brought a stern order to remove the flag. The contrite division commander, Captain William Groverman, admitted his error but made clear that the flags—the personal property of the ships' captains—

never flew over or in place of the Stars and Stripes. "It's a very sensitive subject," Groverman commented when pressed for more details. The Associated Press observed that the flags were "false colors," since most of the crewmen in the Dixie Division were New Englanders.[13]

Nowhere was the influence of the flag fad in the U.S. military more evident than among the troops in and around Korea during the war of 1950–1953. There the flag was not only a novelty and a logo of a sometimes pugnacious (white) southern identity, but it also filled a patriotic vacuum. Because U.S. forces were fighting under the auspices of the United Nations, American servicemen in Korea carried the UN banner, not the Stars and Stripes. Patriotic American boys looked around for alternatives. State flags, especially those of Texas and Arkansas, were evident, but the Confederate flag, the "rage" in the land they left behind, was the clear favorite. Chapters of the United Daughters of the Confederacy were busy filling requests from servicemen for battle flags. "The banner has taken a place of honor with us and has been placed in the most prominent spot, our headquarters," wrote a member of the 822nd Engineer Aviation Battalion to the Savannah, Georgia, UDC chapter. "It is a symbol that we of the South can cherish and hold dear in these trying times. Our morale has been el[ev]ated to an all-time high." UDC officials explained that flying Texas or Confederate flags "was the only way the soldiers in Korea could show they were Americans." It also fulfilled one of the UDC's educational objectives: "The southern boys glory in telling their Yankee buddies what our Flag means."[14]

A half-century later, Korean War veterans who displayed Confederate flags did not recall a flag fad in the United States or being influenced by the wider popular culture. Instead, they recalled being inspired by an awareness of southern heritage or by their interest in Civil War history. The veterans insisted that they and others who flew the Confederate flag were patriotic Americans and proved it on the battlefield. As in World War II, southern servicemen who displayed the flag compelled their "Yankee" comrades to salute it. Others wisecracked that the "Yankees" were finally fighting on the "right side"—for *South* Korea. Soldiers raised the flag on navy transports and army vehicles, on poles at rear area installations, and on makeshift poles over hard-won ground at the front. As Marine Captain Julian Dusenbury had done in 1945, soldiers carried the flag as a good-luck charm or a morale builder.[15]

Many of the men who displayed the Confederate battle flag or supported its display were not southerners. The *New York Times Magazine* in October 1951 showed a marine officer from Staten Island holding the Confederate flag. The soldier wrote the paper explaining that he had received it as a gift from a southern friend with whom he had attended Tulane University. The friend believed the symbol appropriate, since he was fighting for *South* Korea. "The U.N. flag was far too impersonal," wrote the marine. "In fact, most of us did not know what the U.N. flag looked like until we reached Pusan . . . The reason I'm telling you all this is to establish a better background for the appearance of the Confederate flags in Korea. Many boys over here are true southerners and take pride in showing it, as do the Texans with their Lone Star banner. Symbols of home, however controversial, are always the subject of good-natured kidding among fellows from the different states." The boys in Korea, he assured his fellow New Yorkers, "are right in there, slugging it out for the greatest inspiration of all—our Stars and Stripes."[16]

Another New York marine in Korea had a different reaction to the Confederate flags he encountered. In an effort "to give the Confederate emblem some healthy competition," he proposed raising a New York City flag over his base. New York City Hall responded by sending one hundred city flags to servicemen in Asia. The instigator of the scheme allegedly declared upon unwrapping his flag, "Now, let's see those Rebels raise their flag. I'll fly this thing higher than anything else." A Texas-born army officer in Company E, 38th Infantry Regiment, kept a Confederate battle flag in his bunker on the front and flying from his tent while in reserve. Two men in his company, one from Brooklyn, the other from the Bronx, threatened "retaliation" and ordered a New York City flag. He still had a photograph of the two men posing with their city flag forty-seven years later.[17]

Fought as it was in the open, even on the pages of American newspapers, the rivalry between the Confederate battle flag and other flags challenged service regulations. These regulations were rarely enforced and widely ignored. A veteran of an elite air force unit known as the Mosquitoes described his comrades as "flamboyant" men who flouted regulations about dress and appearance as well as flags. In Korea, as in bases in the United States and Europe, the military in 1951 tried to curb excessive Confederate flag use. Even then, soldiers were able to ignore the regulations.[18]

The flag fad in Korea occurred during the first stages of the racial integration of America's armed services. Confederate flag wavers in Korea insisted that the black soldiers in their units did not protest or object openly to the rebel banner. However, it was a new African-American company commander who compelled a white Georgia infantryman to remove a Confederate flag from a tall pole on the company street. Men on the battlefront found it easier to ignore what they considered trivial orders and, they claimed, easier to comprehend that Confederate flags were in a real sense "American" flags—reminders of home and sources of good-natured regional rivalries among American soldiers. By the end of the decade—owing largely to the racial strife that followed the U.S. Supreme Court's 1954 decision in *Brown v. Board of Education*—rebel flags at U.S. military bases were more likely to be interpreted as symbols of racial intolerance.[19]

The flag fad infiltrated American patriotic organizations as well. The Gastonia Chapter of the UDC presented a full-sized Confederate flag to the color guard of the American Legion Drum and Bugle Corps of Gastonia, North Carolina. "The Stars and Bars [sic] and Confederate caps were very much in evidence" at the October 1951 American Legion convention. There was apparently no controversy about the rebel banner. In contrast, the flag became a divisive sectional issue at the August 1951 convention of the Veterans of Foreign Wars (VFW). The Confederate flag had become popular as part of VFW events; a VFW post in Bristol, on the border between Virginia and Tennessee, even claimed proudly that its use of the Confederate flag launched the nationwide flag fad. In response, a Massachusetts convention delegate called for an investigation of southern VFW posts using Confederate flags in their formations.

Amid hoots and rebel yells, the Alabama commander warned "that if you try to drive the Confederate flag from this organization, you're driving the South out of this organization. We of the South are proud of our flag. Yankee Doodle is played and we never object." Other northern delegates hastened to assure their southern counterparts that there would be no investigation.[20]

The testiness of these exchanges suggested that there was more to the flag fad than jocular sectional rivalry. Even as most pundits pronounced it a harmless passing phase, others probed the fad's potential meanings. "Some interpreted all this as an anti-Truman gesture, others possibly more intellectual as a revival of interest in states' rights," wrote *Life* magazine. "Most people, however, recognized a fad when they saw one." "Diehard federalists," wrote John Long in the *New York Times,* see in the fad "a dark Dixiecrat plot to undermine the Union." While Long dismissed such fears, he did acknowledge that "States Righters" perceived the flag as "a protest against the whole 'Fair Deal' administration." The historian Merton Coulter dismissed such association as "the foolish fears of some unbalanced critics of the present national scene."[21]

Despite Coulter's dismissive attitude, there was abundant testimony that anti-federal ideology indeed lay behind the flag's popularity. "The Truman Democrats have been trying to move in and tell the South how to live," explained one southerner. "We resent it and flagwaving expresses our general attitude." A Chicago woman bought a large battle flag from a Savannah, Georgia, store and told the clerk that she was sick of the Truman administration and that she replaced the Stars and Stripes in front of her home with the battle flag and tacked up a sign reading "We have seceded from the Union." Roy V. Harris, the king maker of Georgia politics and editor of the segregationist weekly *Augusta Courier,* believed fervently that the flag had "become associated with the movement to defeat Truman from one end of the nation to the other and most of the people who carry this flag do so as an expression of their sympathy for the southern cause and their opposition to the President." Warming to his subject, Harris declared that the flag was "a symbol of rebellion of the white people of this nation against Harry Truman and his damnable schemes." He urged his readers to "get your Confederate flag today and raise it." Following his own advice, Harris added a flag to the masthead of his five-year-old paper the following week and kept it there for decades.[22]

Even flag defenders who dismissed fears of the flag's sinister meaning betrayed an ideological edge. H. Norton Mason, Jr., adjutant-in-chief of the Sons of Confederate Veterans, explained that the flag owed its popularity to a "revival of interest in the Confederacy and the principles on which it was founded." People were obviously growing wary that "with an overbalance of power the federal government will usurp powers reserved to the States and to the people in the Bill of Rights." "As the people of the South show their true colors, they are reaffirming their faith in the right of free men to govern themselves," he explained. "In its true place, the Confederate flag can only be a symbol of the truly American devotion to the principles of democratic government, which guarantees a federal union of sovereign states, each respecting and protecting the rights of others." To the widely quoted warning by a Sons of Union Veterans (SUV) chaplain that the flag fad was "dangerous," Mason responded that the SUV or its members may be "determined to continue fighting the southern people and the ideals for which we stand." Mason seemed oblivious to the reasoning that the flag's association with Confederate states' rights principles was exactly what its detractors feared and loathed. The SCV's commander-in-chief in 1950 urged white southern men to join the organization to defend the southern "way of life." "We need increased membership of Confederate ancestry in our fight to preserve these traditions," which included "certain regulations regarding race segregation."[23]

Not surprisingly, organs of African-American opinion were most acutely aware of the flag fad's ideological overtones. Claude Barnett's American Negro Press reported approvingly that an African-American Chicago minister and alderman nipped in the bud a Rebel Day event planned at a Hyde Park high school. Seven southern-born students had distributed Confederate flags and convinced fellow students to dress up for the day. Alderman Archibald Carey scored a day that "commemorates a rebellion against the government of the United States . . . and exalts the flag of the Confederacy which was once the rallying point of an uprising against the Republic." The *Chicago Defender* was willing to concede the innocent side of the "flag craze" but believed that it was in large part a reaction against the "remarkable progress" of black Americans and expressed a desire to stop "the phenomenal advancement of the Negro toward first class citizenship."[24]

The *Afro-American,* published in Baltimore and Richmond, in early 1952 warned that the flag fad was part and parcel of the United Daughters of the Confederacy's effort to rewrite history and deny that the war was a rebellion against the Union. "Real Americans," the paper insisted, recognized the flag fad for what it was—"an attempt to popularize the South's opposition to Civil Rights."[25] A later issue equated the Confederate flag at home with the hammer and sickle flag abroad. For those who would dismiss the flag fad as harmless, a sermon-like editorial drew historical parallels with the rise of Mussolini and Hitler. "KEEP YOUR EYES ON THOSE CONFEDERATE FLAGS!"

> Stop a moment! Ask yourself what sinister forces are behind this sudden craze to make the whole nation rebel conscious?
>
> Stop a moment! Ask yourself why this fad broke out apparently from nowhere on the very heels of the political movement of the Dixiecrats and their unsuccessful attempt to wrest the reins of power from the Democratic party.
>
> Stop a moment! Ask yourself if the South is not now trying to accomplish by fiat what they failed to gain first by arms and later by ballot.
>
> Are these Confederate flags and emblems but an opiate to lull the rest of America into casual acceptance of symbols which if presented in their true light would be rejected and abhorred?
>
> Have we so soon forgotten what the Confederate flag represents?

The Confederate flag stands for slavery and human degradation.

The Confederate flag stands for rebellion and treachery.

The Confederate flag stands for bloodshed and segregation.

The Confederate flag stands for oppression and disfran-
chisement.

The Confederate flag stands for white supremacy and
everything in which democracy and Christianity are opposed.

These are no laughing matters.

To the plea from American servicemen, Confederate descendants, and
trinket merchants that they "mean no harm" in flying the flag, the *Afro-
American* answered that the conquered and their progeny never lose hope
"that a lost cause may someday be regained."

AWAKE AMERICA!
Let us not become so intent in watching the enemy beyond
our borders, that we are blind to the enemy within our
gates.[26]

The influential *Pittsburgh Courier* was among the most vocal critics of
the Confederate flag fad, and the most prominent voice to link the flag
with slavery and racism. Several articles in the September 29, 1951, *Courier* berated the reappearance of an "odious symbol of slavery and servi-
tude of Negroes in the South." While the paper acknowledged that the
flag's popularity was another teenage fad, it could not dismiss the flag fad
as a trivial matter. "Once this flag was proudly waved by southerners—
hate-filled southerners—who were locked in a deadly struggle with their
own country, the United States of America, in open rebellion against the
United States. They lost their fight, but now—some ninety years later—
this Confederate flag is being waved again. It is not a good omen for a nation which is pleading for unity in the face of world communism."[27]

Particularly troubling to the editors of the *Courier* was the presence of the rebel flag in the armed forces. The *Courier* expressed outrage that the secretary of defense's "confused spokesman" was apparently ignorant of or indifferent to the army regulation against unauthorized flags. However, in response to a *Courier* story about Confederate flags used by men in the 82nd Airborne Division, the Pentagon did order an investigation headed by an African-American officer. The *Courier* referred to the battle flag as "that 'emblem of disunity'" and quoted equally outraged statements by unnamed U.S. senators who determined to enforce regulations against the flag.[28]

The leader of a Virginia-based organization, the American Council on Human Rights, echoed this fear of disunity. Elmer Henderson cautioned that while the flag fad might be "meaningless," it was inspired by the Dixiecrats and indicated a revival of the Ku Klux Klan. "Unless challenged in an effective manner it could lead public opinion into reactionary channels that could set back our grand march toward civil and human rights." One symbolic measure he suggested was to combat the Confederate flag by flying U.S. flags on cars and street corners. "These could show southerners who are reviving the dead hand of the past our allegiance to which our children in schools pledge allegiance every morning, and the flag we salute in gatherings as the national anthem is played." The U.S. flag was "a symbol of faith in the ultimate victory of the principle of equality of citizenship for all without regard to race or color in the United States."[29]

The political use of the flag disturbed not only African-American editors but also the primary keepers of the Confederate flame—the United Daughters of the Confederacy and, to a lesser degree, the Sons of Confederate Veterans. Beginning in 1948, the UDC sought to prevent political groups from appropriating the flag and to prevent misuse of the flag by souvenir manufacturers and overzealous youths. The Kappa Alpha Order, whose members helped to launch the flag into American popular culture, also sought to control and limit flag use. Unlike the African-American press, these Confederate heritage organizations did not believe that the flag carried threatening meanings but were concerned that they would lose control of the flag and its meaning.

As the pundits of 1951 predicted, the flag fad did fade. Sales of Confederate flags dipped in 1952 and the phenomenon disappeared from national headlines. The *Montgomery Advertiser* in late 1953 declared the fad dead.[30] But the intense popularity of the Confederate battle flag during this period had significant long-term effects. Continuing the trend evident before World War II and accelerated in 1948, the fad fixed the flag's place as a cultural icon. Uses that were rare before World War II became commonplace in the 1950s.

The pattern of flag use in the 1950s underscored the important and fundamental transformation that had occurred since before World War II. Brought dramatically to national attention, the Confederate battle flag acquired visibility and familiarity far beyond the South. The transformation culminating in the flag fad also stripped off the shroud of reverence that prevented the flag's admirers from using it outside of Confederate memorial rituals and introduced it into arenas in which people who had no reverence for it felt free to use it in trivial, even irreverent ways. While the flag was and is a sacred symbol to Confederate heritage organizations and to countless individuals, those organizations and people lost exclusive control over the flag's symbolic meaning as a result of the flag fad. The flag took on new identities as a logo for the South and a symbol of rebelliousness that had national currency and appeal. Simultaneously, the Dixiecrat use of the flag endowed it with a more specific connotation of resistance to the civil rights movement and to racial integration. The escalation of the civil rights struggle in 1954 revealed just how powerful a symbol of resistance the Confederate flag could be, and it forever changed the terms of discussion over the flag's meaning.

In the years during and immediately after the flag fad, the use of the Confederate battle flag in college campus traditions and in the wider American culture became fully entrenched. Kappa Alpha fraternity's use of the flag in Old South rituals flowered in the 1950s, despite the national office's injunction against it. The KA tradition received a lot of national attention during the flag fad, most notably a feature spread in the May 22, 1950, edition of *Life* magazine. Photographs of the KA chapter at Auburn University introduced a national audience to the Old South

Ball and an increasingly popular panoply of related events and gestures: a secession ceremony, a flag-waving parade through downtown Auburn, and a huge Confederate flag on the fraternity house. At the University of Alabama, the flag taken out of mothballs in the summer of 1948 remained out after the fall elections. The 1951 Old South events included Confederate uniforms and flags and white female students in black face. Old South Week in 1954 featured a parade down University Avenue "followed by secession ceremonies and the raising of the Confederate Flag." The University of Georgia and three other KA chapters in state schools co-sponsored an Old South Ball and a flag-festooned parade down Atlanta's famous Peachtree Street. Birmingham-Southern College's Kappa Alpha chapter sponsored a Rose Ball, which in 1952 featured "the largest Confederate flag in the world" as an overhead decoration in the gymnasium. The KA chapter at the University of South Carolina held its first Old South Ball in 1952, replete with a secession ceremony, "pretty girls and southern gentlemen."[31]

In the 1950s the University of Mississippi fully embraced the Confederate battle flag as the all-but-official school symbol. After the fad era had faded, the flag became a visible fixture in Kappa Alpha's traditional Dixie Week. Throughout the decade, the huge battle flag introduced in the fall of 1948 was a fixture at football game half-time shows. It appeared on the cover of several yearbooks and football game programs. The school's majorettes and Rebelettes marched with flags, and at the 1953 Sugar Bowl game the band "unfurled a giant Rebel flag large enough to cover the entire band as it marched before the huge crowd." Beginning in 1956–57 the Ole Miss band sported new uniforms "styled after the uniforms worn by the southern soldiers in the War Between the States," making it more than ever "the band of the South." The battle flag was a symbol that the university proudly and prominently displayed to the world when officials welcomed celebrities and when the band majorettes traveled to Belgium and Holland in 1959. The majorette uniforms featured bibs with battle flag motifs.[32]

Southern schools that Americans usually do not associate with the Confederate flag flirted with it during the flag fad. The flag's lineage at the University of Florida in Gainesville was longer than that of Ole Miss. Before 1948, Florida's Kappa Alpha chapter used the flag in its Plantation Ball rituals, and in 1952 Florida took a step that Mississippi never did: it adopted a variant of the Confederate battle flag as its official school flag. The school approached its centennial in 1953 without ever having had an official school flag. The school sponsored a campus-wide contest in 1951–1952, soliciting ideas from the entire campus community. A committee consisting of the university president and three members of the Art Department chose the design of senior Manuel Fernandez: a rectangular battle flag with a white cross on a blue background, six orange stars (each representing one of the schools in the university), and the school seal superimposed over the cross. Being official did not make the flag popular, however. It was less visible at school functions than was the blue cross on a red field and was replaced as the official school flag in 1961.[33]

The 1950s saw the flowering of another predominantly southern cultural form with which the Confederate flag became associated almost immediately—stock car racing. Born in the South in the mid-1940s, modern stock car racing grew out of the early twentieth-century Daytona Beach races. When the National Association of Stock Car Auto Racing (NASCAR) series began in 1949, three of eight races occurred north of the Mason-Dixon Line, but the South gave stock car racing its character and its symbols. Inevitably, an early program for an Alabama track named the Dixie Speedway featured crossed Confederate and checkered flags as its logo. On a grander scale, the Atlanta International Raceway in 1960 launched the Dixie 500, for which the Confederate flag was the *de facto* logo.[34]

Not accidentally, the link between stock car racing and the Confederate battle flag was strongest in Darlington, South Carolina. Virtually from the beginning of its history as one of sport's premier speedways, Darlington's impresarios played upon southern themes and symbols. The track's signature race was the Southern 500. For the inaugural race on Labor Day 1950, the battle flag was one of the track's logos. Race directors posed with Confederate flags, sold battle flag lapel stickers, dressed flag-carrying majorettes in stylized Confederate flag uniforms, and emblazoned flags on the announcer's desk. The symbolism intensified with the creation of a new race in 1957 held on the weekend closest to Confederate Memorial Day (April 26 in South Carolina): the Rebel 300, subsequently lengthened to the Rebel 500. For more than a decade the race featured a flag-waving "Johnny Reb" who greeted the winner in victory lane. From the Darlington races' origins until the early 1980s, the program for the races featured the battle flag prominently. After officials discontinued sponsorship and promotion of the flag, it nevertheless continued to enjoy cult status among fans in the stands and in the infield.[35]

The marriage of the Confederate battle flag and stock car racing typified the history of the flag in the 1950s. A wide variety of organizations, schools, institutions, and events in some way identified with the South as a region or even a compass point and adopted the ubiquitous and eye-catching banner as their symbol. A textbook example was that of the Richmond, Virginia, chapter of the Power Squadron, a nationwide club of powerboat enthusiasts. Founded in 1953, the chapter in the former capital of the Confederacy thought it natural to use as its flag, or burgee, a triangular pennant with Confederate battle flag design. The flag also became the logo for a Texas-based organization dedicated to preserving and flying World War II combat aircraft. Formed in 1951, the group purchased its first plane in 1957. Someone surreptitiously painted "Confederate Air Force" on the plane's nose; the group embraced the name and, along with it, the battle flag as an official insignia. The group's Confederate symbolism and playful allusions to the Old South flourished into the late 1970s, but its leadership abandoned the flag and in October 2000 voted to change the name.[36]

In the mid-1950s and early 1960s the battle flag became allied with Chattanooga's Cotton Ball, one of the South's most elaborate society events. Inaugurated in 1932 by a daughter of a Confederate veteran "to perpetuate the vanishing glories of the Old South," the Cotton Ball was (and still is) basically a debutante ball, but with a special twist: participants in the ball had to have Confederate ancestry. The first balls featured children in black face, the playing of "Dixie," and ubiquitous American flags, but apparently no Confederate flags. The flag was evident first in

1938 on the 75th anniversary of the battles around Chattanooga and as one of four flags on a medal in 1940. Frequent and substantial use of the battle flag began in 1956 with a ball dedicated to the theme of the Stars and Bars. For the first time, the battle flag was the primary decoration, and Confederate themes were part of the pageantry. Too late to have been a direct result of the flag fad, the 1956 ball suggests another link between the popular use of the flag and an increasing sense of white southern identity. Notes written for the ceremony introduced the girl representing the "Spirit of the South" with the line: "In these trying times may the Spirit of the South never die—and very much alive—representing the Spirit of the South—Miss Barbara Willingham." The Cotton Balls in 1960, 1962, and 1963 also featured Confederate battle flags in the decorations and ceremonies. Finally, in 1966, the ball adopted an official coat of arms that featured a battle flag motif on a shield. This coat of arms was the ball's most visible decoration into the 1990s.[37]

The Cotton Ball's adoption of the flag revealed two other influences at work in the late 1950s and early 1960s: white southern resistance to civil rights and the commemoration of the Civil War Centennial. The coincidence of these events complicates the effort to understand or assign motives for flag use. The assault on racial segregation by the federal government and by southern blacks intensified white southerners' consciousness of their traditions and symbols at the same time that a federal initiative encouraged all states to develop and promote their Civil War history and resources. This was the era in which Georgia, Alabama, and South Carolina incorporated the battle flag into their official symbolism, setting the stage for the rancorous flag wars of later decades.

It became a popular aphorism in the early 1960s that "the South may have lost the war—but it's sure going to win the Centennial." Southern states debated whether to participate in an event that commemorated southern defeat, but decided that the centennial was an opportunity to advertise the region to a national, even international, audience and to win support for the southern perspective on struggles past and present. Virginia Governor J. Lindsay Almond told his state's commission that the centennial was an opportunity to emphasize "the basic underlying principles in defense of which the war was fought," namely, states' rights. In his address to the Confederate States Civil War Centennial Conference (a consortium of the southern state commissions), Mississippi Governor Ross R. Barnett alluded playfully to the commercial and public relations opportunities that the centennial presented. "The Centennial is the first opportunity we have had in a hundred years to make the Yankees pay for the War and like it," he quipped, quoting a friend. "Further, I believe that the kind of people who can and will come South will be the kind of people we want to come—and I don't mean 'freedom riders.'" Barnett echoed Almond in anticipating that the centennial would bring "respectful attention" to the modern South, especially its "precious heritage of local self-government" and resistance to "centralization of power in the National Government." The centennial gave the South an opportunity to draw attention to its cause. "Through the centennial," South Carolina's chairman, John A. May, concluded, "I think the nation now knows the principles for which the South stood and the thinking of its leaders."[38]

Inevitably, the Confederate battle flag was a prominent, officially sanctioned symbol during the centennial observations. Several southern states featured the battle flag without the U.S. flag on their state commission logos. Participants carried it in reenactments of battles and major events. The U.S. Civil War Centennial Commission used the flag—in conjunction with the Stars and Stripes—in and on official publications. A centennial parade in Jackson, Mississippi, featured a group representing the University Greys and the Ole Miss band carrying "the giant Confederate Flag which the band has made famous here and in Europe." The Virginia Civil War Centennial Commission declared the first week of celebrations "flags and flowers" week and encouraged everyone to display American, state, and Confederate flags.[39]

In response to queries about where and how to display the Confederate flag, North Carolina's Department of Archives and History proposed a resolution delineating "proper usage and procedure." The nonbinding suggestions deemed it proper to fly the Confederate flag over the state capitol and other state and local government buildings on Confederate Memorial Day (May 10) and other appropriate occasions, as long as the

Stars and Stripes was displayed according to U.S. government regulations. "The Confederate flag may appropriately be flown over or on any
private property in the state," the resolution advised. Florida allowed the
battle flag to be raised over the state capitol in Tallahassee for one day in
March 1963 to commemorate the 98th anniversary of the Confederate
victory that saved the city from Federal occupation. Even Arizona, which
was occupied briefly by Confederate troops in 1862, flew a Confederate
flag on the state capitol on January 8, 1961, the opening day of centennial commemorations.[40]

With the officially sanctioned flag display came a flood of tacky souvenirs and promotions. "The Civil War Centennial is one of the most
mouth-watering marketing situations to come along in years," salivated
one trade magazine. Merchants sold "turncoats" (blue on one side, gray
on the other) for dogs; neckties that featured U.S. and Confederate flags
at the top and the increasingly popular slogan "Forget Hell" at the bottom; and flag-decorated music boxes (made in Japan) that played "Dixie."
The *Atlanta Constitution's* Ralph McGill and other commentators deplored such commercialism and the theatrics of the centennial, which,
they believed, trivialized the war and the people who fought it.[41]

The 1957 legislation authorizing the Centennial Commission hoped to
carry out the commemoration "free from stains of commercialism or
vulgarity." The commission formed an advertising committee that distributed a pamphlet entitled "Aids to Advertisers." The pamphlet featured suggestions for advertising "tie-ins" and a list of Dos and Don'ts to
marketers, including an admonition not to "debase flags, symbols, or insignia by misusing them for commercial purposes." More important, the
legislation also charged the commission with a commemoration that
would not "reawaken memories of old sectional antagonisms and political rancor," which proved difficult to accomplish in the context of the
civil rights movement.[42]

The souvenir business worried some observers not because of vulgarity or commercialism but because it seemed to create public enthusiasm
for the Confederacy. "There were more Confederate flags sold during
the first year of the Civil War Centennial (1961) than were sold through-

out the South during the war itself," noted one disapproving columnist. "The enterprise of manufacturing Confederate flags and other secession-ist paraphernalia, never in a languishing state, threatens to become a ma-jor industry before taps sounds the end of Appomattox day in 1965," warned the African-American historian John Hope Franklin in 1962. Liberal critics were distressed that the official centennial proceedings not only gave equal treatment to North and South—including "reverence as much for the Stars and Bars as the Stars and Stripes"—but even seemed to favor the South and, ominously, gave the southern state governments complete control over the ideological content of celebrations in their states.[43]

Concerns over the South "winning the Centennial" probably would have existed regardless of the political climate of the early 1960s. The Civil War was, after all, a war fought over real and divisive issues and one in which the winners, losers, and victimized neutrals lived together in one country afterward. The issues of the war were not historical memo-ries in 1961 but were front-page news. "It would be ironic, not to say tragic, coincidence," mused C. Vann Woodward on the eve of the centen-nial, "if the celebration of the anniversary took place in the midst of a cri-sis reminiscent of the one celebrated." Another historian, Charles Sellers, echoed Woodward. "Will history repeat itself? Will the Sumter centen-nial find southerners once again defending their southernism in desper-ate, increasing revolt against the larger society of which they have always been a part, against social values which they have always shared?"[44] This was, of course, exactly what did happen in the late 1950s and early 1960s. One result of the coincidence was to cast a shadow of doubt over the status of the Confederate flag as a neutral commemorative symbol or an innocent totem of a youthful fad.

Chapter 7

"Symbol of the White Race and White Supremacy"

After years of preparation, the Civil War Centennial celebrations began in April 1961 when dignitaries from around the country descended upon Charleston, South Carolina, to commemorate the event that lit the fuse of war: the firing on Fort Sumter. Much to the consternation of the U.S. Civil War Centennial Commission, the inaugural event showcased America's contemporary divisions as much as it commemorated a past civil war. The state delegations were to stay in the prestigious Francis Marion Hotel, but it was reported that, consistent with city and state segregation ordinances, the hotel refused to register an African-American delegate, Madaline Williams of New Jersey. While commission officials declined to force the issue and the hotel insisted that Mrs. Williams had never requested a room, President John F. Kennedy in late March asked the hotel to compromise its segregation policy. The hotel refused. The New Jersey and New York delegations pulled out of the hotel. The New York delegation announced that it would observe the Sumter centennial in Boston by laying a wreath at the monument honoring Colonel Robert Gould Shaw and the U.S. Colored Troop regiment, the 54th Massachusetts.

Confronted with the hotel's dogged commitment to law and custom, the commission moved its accommodations to a nearby U.S. military base. "It had been impossible to dissociate the racial issue from the Civil War while it raged (as evidenced by the 1863 New York draft riots)," observed the commission's subsequent chairman, historian Allan Nevins; "it was now impossible to dissociate it entirely from the centennial commemoration."[1]

The tension escalated during the Sumter commemoration itself. The keynote speaker, *Saturday Evening Post* associate editor Ashley Halsey, a native South Carolinian, took the opportunity to express his disdain for what he believed to be the deliberate confrontation provoked by the New Jersey delegation. Halsey related a story of his unreconstructed grandmother hanging out "an enormous Confederate flag" during Franklin D. Roosevelt's visit to Charleston in 1936 and declared that current events compelled him to show "our flag" again. He argued that the Civil War was not caused by slavery, that secession was understood to be constitutional in 1861, and that the Fourteenth and Fifteenth Amendments to the Constitution were not passed legally. Those amendments "which were railroaded into our Constitution are today the basis of our present racial unrest." Once asked, "Why won't the South give the Negroes their rights?" Halsey replied that "the South *never* has consented to those rights."[2]

In January 1963, one hundred years after Abraham Lincoln's Emancipation Proclamation declared free those slaves living within Confederate lines, a new governor took the oath of office in Montgomery, Alabama. George Corley Wallace reminded white Alabamians of their grievances against the North during the Civil War and Reconstruction and promised them that he would never again sacrifice the southern "way of life" to the federal government. Standing at a podium flanked by a Confederate battle flag as well as the Stars and Stripes and the state flag, Wallace intoned:

> Today I have stood, where once Jefferson Davis stood, and
> took an oath to my people. It is very appropriate then that
> from this Cradle of the Confederacy, this very Heart of the

Great Anglo-Saxon Southland . . . we sound the drum for
freedom . . . Let us rise to the call of freedom-loving
blood that is in us and send our answer to the tyranny that
clanks its chains upon the South. In the name of the greatest people that have ever trod this earth, I draw the line in
the dust and toss the gauntlet before the feet of tyranny
. . . and I say . . . segregation now . . . segregation tomorrow . . . segregation forever."[3]

Two years later, the commemoration of the event that effectively
ended the Civil War—Lee's surrender to Grant at Appomattox—found
the country absorbed with news coming from Alabama. Several weeks
earlier, civil rights marchers led by Dr. Martin Luther King, Jr., completed a four-day trek from Selma to Montgomery intended to build support for the passage of a federal voting rights act. As the marchers made
their way along the highways of central Alabama, they were taunted by
small groups of young men with Confederate flags and flag-emblazoned
clothing. When they arrived in Montgomery carrying the Stars and
Stripes, at least one white man greeted them defiantly waving a small
Confederate flag. One hundred years to the day after Lee's surrender,
Time magazine carried a feature article on Ku Klux Klan violence and a
photograph of Imperial Wizard Robert Shelton of Tuscaloosa, with his
favorite totem: a Confederate battle flag.[4]

Such events in the 1960s, especially the searing images of Shelton and
other Klansmen posing with Confederate flags, intensified the flag's association with segregation and racism. Not without merit, flag defenders
today complain that the symbolic impact of flag-toting Klansmen has
been far out of proportion to their numbers and their place in American
society. The news media, for whom Klansmen with flags present irresist-
ibly powerful images, have allowed the Ku Klux Klan to seize control of
the Confederate flag's imagery in the late twentieth century.

The Ku Klux Klan was not the only group of white southerners that
used the flag as a racist symbol in the 1950s and 1960s. Ordinary white
southerners protesting integration carried the flag, along with signs

whose messages concerning race were unmistakable. A consummate politician, George Wallace made the battle flag his symbol not because it resonated with Klansmen but because it resonated with white Alabamians in general.

Civil rights leaders came to view the Confederate battle flag as a symbol of racism because they encountered it in situations in which white people *intended* it as a symbol of racism. The late legendary Congress of Racial Equality leader James Farmer saw the flag as a symbol of "aggressive racism." He remembered seeing Confederate flags whenever he was conscious of "people assembling for racist purposes." Civil rights lawyer Oliver Hill also associated the flag with encounters during "massive resistance days." "It was always used by ardent segregationists," he recalled, and it will always mean "ardent segregationism" to him.[5] For many African Americans, the battle flag evokes a dark sense of physical threat, often because of actual experiences in which the flag accompanied groups of people intent on doing them harm.

It is easy to both exaggerate and minimize the prominence of the Confederate battle flag as a racist symbol. In contrast to James Farmer's experiences, civil rights pioneer and NAACP chairman Julian Bond remembered no direct confrontations with racists waving Confederate flags. The flag, he recalled, "wasn't ubiquitous" among hecklers and segregationists. Indeed, more episodes of racial violence and intimidation occurred in the civil rights era and in the decades before with no Confederate flags present than with flags flying. Nevertheless, because of the very real events that did occur, Julian Bond "always associated it with people who meant me ill."[6]

Since the mid-twentieth century, when the flag escaped the exclusive control of Confederate heritage organizations and entered American popular culture, it has been brandished by racists who believe that its meaning is, and always was, white supremacy. Beginning with the Confederacy itself, whenever the racial order of the South has come under serious challenge, defenders of the status quo have found the Confederate battle flag a powerful symbol for their opposition to change. Prompted by northern urban activists and northern African Americans within the Democratic Party, the federal government in the 1940s had once again begun to challenge the South's racial status quo.

Not coincidentally, the 1940s also saw both the first association of the flag with a major political movement (the States' Rights Party) intent on preserving the segregationist status quo and the first documented use of the flag in the rituals of the Ku Klux Klan. Klanbuster Stetson Kennedy described the flag's use in Atlanta in 1943–1944. Faced with federal legal action, the centralized KKK disbanded in June 1944 but continued to exist in the form of local chapters and splinter organizations using the Klan name. Under the leadership of Dr. Samuel Green of Atlanta, the Klan enjoyed one of its periodic revivals beginning in late 1945, replete with the obligatory cross burnings on Stone Mountain. Unlike earlier incarnations, the new Klan employed Confederate symbols regularly. A *Life* magazine article in May 1946 featured photographs of a Klan ritual using the trinity of (unofficial) modern Klan symbols: the Christian cross, the American flag, and the Confederate flag.[7]

Green's Klan spread from Georgia to neighboring states, especially Alabama. One of the revived Klan's most eccentric leaders, Dr. Lycurgus Spinks of Montgomery, Alabama, founder of the Knights of the Ku Klux Klan of America, made the Confederate flag a personal symbol. Posed before the U.S. flag and Confederate battle flag and dressed in the colorful robes of a self-proclaimed "imperial emperor," Spinks received the bemused attention of national news media.[8]

The ideology and motives of the revived Klan were clear from a speech that Samuel Green gave at a rally and "naturalization" ceremony in Tarrant, Alabama, in April 1949 shortly before his death. Speaking on a softball field with U.S. and Confederate flags waving, Green explained that "God segregated the races. There is no law that can be passed by Harry Truman, or Congress, or by the Legislature of your state that can supersede the law of the Lord."[9] Green's death nipped in the bud the Klan's revival, but the late 1940s showed that the Truman administration's assault on segregation was as conducive to Klan activity as it was to mainstream political revolt.

Developments beyond the Truman administration's civil rights agenda

weakened the foundations of the South's "Jim Crow" system and provoked Confederate flag-waving by defenders of that system. The legal
strategy of a reinvigorated NAACP challenged "separate but equal" segregation laws where they were most vulnerable—by demonstrating that
separate invariably meant inferior schools and accommodations. The
courts agreed and compelled states with segregation laws to spend more
money on facilities for blacks. Southern white liberals spoke more
openly and confidently about a South without segregation, while conservatives realized that only by spending more on black schools could they
avert a court-ordered end to segregation. The backlash against these
threats to the southern "way of life" clearly fueled the early 1950s flag
fad. Roy V. Harris, the recently retired speaker of the Georgia House of
Representatives and editor of the *Augusta Courier,* minced no words in
linking the threat to his embrace of the Confederate flag in 1951. "The
Confederate flag is coming to mean something to everybody now. It
means the southern cause. It means the heart throbs of the people of the
South. It is becoming to be [sic] the symbol of the white race and the
cause of the white people. The Confederate flag means segregation."[10]

The spark that ignited segregationist resistance at every level of white
southern society was the 1954 U.S. Supreme Court decision in *Brown v.
Board of Education, Topeka, Kansas.* On May 17, 1954—dubbed "Black
Monday" by segregationists—the U.S. Supreme Court unanimously
ruled that "separate but equal" schools for white and black students violated the U.S. Constitution. A year later, the Court with intentional ambiguity advised lower courts to desegregate public schools "with all deliberate speed." The *Brown* decision made a moderate pace of educational
change untenable and unleashed an angry and often violent campaign to
preserve legalized segregation. The Confederate battle flag was a favorite
symbol in the hands of those white southerners who fought, into the
1970s, to preserve the old order.

Almost without exception, southern political leaders announced their
unequivocal intention to circumvent the integration of public schools—a
posture that came to be known as "massive resistance." State legislatures
and the southern congressional delegation echoed this resolve. In their

1955 and 1956 sessions the southern state legislatures crafted plans that subverted *Brown* and effectively delayed school integration until subsequent U.S. Supreme Court decisions handed down in the late 1960s. As the Virginia General Assembly began a special session to pass massive resistance ordinances, a group of ardent segregationists stood in the gallery waving small Confederate flags. The same session of the Georgia legislature that passed the massive resistance plan also incorporated the Confederate battle flag into the state flag. While defenders of the flag in the 1990s have argued accurately that there is no "smoking gun" linking the two events, historians have demonstrated that the flag change was a symbolic counterpart to the new segregation laws.[11]

During the height of the civil rights movement in the 1950s and 1960s, the Confederate battle flag became the opposing symbol to the Stars and Stripes. Identifying themselves with American principles and patriotism, civil rights protesters marched with the Stars and Stripes. Segregationists often played into the protesters' strategy by taunting them with Confederate flags. Even an exchange of stunts evidenced the Confederate flag's oppositional meaning: after a Chicago pilot, in the wake of the *Brown* decision, dropped copies of the U.S. Constitution over the South, an Oxford, Mississippi, disc jockey flew to Chicago and dropped 20,000 small Confederate flags over the Windy City.[12]

Grassroots organizations emerged to contest integration and to wave the flag. Inspired by Mississippi judge Tom Brady's speech "Black Monday," delivered weeks after the decision, Robert Patterson of Clarksdale, Mississippi, formed the first of a sprawling network of "Citizens' Councils" in July 1954. The Citizens' Councils used political and especially economic pressure to punish black activists and to enforce white unity on the segregation issue. Among the councils' activities were educational campaigns, including the distribution of pro-segregation textbooks and speakers in public schools. A 1957 *Manual for Southerners* made explicit the organization's ideology and its understanding of a popular catchphrase:

> Do you know what part of the country you live in? You
> live in the South. You know you live in Mississippi. Missis-

sippi is a state in the South. The South is a big part of the
country.

Negroes and white people do not go to the same places
together. We live in different parts of town. And we are
kind to each other. This is called our Southern Way of Life.
We do not mix our races. But we are kind to each other.[13]

From Mississippi the Citizens' Councils spread throughout the South
and formed a federation that claimed as many as 500,000 members
(though some sources estimate membership to have been half that). The
councils insisted that constitutional issues were at the heart of their resistance to *Brown*. Echoing the Dixiecrats of a few years before, they argued
that all Americans had something to fear from a federal government that
could force the end of legalized segregation. At the same time, however,
the councils unapologetically proclaimed the religious, moral, and scientific necessity of racial segregation. Constitutional and economic arguments were for the Citizens' Councils, as they had been for the fathers of
the Confederacy, a means to preserve a "way of life" based on the racial
status quo.[14]

Considering the strong ideological link between resistance to federal
interference in southern race issues in the 1860s and the segregationist
backlash of the 1950s, it is not surprising that the Confederate battle flag
was a central icon of the Citizens' Councils. Under Robert Patterson's
leadership, the organization's headquarters was a "one-room, Confederate flag-cluttered office" in Clarksdale. Patterson spoke at a podium
decorated with a full-sized battle flag. The organization's logo featured
crossed U.S. and Confederate battle flags with the motto "States' Rights
/ Racial Integrity." The Association of Citizens' Councils of Mississippi
offered for sale a variety of pamphlets, including Brady's "Black Monday"
speech, "A Christian View on Segregation," "The Ugly Truth about the
NAACP," "Interposition, the Barrier against Tyranny," and single-sheet
publications on such topics as "Is Segregation Unchristian?" and "The
Confederate Flag." The Mississippi Citizens' Councils also distributed a
bumper sticker featuring a rectangular battle flag and the slogan "Support your Citizens' Councils." The newspaper of the Citizens' Councils

of America ran a regular column, "A Southern Viewpoint," and used a battle flag as the column's masthead. Roy Harris, the editor of the *Augusta Courier* who proudly carried the sobriquet of "Mr. Segregation," was president of the Citizens' Councils in the 1960s. Like Patterson, Harris addressed his audiences from a stage decked out not only with the council logo but a Confederate battle flag.[15]

Similar groups, including a Citizens' Councils network, proliferated in Virginia. One of them, the "Virginia League," steeped itself in Confederate imagery, offering for sale pictures of Robert E. Lee and Stonewall Jackson. The organization's newspaper, *The Virginian,* printed a quotation from Douglas Southall Freeman's *Lee's Lieutenants* on the value of Christianity to Confederate troops and then urged modern-day southerners to keep the faith "undefiled by apostasy and undiluted by compromise." In March 1956 *The Virginian* began using a masthead of an aged Confederate officer in full uniform and battle flag proclaiming "My country's calling on her sons to meet the foe!" With the guidance of adult segregationist activists, a group of teenagers in Clinton, Tennessee, founded Tennessee White Youth in November 1956. Described as a "Citizens' Council-type organization for teenagers," its founders wore turtlenecks emblazoned with the battle flag when they received their organizational charter.[16]

Confederate heritage organizations did not advocate use of the battle flag as a symbol of defiance, but leaders of the Sons of Confederate Veterans sympathized explicitly with the fight against integration and even tried to align the SCV with the segregationist cause. "If you believe the true reasons for the War Between the States and that your ancestors were right in fighting for the privileges of each state to govern itself, it is your duty to assist in forming a larger organization that we may exert influence in the affairs of our state and nation," declared SCV Commander-in-Chief Belmont Dennis in January 1951. "We are against the national Administration's effort to eliminate segregation in our Southland." Hatley Norton Mason, of Virginia, adjutant general of the SCV in the early 1950s, served later as president of the Virginia Defenders of State Sovereignty and Individual Liberties. He warned of groups "working to destroy the South and to some extent aimed at destroying the white race in America, then take over." In 1957 he invited his cousin, Judge Walter B. Jones of Alabama (famous for declaring the NAACP illegal in Alabama), to come to Virginia and "meet some of our Patriots who live around Richmond, who will also speak & are members of the S.C.V."[17]

John D. Long, the South Carolina politician who was responsible for placing the Confederate flag in both chambers of the state legislature, in March 1957 resolved that "the Battle Flag of the southern Confederacy inspires our dedication to the resurrection of truth with glorious and eternal vindication." In 1944, in the face of the first rumblings of federal civil rights initiatives, he proposed a resolution declaring the state assembly's "allegiance to established White Supremacy as now prevailing in the South and pledging our lives and our sacred honor to maintain it, whatever the cost, in war and in peace." He reminded his fellow senators in May 1961 that since the end of the Civil War "the North has never ceased to carry on and wage unrelenting Black War against the South and the white people of the South, seeking to destroy our way of life."[18]

The implication of this well-established pattern is that Confederate heritage leaders were not apolitical and that they saw links between the Confederate cause and the cause of segregation. While it is notable and significant that flag defenders refrained from dragging the flag into the struggles over segregation, it is also significant how many people who revered and protected or promoted the flag also held segregationist views and drew direct links between their Confederate heritage and the fight to preserve segregation. Their own segregationist tendencies may have muted their opposition to others who used the flag as a segregationist symbol.

The *Brown* decision gave rise to other organizations that were more overt and violent in their expressions of racism and resistance. The Klan revived yet again, especially in Alabama, where violence and intimidation of blacks escalated. A wave of Klan bombings gave "Bombingham" its unwanted nickname years before the infamous 1963 church bombing that killed four schoolgirls. Klan rallies throughout Alabama after *Brown* almost inevitably occurred under the Confederate battle flag. The imperial wizard of the Gulf Ku Klux Klan in Mobile, Alabama, operated a gun shop bedecked with a huge Confederate flag on the wall. The leader of the Klan in Birmingham, Alabama, called his group the "Original Ku Klux Klan of the Confederacy."[19]

The Klan leader associated most closely with the flag was a Tuscaloosa, Alabama, tire salesman, Robert Shelton, who became imperial wizard of the newly formed United Klans of America, Knights of the Ku Klux Klan, in 1961. Like Patterson of the Citizens' Councils, Shelton displayed a Confederate battle flag in his office, along with a U.S. flag and a portrait of Alabama Governor George C. Wallace. Thanks to the intense scrutiny of the Klan during the height of the civil rights movement and to his own flamboyance, Shelton solidified the already strong association between the Klan and the Confederate flag. Klan leaders following Shelton insisted that the flag stood for racial purity and that Confederate heritage leaders who denied this were evading the truth.[20]

The late 1950s also saw the rise of a loosely knit organization of right-wing groups that called themselves the Confederate Underground. The Underground's most infamous act was the bombing of Atlanta's oldest and wealthiest synagogue in the early morning of October 12, 1958. "General Gordon of the Confederate Underground" called United Press International to claim responsibility for the bombing and warn that henceforth bombings would not be empty buildings. The Confederate Underground and the "Confederate Army" also bombed a Jewish temple in Nashville, Tennessee, and threatened other bombings. The linkage between anti-Semitic violence and Confederate identity drew outraged comments from editor Ralph McGill and President Dwight D. Eisenhower.[21] For one of the men implicated in the activities of the Confederate Underground, Jesse B. Stoner, associating the Confederacy with anti-Semitism and racism was a life-long crusade.

Born in North Georgia in 1924 and orphaned at age sixteen, Stoner was a member of the Columbians, the neo-Nazi youth group that investigator Stetson Kennedy exposed. There was nothing subtle about Stoner's racism. At age eighteen he petitioned Congress to declare Jews "the children of the Devil" and at twenty-one he headed his own J. B. Stoner Anti-Jewish Party, urging that Jews be "put to death." He had always been a racist, he declared proudly. "I never did like niggers," he stated simply in 1974. "Still don't like niggers. I don't like niggers because they're a threat to the white race, the white civilization." Throughout the 1970s, Stoner ran for several offices in Georgia, garnering more than 73,000 votes for lieutenant governor in 1974. In 1977 he was indicted for involvement in a Birmingham, Alabama, church bombing. Sentenced in 1980 to ten years in prison, he fled instead, evading capture until 1983. Stoner's personal logo was a Confederate battle flag he carried along with a handkerchief in his breast pocket; the nattily dressed professional racist also sported a Confederate flag bow tie. His campaign advertisements, adorned with battle flags, featured his electioneering slogans, "The White People's Candidate" and "Champion of White Supremacy," and his plans for driving all black people out of Georgia.[22]

Stoner and another former Columbian, Edward R. Fields, were the founders and leaders of the right-wing organization that most explicitly associated the Confederate flag with racism: the National States' Rights Party. Organized in August 1958 in Knoxville, the NSRP incorporated the United White Party and the Christian Anti-Jewish Party and was as anti-Semitic as it was racist in its rhetoric. The battle flag was as much a personal totem for Fields as it was for Stoner. The flag was ubiquitous in NSRP functions and publications, especially its newspaper, *The Thunderbolt*. "Our Proud Banner," as the party dubbed the flag, regularly adorned the podium or hall when party representatives spoke. Stoner and Fields explicitly viewed the battle flag as a symbol of their cause and their acts.[23]

"Raise That Confederate Banner," *Thunderbolt* exclaimed proudly when describing how a party officer in Atlanta carried a battle flag while leading a demonstration against race-mixing in the schools. The party applauded the students at the University of Mississippi who waved the flag in their resistance to the school's integration in late September 1962. "The Confederate Flag has become the symbol of FREEDOM to Patriotic Americans in every section of this land." Recounting a 1965 parade in Bogalusa, Mississippi, *Thunderbolt* declared that "the time has come to raise that Rebel banner" against race-mixing. The leaders of the march carried Confederate flags and wore vests decorated with a flag design. In

1965 the NSRP declared categorically what it believed the flag meant: "The Confederate Flag is no longer a sectional emblem. It is now the symbol of the White race and White supremacy. Fly it on your car and house." Readers could purchase a three-by-five-foot flag for five dollars or smaller versions for twenty cents apiece.[24]

Because Stoner, Fields, and the NSRP wanted the flag to be a battle standard in the new fight for white supremacy, they were not surprised when the flag became a source of interracial friction in the late 1960s and early 1970s. In fact, defending the battle flag, particularly its continued use as a symbol of resistance to integrated public schools, gave the NSRP a new popular issue on which to build its base. "Traditions and heritages that are sacred to a people often bind them together in a common defense of their common way of life," observed an article in *The Thunderbolt.* "So it is with the Confederate flag, singing of the song, 'Dixie,' and the use of the name 'Rebels' by schools and their football teams in the South . . . Therefore the Confederate flag has become a symbol of resistance for all Whitefolk, both North, South, East and West in the fight against forced race mixing. The enemy is very astute on these matters and has moved in several states to outlaw the use of the Confederate symbols by young white students." In response to this organized campaign, the NSRP urged white southerners to use "the flag of our forefathers" more than ever. Fields traveled to Jacksonville and New Orleans to rally flag supporters.[25]

The virulent and proudly overt racism of the NSRP had enormous shock value and generated quotable rhetoric, but it came from a fringe group that did not wield much popular influence. More significant and more influential than the racist use of the flag by marginal groups was its use by ordinary mainstream citizens protesting against integration. If extremists alone had used the flag as a racist symbol, it would be possible to dismiss its racist connotation as an aberration, a meaning conferred by people whom the wider society holds in well-deserved contempt. Instead, the pattern of racist flag use suggests that it was not only the Ku Klux Klan and the J. B. Stoners who understood the flag to symbolize their belief in the inferiority of African Americans and the necessity of separating the races.

The collection and interpretation of evidence for the Confederate flag's racist use present significant challenges. They depend upon eyewitnesses or photographers troubling to notice and document the flag's presence as a symbol of segregation or white supremacy. Because of its visual and symbolic power, the Confederate flag may have arrested attention out of proportion to its presence or importance. While condemning the use of the flag by "red-necked Klan-type individuals" at a May 1967 Richmond rally for George Wallace, the *Richmond Times-Dispatch* also chastised television cameramen for seeking out the "tiny fraction" of flag wavers in the crowd of 4,600 people and creating the perception that nearly everybody waved flags.[26]

Eyewitness accounts and photographic evidence suggest that the flag was present at most of the notable demonstrations and incidents during the civil rights era from 1954 through the busing crisis of the 1970s. Often, a few people—sometimes known racist rabble-rousers—were responsible for the flag's presence. On other occasions, however, the masses of white segregationists wielded flags of their own accord. It is possible that eyewitness accounts and photographic evidence might well have *under*represented the flag's presence as a symbol of protest precisely because it had become so commonplace that it did not warrant attention.

Fixing attention on the presence or absence of Confederate flags also has the potential of distracting attention from the presence of other symbols. The Stars and Stripes was also an effective and ubiquitous symbol in the hands of segregationists—from Klansmen to ordinary citizens to prominent politicians like George Wallace—during the civil rights era. While the Confederate and American flags frequently faced off in symbolic opposition to each other, more often than not segregationists employed the two flags together, sending the clear message that they believed segregation to be consistent with both southern and American values.

The primary battlegrounds over racial integration were public schools and universities. As handfuls of African-American children applied for admission into previously segregated schools, white authorities erected legal or administrative roadblocks while white communities staged mass demonstrations. One of the first battles occurred at the University of

Alabama in Tuscaloosa in February 1956 when Autherine Lucy arrived there to begin classes. Admitted into the university by the school's administration, Lucy began classes on Friday, February 3. The school's conciliatory response to court-ordered integration enraged segregationists. At midnight, a large crowd (estimated between five hundred and twelve hundred) marched behind a group of students carrying a Confederate flag from campus to a flag pole in downtown Tuscaloosa, singing "Dixie" and chanting "Keep 'Bama white" and "To hell with Autherine." At the flag pole the crowd heard a rabble-rousing speech from the leader of the march, student Leonard Wilson. An avowed racist and member of the Selma Citizens' Council, Wilson displayed a Confederate battle flag in his room and used the flag as a personal symbol during his angry activism in Tuscaloosa.[27]

Led again by Leonard Wilson, hundreds of students gathered at the flag pole again late on Saturday night, then marched back to campus to find Autherine Lucy. Upon discovering that she was not on campus, the crowd confronted university president Oliver Cromwell Carmichael. Someone held aloft a Confederate battle flag while Wilson addressed the crowd at the flag pole, and others carried smaller flags as they marched. Following yet another demonstration, university trustees finally suspended Autherine Lucy for her own protection. A month later, the administration also expelled Leonard Wilson.[28]

Confederate flags were present during the first major showdown over the integration of a public school a year later. After more than a year of planning a strategy of gradualism, the school board of Little Rock, Arkansas, in September 1957 admitted nine African-American students into the all-white Central High School. Although Little Rock had already integrated its bus system and restaurants, opponents of school integration mobilized resistance around the state against integrating Central High. Arkansas Governor Orval Faubus, who had once cultivated a reputation as a moderate, succumbed to the pressure and called in the state's National Guard to keep the black students away and maintain order at the school. President Dwight D. Eisenhower reluctantly called in the U.S. Army's 101st Airborne Division and federalized the Arkansas National Guard to ensure the safety of the black students. Integration "at the point of a bayonet" provoked outrage throughout the South, and Faubus struck back by closing Little Rock's schools during the following school year.[29]

On September 3, 1957, when the "Little Rock 9" first attempted to enter the school, they were turned away by the National Guard and by crowds of white students, parents, and outsiders. A small group of boys wore Confederate kepis and waved a Confederate flag, while a group from the rabidly segregationist Mothers League sang "Dixie." Subsequent confrontations between authorities and protesters brought out white youths wearing leather jackets with Confederate flags and skull motifs and singing "Dixie," while protesters at North Little Rock High School hung an effigy of a Negro with a sign reading "To hell with integration." Segregationists distributed badges and window stickers with the message "I like Faubus" and a picture of a Confederate battle flag to "let others know that you do not intend to dance to the tune of the NAACP." Two years later, when Central High and other Little Rock schools were integrated and reopened, protesters carried Confederate flags and signs that proclaimed "STOP the Race Mixing March of the Anti-Christ" and "Race Mixing Is Communism."[30]

Segregationists carried Confederate flags in subsequent confrontations over school integration—in New Orleans in 1960, Atlanta in 1962, and Birmingham in 1963. The courts stayed a decision to open integrated schools in New Orleans in September 1960, but integrated schools opened two months later. A large parade of segregationist students and mothers converged on City Hall downtown and was broken up by police and water hoses. Some of the students wore Confederate hats and carried small rebel flags. The crowd draped a Confederate flag around the base of the George Washington statue while someone rushed up to display a flag on the Civic Center.[31]

The desegregation crisis in Birmingham occurred in two waves. Court orders to integrate two high schools in September 1957 brought forth large groups of white protesters. At Woodlawn, students raised two Confederate flags on the school's flag poles, displayed a sign reading "Stay out niggers," and yelled "No Negroes will get by us." Six years later, during the period that the city's violent repression of civil rights marches riveted national attention on Birmingham, similar scenes occurred at Graymont Elementary and West End High School. Despite the willingness of Birmingham school officials to obey the court order, Governor George C. Wallace and hardcore states' rights advocates encouraged resistance. Leading the flag-waving protest at Graymont were Ed Fields and Jerry Dutton of the National States' Rights Party. At West End, the flag waving emanated more clearly from the masses of parents and students. The scene resembled a sporting event, as a student played "Dixie" on his trumpet while other students clapped, cheered, waved Confederate flags, and chanted "Go home, nigger! Go home, nigger!" "Hit 'em back, hit 'em back—harder, harder!" and "Two, four, six, eight, who do we appreciate? Wallace, Wallace, Wallace!" The *Birmingham News* editorialized against those who "stand outside a school building and wave Confederate banners and bleat appeals to false patriotism." The flag, the editors wrote, was a "revered" emblem and was not intended to be "a symbol of hate, bigotry and discord." Clearly, however, those who marched at West End High School believed that waving the battle flag was an appropriate expression of their determination to keep their schools white.[32]

The most historically significant civil rights incident for which the Confederate flag became a symbol was the 1962 integration of the University of Mississippi by student James Meredith. The flag's place in the "Meredith riots" and their aftermath suggests how easily a symbol of a southern school's identity could be transformed into a symbol of segregation and white supremacy—and how the identity of a southern school was in fact intertwined with white supremacy and segregation. Between 1947, when it was first introduced at Ole Miss, and 1962, the Confederate battle flag became the all-but-official school symbol. Wearing stylized Confederate uniforms, the band carried a huge battle flag onto the football field at halftime, while Ole Miss fans waved flags in the stands. The flag also figured prominently in the social life of fraternities.

When an Associated Press photographer captured a group of Ole Miss male students holding a large Confederate battle flag on the day that black student James Meredith arrived on campus, the scene resembled earlier photographs of students at campus social events. The incident was hardly isolated. Ten days earlier, on September 20, 1962, anticipating Meredith's scheduled arrival (later delayed), students sang "Glory, Glory, Segregation" to the tune of the "Battle Hymn of the Republic," while a group of students lowered the American flag from the campus flag pole and raised a Confederate flag. A senior class officer was able to replace the American flag almost immediately. During the following week, the school spirit of another football season merged with the growing excitement over Meredith's imminent arrival. Confederate flags abounded on car antennas, and local radio stations played "Dixie." On September 29, at a football game played in Jackson, Mississippi, the stands turned into "a sea of Confederate flags" as Governor Ross Barnett addressed the crowd at halftime. "I love Mississippi!" he declared, riding a wave of popularity as the man who defied federal authority. "I love her people—her customs! And I love and respect her heritage!"[33] The scene left no doubt that the Confederate flag was part of a heritage which included segregation as an integral part.

When the state exhausted its legal maneuvers, Monday, October 1, was chosen as the date on which Meredith would register for classes. As students returned to campus from the weekend's activity, reporters descended on Ole Miss and noted the proliferation of Confederate flags. Some reporters mistook the battle flag design of the band's uniform as a special anti-Meredith gesture. Real segregationist gestures were not easy to miss. Unusual even for Ole Miss, flags hung from dormitory windows and automobiles, while a gathering crowd chanted "Two, one, four, three, we hate Kennedy" and "We want Meredith. Get a rope." In the afternoon, the crowds grew restive. Students (or, according to university officials, "outsiders") carried Confederate flags and signs reading "Yankee Go Home!" The students jeered the helmeted U.S. marshals sent to Oxford to protect Meredith. Whenever a Confederate flag appeared, the students broke into cheers. Students attempted again to raise a Confederate flag on the pole in front of the Lyceum. They succeeded, and the flag remained there overnight. As night fell, a battle erupted between rock-throwing students and rifle-brandishing marshals. Reporters were caught in the crossfire. A young local man and a French reporter were killed. Despite the night of violence, James Meredith registered for classes the next morning as scheduled. Federalized National Guard troops cordoned off the campus and searched everyone entering.[34]

Once the smoke had cleared, James Meredith and the National Guard troops were still at Ole Miss, and the Confederate flag remained the primary symbol of resistance to integration. Beginning in October 1962 and continuing for more than two years, a group calling itself the Rebel Underground published an occasional newsletter declaring its opposition to "Brotherhood by Bayonet." The masthead for the newsletter was a Confederate battle flag. Consisting largely of diatribes against "carpetbaggers and scalawags on the faculty" (specifically James W. Silver and Russell H. Barrett, chroniclers of the school's time of troubles), the Underground also articulated the blend of states' rights theory and racism underlying the segregationist argument. Appealing to students at Ole Miss and throughout the South to resist integration and the destruction of the Bill of Rights, the Underground also decried "racial amalgamation" and "mongrelization." As the Underground faded into inactivity, another organization, the Conservative Students' Association (or CSA) formed late in 1964 to fill the "conservative vacuum" on campus. The CSA, like the Rebel Underground, featured a Confederate battle flag on its literature.[35]

In addition to the "carpetbaggers and scalawags" whom the Underground sought to stigmatize, other university staff and faculty members hinted that the battle over integration had tarnished the Confederate flag as a school symbol. Band director Lyle Babcock proposed that the band change its uniform from the stylized Confederate uniforms adopted a few years earlier. "I don't want to give anyone the idea that I'm ashamed we are the Ole Miss Rebels but it can be overemphasized," Babcock commented. "In some instances, it would not be in the best interests of the University to push this southern traditionalism." Governor Ross Barnett did not agree. Declaring "We are proud of our heritage," Barnett overruled Babcock's decision.[36]

There was no subtlety or ambiguity in Assistant Professor of Art George Raymond Kerciu's portrayal of Ole Miss's "southern traditionalism." In April 1963 Kerciu (who hailed from Detroit) opened an exhibit of his own work at the university's fine arts gallery. The show included five canvasses depicting Confederate battle flags with racial epithets and slogans—paintings intended to portray the campus on the night of the Meredith riots. University officials ordered the paintings removed after receiving complaints from the Citizens' Councils and the United Daughters of the Confederacy. A small group of students and the student newspaper rallied to Kerciu's defense. His paintings, Kerciu insisted, were "only recordings of the things I've seen and heard on this campus . . . As for the Rebel Flag, it was part of this atmosphere—part of all the statements that have come out. Now all these people seem unwilling to admit that they made these statements. It's not my statement, it's theirs." A university law student brought charges against Kerciu under the state's flag desecration law. Kerciu was arrested, then released, and the charges were not pursued. Part of the small circle of faculty members who openly supported James Meredith's admission, Kerciu left the university at the end of the term.[37]

From Ole Miss, the high-profile civil rights battles moved east to Alabama, where George Corley Wallace was inaugurated as governor in January 1963. Symbolically positioning himself on the spot where Jefferson Davis accepted the Confederate provisional presidency in February 1861, Wallace explicitly linked his stand against federally mandated integration with the Confederacy's resistance to federal interference with slavery. His inaugural address included the infamous declaration (written for him by Asa E. "Ace" Carter, founder and leader of "the original Ku Klux Knights of the Confederacy") that he stood in the shadow of Jefferson Davis and affirmed his stand for "Segregation now, segregation tomorrow, segregation forever!"[38]

The battle flag was not merely a symbolic element in the choreography of Wallace's inauguration. The battle flag was a ubiquitous symbol during his campaign for governor in 1958 (which was unsuccessful) and again in 1962; it was plastered on the windows of automobiles, along with his photograph or name and the slogans "Wake Up! Let's Fight" and especially "Stand Up for Alabama"; it flapped from the cabs of sound trucks and from makeshift speakers' platforms; and it was waved by Wallace supporters at rallies and conventions. The battle flag (along with the Stars and Stripes and the state flag) stood prominently behind his desk in the Governor's Mansion and appeared in many official portraits and photos of Wallace as he met with visitors. "The Confederate Flag is becoming just as much a symbol of the Wallace administration as his campaign slogan," noted the *Birmingham News* in April 1963. In fact, two painted battle flags adorned the fuselage of Wallace's plane, along with the ubiquitous "Stand Up for Alabama." During his surprisingly strong bid for the presidency in 1964, the slogan on the plane was changed to "Stand Up for America" and one of the two battle flags was transformed into a Stars and Stripes. Wallace's Alabama State Patrol vehicles also sported front license plates with Confederate flags, and troopers wore flag decals on their white helmets.[39]

The most conspicuous and controversial of Wallace's many Confederate flag gestures was to fly it on the dome of the state capitol building. Soon after Wallace took office, Alabamians and citizens of other states noticed that the Confederate flag flew below the state flag on the capitol dome and that the U.S. flag was conspicuously absent. Given Wallace's states' rights, anti-federal ideology, the message seemed obvious. Responding to the hundreds of letters complaining about this apparently unpatriotic gesture, Wallace usually explained that the Confederate flag was an appropriate symbol for Alabama to fly during the Civil War Centennial. Far from being an anti-American gesture, the Confederate flag was "part of the American flag and part of the American heritage and tradition." He assured his critics that no flag flew or should fly above the Stars and Stripes, which had a position of honor on the capitol grounds on a pole erected in the World War I era.[40]

Wallace's letters were inconsistent on the critical point of when the battle flag went up on the capitol. To some he insisted that the flag had been on the dome already when he became governor; to others he proudly claimed credit for putting it there himself. In fact, Wallace had the flag put up on the capitol on April 25, 1963, the day that U.S. Attorney General Robert F. Kennedy traveled to Montgomery to meet with Wallace about the integration of the University of Alabama. The following day was Confederate Memorial Day, but Alabama had no tradition of putting a Confederate flag on the capitol dome for the occasion and Wallace never claimed Confederate Memorial Day as his motivation. Regardless of the explanation he offered for when and why the Confederate flag flew, Wallace told supporters and detractors alike that "it shall fly here as long as I am Governor." Indeed, the flag flew throughout Wallace's four terms and beyond.[41]

Wallace was very consistent in his defense of the Confederate battle flag and in linking it with the states' rights stance that brought him to national prominence. "I love the Confederate flag and the Alabama Flag as I love the American Flag," he wrote to a Texas woman, "and in my judgment, it is appropriate for the Confederate Flag to be so displayed. Those who fought and died under the Confederate Flag were people who believed in a cause—there were those on both sides—and today the descendants of the brave men of the North and the South must join together if we are to save this Nation from many of the dangerous trends facing it."[42]

To a Nebraska schoolgirl he stated more explicitly the cause for which Confederates fought: "We fly the Confederate Flag out of respect for the dead and wounded of the Civil War who fought so valiantly for States' Rights." When the Confederate flag was at the center of a disturbance at an Alabama public school, Wallace speculated that it "was not flown out of disrespect for the flag of the United States, but as a symbol of resistance to what the people of that small town felt to be the undue interference in their local affairs." Speaking no doubt for himself, too, Wallace (a U.S. Army veteran) assured a correspondent from Illinois: "There is no part of the country which is more loyal to the American flag than the great southern region of the country." Several correspondents who shared Wallace's professed love of the Confederate flag charged him with misusing it for political purposes. Perhaps with puckish purposefulness, Wallace replied to one by assuring him that the Confederate flag flew proudly on the capitol dome and elsewhere in the state. "Apparently, you did not get the point of my letter," the man replied. "We should accept the flag as part of our heritage and not desecrate its proud symbol by using it the way you do."[43]

Other politicians renowned for their resistance to civil rights followed George Wallace and Ross Barnett in embracing the Confederate battle flag as a personal totem. Lester G. Maddox, the self-made Georgia businessman who closed his successful Pickrick fried chicken restaurant rather than integrate it as required by the 1964 U.S. Civil Rights Act, parlayed his states' rights principles into election as Georgia's governor in 1966 and (because Georgia's constitution barred him from running for a second consecutive term) a landslide victory as lieutenant governor in 1970. Like Wallace, Maddox campaigned with the battle flag, and he sold battle flag souvenirs to support his cause.[44]

The height of the civil rights movement saw Confederate flags used routinely by the segregationist resistance. In early 1960 black students from southern colleges orchestrated "sit-ins" to force the integration of lunch counters. Trained in the techniques of nonviolence, the students remained at the counter waiting for service, enduring taunts and occasional assaults. In at least three cities—Jacksonville, Florida; Greensboro, North Carolina; and Richmond, Virginia—the students faced harassment from white students bearing Confederate flags. In Jacksonville, at least twenty students wielded axe handles topped with Confederate flags. Another 100 flag- and stick-wielding men stood in reserve a few blocks away. The flag-bearing youths in Greensboro gave way to black football players carrying American flags. "Who do you think you are?" demanded the whites. "We the Union Army," the black students replied. In Richmond, white toughs waved battle flags when they confronted the black sit-in strikers, some of whom carried the Stars and Stripes. Led by a strong local Ku Klux Klan and the loud presence of National States' Rights Party leader J. B. Stoner, segregationists in St. Augustine, Florida, fought back against integrationist pressure in the summer of 1964, flags flying high. A store that usually sold about a dozen Confederate flags per year sold thirty-six dozen in ten days in June 1964. Those who purchased the flags brought them along to anti-integration rallies; an estimated six to seven hundred flag-waving protesters listened to fiery speeches at a rally on June 21, and fifty cars flying flags drove up and down the beach a week later.[45]

Fourteen years after the *Brown* decision, subsequent court decisions finally overcame the last legal resistance to school integration and the civil rights struggle moved into a new phase. The battle flag moved with it. In newly integrated schools the battle flag became a popular symbol among white students and occasionally provoked disturbances and led to court decisions prohibiting students from wearing or displaying Confederate symbols. In the early 1970s, courts throughout the country ordered the busing of black and white children to achieve substantial school integration. At rallies in Richmond, Virginia, and Louisville, Kentucky, protesters carried Confederate flags along with signs expressing their opposition to busing.[46]

The growing notoriety of the flag as a symbol of ardent segregationism brought a predictable reaction from supporters of civil rights. Anticipating the language and the demands of civil rights activists twenty-five years later, a few voices in the 1960s declared the Confederate battle flag a racist symbol and demanded its removal from public places. The NAACP protested the participation by a group of gray-clad men marching with a Confederate flag in a Philadelphia Memorial Day parade in 1959. Citing use of the Confederate flag as a symbol of protest against civil rights groups in the Bronx, a New York City council candidate proposed a ban on all public display of Confederate flags. The city "cannot continue this underwriting of the symbol of bigotry," he argued.[47]

One of the nation's first Confederate "flag flaps" (as later headline writers dubbed these controversies) occurred in San Francisco in 1964 with the inclusion of a Confederate battle flag in a "pavilion of American flags" at City Hall. Although the display's sponsor insisted that there were "no political overtones" intended, civil rights leaders denounced the Confederate flag as "a symbol of hate" and a "badge of slavery" and called for its removal. Several weeks later, during a human rights rally, someone stole the flag. Its sponsors replaced it with a Confederate Stars and Bars, then with a thirty-seven-star U.S. flag. Twenty years later, another historical flag display at the same location provoked a member of a radical group to tear down and burn the flag. The city replaced it with a flag commemorating California Union soldiers in the Civil War.[48]

The flag's reputation as a racist symbol, along with the racial turmoil of the 1960s, also lowered official tolerance for the flag in the U.S. military. An investigation of alleged racial discrimination in the armed forces in 1960 recommended directives "prohibiting the use of symbols of racial intolerance such as 'The Rebel Flag' and 'The Burning Cross' by any Service Unit." The recommendation stemmed from the use of both symbols between 1958 and 1960 by a fighter squadron stationed in Japan that called itself the Rebel Outfit. Originally introduced by the lieutenant colonel as "a morale gimmic [sic]," the flag's "connotations of racial intolerance stimulated acts of intimidation and intolerance upon and discrimination against Negro personnel."[49]

A similar incident arose during the height of the Vietnam War when a Georgia congressman raised the alarm about "censorship" and prejudice toward southern states. The Georgia General Assembly spent some ten thousand dollars each year sending state flags—which, since 1956, featured the Confederate battle flag—to servicemen. Some of the servicemen folded over the blue field with the state emblem to make a plain Confederate battle flag. A constituent complained to a Georgia congressman about an order that banned Confederate and southern state flags from the barracks. The Defense Department explained that the order was issued by the commanders of the First Marine Aircraft Wing in Vietnam following the murder of Dr. Martin Luther King. The commanders forbade "the outward display of the Confederate flag" (and the state flags on which it appears) in order "to reduce the likelihood of any racial tensions within the wing." The Pentagon further stated that there was no policy forbidding individual use of Confederate or state flags within the service.[50]

The April 1968 flag order presaged the pattern of controversies that became familiar in subsequent decades. Declaring the Confederate flag a symbol of racism, African-American activists pressured governments and institutions to stop displaying or endorsing its display. As governments and institutions became more responsive to these demands and even acted preemptively out of sensitivity to African-American perceptions, Confederate heritage groups and other flag defenders expressed their outrage and asserted their right to play a role in determining public symbolism. Beginning in the late 1960s, public schools and college campuses became battlegrounds over the flag, and the controversies soon spread to engulf local and state governments.

Historians cannot say whether the flag controversies of our own time would have occurred if the battle flag had not become an overt and intentional symbol of racism in the 1950s and 1960s. The preeminent symbol of our country's most significant dissident political movement is destined to be controversial, especially when that movement was so closely related to racial issues. If the symbol were merely a historical one, however, the passions surrounding it would not have been so strong or immediate. Instead, the Confederate flag is not simply a symbol of perceived racism in the country's distant past but a symbol of explicit racism in the recent past and in the present. Sometimes consciously, those who have used the Confederate flag as a racist symbol in recent decades have solidified the perceived link between modern racism and the Confederacy.

Many opponents of civil rights insisted that they were motivated by a desire to preserve constitutional liberty, not by racism, and that the Confederate flag symbolized that struggle for principles—the same principles for which their Confederate forebears fought. Even if we accept this argument at face value, African Americans still have ample reason to associate the Confederate flag with ideas and with people who are determined to use legal means and violence to deny them the rights and privileges that other Americans enjoy. Confederate flags displayed on or in public buildings imply reverence for a time when African Americans were second-class citizens—when they were denied fundamental rights and suffered intimidation and physical harm if they tried to claim those rights. Because this is precisely what some people intend the flag to communicate, many modern African Americans understandably view the battle flag as an implied threat.

In 1995 the southern novelist and historian Shelby Foote ruminated on the damage done to the Confederate flag's reputation during the civil rights movement: "The fault that so many blacks are upset about it lies with me and others who failed to speak up back when integration was starting in the South . . . Too many of us said that if others are sending their riffraff here to tell us what to do, then we'll let our riffraff take care of them. And they did, committing outrageous acts while waving that rebel flag. We should have spoken out to protest that."[51] Contrary to Foote's after-the-fact observation, white southern opinion makers and lawmakers did protest the flag's use by the Ku Klux Klan and other racists during the height of the civil rights era. Alabama's Klan-fighting attorney general Richmond Flowers wrote in *Look* magazine in 1966:

> Today the flag for which my grandfather fought is desecrated. The Stars and Bars [sic] should be a thing of honor. Instead, flaunted by racists whose forebears may never have served under it, it has come to mean one thing: hate. Our Confederate ancestors would spin in their graves if they saw their flags in the hands of those who trample upon everything they fought for. It deserves a better place in history than on car bumpers or on the bloody robes of the killers, floggers and night riders who call themselves the Ku Klux Klan.[52]

For several years before, liberal southern newspaper editors similarly protested the desecration of the flag by racists. "The Confederate flag is being used in Alabama in a manner which represents a gross perversion of the things it stood for a century ago," wrote *Richmond Times-Dispatch* editor Virginius Dabney in reaction to scenes broadcast during the Selma to Montgomery march in 1965. "In Selma on Sunday the flag of the Confederacy was being waved or displayed by the trashier white elements in and around the town—Ku Kluxers and slack-jawed juveniles." While Dabney and his newspaper sympathized with "dignified, forceful and properly-represented arguments" against the "unconstitutional voting bill," he and other "true southerners" disapproved of seeing the Confederate flag "dragged into today's interracial controversies, where it is almost invariably made to seem synonymous with 'bigotry' or 'racism.'" "It is," Dabney concluded, "high time somebody moved forcefully to stop this wholesale misrepresentation of a revered symbol." A year earlier, Dabney had written another editorial insisting that "the Confederate flag should not be used today except in connection with dignified Confederate observances and anniversaries—such as Confederate parades or as a decoration for Confederate monuments."[53]

The Pulitzer Prize–winning editor was not alone in this appeal for action. *Atlanta Constitution* editor Ralph McGill, who had protested the flag's use during the 1948 Dixiecrat convention, echoed Dabney's criticism and his belief that the white South's lower-class elements were the primary offenders. The battle flag, he wrote, "has become degraded to the place where it is sold in variety stores for sideburned, leather-jacketed teenagers to tie on the radio aerial or windshield of their hot rods. The flags so reverently furled at Appomattox now are companions of the burning cross of the Ku Kluxers." Raleigh *News & Observer* editor Jonathan Daniels similarly noted that the flag "is often just confetti in careless hands now." Even *The New York Times* editorialized after the September 1963 16th Street Baptist Church bombing in Birmingham, Alabama: "The desecration of the Confederate flag, waved by rabble-rousers in Alabama, is a desecration of the American flag everywhere."[54]

While being dragged into interracial controversies represented a major change from the flag's use in the era before World War II, it is not exactly accurate to say that this use was a "gross perversion" of its original meaning. The flag's latter-day association with racial controversy has had more to do with a change in its relationship to society than with a change in its inherent symbolic meaning. Before World War II, the flag was a staid symbol of an established, explicitly white supremacist social order in the South that enjoyed the tacit support of the federal government. After the fight over civil rights was joined, the flag became, in some hands, a belligerent symbol of an order under attack by the federal government. In circumstances and in attitude, there is a fundamental difference between a symbol of the status quo and a symbol of protest. It was the circumstances of protest that called forth "slack-jawed juveniles" to flaunt flags and heckle civil rights marchers on the road to Montgomery. The flag's previous immunity to racial controversy relied on a consensus belief that the flag represented the soldierly valor of Confederate soldiers, which everyone could respect. This was an artificial consensus rooted in an explicitly white supremacist order in the South and its toleration by the rest of the nation. Once that order began to crumble and the toleration ended, so, too, did the flag's exemption from racial controversy.

Being dragged into racial controversies and becoming "confetti in careless hands" not only drew comments from the pens of editorial writers. It also sounded a clarion call to the traditional defenders of the flag and elicited action from southern state legislatures. The campaign to remove the flag from careless hands warrants closer study.

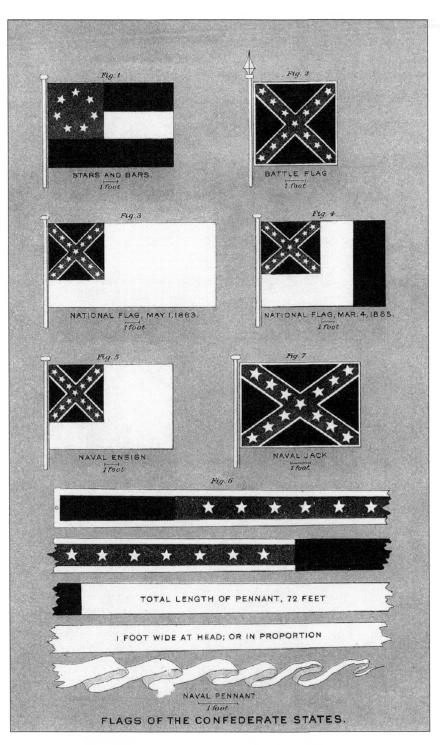

Fig. 1

STARS AND BARS.
⊢ 1 foot ⊣

Fig. 2

BATTLE FLAG
⊢ 1 foot ⊣

Fig. 3

NATIONAL FLAG, MAY 1, 1863.
⊢ 1 foot ⊣

Fig. 4

NATIONAL FLAG, MAR. 4, 1865.
⊢ 1 foot ⊣

Fig. 5

NAVAL ENSIGN.
⊢ 1 foot ⊣

Fig. 7

NAVAL JACK
⊢ 1 foot ⊣

Fig. 6

★ ★ ★ ★ ★ ★

★ ★ ★ ★ ★ ★

TOTAL LENGTH OF PENNANT, 72 FEET

1 FOOT WIDE AT HEAD; OR IN PROPORTION

NAVAL PENNANT
⊢ 1 foot ⊣

FLAGS OF THE CONFEDERATE STATES.

1. The United Confederate Veterans in 1904 officially defined the patterns and proper dimensions of the successive Confederate national flags, battle flag, and naval flags. The UCV declared the square St. Andrew's cross flag as "the battle flag," even though Confederate military units carried many other battle flag patterns during the war.

2. Congressman William Porcher Miles of South Carolina championed the saltire or St. Andrew's cross pattern first as a national flag design.

3. Miles recommended it to General Pierre Gustav Toutant Beauregard as the battle flag for the Army of the Potomac (later the Army of Northern Virginia) in 1861. Beauregard subsequently introduced it to other armies and departments throughout the Confederacy.

4. The battle flag of the 48th Virginia Infantry reveals the main features of the Army of Northern Virginia pattern: the square shape, wide border, and five-pointed stars, as well as the unit identification and the battle honors indicating the engagements in which the unit participated. A Michigan soldier captured the flag at the battle of the Wilderness in May 1864.

5. Pvt. Marshall Sherman of the 1st Minnesota Infantry received the Medal of Honor for capturing the flag of the 28th Virginia Infantry at Gettysburg. He later borrowed the flag from the War Department, but failed to return it. Sherman's descendants donated the flag to the Minnesota Historical Society. A century later, the flag became a political issue when Civil War reenactors and Virginia political officials demanded that it be returned, while the Minnesota Historical Society and state officials refused, claiming that the captured flag was also a legitimate piece of their state history.

6. Soldier-artist Allen Christian Redwood of the 55th Virginia Infantry depicted the opening phase of the battle of Gettysburg on July 1, 1863. The Confederate battle flag visible in the foreground is that of Redwood's own unit.

7. Richard Norris Brooke's melodramatic painting captures the grief that Confederate soldiers felt when they furled their battle flags at Appomattox.

8. Corporal Thomas Colley, a veteran of the 1st Virginia Cavalry, posed in 1897 with his unit's battle flag.

9. On the stage or lectern and placed on graves, battle flags became part of the Confederate Memorial Day ritual by the end of the nineteenth century and continue to be in the early twenty-first.

10. Aged residents of the Lee Camp Soldier's Home in Richmond, Virginia, raised the battle flag during the 1932 United Confederate Veterans reunion.

11. In May 1909, Alabama United Daughters of the Confederacy and local dignitaries gathered in Huntsville to celebrate the return of a battle flag that the 4th Ohio Cavalry had captured from a Confederate unit during the battle of Selma 44 years before. Ironically, the honored flag was the only one of the dozens on and around the stage that was not an oblong St. Andrew's cross pattern (which a published account misnamed the "stars and bars").

12. Lieutenant Thomas M. Davis, U.S. Naval Reserve, of Columbia, South Carolina, raised a Confederate battle flag on Okinawa, April 4, 1945. Marines later raised a larger Confederate battle flag over Shuri Castle on Okinawa after two months of fierce fighting. The flag was a popular totem for Southern-born American servicemen in World War II, Korea, and more recent wars.

13. Robed, hooded, and armed, Ku Klux Klan members participated in Atlanta's 1939 Confederate Memorial Day parade. This photograph is among the earliest pieces of evidence of the Confederate battle flag's use by the Klan.

14. The scene inside the Birmingham City Auditorium on July 17, 1948, after the States' Rights ("Dixiecrat") Party nominated Governor J. Strom Thurmond, of South Carolina, for President. College students serving as delegates brought the Confederate flags onto the convention floor.

15. In the fall of 1948, the University of Mississippi home economics department sewed the huge Confederate flag that became part of the school's gridiron tradition during the 1950s.

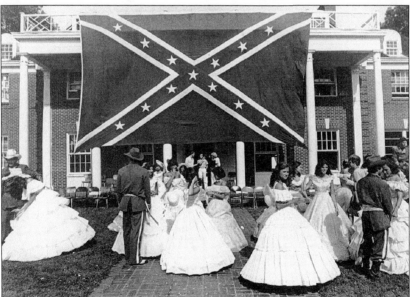

16. Students from the University of North Carolina claimed to be among the first to cheer on their football team with Confederate flags. A pair of freshmen posed with their flag amid the bright lights of New York City, where the Tar Heels played Notre Dame in 1949.

17. The Kappa Alpha fraternity house at Auburn University boasted a huge Confederate flag as a backdrop for the Order's annual Old South weekend.

18. Three members of the 31st Infantry ("Dixie") Division Band, all from Montgomery, Alabama, discuss a sheet of music in front of their bandroom quarters at Fort Jackson, South Carolina, in December 1951. The Confederate flag became a de facto symbol of the Dixie Division in the early 1950s.

19. Newspapers in 1951 reported that half the vehicles of the U.S. Army's 28th Division flew Confederate flags during the Operation Southern Pines training exercise. Richmond cartoonist Fred Seibel speculated on the reaction of one former U.S. Army commander.

20. A young woman identified as "Miss Dixie" 1951 posed wearing a Confederate flag halter top during the so-called "flag fad" era. For keepers of the Confederate flame, "Miss Dixie" also raised the specter of the misuse of a sacred symbol.

21. A Confederate flag topped the pyramid in a water ski show at Cypress Gardens, near Winter Haven, Florida, 1957. In other shows, the water skiers used American flags or solid color flags.

22. Lycurgus Spinks was self-proclaimed "Imperial Emperor" of the Knights of the Ku Klux Klan of America. He surrounded himself with what became a trinity of KKK symbols in the 1950s and 1960s: the Confederate flag, the Stars and Stripes, and the Christian cross.

23. A former king-maker of Georgia politics, Roy V. Harris became a leader of the White Citizens Councils and editor of the proudly segregationist *Augusta Courier*. Both the Citizens Councils and the *Courier* featured a battle flag in their logos.

24. The Confederate flag was a personal totem and powerful campaign symbol for Alabama Governor George C. Wallace. In 1963, he had the flag placed over the state capitol building.

25. A Virginia teenager went door-to-door rallying people to resist federally mandated school integration. With his Confederate flag, hat, states' rights bumper sticker, and eye patch (the result of an accidental self-inflicted gunshot wound), he went to the Virginia State Capitol building to cheer on the General Assembly as it passed "Massive Resistance" laws.

26. A lone Confederate flag waved as Arkansas Governor Orval Faubus read a statement of protest at Little Rock's Central High School on the day that he and the school yielded to court-ordered integration in 1959.

27. Students in Birmingham, Alabama, students carried Confederate flags in their 1963 march to protest integration.

28. Cartoonist Pat Oliphant lampooned the appeals made for protecting the Confederate flag from desecration.

29. Signs for businesses with "Southern," "Dixie," or "Rebel" in their names seemed incomplete without an accompanying logo in the 1950s and 1960s. By the early twenty-first century, they were a vanishing breed.

30. The United Daughters of the Confederacy emerged as one of the most vocal organizations opposing the "misuse" and proliferation of the flag. UDC members posed with an original battle flag carried by a unit in Thomas J. "Stonewall" Jackson's command.

31. Confederate flag "bug screens" on freight-hauling trucks are a familiar sight to travelers on America's highways. By the 1970s, the Confederate flag became a totem of the independent trucker as well as the biker, "redneck," and "good ol' boy."

32. The Dodge known as the "General Lee" was a bona fide character in the 1979–1984 television show "The Dukes of Hazzard" and helped define the Confederate flag as a symbol of the "good ol' boy." Twenty years after the show's demise, the actor who played the character Cooter attracted visitors to his rural Virginia store with a replica of the General Lee.

33. Mourners gathered at a Confederate Flag Day memorial service for Michael Westerman, a Kentucky teenager killed apparently because of the Confederate flag he flew on his pickup truck.

34. Louisville, Kentucky, 1975. As the school integration battles of the 1950s–1960s became battles over busing in the 1970s, opponents of forced integration continued to reach for the Confederate battle flag. Modern school policies restricting display of the Confederate battle flag originated as a result of its use as a symbol of resistance to integration.

35. "You Wear Your 'X' and I'll Wear Mine." Reflecting a wider 1990s trend, the competing cultural symbols of the Confederate flag and Malcolm X became a source of friction at Stonewall Jackson Middle School in Hanover County, Virginia.

36. University of Mississippi football fans, ca. 1964. By 1997, after much controversy, the school's administration, faculty, alumni association, and student government voted to distance Ole Miss from the once-ubiquitous Confederate flag.

37,38,39. The prolonged battle over the Confederate flag on South Carolina's capitol dome featured numerous confrontations between pro-flag and anti-flag protesters. Peggy Peattie, photographer for *The State,* captured the scenes and the moods of those confrontations in Hilton Head (opposite top) and Myrtle Beach (opposite bottom and above).

40. The Georgia State flag, 1955–2004: (a) the state flag used from 1905 to 1956 inspired by the Confederate Stars and Bars; (b) the flag adopted in 1956 featuring the Confederate battle flag; (c) the blue flag adopted in 2001 at the behest of Governor Roy Barnes and replaced in 2003 by (d) a flag resembling the pre-1956 flag and modeled even more closely on the Stars and Bars. Georgia voters approved this flag in a 2004 referendum.

41. A 2001 referendum presented Mississippi's citizens with a choice between two state flags. The only substantive difference was the presence or absence of the St. Andrew's cross motif. The existing flag with the St. Andrew's cross won by a 2–1 margin.

42. Designed and informally adopted in the aftermath of the 1950s flag fad, the insignia of the Virginia Air National Guard was removed from planes and other squadron property in 1992 after the complaint of an African-American squadron member.

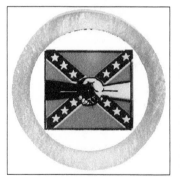

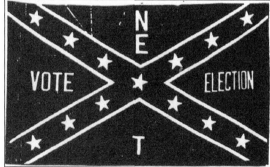

43. The unofficial symbol of the Southern Students Organizing Committee, ca. 1964.

44. "Ballot" created by Charles Nixon of Richmond, Virginia, in 1988.

45. The marriage of the Confederate battle flag and country-western icon Hank Williams, Jr.

46. A battle flag decorated the grave of a soldier buried in the Beauvoir Confederate cemetery, Biloxi, Mississippi. Amid the many controversies surrounding public display of the Confederate flag, it has continued to serve as a memorial symbol for Confederate soldiers.

Chapter 8

"The Perverted Banner"

By 1965, when Raleigh *News & Observer* editor Jonathan Daniels lamented that the Confederate flag had become "just confetti in careless hands," many different kinds of hands had seized the flag. Like-minded observers before Daniels had ridiculed "those silly little Confederate flags" that were being "brandished promiscuously by gin-soaked football rooters"; bemoaned the flags adorning the "bloody robes of the killers, floggers and night riders who call themselves the Ku Klux Klan" and the leather jackets of "slack-jawed juveniles"; and accused the Dixiecrats of "prostituting" the flag for political purposes.[1] The outrage and harsh words directed at the "careless hands" that picked up the flag in the decades after World War II suggested that something unprecedented was occurring. While the battle flag was certainly a familiar part of the southern landscape before World War II, the nature of its presence changed dramatically after 1948. The reaction to this change was almost immediate, and it came first from the organization that had been in the forefront of promoting reverence for the flag: the United Daughters of the Confederacy (UDC).

The president-general of the UDC in November 1948 reacted to the "urgent call" she received to rule on the late presidential campaign:

> Now all good Daughters know that after that sad day at Appomattox, when the South surrendered to the weight of numbers, the flag of the Confederacy was furled forever . . . It is now a sacred symbol to be used only by Sons and Daughters of the Confederacy . . . Our flag is not to be used in connection with any political movement—we are not in politics . . . If we regard our flag "with affectionate reverence and undying remembrance" we must not permit improper use of it—and should let this be understood by the people at large. If the misuse of our flag occurs again— it will be our fault.[2]

At its November 1949 annual convention, the organization that had been the principal keeper of the Confederate flame for more than a half-century expressed concern that "in certain demonstrations of college groups and some political groups at times the Confederate Flag or insignia has been displayed with seeming disregard of its significance." The UDC did not limit its disapproval to words, but also took action. An ad hoc committee submitted to the convention "Legislation to Protect the Confederate Flag from Misuse"—legislation that borrowed directly and explicitly from existing laws protecting the Stars and Stripes and some state flags. "It is the opinion of this committee that any display of the Flag not relative to the Patriotic ideals of the Organizations Commemorative of the Confederacy would result in disrespect of the Flag."[3]

Notwithstanding this forceful report, the new Committee on Legislation to Protect the Confederate Flag from Misuse declined to lobby for state legislation, citing the war in Korea and the paramount importance of having U.S. soldiers fight under the United States, not the United Nations, flag.[4] Without patrons and without a push from the UDC, the legislative campaign languished for a decade.

By the mid-1950s, the committee on flag legislation evolved into the Committee to Protect the Confederate Flag from Desecration that still survives a half-century later. In name and in purpose, the committee was modeled after those of other patriotic organizations, specifically the Daughters of the American Revolution. Early in the twentieth century the DAR's flag committee had lobbied successfully for state laws to protect the United States flag from desecration and to elevate the Stars and Stripes to the status of a sacred icon. Inadvertently, the DAR had been responsible for passing the Mississippi law that protected the Confederate flag as well as the Stars and Stripes. That the UDC had not created an analogous flag committee until 1950 suggests that faithful Confederates saw little or no evidence of flag desecration to be deterred or punished. Instead, the significant UDC attention to Confederate flags before 1948 involved determining the creator of the first national flag and the proper shape of the battle flag and distributing proper Confederate flags and information about them as widely as possible.

Use of the Confederate flag within the organization itself was a primary concern for the UDC, particularly the relative status of the U.S. and the Confederate flags within UDC rituals. In 1947 the Alabama Division of the UDC adopted "Rules for Flag Display" that other state divisions emulated. Reflecting the Confederate memorial tradition of "dual loyalty" to the United States and to the memory of the Confederacy, the rules emphasized the symbolic and physical primacy of the national standard. The Confederate flag, the rules insisted, "is the sacred emblem of the South. It has been hallowed by the blood of our people. It is an emblem, not of hatred, strife, or defeat, but of love, courage and sacrifice." Accordingly, it should be displayed with respect, not as drapery or on cars, trains, or other vehicles, and not carried in public if not on a staff.[5]

In 1961 the UDC's national convention adopted a set of "Traditions and Code for Correct Use of the Confederate Flags / How to Display and Respect Our Flags." In contrast to the veiled legalistic language of the model legislation to protect the flag, the UDC's code detailed the "do's" and "don'ts" of Confederate flag use. Not surprisingly, the code addressed many of the popular uses of the flag. It forbade the display of advertising signs on flag staffs or halyards and the use of flag images on "clothing of any kind" or on mugs, napkins "or anything that is designed for temporary use and discard," including athletic uniforms. Flags should not be draped or flown on cars except when carried properly on staffs "for special Confederate observances." In ceremonies unveiling Confederate monuments, the flag should not be used as the veil.[6] The codes for proper flag use gave the UDC a firm foundation on which to stand as its leaders became increasingly vocal arbiters of popular flag use.

The nationwide flag fad of the early 1950s presented philosophical and practical dilemmas for these guardians of the Confederate flag. Did the flag's popularity and the diverse forms that this popularity took represent "misuse" of the flag? Several UDC leaders loudly protested the trivialization of the flag during the fad, but the official reaction was more ambivalent. "I think it's terrible the way [flags] are on all those cars," commented the past president of the Richmond chapter. Typically, however, she qualified her objection by adding: "But isn't it awful that our wonderful flag was so little known before." Echoing this reasoning was the chairman of the national Committee on Legislation to Protect the Confederate Flag from Misuse, who pointed out the potential benefits of the fad. "Youngsters flying Confederate Flags from the hoods of their cars, in their fraternity houses, and on their caps are sure to discuss the Flag and develop a feeling for it. They ask questions and read about it, and soon they are 'sold' on the South and its brilliant history," she argued. While misuse of the flag can be "distressing," she conceded, it was usually the result of ignorance, not malevolence. "Schools using Confederate uniforms, caps, and emblems are exemplifying the southern spirit." The UDC should "lose no opportunity to furnish accurate and adequate explanation and instruction, rather than discourage and antagonize."[7]

With the passing of the flag fad after 1952, the question of whether to censure or channel the popular enthusiasm lost its urgency. In 1954 the UDC committee chair sent to one hundred present and former UDC officers around the country a questionnaire about flag use and abuse. The seventy-nine responses were virtually unanimous in declaring that no violations of proper flag use were occurring in their states or communities. With few dissenters, the respondents approved "a positive campaign of education as to the correct use of the Confederate Flag" and agreed that "the use of the Confederate Flag on beverage glasses, neckties, scarves," and so on constituted "a violation of the proper use of the Confederate Flag." Consistent with its new desire to "accent the positive," the committee suggested changing its name to Committee to Promote the Correct Use of the Confederate Flags.[8]

The UDC remained vigilant about misuse, however trivial. A Chicago committee chair requested that a person remove a flag from a car radiator. In California, a chapter demanded a public apology from the sponsors of the *Red Skelton Show,* which, on June 4, 1957, included a skit in which a comedian dressed like a tramp rose from behind a bar waving a Confederate flag. "This sort of action by the comedian was contrary to the spirit of the courageous men who followed Robert E. Lee," the resolution noted.[9]

Like the UDC, the Kappa Alpha Order expressed concern over the flag fad but similarly directed its efforts at regulating flag use within its own organization. Kappa Alpha's national leadership was very forthright in acknowledging the fraternity's role in launching the flag fad and equally forthright in attempting to stop it. The Advisory Council of Kappa Alpha issued a "statement of principles" at its 1951 meeting. "We are aware of and deplore the indiscriminate misuse and abuse of the Battle Flag by those who would make it a political symbol; and by those who would derive financial gain from it by promoting its sales or using it in advertising their merchandise," the statement declared. "The Advisory Council believes that we can and should, by our conduct, demonstrate the honor and respect which we feel and which the flag of the Confederate States of America deserves. As we were largely responsible for popularizing its display today so we can help to restore respect for it by promptly disassociating ourselves from all manner of cheap, tawdry and vulgar exhibitions; and by limiting its use among us to such places and occasions as are fit and becoming." Specifically, the Advisory Council requested that its members cease using the flag on neckties, caps, and automobile windshield stickers. Fifteen years later, KA reiterated this policy and further requested its members to cease all public display of the battle flag symbol.[10]

In the 1950s, Confederate heritage groups also turned their attention to the flag's appropriation by racists. Without mentioning the Ku Klux Klan by name, an Alabama chapter in 1957 reported that "hooded groups have been seen parading the streets in cars flying the Confederate Flags." The chapter denounced these "'ugly, unchristian, and unpatriotic acts.'" Seven years later, a North Carolina chapter objected to "the use of Confederate Flags as symbols of picketing, demonstrations and protesting." The Correct Use committee chair wrote to *Life* magazine protesting the publication of a picture of KKK Imperial Wizard Robert Shelton in front of the Confederate flag. *Life* replied sympathetically but emphasized that it was the Klan, not the magazine, misusing the flag.[11]

The Sons of Confederate Veterans, just then emerging from a moribund period, recognized the Klan's threat several years earlier. In response to a report that a Florida Klan group was reorganizing itself as an "American Confederate Army," Commander-in-Chief William Beard of New York wrote an open letter in 1952 condemning "any attempt to use the word 'Confederate' by those in sympathy with the principles of the second Ku Klux Klan." "No one has the moral right to use or display the Confederate Flag or any other article of dress bearing the Confederate Flag unless he feels the Affection, the Reverence and undying Remembrance with which we salute the Confederate Flag," declared Beard.[12]

In February 1958, newspapers reported that the legislature of South Carolina adopted a resolution denouncing William D. Hartman, formerly of North Carolina, and an executive with the Martex Corporation as "an unworthy American" because he sponsored a line of "Dixie beach towels" bearing the Confederate battle flag. The legislature's concurrent resolution noted that Hartman's act "constitutes a veiled attack, parading in the garb of legitimate advertisement, on the valor, courage and sacrifice of the Men in Gray who followed the immortal Robert E. Lee in defense of what was then, and is now, a burning question among all of the States of this Union—'What rights are reserved to the States?'" The towel had the effect of undermining the unity and common purpose that was essential for the United States to play its role in the world. "Certainly the buying public, both of the North and of the South, do not approve of such a crude method of advertisement, even if it serves to get a few fanatics to buy towels who would otherwise not resort to the use of such commodities," the resolution continued. "We call attention to the gentleman that it is indeed, to say the least, exceedingly bad taste to open old wounds which have been healing for more than three-fourths of a century."[13]

The beach towel incident mobilized Confederate heritage groups in South Carolina in defense of the Confederate flag. Predictably, the UDC and the SCV commended the legislature's resolution. The SCV's national leadership denied vehemently the claims by Martex that anyone authorized to speak for the group had in any way approved or complimented the offending beach towels. Another group that publicly protested the beach towels called itself the Association of Southern Redshirts after the often-violent militias that helped "redeem" the state from Reconstruction rule in 1876, and included in its membership a former Klansman.[14]

This tempest in a teacup galvanized groups in South Carolina to pass legislation protecting the Confederate flag from desecration. The SCV's commander-in-chief, Thomas W. Crigler of Mississippi, noted that his state had such a law and that the state attorney general assured him that the law would punish anyone attempting to sell the Martex beach towel in Mississippi. Prompted by Crigler, the SCV's South Carolina Division commander called for the General Assembly to enact a bill "to prevent the further depredation of our southern heritage." The House of Representatives passed the desecration bill that day, and the Senate concurred within two weeks. South Carolina became the second state to accord Confederate flags the same protection given to the national and state flags.[15]

The law featured the standard language punishing any kind of advertisement placed on a flag or representation of a flag and punishing anyone who would "publicly mutilate, deface, defile, defy, jeer at, trample upon or cast contempt, either by word or act" upon the flag. It also punished anyone who would create, display, sell, or give away "an article of merchandise or a receptacle of merchandise upon which shall have been printed, painted, attached or otherwise placed a representation of any such flag, standard, color, or ensign to advertise, call attention to, decorate, mark or distinguish the article or substance on which placed." This language seemed tailored to prevent any Confederate flag towels from ever gracing the Grand Strand at Myrtle Beach. Echoing this legislation, a handbook issued by the state's Confederate War Centennial Commission emphasized that "the use of the Confederate flag as a design on jackets, underwear, handkerchiefs, paper plates, napkins, and receptacles is generally to be deplored."[16]

Nevertheless, in the subsequent years—the years of the Civil War Centennial—souvenir items bearing the Confederate flag proliferated freely in South Carolina, with no prosecution by the state attorney general. State Senator Earle E. Morris of Pickens County was appalled at the flag's use on towels and garments and determined to stop the "cheapening" of the flag. In April 1966 Morris introduced a concurrent resolution calling for a full-scale investigation of the "misuse" and "outright desecration" of the flag and a report of the results to the 1967 session. The measure passed the Senate but died in a House committee.[17]

While Morris decried the "cheapening" of the battle flag, other advocates of stronger protective legislation took aim at the flag's increasing use by hate groups. Concurrent with Morris's campaign, the Wade Hampton Camp 273, SCV, in December 1965 passed resolutions deploring "the use of the Confederate flag in any phase of racial agitation or controversy, or its commercial exploitation in any 'souvenir' or similar form." An SCV spokesman condemned both the use of the flag by the Ku Klux Klan and by biracial groups of integrationists attempting to "provoke violence" by sitting on Confederate flag beach towels. The resolutions insisted that the flag in its 1861–1865 context "represented no racial animosity or bias but rather the wish of a presumably sovereign people to exercise their constitutional rights of self-determination to solve all their problems including the slavery issue." The SCV resolution urged the legislatures of all former Confederate states to pass laws "banning both the commercialization of the Confederate battle flag and its use as a symbol, uniform insignia or flag by agitators, demonstrators and others who do not display it with the United States flag."[18]

The South Carolina legislature declined to strengthen or clarify the desecration law passed in 1958, but in the following years several other states followed South Carolina's lead. In Florida, the impetus came from another case of disrespectful flag use, and the primary target of the movement was commercial use of the flag. At the behest of the Florida Division, United Daughters of the Confederacy, Representative Mack Cleveland of Sanford introduced legislation in the 1959 session prohibiting use of the Confederate flag, state flag, or state emblem for advertising purposes and punishing any person, firm, or corporation that would "mutilate, deface, defile or contemptuously abuse" these flags or emblems. The provocation was an incident in which a "maverick type" female tennis player wore a Confederate flag on her shorts. It was, Cleveland recalled, "a little bit of an issue" covered primarily in the sports pages. The UDC Florida Division asked Cleveland to sponsor the legislation, which he piloted through the House without opposition, only to see it die in a Senate committee. Two years later, Cleveland's bill passed both houses and a nearly identical bill originating in the Senate also passed and became law. The Senate added a clause that allowed use of the flags "for decorative or patriotic purposes." While the UDC applauded the act, the state NAACP denounced it. "It is deplorable that this flag which symbolizes a cause that was basically opposed to the American democracy should be raised from the dead," remarked NAACP State Field Secretary Robert Saunders. "It is worse that the state should move to punish a citizen who fails to respect it."[19]

Before Florida passed its desecration statute in 1961, Louisiana and Georgia passed similar laws. Both laws included the standard prohibition against mutilation, defiling, defacing, and casting contempt upon the flag. The Louisiana law resembled that of South Carolina and prohibited the placement of marks or advertisements on flags and also prohibited the use of the flag motif on merchandise or anything designed to hold or carry merchandise. The Georgia law was narrower than others and simply prohibited the use of U.S., state, and Confederate flags (national, military, and naval flags) "for the purpose of advertising, selling, or promoting the sale of any article of merchandise whatever within this state." The law exempted use of the flag on the covers of official publications and use of flags for "decorative or patriotic purposes," no doubt inspiring the similar exemption passed in Florida a year later.[20]

North Carolina did not pass legislation, but in 1959 the state's Department of Archives and History drafted a resolution for proper flag use. "As of course you know," wrote the agency's director, "the Confederate Flags have recently been used on dish towels, wash cloths, neckties, and the good Lord knows what else, and some of us who have real respect and reverence for what our ancestors fought for in that period think that such practices are bad. On the other hand extremists on the opposite side have protested the flying of the Confederate flag—well, practically everywhere." The proposed resolution strove to find the happy medium.[21]

Conspicuously absent from the roll call of states passing protective legislation was one most closely associated with the battle flag: Alabama. Alabama did not adopt legislation protecting the flag. A 1977 act declared it a misdemeanor to desecrate in a public place the U.S. or Alabama flag "or any other object of veneration by the public or a substantial segment thereof," but it is not clear that it embraced the battle flag. Ten years earlier, the legislature passed and Governor Lurleen (Mrs. George C.) Wallace amended and signed a strange joint resolution requesting Alabama's state-supported institutions of higher learning to fly the state flag and the Confederate battle flag along with the Stars and Stripes and play "Alabama" and "Dixie" along with the "Star Spangled Banner" at homecoming festivities. The joint resolution reasoned that "people throughout the United States are thankful for the leadership Alabamians are giving in the present fight for the preservation of the right of the people to govern themselves" and that the Alabama state flag and Confederate battle flag "have today become beacons for those who believe in local self-government, private property rights and individual liberty and freedom." A disapproving *Montgomery Advertiser* ridiculed the measure and asked: "Has anybody given any thought to what will happen at Alabama State [a historically black college] when they take on Tuskegee Institute?"[22]

Flag-protection advocates even endeavored to have the U.S. Congress pass legislation. Judge William M. Beard, who had been commander-in-chief of the Sons of Confederate Veterans during the flag fad, wrote to the Civil War Centennial Commission in June 1959 suggesting that legislation to protect the battle flag from commercial misuse would be "one of the most appropriate ways in which we could celebrate the 100th Anniversary of the War Between the States." The commission's executive director, Karl Betts, expressed "complete accord" with Beard's opinion that the battle flag "has been terribly misused for commercial and purely unpatriotic purposes" and that something should be done about it. Cautioning that Congress would be reluctant to enact such legislation, Betts suggested instead that civic, patriotic, and historical groups around the country pass resolutions "to make it more of a national issue" and help stop "the present disgraceful tactics." Congressman Wint Smith of Kansas, to whom Betts sent his communications with Beard, expressed sympathy with the proposal and wished "that there was some way we could acquiesce without giving our formal approval. We have still got to watch very carefully not to inflame either side on this matter." He predicted that the legislation would "run into a lot of trouble" if introduced in Congress. The proposal for national legislation to protect the Confederate battle flag died.[23]

Thus, by the first year of the Civil War Centennial, five former Confederate states had enacted laws ostensibly prohibiting and punishing misuse of the Confederate flag. These laws originated primarily in reaction to commercial use of the flag. Yet the years immediately following brought a flood of trinkets and souvenirs featuring the increasingly ubiquitous Confederate flag. In none of the states with desecration statutes was there prosecution of manufacturers or merchants producing or selling Confederate flag souvenirs. The only legal opinion offered on the commercial use of the flag in this era came in Georgia in 1967. The state attorney general in September 1967 issued an unofficial opinion advising the Dixie Crystals company of Savannah that state law prohibited use of a replica of the state flag (which, since 1956, featured the battle flag) on its sugar packets.[24]

On those occasions when states chose to wield their flag desecration statutes, the purpose was not to prohibit commercial use of the flag but to punish "radicals" who mutilated or desecrated the flag as part of a protest against racism. University of Mississippi art professor George Raymond Kerciu was arrested on these grounds in April 1963, then released on bond; the law student who had brought the charges later dropped them.[25]

On February 17, 1969, South Carolina state officials arrested University of South Carolina student Brett Bursey and charged him under the flag desecration law. Bursey, a member of the radical activist group AWARE, burned a Confederate flag on Lincoln's birthday as part of his group's effort to rid the campus of Confederate vestiges. A leader of the Columbia Chapter of the UDC brought the incident to the attention of the state attorney general, who advised her about prosecution under the statute. "A suit may be commenced by any person who is in a position to sign a warrant charging an individual with the offense," he wrote, and the charges should be made "immediately" after the offense. Police arrested Bursey that same day. He was released on bond and was never prosecuted, but the charges were never dismissed. More than twenty years later, as the editor of an alternative weekly paper in Columbia, Bursey was a vocal member of the coalition calling for the removal of the Confederate flag from the South Carolina state house. Still technically charged for his 1969 desecration offense, Bursey joked that he was "the oldest living Confederate prisoner of war" and still sought his day in court.[26]

Similarly, it was demonstrations against the flag, rather than commercial use, that moved the Virginia General Assembly to pass a flag protection measure. In November 1969 a group of thirty-five protesters (primarily African Americans) publicly trampled, dragged, and tore up the Confederate flag in Alexandria. The protest followed several racial incidents involving local police and took place one year after a bitter controversy over the city's display of Confederate flags on downtown streets.

The Virginia General Assembly responded in early 1970 with a joint resolution requesting that "persons harboring antagonism toward Confederate flags" respect the rights of those who cherish the flag. The resolution also censured and deplored any efforts to ban the flag "on appropriate occasions and in appropriate places" and especially censured "the mutilation and desecration of a Confederate flag and any other acts which tend to publicly degrade Confederate flags." Aside from the indirect allusion to "improper" uses and display of the flag, the resolution condemned only those who reacted against the flag's racist uses. The resolution's text made clear the Assembly's favorable attitude toward the flag. According to the resolution, "a majority of Virginians" venerated the flag and believed that the "courageous people" of the Confederacy fought to defend their homes, not to defend slavery. The problem was not with the flag but with the occasional actions of "those viewing the Confederate flags as representative of racial prejudice."[27]

Far from fading away in the face of state regulation and after the end of the Civil War Centennial, the use of the Confederate flag in pop culture became even more prevalent in the 1960s, 1970s, and 1980s. Nothing more dramatically indicates the failure of the regulation efforts than the emergence of cultural types linked closely with the Confederate flag. By the Civil War Centennial, a popular souvenir available throughout the South featured a flag-draped superannuated Confederate soldier saying "Hell, no, I'll never forget!" More generally, observed one journalist in 1969, the battle flag had become a symbol of "simple rebellion, the degenerate form of any nameless revolt, indeed for any anomic nut with a generalized gripe."[28]

The decades beginning with the 1960s brought the flag some of its most powerful symbolic associations. It adorned bug screens covering the front grills of freight-hauling trucks; it was framed by gun racks in the back of pickups; it was emblazoned with the garish logos of motorcycle enthusiasts. These images—including a continued association with stock car racing—have become veritable clichés of Americana, immediately recognizable in cartoons, films, and other forms of popular culture. The Confederate flag has proven to be an effective symbol for the fierce independence and individual rebelliousness common to all these types of people. "We fly the rebel flag because it's our belief—to be able to do what you want to do. We're 100 percent rebel," a Kansas man told a reporter. In an attempt to appeal to the self-declared "rebels of the road," a southern California businessman in 1980 renamed his truck stop chain "Dixxie Diesel" and raised 30-foot-long battle flags over each of his four stations.[29]

In this era the flag assumed a powerful new meaning as shorthand for "redneck" or "good ol' boy." For people outside the working-class southern culture from which this image emerged, a "redneck" was a threatening figure to be avoided. For those within the culture, "redneck" was not necessarily a pejorative term, but connoted being "down to earth" in every respect—rough around the edges, to be sure, but decent, hardworking Christian people with strong moral values. Several 1970s country and southern rock bands proudly embraced the redneck image along with the Confederate flag, most notably Hank Williams, Jr., Alabama, and Lynyrd Skynyrd, whose "Sweet Home Alabama" (1974), with its pugnacious reply to singer Neil Young's criticism of the "Southern Man," quickly became—and remains—a white southern anthem. Williams coupled a tough, slightly uncouth image with a flag-toting, pro-South belligerence, most notably in his 1988 "If the South Woulda Won." More recent groups, such as Tom Petty and the Heartbreakers and Confederate Railroad, continue southern music's tradition of waving the flag.[30]

The television series *The Dukes of Hazzard,* which aired on CBS from 1979 to 1984 (and has, to date, spawned two "reunion" television movies), solidified an emerging image of the Confederate flag as the totem of the hard-fighting, fast-driving, fun-loving but pure-hearted "good ol' boy." The series built upon the 1977 film *Smokey and the Bandit,* in which Burt Reynolds's character drove a Trans-Am with a Georgia state flag license plate. The *Dukes of Hazzard* was a major hit, ranked third in the TV ratings in 1980–1981, with forty-six million viewers. The Confederate flag was painted onto the roof of a bright orange 1969 Dodge Charger named the "General Lee." The producers considered the car a bona fide star of the show. Appearing in thirty to thirty-five percent of each show and responsible for $100 million in annual sales of toys, party goods, musical instruments, towels, and other retail products bearing the Confederate flag, the car accounted for more than half of the sixty thousand fan letters that the show received each month. So profitable was the "General Lee" and its flag that the show's producer, Warner Communications, aggressively (and successfully) protected its trademark in federal court, winning at least two cases against manufacturers of copycat toy cars. The court decided that protecting the logo of the orange car with the flag and the numbers "01" did not grant "an eternal monopoly on the shape or form of some useful object."[31] Absent from the court opinions was any discussion whether the "General Lee" violated the "proper use" of the Confederate battle flag. In federal court and in the national marketplace, this kind of "misuse" was a nonissue. More than fifteen years after the show's demise, *The Dukes of Hazzard* commands a cult following, and a small fleet of full-size "General Lee" 1969 Dodge Chargers make guest appearances at special events throughout the South.

The occasional efforts to restrict use of the Confederate flag in pop culture have arisen from sensitivity to its racial overtones, not from concerns over flag desecration. As stock car racing became a mainstream and enormously successful commercial sport, race officials quietly ended the official use of Confederate symbols. In 1993 NASCAR barred a car sponsored by the Sons of Confederate Veterans bearing the organization's battle flag logo. A year later, Harley-Davidson, makers of the popular American motorcycle, forbade the use of logos and the sale of products bearing the Confederate flag; the Milwaukee-based company acted after receiving a protest from a local civil rights activist. The chairman of the heritage committee at the Wisconsin Division of the SCV reacted by broadcasting the alarm to the community of Civil War enthusiasts and urging everyone to write to Harley-Davidson in protest. In defending the use of the battle flag in a way that had once been defined as "desecration," the chairman used the "slippery slope" argument: "If Harley-Davidson's actions, indeed the actions of all who seek to remove from public display any portion of the Confederate battle flag, go unchallenged, then in the very near future, we will be unable to display our flag at graveside memorial services, on our lapel pins, from our homes, on Confederate Memorial Day, or even at reenactments without first having to prove that we are not racists." Within months, Harley-Davidson reversed its decision, and declared that local motorcycle dealers could decide for themselves whether or not to incorporate the Confederate flag in their logos. This "heritage victory" highlighted the irony of the continuing fight to protect the Confederate flag: in order to refute the charge that the flag is racist, its defenders had to support the right to "desecrate" it commercially.[32]

This irony illustrates the inconsistency in the arguments of flag defenders. In 1997 the journalist, SCV activist, and flag historian Don Hinkle declared that "anyone who uses the Confederate battle flag for any purpose other than to honor the Confederate dead is desecrating a sacred symbol." But when he addressed the civil rights community's growing objections to public display of the flag, Hinkle compromised this straightforward delineation of proper flag use and defended and apparently celebrated the right of individuals to display the flag on clothing items, souvenirs, and even tattoos. He did not explain how exactly a tattoo of a Confederate flag and the cartoon character "Tasmanian Devil" honored the Confederate dead.[33]

Confederate heritage organizations have long been acutely aware that improper use of the flag injures its reputation and causes problems for those who display it properly. Hinkle conceded the "serious damage done to the flag during the early 1960s," especially by the Klan. Continuing the work begun in the 1950s, the SCV has stepped up its attack on the Ku Klux Klan, whose appropriation of the flag has garnered disproportionate attention and influence. In August 1989 the SCV adopted unanimously a resolution condemning "in the strongest terms possible the inappropriate use of the Confederate Battle Flag or any other flag, seal, title or name bearing any relationship whatsoever to the Confederate States of America or the armed forces of the Government of the Confederate States of America by individuals or groups of individuals, organized or unorganized, who espouse political extremism or racial superiority." When the SCV tried to gain formal trademark control of the flag, it learned that the courts considered the flag to be in the public domain. Not only was the SCV unable to gain exclusive use of the flag, it also had to fight off a lawsuit from the maverick leader of another heritage organization, the Confederate Memorial Association, of Washington, D.C., who claimed that the SCV itself was desecrating the flag.[34]

Even if flag defenders had aggressively acted to prevent or punish commercial appropriation of the flag, it is doubtful they could have succeeded. In 1989–1990 the U.S. Supreme Court handed down two landmark decisions *(Texas v. Johnson* and *United States v. Eichman)* invalidating state and federal laws prohibiting burning of the U.S. flag. The Court deemed burning the national flag as an act of free speech, which is protected under the First Amendment to the Constitution. The flag of a defunct secessionist nation obviously could not claim protection that the courts denied to the U.S. flag. The majority in the *Johnson* decision warned that "to conclude that the government may permit designated symbols to be used to communicate only a limited set of messages would be to enter territory having no discernible or defensible boundaries." By this logic, the government could extend the same protection to state flags, the presidential seal, or other symbols chosen according to "political preferences"—a clear violation of the First Amendment.[35]

How, then, is it possible to prevent desecration of the Confederate flag? Confederate heritage groups in recent years have pursued a logical two-track approach to defending the flag: persuade the media not to give coverage to the misuse of the flag by the KKK and other extremists while simultaneously offering models of proper, reverent flag use. Theoretically, it may be possible to teach a critical mass of Americans by word and example to believe that the Confederate flag is a positive or at least a benign historical icon. But as long as hate groups and ordinary people use the flag as a racist or politically charged symbol, and as long as the flag maintains its status as a signal of countercultural rebellion and militant individualism, the education campaign will fail to overcome stiff resistance to the Confederate flag.

Another component of the modern effort to protect the flag has been to redefine "desecration" in ways that allow or condone uses that earlier generations believed brought disrespect to the flag. Early guardians of the flag perceived that the greatest threat to it came not from outsiders intent on dishonoring it but from insiders whose enthusiasm for the flag was not tempered with proper reverence for it. The campaign to protect the flag carried generational and class overtones. Flag guardians censured the "undignified" and "disrespectful" displays of the flag by "slack-jawed" or "lantern-jawed" youths behaving badly—either by pulling down goal posts after football games or taunting civil rights marchers. But at some point, the flag's guardians became more concerned with silencing those who reacted against the flag's segregationist use than with punishing those actually guilty of that form of flag desecration.

In 1960 *Atlanta Journal* editor Ralph McGill warned southerners about the consequences of unregulated use of the Confederate flag:

> It is a noble banner, and one greatly revered by friend and foe alike. But the trouble is that the heirs of the past and of those who fought and died for it unfurl the flag at the drop of a hat, and, often, for the most unworthy, dubious, and shabby causes.
>
> One sees the flag embroidered on the leather jackets of tough young hoodlums, brought to court for the most shocking crimes . . . It gives one pause to see the honored flag being carried by hard-eyed or slack-faced men in a KKK demonstration against the Constitution of the United States and the courts which must inforce its provisions. To see the banner displayed at meetings of extremists where there are incitements to violence, such as destroying schools, is disturbing and dismaying . . .
>
> The noble flag is now unfurled over hot dogs, hamburgers, and peanuts. There is no objection. This is precisely the point. It is in grave danger of becoming the symbol of unworthy men, ideas, motives, and objectives . . .
>
> This is no way to honor a flag. Those who live and re-

vere it must rally around it. The South needs to reread Father Ryan.[36]

McGill recognized a fundamental truth: that the best way to protect a symbol's historical integrity is to ensure that it remains a historical symbol and keep it off the modern symbolic landscape.

Instead of rereading Father Ryan or heeding the advice of Ralph McGill, flag guardians of recent decades have concentrated on defending the right to unfurl the flag. As a consequence, they aided and abetted the outcome they hoped to avoid: loss of control of the flag and its meaning. Torn between a desire to control the flag's meaning and a desire to convert others to their understanding of it, today's guardians have allowed themselves to become parties to its proliferation. Instead of censuring everyone who unfurled the flag for "unworthy, dubious, and shabby" causes, defenders of the flag now support almost everyone who uses the flag except extreme racists. Yesterday's "desecration"—depicting the flag on beach towels, T-shirts, neckties, and bumper stickers—has become today's "honor."

Indicative of where this has led in recent decades are businesses that cater to a growing flag-waver market. The Cavalier Shoppe in Bruce, Mississippi, located a few miles from the University of Mississippi, opened in the late 1960s as a "classic men's store" with a conscious traditional southern flavor. "We are committed to God our Saviour and Lord, our Country, Mom, Pop, Dixie, Taters, Grits, Poke Salad, Black-Eyed Peas and southern Pecan Pie," declared the store's catalogue. In the early 1990s the proprietors began marketing a breathtaking assortment of "Rebel Flag" items, reacting, they explained, "to the onset of rebellion against the Flag by various groups along with the timidety [sic] of politicians, businesses and professional people who would not defend the Flag." By 1995 the owners confessed that "our wildest aspirations have been surpassed." The Cavalier Shoppe advertised coats, jackets, shirts, T-shirts, sweat shirts, skirts, neckties, aprons, hats, shorts, pajamas, golf socks, bikinis, belts, mittens, umbrellas, clocks, key rings, Frisbees, decals, patches, letter openers, pins, knives, lighters, tote bags, folding camp stools, golf balls, baby diapers, and dog collars bearing the Confederate naval jack.[37]

A few years after the Cavalier Shoppe urged its customers to "Wave a Rebel Flag!" the Georgia-based Dixie Outfitters launched an enormously successful line of clothing that featured the battle flag with sporting dogs, fish, wildlife, horses, rodeo scenes, cars, trucks, motorcycles, and "Confederate legends." Echoing the language of the Cavalier Shoppe's proprietors, the Dixie Outfitters' mission statement declared that the company was proud in being southern and "proud of our ancestors who fought and died in the Civil War for the South." "We believe the real meaning of the Confederate Flag has been distorted by various groups for their own purposes. We strive to feature the Confederate Flag in the context of history, heritage, and pride in the southern way of life." The flag was a "symbol of less government, less taxes, and the right of the people to govern themselves."[38]

The Cavalier Shoppe, Dixie Outfitters, Confederate Supply, and other commercial operations exemplify the place of the Confederate battle flag in American life at the dawn of the twenty-first century. Although the baby diaper and dog collar may fulfill someone's idea of comic hyperbole, the generations of Americans who have stopped by Stuckey's stores in their travels through the South are not shocked or outraged by the Cavalier Shoppe's product line. This in itself is powerful testimony to fundamental changes in the flag's status that occurred in the preceding half-century. It was inconceivable in 1945 that the battle flag would be emblazoned on clothing or novelty items. Much of the change, of course, reflects the revolution in fashion and the emergence of a popular culture that regards every space as a potential billboard. It was inconceivable in 1945 for Americans of all ages and classes to go out in public with T-shirts emblazoned with emblems, logos, and messages of every description. Over time, people became accustomed to and comfortable with the inconceivable.

It also reflects changed attitudes toward the battle flag, the Stars and Stripes, and other symbols that command reverence among the American people. Once defined as desecration, displaying the American flag on a T-shirt or baseball cap is now an act of patriotism. Similarly, reverence and respect for the Confederate battle flag no longer demand that it be confined to appropriate ceremonies and rituals; on the contrary, respect has become equated with flaunting it whenever and wherever it is most likely to command attention. Although this ethos is in step with modern American culture, it blurs the distinctions among expressions of reverence, desecration, and belligerence, and this blurring has serious consequences for the flag's image and meaning.

In more recent decades, defending the flag against those who would remove it from public places has become the definition of "protecting" the flag. The rallying cry of today's flag defenders is "Keep It Flying." Waving the flag has become a gesture of defiance against what the Dixie Outfitters euphemistically called "various groups"—no doubt referring to the NAACP and other civil rights organizations—that have rebelled against the flag. This rallying cry animates the pro-flag forces in the battles over the flag that have dominated the flag's history since the 1960s.

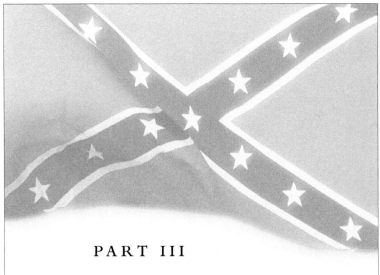

PART III

Flag Wars

The radically different perceptions of the flag's meaning have precipitated hundreds of incidents and public debates. These flag wars—or "flag flaps," as newspaper headlines dub them—began in the mid-1960s and have occurred in two waves, the first in the 1960s and 1970s and the second from the late 1980s into the new century. The first wave anticipated the issues and arguments of the second. The major difference was the considerable increase in African-American political strength and leverage. The flag wars are today's current events, but they represent a major chapter in the continuing history of the Confederate battle flag. The flag has been the subject of more news coverage and commentary since 1970 than in the century before. More important, the flag wars are fundamentally about history. They are debates about the meaning and the relevance of history, and they often result from flags placed on the landscape in the decades before the 1960s.

Chapter 9

"Vindication of the Cause"

On January 14, 1995, on a highway just south of the Kentucky–Tennessee state line, a car carrying four black youths pulled alongside a red pickup truck flying a large Confederate battle flag. Seventeen-year-old Freddie Morrow fired a .32 caliber pistol at the truck. One shot struck the driver, a white nineteen-year-old named Michael David Westerman, in the heart. From the passenger seat, Westerman's wife managed to get control of the truck and drive her husband to a hospital. He died the next day. "I've talked to all of them," a policeman said of the suspects, "and the only thing that might have motivated them was the fact that the truck had a Rebel flag on it." Two cars of young black men had been pursuing Westerman's truck from the time it left a convenience store in Guthrie, Kentucky, home to Westerman and most of the teenagers. Several of the youths later alleged that the driver reached back and defiantly shook the large Confederate battle flag flying over the truck bed; one of the youths claimed that he heard someone call "Nigger!" from the truck.[1]

"Killed for Flying Confederate Flag! South-Hating Liberals Are to Blame for This!" screamed the headlines of the racist newspaper *The Truth at Last* (successor to *Thunderbolt*). The aptly named magazine *South-*

ern Partisan proclaimed Westerman the "most recent martyr" of the Confederacy, a young man "shot for his heritage." Self-styled Confederate Americans seized upon the senseless murder as an opportunity to show the logical consequences of anti-southern (that is, anti-Confederate) rhetoric. A month after the murder, more than four hundred members of Confederate heritage groups descended on Todd County from as far away as North Carolina and Missouri for the observation of Confederate Flag Day (March 4). Gathered at Westerman's flag-festooned gravesite, mourners carried a flag emblazoned with "Michael David Westerman 1975–1995 Martyr." The mourners moved in a flag-waving convoy to the Jefferson Davis monument in nearby Fairview, Kentucky. The Sons of Confederate Veterans gave Westerman's father a certificate declaring his son a posthumous member of the organization. David Westerman in turn presented the SCV with the flag that Michael had flown on his truck.[2]

The memorial ceremony also offered disturbing reminders of why many black and white Americans view the Confederate flag as a threatening racist symbol, a red flag capable of provoking a violent reaction. Right-wing extremist groups, including the Council of Conservative Citizens (successor to the Citizens' Councils) and the Ku Klux Klan, joined the SCV in mourning Michael Westerman. Hooded Klansmen handed out segregationist literature. A few skinheads were present but kept their distance from the ceremonies. Addressing the crowd at the Jefferson Davis memorial, spokesmen for two politicized heritage groups used the opportunity to find larger meanings in Westerman's murder. R. Lee Collins, founder of the Heritage Preservation Association, warned of the threat to southern heritage from "the goose-stepping storm troopers of the political correctness movement." Dr. Michael Hill, of the Southern League, warned of "mongrelized multiculturalism." According to Hill, Westerman's murder fit the pattern of the incidents at Ruby Ridge, Idaho, and Waco, Texas, in which innocent people died because they had armed themselves and defied the federal government. "It is open season on anyone who has the audacity to question the dictates of an all-powerful federal government or the illicit rights bestowed on a compliant and deadly underclass that now fulfills a role similar to that of Hitler's brown-shirted street thugs in the nineteen-thirties," Hill said.[3]

While Westerman's murder was a rare example of extreme violence apparently resulting from a reaction to the Confederate battle flag, it may have been related to a dispute over the flag which was almost textbook in its origins and course. At the time of the murder, Todd Central High School (from which Westerman graduated in 1993) had been torn by a dispute over the school's team name, the Rebels, and its Confederate flag symbol. Todd County, Kentucky, was the birthplace of Confederate President Jefferson Davis and the site of an obelisk erected in 1924 by the United Daughters of the Confederacy as the Jefferson Davis memorial. Black residents, representing forty percent of the county's population, were pressuring the school system to change the high school's Confederate symbols. In the wake of the Westerman murder, which black and white residents condemned, defenders of the symbols successfully fought against the change.[4]

The Todd County school fight and the Westerman murder came in the midst of a wave of flag controversies that began in the late 1980s and continued unabated into the new century. Fueled by radically different perceptions of what the flag meant and what should be done with it, these controversies were played out in public schools, colleges and universities, and local and state governments. Although the variety of flag flaps seemed endless, there were important consistencies in the nature of the disputes and the identity and character of the disputants. Many flag flaps conformed to a predictable scenario because they involved officially sanctioned public symbolism. Whether the emblems in question were state flags, city seals, school mascots, flag displays on public property, or the insignias of organizations that received public support, the issues and questions involved were nearly identical:

· Should a government or public organization use a symbol that part of the public finds offensive?

· Conversely, should a government or public organization choose its symbols in deference to the feelings of a minority of its population at the expense of the sensibilities of its majority?

· Are public symbols subject to majority rule?

· Is the historical fact of the Confederacy's existence and the continued loyalty that many people feel to its memory more, or less, important than the offense that Confederate symbols give to black citizens?

· Are flags and other Confederate symbols neutral war memorials and reminders of historical fact or are they ideologically charged instruments that empower one group at the expense of others?

Typically, the disputes were argued and adjudicated in the political forum; quite often they found their way into the courts.

Other flag flaps occurred when individuals wear or display the Confederate flag, usually in public settings, most commonly at public schools and universities. Such controversies typically revolved around the rights and limitations of free speech and how the exercise of free speech affected the educational environment:

· Is it inherently disruptive when an individual displays a flag or wears a flag emblem on his clothing?

· If disruption occurs, is it the fault of the person displaying the flag or of the person who feels offended or threatened and reacts accordingly?

Private organizations and businesses occasionally sparked controversies by forbidding their members or employees from wearing or displaying the flag. Laws favored the rights of businesses over the rights of members or employees, leaving them little recourse. The Boy Scouts of America announced in August 1991 that it would no longer allow use of the Confederate battle flag at official scout functions. The flag had for decades been a common emblem on T-shirts and patches and appeared on the insignia of several districts in the South. A white eighteen-year-old South Carolina scout complained that "blatant exhibitionism" of the flag at the annual convention of the Dixie Fellowship (involving scouts from the Carolinas and Georgia) deterred African-American boys from joining, prompting the Boy Scouts to ban official use of the flag.[5]

In 2000 the DuPont Corporation's Spruance plant outside Richmond, Virginia, banned representations of Confederate battle flags on company property after receiving complaints from employees. The plant manager explained that the ruling was consistent with policies that prohibit signs or pictures considered "obscene, disruptive or inflammatory," and insisted that private companies had a right to restrict expression on their property; civil libertarians agreed. Whatever the legal realities, disgruntled employees began a flag-waving vigil outside the company gates and continued to maintain the protest more than two years later.[6]

When SCANA, a private power company that provides most of South Carolina's energy, adopted an anti-flag policy in 2002, outraged employees found a powerful ally in Senator Glenn McConnell, president pro tempore of the state Senate and owner of a North Charleston Confederate memorabilia store. SCANA prohibited its employees from driving company vehicles to Maurice's Barbecue, a business that displayed the Confederate battle flag and whose owner appeared to defend slavery because it brought blacks to a better life in America. The SCV threatened to sue SCANA; Senator McConnell proposed a bill to strip SCANA of state contracts and to issue licenses to competitors.[7]

Flag flaps awakened and unleashed enormous public interest and emotion—especially among flag supporters. Whenever people were invited to register their opinion on the issue, they did so in large, often unprecedented, numbers. The city council of Alexandria, Virginia, received five times the volume of letters and calls (overwhelmingly pro-flag) about a 1968 proposal that the city cease public display of the Confederate flag than it had received when it raised taxes six months before. Unscientific surveys in Montgomery, Alabama, and Danville, Virginia, in 1988 and 1993, respectively, garnered twice as many calls as any issue previously featured in the opinion surveys.[8] The vast majority of calls on the flag issue came from people defending the flag against its detractors. Although many Americans, especially northerners, are incredulous over it, the Confederate flag generates enormous grass-roots interest wherever it becomes an issue.

Although the flag wars elicited strong feelings and engaged individuals on all sides, they were fought largely by organizations—civil rights groups on one side and Confederate heritage groups on the other. In particular, the NAACP and the SCV roamed the flag-debate landscape like professional gladiators ready to do battle. As the flag issue gained regional and national prominence, spokesmen for those organizations became frequent guests on national television and radio talk shows. Both sides insisted that if people were properly educated about the Confederacy and the flag, they would understand and support their position.

Confederate heritage spokesmen charged that the flag flaps were products of a prejudice against Confederate symbols by African-American organizations, notably the NAACP. P. Charles Lunsford, chairman of the SCV Heritage Defense Committee, claimed that there had been no complaints against Confederate symbols "until the mid-1980's when the NAACP took it upon itself to declare war on Confederate Americans." The journalist and historian Don Hinkle agreed that the NAACP "and the politically correct movement" were responsible for making the flag a "political issue." Posing the obvious question, Hinkle asked, "So why did the NAACP wait 135 years [sic: The NAACP did not exist until 1909] to launch an attack on the Confederate battle flag?" The answer accused the NAACP of self-interested cynicism. "Declining membership and internal controversy plagued the NAACP in the late 1980s and early 1990s under the leadership of Benjamin Chavis, who was eventually booted out the door by the membership." Repeating an oft-made charge, Hinkle concluded: "It appears that the attack upon the flag by the NAACP was a calculated undertaking designed to whip blacks into an emotional tizzy and bolster the organization's pocketbook."⁹

The most frequently cited evidence of the NAACP's "declaration of war" against the Confederate heritage was an alleged 1991 resolution on NAACP letterhead circulated by southern heritage organizations. In uncharacteristically intemperate language, the resolution described the battle flag as a symbol of "tyrannical evil," and "an abhorrence to all Americans and decent people of this country, and indeed the world and is an odious blight upon the universe." It contended that "African-Americans had no voice, no consultation, no concurrence, no commonality, not in fact nor in philosophy, in the vile conception of the Confederate Battle Flag containing the ugly symbol of idiotic white supremacy, racism and denigration." It rejected the battle flag as an appropriate symbol on state flags and resolved "that the National Office of the NAACP and all its units commit their legal resources to the removal of the Confederate Battleflag from all public properties." The NAACP confirmed that the 1991 convention had approved this resolution, but NAACP chairman Julian Bond denied the validity of a "bogus" resolution that has the NAACP calling for "the removal of the Confederate flag *from all public and private places.*" The NAACP restated its consistent position in 2001, calling "for the immediate removal of the Confederate battle flag and/or Confederate emblems from any and all public sites in this country except at historical museums."[10]

While the NAACP was often the protagonist in flag flaps, attempts to portray the civil rights organization as a self-interested troublemaker are disingenuous. Those who charge that the battle flag only became a problem when the NAACP began exploiting it in the 1980s and 1990s have short memories or have not examined the issue very closely. African-American protests against the flag began almost immediately after it became a visible symbol in the late 1940s and early 1950s. Confederate heritage groups themselves reacted at the same time against the wider and careless use of the flag.

Civil rights coalitions targeted the flag as a racist symbol as early as the 1960s. In 1961, for example, the NAACP's Virginia State Conference protested the use of a Confederate battle flag on automobile license plates in Spotsylvania County. Lester Banks, executive secretary of the state NAACP conference, called the plates "an unforgivable insult" to county blacks and urged them to resist the inclusion of the battle flag on license plates with the same "patriotism and fierceness" as they would a Nazi swastika. County officials allowed residents to tape or paint over the flag and pledged to use a different motif on the 1962 plates. The state conference of the NAACP made available five hundred weatherproof stickers bearing the American flag and the inscription "One Nation Indivisible" which citizens could use to cover the Confederate flag. A 1972 editorial in the NAACP's magazine, *The Crisis,* stated the organization's position toward the flag and the song "Dixie." Although individuals had a First Amendment right to unfurl even offensive symbols, "the display of divisive symbols by public institutions and agencies should certainly be subject to government regulation. In the present climate the banning of such symbols in schools and other public institutions is essential if further polarization of the races is to be avoided."[11]

The charge that the NAACP exploited the flag issue to raise funds and recruit members may not be completely without foundation. The late civil rights leader James Farmer, although not a spokesman for the NAACP, defended using the flag issue to galvanize support for civil rights causes. "We don't have 'Bull' Connor to rally [people] around," Farmer explained in 1994. The NAACP, America's most venerable civil rights organization, was ailing in the late 1980s. While its critics portrayed it as a well-funded, powerfully connected liberal leviathan, in fact the organization suffered from enormous debt, declining membership, internal dissent, and a leadership crisis culminating in the firing of President Benjamin Chavis in August 1994 and the defeat of veteran chairman William Gibson in February 1995. Without the stark moral alternatives of the 1950s and 1960s, the campaign for racial justice was losing momentum.

The Confederate battle flag had a clear and threatening meaning for blacks, especially those who were more educated and affluent.[12] African-American activists likened the Confederate battle flag to the Nazi swastika. Regardless of what benign meaning each symbol may have had originally, they argued, both had become anathema to Jews and blacks, respectively. More immediately, the Confederate flag had become the symbol of the Ku Klux Klan and other racist hate groups. Use of the same flag by governments and by publicly accountable organizations made them guilty of racism by association. Whether or not such reasoning was logical or valid, it made for powerful politics. Civil rights groups argued that the case against the flag was not merely the politics of symbolism; the flag expressed a Confederate mindset that could pose a tangible threat to civil rights.

The NAACP case against the flag was calculated to revive indignation against tangible, overt, state-sanctioned discrimination. The paucity of such tangible discrimination and the complexities of civil rights issues in the 1980s and 1990s had hampered the NAACP's work. The presence of Confederate battle flag emblems over two southern state capitols and on two state flags seemed to provide evidence that, even in the age of affirmative action and civil rights laws, southern states did not accept fully the equality of their black citizens. That three of those battle flags were apparent legacies of the era of "massive resistance" against integration reinforced the usefulness of the flag issue for the NAACP.

In presenting the case against the flag and in jousting with flag supporters, the late Earl T. Shinhoster, the NAACP's southeast regional director who subsequently became national field secretary and interim national director, maintained that the organization wanted only to end the use of the flag on official state symbols. A state flag, he insisted, was a "public policy instrument" which ought to represent the people who constitute the public. The battle flag "should be relegated to a museum." Shinhoster noted that the SCV and other heritage groups should be leading the movement to "retire" the flag to museums, since only by doing so could they protect it from misuse and preserve its value as a tool for historical education.[13] Local activists in the NAACP and other civil rights organizations, such as the Southern Christian Leadership Conference (SCLC) and the Southern Poverty Law Center (SPLC), and websites such as "The Temple of Democracy" also campaigned against official use of the Confederate battle flag.

The well-established Sons of Confederate Veterans emerged as the most visible, active, and effective defender of the flag. Founded in 1896 as an auxiliary to the United Confederate Veterans, the SCV was, from its origin, dedicated explicitly to defending the reputation of Confederate veterans and the cause for which they fought. Decades after the death of the last Confederate soldier, the SCV and the UDC still survived and occasionally thrived, observing the traditional Confederate holidays and continuing faithfully the patriotic, historical, and educational work of their predecessors. Both the SCV and the UDC carried forward into the twenty-first century, virtually unchanged, the "Lost Cause" historical interpretations and ideological vision formulated at the turn of the twentieth.

General Stephen D. Lee in 1906 gave to the SCV a "charge" that remained the foundation of its mission a century later: "To you, Sons of Confederate Veterans, we submit the vindication of the Cause for which we fought; to your strength will be given the defense of the Confederate soldier's good name, the guardianship of his history, the emulation of his virtues, the perpetuation of those principles he loved and which made him glorious and which you cherish. Remember, it is your duty to see that the true history of the South is presented to future generations."[14] Significantly, Lee charged the Sons not only with honoring the soldiers but with "vindication of the Cause." This statement underscores the futility of trying to divorce the defense of Confederate symbols and the honor of Confederate soldiers from the cause for which the soldiers fought.

During the flag wars of the late twentieth century, the SCV lived up to its charge. From the time of the flag fad in the early 1950s, SCV officials defended the integrity of the battle flag against trivialization and against those who insisted that its display was unpatriotic or racist. SCV spokesmen reiterated the consistent argument that the South fought a legitimate war for independence, not a war to defend slavery, and that the ascendant "Yankee" view of history falsely vilified the South and led people to misinterpret the battle flag. The re-emergence of the battle flag issue in the late 1980s found a newly reinvigorated SCV ready to defend the flag and "keep it flying" wherever it was. Ironically, the NAACP's campaign to end publicly sanctioned display of the flag gave the SCV exactly what the battle flag gave to the NAACP: an emotional and effective recruiting tool. The SCV seized the opportunity to present itself as a high-profile defender of the flag and of the honor of the men who carried it, and in the process doubled its membership.[15]

In the mid-1980s the SCV formed a Save the Flag Committee, which was changed in 1989 to the Confederate Heritage Committee. The committee served as a clearinghouse for alleged "heritage violations" and coordinated the censure of "heritage violators." "All over the Confederation, our history is being challenged; our Confederate heritage is under relentless attack," warned the SCV's "Attacks on the Colors" column in 1991. "At no time since its inception in 1896 has the SCV faced more numerous or more dangerous assaults than at the present time." "Heritage, Not Hate" became the ubiquitous slogan of the flag defenders. The SCV identified and endeavored to punish political, cultural, and business leaders who perpetuated negative depictions of the battle flag, and it officially condemned the Ku Klux Klan and other hate groups for adopting and misusing the flag—the most obvious source of the flag's negative publicity.

The SCV also challenged the customary portrayal of African-American opposition to Confederate symbols by publicizing the views of strongly pro-Confederate black activists, most notably Dr. Leonard Haynes and H. K. Edgerton. A former NAACP officer in Asheville, North Carolina, Edgerton became affiliated with the Southern Legal Resources Center (SLRC) and a spirited speaker for southern heritage. In 2002–2003 he staged a 1,300-mile march across the South wearing a Confederate uniform and carrying a battle flag. The SCV also celebrated the alleged contributions of the thousands of slaves and free blacks in Confederate armies and magnified the evidence of their formal enlistment and participation as combat soldiers. The existence and contributions of "Black Confederates" was a none-too-subtle attempt to rebut the charge that Confederate symbols were inherently racist.[16]

Largely as a reaction to organized campaigns against the battle flag, the song "Dixie," and other Confederate symbols, Confederate heritage groups and publications proliferated in the late 1980s and 1990s. They shared the conviction that most books and programs about the Civil War were biased in favor of the North and continued to crank out their own books, articles, and public programs designed to show that the Confederate cause was just. Far from being descendants of oppressive slave owners, Confederate Americans portrayed themselves as victims—an oppressed minority threatened with "cultural genocide." Black and liberal attacks on the Confederate battle flag were a manifestation of that process, and therefore defense of the flag was part of a battle for self-preservation.

Charles Lunsford, a Georgia state government employee who was the SCV's most visible spokesman on heritage issues, articulated this argument in language that turned on its head the oft-used analogy between the battle flag and the Nazi swastika: Why were Confederate symbols coming under attack? asked Lunsford. The reason, he answered, was simply hatred, vengeance, and retribution, "an effort to take from white southerners the last reminders of their noble ancestors—the symbols." Lunsford argued that Confederate Americans were in a position analogous not to the Nazis but to their victims. Persecution, such as that which Confederate Americans were suffering, "has happened before in other places, in other times." The Nazi persecution of the Jews began with "a campaign of hatred" in the 1930s. "Jews were made to seem simple, base and less cultured than the majority population. Then their sacred symbols were attacked and banned. We all know what happened next. Sobering, isn't it."[17]

Other flag defenders echoed this message of historical and contemporary victimization. "The money and power that is behind the NAACP is vast," warned the editor of *Southern Heritage Magazine.* "They can win if we don't get smart fast. If we allow the Yankee myth to perpetuate through the liberal media establishment, then we are doomed to run aground with white flags of surrender." "Our goal," he insisted, "must be to discredit the Yankee myth builders who have maligned the South. The people of the South have worn the saddle of slavery for far too long. We suffered the injustice of Reconstruction. We now suffer their shroud of racism and are force-fed the notion that 'it's a southern thing.'" The Confederate Society of America pledged "to stop this historical revision and the Confederate bashing that is so prevalent today and to fight the evil forces of ongoing governmental encroachment in the lives of Americans." "The Confederate Movement is growing," declared CSA founder David Martin in his publication *CSA News.* "For 128 years the Confederate people have been a subjugated nation, and we have declared 'Enough!' The time is now! Our Cause is just! We must not fail!"[18]

Similar alarmist rhetoric characterized the Heritage Preservation Association, an unabashedly activist organization which grew out of the defense of the Georgia state flag. Founded in 1992 by R. Lee Collins, the

HPA temporarily eclipsed the SCV as the most ardent and aggressive defender of the flag. Chapters were formed in communities such as Cumberland, Maryland, where publicly sponsored flag displays were threatened or removed. Among its most vocal members was Charles Lunsford, who resigned his position with the SCV while denouncing the SCV's leadership for compromising on vital questions.[19]

Lunsford and an increasing number of activists warned that the forces arrayed against Confederate Americans would not be content with removing Confederate battle flags from public places but wanted to eradicate all vestiges of "southern" (that is, white southern) culture. "It's not everything Confederate, it's just the Battle Flag, which has been used by hate groups," was among the most common and effective arguments that Lunsford encountered between 1987 and 1993. "All that I need to refute that argument is mention the name Carol Moseley-Braun," Lunsford wrote with a strong sense of vindication.[20]

Indeed, one of the loudest flag flaps of the era occurred when Senator Carol Moseley-Braun (D-Illinois), the first African-American woman elected to the U.S. Senate (and subsequently a candidate for the 2004 Democratic Party presidential nomination), successfully shamed her Senate colleagues into not renewing a congressional patent on the logo of the United Daughters of the Confederacy. The issue first drew public attention in May 1993 when Moseley-Braun's impassioned plea not to give the Senate's "imprimatur" to a Confederate symbol convinced a committee to vote twelve to three against renewing the special patent.[21]

Two months later, Senator Jesse Helms of North Carolina, seconded by Senator J. Strom Thurmond of South Carolina, brought the issue to the floor while Moseley-Braun was attending another hearing and asked his colleagues to rectify the unintended "rebuke" given to the "gentle ladies" of the UDC. Moseley-Braun returned to the chamber and delivered a speech, punctuated by tears and outrage. "The fact of the matter is the emblems of the Confederacy have meaning to Americans 100 years after the end of the Civil War," she said. Quoting from Confederate Vice President Alexander Stephens's infamous 1861 "Cornerstone" speech, she emphasized that the display of Confederate symbols made African Americans "suffer the indignity of being reminded time and time again that at one point in this country's history, we were human chattel." Although she acknowledged the free speech rights of individuals to display the Confederate flag, she declared that the Confederate flag "has no place in modern times. It has no place in this body. It has no place in the Senate. It has no place in our society." A parade of senators followed her to the microphone, praising Moseley-Braun's "powerful" speech and agreeing that it was not appropriate for the Senate to endorse Confederate symbols. In the end, the full Senate voted seventy-five to twenty-five not to renew the patent.[22]

This incident—the only notable flag flap to be fought within the halls of the U.S. Congress—was rife with ironies. For one thing, it turned a critical spotlight on a heritage organization that had maintained a low political profile for decades. Although it had been in the front lines of defending Confederate heritage early in the twentieth century, the UDC in the century's last decades had yielded political leadership to the men's organizations. Furthermore, the symbol immediately at issue was the Stars and Bars proper, not the battle flag. Although Moseley-Braun spoke generally about Confederate symbols, her office later explained that the Stars and Bars was the objectionable symbol because it represented the government that rested on the "cornerstone" of slavery. In the battles over the battle flag, many moderates on both sides of the flag issue had found the Stars and Bars to be an acceptable compromise symbol. It found favor with moderates for the same reason that it was popular in 1861 and unpopular in 1863: it resembled the Stars and Stripes and was not a potent symbol of mature Confederate nationalism. Many people simply did not recognize it as a Confederate symbol at all. If, as Moseley-Braun insisted, the Stars and Bars was subject to the same harsh rhetoric as the battle flag and if the formal renewal of a meaningless special patent on the logo of a patriotic organization elicited protest, what place could Confederate heritage organizations hope to have in American society? Although Moseley-Braun won applause in some circles for her principled stand against vestigial Confederate symbols, others joined Lunsford in believing that her actions signaled an unwarranted attack on history and a chilling display of political correctness run amok. Where would it all end?[23]

The answer, clearly, was that it would not end with flags. Civil rights groups called for the removal of Confederate monuments, especially those dedicated to the memory of Nathan Bedford Forrest—the Confederate general who had made his prewar fortune as a slave trader, had allegedly ordered the murder of surrendered black soldiers at Fort Pillow, Tennessee, in 1864, and had served as the Ku Klux Klan's first grand wizard. In Richmond, Virginia, in 1999 a black city councilman protested the inclusion of a banner of Robert E. Lee in a gallery of banners placed on the city's flood wall. After much debate, the banner was placed after all, only to be burned by a vandal, then replaced.[24] Richmond officials did rename two city bridges that previously had borne the names of Confederate generals.

These battles over Confederate symbols, monuments, and names were, in turn, part of a wider war over the interpretation and teaching of American history. Conservative groups reacted with outrage to museum exhibits such as "The West as America" and the aborted "The Last Act" (about the *Enola Gay,* the decision to use the atom bomb against Japan, and the end of World War II), both of which questioned basic articles of faith in American history. When a panel of scholars created "national history standards" that highlighted the contributions of people other than European males, conservative groups furiously denounced "politically correct" historians for "hijacking history."

Much of the verbal flak in the public "history wars" was racial in nature. While African Americans continued to believe that school curricula and official histories neglect the contributions and roles of their forebears, many white Americans expressed resentment over having black history "crammed down their throats" in the form of Black History Month observances. Critical evaluations of founding fathers found their way into the public policy realm. Most notorious was the elimination of George Washington's name from a New Orleans public school in accordance with a new regulation that prohibited naming any schools after slaveholders.[25] African Americans, it seemed, were allowed to celebrate their history but European Americans were supposed to be ashamed of theirs. This perceived unfairness animated discussions over the "history wars" and over the Confederate flag.

The Confederate heritage movement spawned several organizations dedicated explicitly to white southern separatism. The League of the South was founded in 1994 by intellectuals steeped in the tradition of the Southern Agrarians—writers and scholars in the 1920s and 1930s who viewed the South as a cultural bulwark against an all-powerful central-ized industrial state. This intellectual tradition, passed down faithfully through the generations, revered Confederate heritage and symbols as an inseparable part of the cultural legacy. The league's ideology rested also on the theory of one of its founders, the historian Grady McWhiney, that the South was culturally distinct in large part because its people de-scended from the Celtic fringes of England, whereas the North drew its heritage from the Saxons.

In 1999 the league gave birth to the Southern Party which sought to elect local candidates committed to secession. Although both organi-zations ostensibly welcomed African Americans and non-Celtic ethnic whites, they unashamedly promoted the superiority of America's "histor-ically European and Christian ethic, linguistic and cultural core" and exploited the frustration and anger of white southerners of Confeder-ate ancestry disgruntled with modern culture's hostility toward their heritage.[26]

The Confederate heritage movement was linked both in ideology and in membership with conservative backlash politics. In the view of south-ern conservative writers, defense of the Confederate flag—as an of-ficially sanctioned symbol of which the white majority approved—was linked inextricably to the defense of the constitutional principles over-thrown in the 1860s and further eroded in the 1960s. "At what time and place did we consent to a government that taxes the middle class to the point of robbery just to maintain a free loading liberal voting welfare class?" asked James R. Kennedy and Walter D. Kennedy, authors of the manifesto *The South Was Right*. "When did we consent to the surrender of local control of our public schools? Where can it be shown that we have consented to reverse discrimination, minority set asides, and forced affirmative action? At what time and place did we give our unfettered consent to a discriminatory South only Voting Rights Act that prevents southerners from establishing reasonable voting qualifications?"[27] The editors of *Southern Partisan* and *Southern Heritage Magazine* also defended the flag as a symbol they believed represented ideals which were not only right in the 1860s but equally valid today.

Just as the early backlash against civil rights gained a national following in the campaigns of Barry Goldwater in 1964 and George Wallace in 1964, 1968, and 1972, conservative southern ideology was not restricted to the South. As more white Americans grew disgusted with the federal government's interference in their lives, the decay of moral standards, and the perceived preference given to African Americans, pro-Confederate writers saw victory on the horizon. The November 1994 elections brought Republican majorities to the U.S. House and Senate, Republican governors to thirty state houses, and a highly touted states' rights–based "Contract with America."[28]

Seen in some quarters as an appropriate symbol for the conservative populist backlash and viewed sympathetically by others as a victim of political correctness and anti-white feeling, the Confederate battle flag was very much a political symbol in the 1990s. The explicit linkage between support for the flag and a conservative ideological counteroffensive underscores a fundamental inconsistency in the pro-flag argument. Flag defenders since the days of Carlton McCarthy have insisted that the flag was a war memorial to the Confederate soldier, a memorial that people could and should honor regardless of what they believe about the Confederate cause. Without going so far as the National States' Rights Party and declaring the flag a symbol of white supremacy, modern ideologues consciously made it a politically charged banner. As it was during the 1948 Dixiecrat campaign and in the subsequent fight against integration, the flag was a historically logical symbol of such a movement. But how could the mainstream American population accept a flag that was the banner of a reactionary ideology and political movement as if it were an apolitical war memorial? Collectively, flag defenders were sending mixed signals.

The NAACP and other flag detractors also sent mixed signals that undercut the veracity of their case. The limited campaign against battle flags that have the imprimatur of sovereignty seemed to mask a deep-seated hatred of flags, monuments, and any tangible evidence of Confederate memorials on the public landscape. While this position may have been perfectly consistent and understandable for African Americans determined that the Confederate South shall never rise again, it played into Confederate heritage warnings about a hidden agenda and, indeed, into their claims of "cultural genocide."

The flag wars were usually not shooting wars, although the opposing sides could point to instances in which flag wavers committed racist crimes and flag haters attacked people who sported flags on their homes or vehicles.[29] With Michael Westerman's murder as an obvious exception, the flag wars were not a matter of life and death. They were, however, a matter of importance to America's cultural and political life. Far from being anachronistic symbolic sideshows or mere echoes of long-finished battles, the flag wars were indicators of deep fissures related to race and constitutional issues. Although they have occurred in our own time, the flag wars were as much about history as they were about contemporary political, social, and cultural issues. Flag wars were often battles over the symbols that earlier generations placed on the American landscape. The anger, frustration, and resentment that animated the flag wars revealed extremely divergent perceptions of the Civil War and of the rights and obligations of the winners and losers of that war in the present and in the future.

Chapter 10

"The Bitterest Battleground"

Tension and bitterness filled the air during the fifteen-minute ceremony. Students, some of them wearing what a reporter characterized as "in-your-face Confederate flag T-shirts," booed as a color guard stepped forward, struck the school's Confederate battle flag, and replaced it with a new flag bearing the name Rebels. Students continued to boo when the principal of Thornton Fractional High School commended the students for dealing with what he called "a painful chapter, but an educational experience for all of us."

The ceremony was a somewhat anticlimactic end to eleven months of controversy surrounding the school's Confederate flag. Typical of other such controversies, parents opposing the flag change formed a committee, Citizens for a Confederate Flag, circulated a petition to put the issue on the local election ballot, and threatened voter retribution against school board members. Parents of white students asked why the wishes of the majority should be ruled by the whims of the school's minority (ten percent) black population. "The flag wasn't doing anything . . . people are just using it as an excuse, something to blame for other problems," remarked one student.[1]

Not so typical of other flag controversies was the location of the school: suburban Chicago. Thornton Fractional School adopted the Rebel team name and the battle flag symbol not because it had any association with Confederate heritage, but because the school was born when the growing school district was separated into northern and southern divisions in 1958. The students of Thornton Fractional South—then all white—accordingly adopted "southern" (Confederate) symbols. The school had only a handful of black students until the early 1990s. Black students claimed that while they had resented the flag, they either "blacked it out" or "learned to live with it" because they did not believe they had any alternative. Speaking only for themselves, the parents of two black students complained about the flag at a March 1993 school board meeting and brought the issue into the open.[2]

The white parents who organized in support of the flag were themselves graduates of Thornton Fractional and cited the school's heritage as the chief reason for retaining the symbols. The mother who formed Citizens for a Confederate Flag soon dropped her support after seeing a television show linking the flag to neo-Nazi groups; she favored instead a school dress code banning any symbol "demeaning to anyone." The protest against the school's policy continued without her but failed to get the issue on the November 1993 ballot and eventually fizzled. Thornton Fractional School lost its Confederate flag as the community faced new allegations that it had illegally prevented a black evangelical church from acquiring property and relocating there.[3]

A 1991 flag controversy in the heart of the old Confederacy turned out much differently. At James F. Byrnes High School in Duncan, South Carolina, a suburb of Spartanburg, a week of pro-flag demonstrations followed the suspension of five students for violating a district-wide ban against wearing Confederate flags or other disruptive symbols. The ban had been adopted in 1970, a year after the integration of the district's schools, when Confederate flags were linked explicitly with resistance to desegregation. The suspensions culminated a month of tensions that apparently began in February with white resentment over the school's "multicultural" programs and with the suspension of a student who refused to remove a Confederate flag sticker from his truck parked in the school parking lot.[4]

In deliberate defiance of the ban, at least ten students wore Confederate flag clothing to school on Monday, March 4. The school evicted the students when they refused to remove the flags. Further evictions occurred on Tuesday. The protest became formal and organized on Wednesday when an estimated eighty students and parents demonstrated at the school. On Thursday, cars and trucks drove by the school flying Confederate flags while students marched down the sidewalk in front of the school yelling "Rebel! Rebel!" and "God bless the flag!" As many as one in six students, fearful of violence, stayed out of school during the week, while police patrolled near the school and officials threatened suspensions of flag-waving protesters. The school carried through with its threat and suspended several students.[5]

The parents of five suspended students formed a Rebel Support Group and brought suit against the school district and officials of Byrnes High School. The class-action suit alleged violations of the students' First, Fourth, Fifth, and Fourteenth Amendment rights. It pointed out inconsistencies in the specific charges against the students and in the school's tolerance of flags and other insignia. Indeed, the school yearbook featured U.S. and Confederate battle flags on its cover and throughout its pages, and the alma mater included the lines: "Where a Rebel Standard flies / Proudly floating free." The terms of the school's dress code, which prohibited "garments with slogans, patches, or buttons that are suggestive, vulgar, racially intended, or provocative" and allowed officials to prohibit clothing deemed disruptive, were, the suit contended, "overly broad" and "lend themselves to arbitrary, capricious and discriminatory application." The suit sought a permanent injunction against enforcement of any policy prohibiting the display of "representations of the Confederate Battle Flag by students."[6]

Before the case reached a court hearing on April 22, 1991, the parties agreed upon a settlement in which the school district agreed to reinstate all suspended students and expunge their records. The school district's multicultural program (which had been adopted a few years earlier as a substitute for Black History Month) would be expanded "to include the study of Southern Heritage." The moratorium on flags and other symbols "likely to cause a material disruption of the successful operation" of schools would be continued until May 31, 1991, but could be lifted if the symbols no longer carried a potential for disruption. "The elimination of the moratorium is conditioned upon continued peaceful and harmonious student conduct."[7]

The Rebel Support Group claimed victory and southern heritage organizations declared the settlement "an extremely important and far-reaching Confederate victory," which vindicated the constitutionality of displaying the Confederate flag and of aggressive court action. Tempering the victory were remarks that the judge made in presenting the settlement. According to an account by a Sons of Confederate Veterans officer present at the court session, the judge lectured the plaintiffs "rather harshly and quite unnecessarily that they should not 'intimidate' blacks." The judge's tone, noted the editor of *CSA News*, "was apparently an attempt to make the students feel that their stand was somehow wrong."[8]

Together, the Thornton Fractional and Byrnes cases exemplified the varieties of flag controversies that have confronted public schools and the diverse outcomes of those cases. On one hand were controversies involving official sanction of the Confederate flag as a school symbol. On the other hand were controversies involving restrictions of student freedom to wear or display flag emblems while on school property. Occasionally, these "public" and "private" controversies occurred simultaneously. Both types of controversies often ended up in court, where legal precedents allowed public school officials wide latitude in censoring symbols and infringing students' free speech rights.

The Thornton Fractional and Byrnes cases were both part of a second wave of cases that began in the late 1980s. A first wave occurred in the late 1960s and early 1970s as a direct result of school desegregation and usually resulted in the restriction of flag display. Before integration was effectively achieved in the 1970s, many white schools—North and South—adopted the popular Rebels team name and, as natural corollaries, chose the Confederate flag as a symbol and "Dixie" as a fight song, without worrying about offending black students. "Yankees" and "Rebels" were as familiar and, for most, as innocent as "Cowboys" and "Indians."

The innocence of the flag ended in the wake of the 1954 *Brown* decision when students and arch-segregationists used the flag as a symbol of massive resistance to integration. During the prolonged struggle over desegregation, the same flag that was the symbol of so many white schools became a symbol of the fight against the integration of those schools. Opponents of integration in Little Rock in 1957 and in New Orleans in 1960 taunted black students with Confederate flags. Unhooded Klansmen carrying a full-sized Confederate flag stood by while five black students were enrolled in Greensboro's Gillespie School. White students in Birmingham in 1963 carried Confederate flags and signs reading "We Want a White School."[9]

Writer John Egerton saw the battle flag as the standard of the "seg" academies founded in the South to circumvent integration. It flew at Hammond Academy, in Columbia, South Carolina, a school that had lost its federal tax-exempt status because it refused to pledge a policy of non-discrimination. Wade Hampton Academy and other private schools in South Carolina issued their graduates lapel pins bearing the Confederate flag and the word "Survivor." Modeled on pins worn by Confederate veterans, the Survivor pin consciously linked the private schools of the 1960s with Confederate resistance to the federal government in the 1860s.[10]

The flag became a major school issue after 1969 when the Supreme Court ordered immediate and effective integration of schools. With that decision, the meaning of the Confederate flag in schools changed forever. "In what used to be ordinary times, when student bodies were more-or-less homogeneous, agitation over such matters as school songs and colors no doubt could be regarded as 'inconsequential' and 'trivial,'" noted the Atlanta-based liberal organization, the Southern Regional Council (SRC), in 1971. "The point, of course, is that these are not ordinary times and student bodies are not homogeneous." Confederate symbols, the SRC concluded, are understandably perceived by blacks as insensitive or hostile.[11]

Not surprisingly, the Confederate battle flag figured prominently in the efforts to eliminate what the courts deemed as "obstacles" to integration. The plaintiffs in a Louisiana desegregation suit argued successfully that meaningful integration must involve prohibiting the official display at all school functions of "all Confederate flags, banners, signs expressing the school board's or its employees' desire to maintain segregated schools, and all other symbols or indicia of racism." The federal judge observed that "the Confederate battle flag, since the decision by the U.S. Supreme Court on May 17, 1954 in Brown v. Board of Education . . . has become a symbol of resistance to school integration and, to some, a symbol of white racism in general." Black students at a high school in Muncie, Indiana, made a similar argument with a different result. Opened in 1962 during the Civil War Centennial, Southside High School chose the usual panoply of Confederate symbols. The judge rejected the black students' complaint because there was no clear association between the symbols and discrimination against black students. In a suburban Pensacola, Florida, high school, federal district and appeals courts found an explicit relationship between the Confederate flag and racial violence and took the unusual step of issuing an injunction prohibiting the use of Confederate school symbols and the display of the Confederate flag by students. Private display of the flag constituted "fighting words" because the flag had been used in protest to integration. The court decision conceded that students in 1958 had not adopted the Confederate symbols as "racial irritants" and that the symbols did not carry a "racially offensive connotation" to most current white students. But the obligations under the *Brown* decision compelled the court to respect the rights of the minority of students who did regard the Confederate flag as a racist symbol.[12]

A controversy in Chattanooga, Tennessee, in 1970 illustrated dramatically how disagreements over Confederate school symbols could escalate into serious turmoil. The decisions by the federal courts in *Melton v. Young* further revealed the perception of the Confederate flag as a symbol with incendiary potential. The suspension of Rod Melton from Brainerd High School in September 1970 occurred in the wake of severe racial tension—which spilled over from the school into the streets of Chatta-

nooga—related directly to black protests over the school's use of Confederate symbols. Brainerd High was integrated by court order in 1966,
and by the 1969–1970 term the school consisted of 170 black and 1,224
white students. It was one of the best high schools in the city, sending
more of its graduates to college than any other school. Opened in 1962
as one of the city's all-white high schools, it had adopted the customary
trinity of the Rebel name, the "Dixie" fight song, and the Confederate
battle flag as the school symbol. Brainerd High football players "ripped"
onto the field "through the Rebel flag with the enthusiastic support of
both cheerleaders and fans."[13]

In early October 1969 black students expressed their disdain for those
symbols by marching out of school pep rallies and, a month later, by
attempting to burn a Confederate flag on the field during half-time.
Within a week, the school's biracial student Human Relations Council
announced a compromise whereby the school would remain the Rebels
but the Confederate flag would be replaced by a new symbol to be voted
upon by a student referendum; "Johnny Reb" would be redecorated in
school colors; and "Dixie" would be one of several songs in a new school
song medley. Four hundred white students walked out of the assembly
when the compromise was announced. On subsequent days, thousands
of whites rallied with Confederate and American flags in support of the
school symbols, motorcades drove through the streets of Chattanooga
flying Confederate flags, and a local White Citizens' Council leader with
a Confederate flag was arrested for trespassing at the school.[14]

At the end of that week, after a Saturday night football game, violent
confrontations broke out when black youths threw rocks at flag-waving
whites cruising in cars through the town of Brainerd. A crowd of 500–
600 white students and adults gathered in the town the following day,
waving flags and singing "Dixie." Police prevented cars from parading,
and the Chattanooga mayor asked the crowd to disperse and return
home. A few nights later, authorities imposed a city-wide five-night cur-
few, and the school rescheduled all night-time sporting events for after-
noons.[15] More violence between white and black students again erupted
in April 1970, resulting in fires set in the school auditorium and two
two-day school closings.[16]

The school administration and Parent Teacher Association appointed a committee of nine prominent citizens, six whites and three blacks, to recommend solutions to the crisis. "The focal point of the single factor most discussed was the problem of symbols," specifically Confederate symbols, the committee reported in July. The investigation found that the only school symbol adopted officially was the name Rebels. Accordingly, the committee recommended that the Rebels name be retained and that "Dixie" continue to be played, but no more than any other song, and that use of the Confederate flag be discontinued. The school board quickly adopted those recommendations. The regulation was phrased very broadly and stated that "all displays of the [Confederate] Flag and Soldier are removed from the school premises and cannot be used in any display where Brainerd is involved." The school implemented that regulation successfully beginning with the 1970 school year.[17] Beyond this prohibition of Confederate symbols as officially sponsored school symbols, the school board authorized principals to devise codes of conduct for their schools. The code adopted for Brainerd specified that "provocative symbols on clothing will not be allowed."

Rod Melton was among many white students who protested the new policies. On September 9, 1970, the school suspended Melton when he refused to remove a three-by-five-inch Confederate flag patch from his jacket. Students and adults rallied to Melton's cause. A group of forty white male students gathered along a road flying flags and singing "Dixie." Anticipating arguments commonly made in the 1990s, they accused the school of promoting a double standard: "If Negroes can wear Afro hair styles and black fists on shirts to school, I don't see why we cannot wear our flag."[18]

Melton's parents brought a suit against the school board contending that the suspensions violated his First and Fourteenth Amendment rights. The U.S. District Court judge agreed that the school code prohibiting "provocative symbols" was indeed too broad and unconstitutional, but ruled that the prohibition of Confederate flag symbols was prudent and constitutionally valid. The prohibition on flags did not rely upon the validity of the code but on the justifiable limitation of free speech based on the landmark "clear and present danger" test. The judge distinguished the

Melton case from the landmark 1968 decision *(Tinker v. Des Moines Independent Community School District)*, which struck down a regulation prohibiting students from wearing symbolic black armbands in protest of the war in Vietnam. The judge in the *Tinker* case ruled that there was no reason to expect that wearing armbands would affect in any way school operations, and *Tinker* in effect became a test for the abridgment of free speech rights in school settings.[19]

In contrast, the judge in the *Melton* case noted that the "substantial disorder at Brainerd High School" in 1969–1970 "had centered around the use of the Confederate flag as a school symbol, and that the school officials had every right to anticipate that a tense racial situation continued to exist as of the opening of the school in September 1970." The school's prohibition of private display of the flag was based on a clear and present danger, not on disapproval of the symbol or a desire to "avoid the discomfort and unpleasantness that often accompany a controversial viewpoint."[20]

Much of the argument in the *Melton* case concerned the nature of the Confederate flag symbol and whether or not its display should be regarded as disruptive or offensive. Rod Melton's lawyer contended that the flag was a symbol of bravery and honor, not racism. The black students who so vigorously and wrongly denounced and attacked the flag were to blame for the troubles, he argued, and the school board was an accessory for its failure, in the words of the judge, to "educate black students to the true meaning of the Confederate flag." Attorneys for the defense countered by underscoring the clear relationship between the flag and racial strife in the school and by offering evidence of Rod Melton's racist attitudes. For instance, during the 1969–1970 school year, Melton had been suspended for wearing clothing bearing a cross and the letters KKK. Without commenting on the meaning of the Confederate flag itself, the District Court and, subsequently, the Federal Court of Appeals, Sixth Circuit, rejected the portrayal of the flag and Rod Melton as victims.[21]

The Louisiana, Muncie, Pensacola, and *Melton* cases represented a distinct era in the history of the Confederate flag as an issue in American public schools. Influencing all of these decisions was the often traumatic process of desegregating schools and the symbolic role that the Confederate flag played in that process. The flag was sometimes a cause of interracial friction because it was used as a symbol of resistance to desegregation. But the flag was also a cause of disruption because of the divergent perception by black and white students of its meaning. Black students contended that Confederate symbols, especially when officially sanctioned, undermined the objectives of desegregation. In this they found an ally in the federal court system.

As integration (nominal as it often was) took hold in the South and the North, school officials were more sensitive to the feelings of minority groups and, in deference to them, changed names and symbols, including those unrelated to the Confederacy. A year before Thornton Fractional lost its Confederate flag symbol, the team name of another Chicago area high school was changed from the politically charged Redskins to the Redhawks. As late as 1980, Chicago's Pekin High School changed its team name from Chinks to Dragons. Sensitivity, along with more practical considerations, has prompted even schools which used the Confederate flag as a segregationist symbol to quietly remove Confederate symbols. When writer John Egerton returned to the formerly segregated Hammond Academy in 1988, he found the "rebel" flag gone, "unceremoniously retired," he was told, about 1984 when the financially strapped school began seeking wider pools of donors and applicants. The headmaster of the private McCallie School in Chattanooga, where a Confederate flag had once hung from the rafters in the cafeteria, similarly banned the flag in 1993, citing sensitivity to minority feelings.[22]

Statistical evidence substantiates the decline of Rebel team names and symbols. The 1965–1966 school term in Virginia found eleven high schools named Rebels and one named Confederates. By 1971–1972 four of those school names changed. By 1983 only five schools retained the name Rebels, though Lee-Davis High School's teams were still the Confederates. The students and parents of those schools did not always give up Confederate symbols without a fight. Opened in 1936, Fairfax High School had been the Rebels for decades. In 1978 the students voted to al-ter the flag that the "Johnny Reb" mascot carried from a St. Andrews cross battle flag to a blue and gray flag. In 1986, upon receiving complaints from the parents of black students and acting at the suggestion of the school's minority task force, the principal banned the logo altogether and sent home students who wore Confederate symbols to school. White students brought suit, contending that the ban violated First Amendment rights. The Federal District and Appeals courts supported the school. "A school mascot or symbol bears the stamp of approval of the school itself," explained the appellate court opinion. "Therefore, school authorities are free to disassociate the school from such a symbol because of educational concerns." Despite the court's verdict, students at the affluent, overwhelmingly white school continued to challenge the ban, bringing Confederate flags to school and to football games.[23]

A second wave of school controversies involving both the official use and private display of the Confederate flag began in the mid-1980s. Most of the controversies revolved around the rights of students to wear flag symbols on their clothing—what pundits have dubbed "T-shirt cases." With the violence surrounding integration fading into history, the threat that the flag posed to school order seemed remote. Nevertheless, schools imposed, and courts often upheld, restrictions on display of the flag and other potentially disruptive symbols. A judge in a South Carolina case upheld the suspension of a student who refused to take off a jacket with a flag logo, citing a precedent that schools "have a right to prevent the occurrence of disturbances." Because of earlier disturbances at the school, the Confederate flag was presumed to be an inflammatory symbol. The "zero tolerance" exhibited toward Confederate symbols was also related to the widely publicized crackdowns on weapons and such commonplace drugs as aspirin. The U.S. Supreme Court ruled in several cases that public school students did not have the same free speech rights as adults and that free speech in public schools is balanced by "society's countervailing interest in teaching students the boundaries of socially appropriate behavior."[24]

The courts have upheld the suspension of flag-toting students even when enforcement seemed absurdly heavy-handed. The starkest of these cases was the 1998 suspension of a suburban Wichita, Kansas, middle school student for drawing a picture of a Confederate flag in his notebook. The drawing violated a 1995 school district "Racial Harassment or Intimidation" policy. Even though the school conceded that the student did not harass or intimidate anyone with the flag sketch, the court ruled that "school officials had evidence that possession and display of Confederate flag images would likely lead to material and substantial disruption of school discipline, and were not required to wait to take action until such disruption occurred." The 1995 policy specifically prohibited "Confederate flags or articles" along with Ku Klux Klan, Aryan Nation White Supremacy, and Black Power items. The school district adopted it following a series of racial incidents at the high school, including at least one fight over a headband with the Confederate flag design. The suspended student claimed that he had not been informed adequately of the policy, but he had in fact been suspended in late 1995 for using a racial slur and investigated for a second incident in 1998. The issue in the case, the court decided, was not free speech but "a question of the appropriate discipline for a student's willful violation of a school policy." A contemporaneous case in Florida, in which a student was suspended for showing a 4″ × 4″ Confederate flag at lunch, also ended with the courts deferring to school officials.[25]

Aided by libertarians and Confederate heritage groups, students and parents have often fought back and won. The 1991 triumph of the Rebel Support Group in Duncan, South Carolina, was part of a growing trend. When students at Chewning Junior High School in Durham, North Carolina, wore Confederate flag emblems to school on what they declared as Southern Pride Day, school officials decided to stop the unauthorized demonstration at the school house door. School officials detained and suspended fourteen students and fired bus drivers who were in complicity with the students. The suspended students enlisted the assistance of the American Civil Liberties Union and negotiated an out-of-court settlement in August 1989. The school agreed to revise its dress code in accordance with the "disruption" test established by the *Tinker* decision and to hold a series of student assemblies to discuss the issue.[26]

Victories came primarily in cases settled out of court because school districts could not or did not want to afford the legal battles. In 2001 an out-of-court settlement at Varina High School in a Richmond, Virginia, suburb restored a suspended student, expunged his record, paid his legal fees, and convened a student assembly to discuss the meaning of Confederate symbols. In 1996 suspended students in Blackville, South Carolina, won a $5,000 out-of-court settlement that also allowed them to wear their Confederate flag T-shirts to school. Lawyers from the Virginia-based Rutherford Institute handled the Varina case, while the North Carolina–based Southern Legal Resources Center (SLRC) provided legal support for the Blackville students. The SLRC also won the case of a Kentucky student who had been suspended for wearing a T-shirt with an image of Hank Williams, Jr., emblazoned on a Confederate battle flag.[27]

A recurring theme in school flag disputes since 1990 has been the defense of the Confederate flag in the name of cultural parity. With the widespread observance of February as Black History Month in public school systems throughout the nation, white students and their parents sometimes chafed at the apparent hypocrisy of not allowing symbols of "Southern [that is, white southern] Heritage." White backlash against Black History Month was one cause of friction at Byrnes High School and in other school cases. Significantly, even when defense of the Confederate flag has not been an immediate issue, white students have often flaunted the flag symbol as a gesture of contempt for African-American symbols. In rural Amelia County, Virginia, in 1995 a few white students wore Confederate flags on their clothing to protest a black teacher who wore an African-inspired head dress during Black History Month. To the distress of the entire community, the Ku Klux Klan exploited the symbolic showdown to pass out recruiting literature.[28]

A more common scenario for disputes between white and black symbols involved the enormously popular "X" clothing based on Spike Lee's 1992 film about the life of black activist Malcolm X. In a typical incident, when parents in Blackville, South Carolina, filed suit against the school district for suspending students for wearing battle flag T-shirts, they accused the schools of a double standard. The school district dress code prohibited "distasteful or disruptive display of symbols, patches or writing on wearing apparel." The plaintiffs contended that, despite the policy, black students were allowed to wear Malcolm X shirts and "Afro-American solidarity flags and slogans, some of which may be offensive to white students." A white student suspended for showing a small battle flag at Pine Ridge High School in Volusia, Florida, noted that other students were allowed to wear Malcolm X shirts or shirts bearing the flags of other countries. His friends in a self-styled "Hick Corner" complained that Puerto Rican students were able to wear flags on their shirts without punishment. After receiving complaints from white students about Malcolm X T-shirts, a suburban Richmond, Virginia, middle school adopted an informal policy that discouraged students from wearing both the Malcolm X and the Confederate flag. School officials defused the situation with an assembly to discuss "the importance of tolerance and mutual understanding" and effectively lifted the informal prohibition.[29]

The ironic juxtaposition of the St. Andrews cross on the battle flag and the X of Malcolm X epitomized the state of the flag debate in schools at the end of the twentieth century. On the one hand, the two symbols spoke to a racially polarized America. Each X commanded respect within its respective subculture and carried a hostile and aggressive message to those outside. But, on the other hand, the coexistence of the two Xs suggested the possibility of mutual tolerance, though not necessarily of mutual understanding. T-shirts marketed to southern heritage groups featured the distinctively shaped Malcolm X logo with the colors and stars of the Confederate battle flag. A variation on that theme bore the legend "You have your 'X' and I have mine." The slogan offered a pithy summary of the attitudes underlying the second wave of public school flag flaps.[30]

"The bitterest battleground in this war against Confederate Heritage is in our schools," noted a 2001 brochure soliciting funds for Confederate heritage defense. "Posturing or paranoid school officials routinely expel or 'discipline' students who attempt to express pride in their heritage by wearing or displaying Confederate symbols."[31] The public schools may not be the bitterest battleground (the state flag and state capitol flags probably deserve that designation), but they are certainly the most fought over ground. The racial integration of public schools brought into contact and conflict different perceptions, feelings, and family traditions with respect to Confederate flags. Students and their parents look to the schools to confirm or, at least, not to denigrate those perceptions and feelings.

Constitutionally, Confederate symbols are almost incidental to larger school controversies that turn often on questions of authority and discipline. Practically and constitutionally, public schools are permitted to subordinate free speech to order. The effect is to deny Confederate symbols the benefit of the doubt and to empower those (primarily African Americans) who perceive Confederate symbols as inherently racist and threatening. Complaints and reactions against Confederate symbols threaten a school's learning environment and mandate the removal of the provocation. One judicial principle underlying court decisions about flags in schools is that schools "have a duty to prevent the occurrence of disturbances." At least one judge has remarked that Confederate symbols virtually by definition cause "dissension and disruption" and that school officials do not need to wait for a disturbance to act against such symbols.[32] Based largely on the demonstrable record of the flag's association with racist statements and gestures, this presumption of guilt toward the Confederate flag has provoked an increasingly effective backlash in defense of the flag.

Viewed from the wider perspective of the Confederate flag's history, the school T-shirt cases represent an ironic twist. Although students sometimes wear shirts bearing the legend "Heritage, Not Hate," their shirts have often been of the biker or redneck variety, featuring death's heads and country music or rock 'n' roll icons. These shirts are the very kind that earlier generations of white southerners defined as desecration of a sacred symbol. The "slack-jawed juveniles" whom southern editors reviled for waving and wearing the flag as they taunted civil rights activists in the 1960s have become the patriotic Confederate martyrs of the 1990s and beyond.

Chapter 11

"If They Talk about Diversity, They're Gonna Get It"

College students were the primary agents for transforming the battle flag into a popular culture symbol in the late 1940s and have since been among the most frequent casual users of the flag—waving it at sporting events and hanging it on dormitory walls. But in the decades since the 1960s, America's colleges and universities, for pragmatic and ideological reasons, have been among the institutions most sensitive to the flag's racial connotations. Traditions of flag use and of free speech have come up against an intolerance of so-called offensive symbols and language and sparked numerous flag wars on campuses throughout the country. As in the secondary schools, the wars have tended to be of two basic varieties: controversies over officially sanctioned Confederate school symbols and over the rights of individuals to display Confederate symbols on school property or at school functions.

The Confederate flag became part of the fabric of campus life in the mid-1950s. Southern college yearbooks and newspapers were filled with photographs of students with flags at parties and sporting events and on their automobiles. This collegiate adoption of the flag occurred not only at Ole Miss and the universities of Virginia and North Carolina but at smaller schools throughout the South. Walker College in Jasper, Alabama, for instance, named its yearbook *Stars and Bars* and featured an embossed battle flag on the cover of the 1956–1957 issue.[1]

Kappa Alpha fraternity's Old South celebrations were at their zenith and featured the battle flag in elaborately choreographed "secessions" from the Union and other stunts carried out with playful allusions to Old South history. Even with no black students on campus, the flag's users surrounded it with race-conscious imagery and language. The Kappa Alpha entry in the 1959 University of Alabama yearbook, for example, pronounced the fraternity's members the "best cotton pickin'" men on campus. "As our 'slaves' mix our next mint juleps, we look forward to this present year with great expectations and know that the past year will always be remembered as another successful year for the Confederacy of the Kappa Alpha Order." The 1960 Kappa Alpha page drew a picture of an embattled Old South: "Solely surviving among the smoldering ruins of Southern Culture, impervious to the hordes of invading carpetbaggers, loud in the praise of the South, feverishly clinging to the last foothold against the NAACP, we press onward in the seventy-fourth year of Kappa Alpha on the university campus."[2]

Even if intended facetiously, such rhetoric is shocking to the modern reader. It reveals clearly that students who used and revered the flag perceived it in racial terms and used it to emphasize continuity between the antebellum South, Civil War history, and the region's latter-day battles. The 1950s rituals of flag use were perhaps expressions of white pride and support for segregation; at the very least, they were manifestations of the symbolic and ideological environment that flourished in segregated schools. Not surprisingly, Confederate symbols and the rituals surrounding them met with different receptions after integration took hold in the late 1960s.

Assaults, sometimes literal, against display of the Confederate battle flag at colleges began by the late 1960s. An African-American magazine in 1969 described a widespread but uncoordinated "black anti-Confederacy rebellion" on college campuses, which sought to purge the flag, "Dixie," and the Rebel nickname from intercollegiate athletics. The president of the University of Miami took away a flag from white students who allegedly waved it in the faces of black fans. Black students at the University of Texas at Arlington ripped down flags and burned them as they fought off white students defending the flag. A group of students, led primarily by a few white "liberals," demanded that the university president ban the flag at athletic events. At the University of South Carolina, the Association of Afro-American Students asked permission to burn a Confederate flag on campus and, when the administration denied permission, requested an administrative investigation of the flag and "Dixie" at the university. Declaring that "meaningless dialogue has ended and now action begins," the radical group AWARE burned a Confederate flag on Lincoln's birthday in 1969. This incident, which led to desecration charges against AWARE president Brett Bursey, provoked a week of pro-flag demonstrations and a confrontation between pro-flag and anti-flag students. "At one point, several costumed white females paraded a car carrying a black-faced 'corpse' dressed with a Confederate flag." An editorial in the student newspaper predicted confidently that the flag could never be banned from campus—that doing so would be as absurd as putting up "No Smoking" signs in classrooms. Nine months later, black students at Clemson University (also in South Carolina) requested that the school not use Confederate flags or play "Dixie" at football games. The Student Senate instead passed a resolution supporting "Dixie" and the flag at all university functions.[3]

A similar incident occurred in 1971 at the University of Virginia, one of the schools first associated with the flag. Black students were incensed at seeing a group of white students waving a large Confederate banner. UVA had a black quarterback and several other black players. Jack Gravely, a law student who later became president of the Virginia State Conference of the NAACP, explained that the black students believed that "black students should not have to play against the back drop of that flag." After their request to cease waving the flag was spurned, the black students confronted the flag wavers. The flag was toppled during a shoving match, which university police broke up. Seeing the flag at the game "evoked a lot of bad memories, memories I wanted to forget," said third-year law student Leonard L. McCants. "We always looked out for a car or pickup truck with a Confederate flag because we knew the flag meant trouble," McCants remembered. "We knew that inevitably a rock or bottle would be thrown or a gun shot off in our direction."[4]

As at UT Arlington, black students at UVA followed the confrontation with a formal protest to the university. While UVA was no longer among the schools most closely associated with the Confederate flag, the flag was still prominent on fraternity row and at sporting events. The Black Student Alliance was able to link the continued display of the flag with other alleged examples of campus racism, such as the exclusion of black students from an open fraternity party.[5]

The university had earlier agreed to ban the playing of "Dixie" at football games and again proved responsive to the black student demands. Within a week of the football game brawl, the university athletic department announced that henceforth at all campus sporting events students could wave only U.S. flags, Virginia flags, and pennants representing UVA and its opponents. Students vowed to challenge the ban, and the American Civil Liberties Union offered legal assistance. An instructor in the university's ROTC program filed a suit alleging violation of his First and Fourteenth Amendment rights as well as rights under the Virginia Constitution. Before the case had a chance to be heard in court, the university asked state Attorney General Andrew Miller for an opinion. Miller advised the university that the ban was an unconstitutional infringement on free speech rights and would not hold up in court. The university immediately rescinded the ban and dropped charges against five students who had violated it by displaying a protest banner at a football game.[6]

In subsequent decades, administrators at schools where the Confederate flag had enjoyed the status of an unofficial school symbol often agreed to or initiated restrictions on flag use. Responsive to the sensitivities of the growing black populations on campus, university officials at even the most conservative schools in the country debated the continued use of the flag.

Among those schools were the nation's last two state-supported military colleges: the Citadel in Charleston, South Carolina, and Virginia Military Institute in Lexington. Both schools celebrated the contributions of their cadets to the Confederate army during the Civil War. In 1971 Christopher Lewis, one of the first African-American students at the Citadel, protested the school's use of a Confederate flag on parade and at sporting events. He designed and carried what he called an "anti-flag flag" featuring a black fist grasping a Confederate flag. Although threatened with violation of the state's flag desecration law, Lewis won his point and the school temporarily ceased using the Confederate flag in official ceremonies. Flag use resumed, however, after Lewis left the school.[7]

Twenty years later, a Citadel cadet argued to a committee investigating racism on campus that the Confederate flag had no legitimate connection with the school, and the committee recommended that the school stop using the flag and playing "Dixie" at sporting events. Agreeing that there was "no legitimate tie" between the Citadel and the flag, the committee declared the flag "one of the most sensitive and divisive issues related to race relations" on campus. The student who brought the complaint asserted that one-third of the students he polled found the flag offensive. The committee's survey, however, found a sharp racial division over the flag: ninety-one percent of the white students believed the flag should be used at football games, while only ten percent of the black students (who constituted seven percent of the student body) agreed. The college administration, however, disregarded the committee's recommendation and instead urged cadets to be sensitive to blacks' perception of the flag.[8]

Although steeped in Confederate history, VMI began de-emphasizing Confederate symbolism when it first admitted black cadets in 1968. The defining moment in the school's history was the participation of the cadets in the nearby Battle of New Market in May 1864. A solemn ceremony honoring the ten cadets who died in the battle once included the playing of "Dixie" and the decoration of the New Market cadets' graves with battle flags. The school ceased playing "Dixie" and placing the flags in the 1970s. A last vestige of the flag's presence was its inclusion on class rings—the design of which was left to each class. The class ring of 1867 included a flag. The flag became a virtual fixture after 1940: thirty-seven of the subsequent fifty-one classes chose to include the emblem. As the number of black cadets grew (to 80 out of a student body of 1,300 in 1992), the flag became an issue of debate.

The class of 1994 agonized over the issue and finally chose to use the stars and bars, not the battle flag, on a broken staff. The college administration, however, decreed that no Confederate flag could be used on the ring. The flag "is no longer an appropriate symbol because of the confusion it causes as to what's being commemorated," explained Superintendent John W. Knapp, VMI Class of 1954, whose own ring includes a battle flag. Colonel Royce Jones, director of cadet affairs, served on the class of 1955 committee that designed the class ring, which featured a battle flag. "It was never an issue because nobody seemed to care back then, and a lot of us care now."[9]

The pressure to cease public display of Confederate flags especially affected the collegiate organization most directly associated with the flag—the Kappa Alpha Order. Founded in 1865 at the college of which Robert E. Lee was then president, Kappa Alpha steeped itself in the lore of the Old South. Officials of the fraternity believed, not unreasonably, that Kappa Alphans' use of the flag had been the cause of the early-1950s flag fad, and, accordingly, they took the lead in discouraging members from using the flag. The 1951 statement of policy issued by the Kappa Alpha national office was merely a "request" to members, and many Kappa Alphans continued to use the flag. The 1966 prohibition on flag use applied only to chapters in Virginia.

But in the wake of the late 1960s campus flag battles, the order in 1972 passed (and amended in 1978) a regulation reminding Kappa Alphans that the Confederate battle flag was not and never had been the flag of the fraternity. The regulation left flag use to members' discretion, "so long as the display is in good taste and not expressly prohibited by the administration of the respective educational institutions." Concerned for the order's public image but also reluctant to dictate to its chapters, Kappa Alpha in 1991 objectively explained why the growing multiculturalism movement on college campuses often ensnared KA chapters in controversies, and the leadership advised chapters on how to avoid such controversies. Some chapters, KA leaders suggested, had made the difficult decision to cease display of Confederate flags. "As gentlemen, they realized their actions did truly offend their accusers and therefore obscured the principles for which the chapter really stands."[10]

As the Executive Office warned, Kappa Alpha chapters that nevertheless continued to use the flag in the 1980s and 1990s often found themselves at the center of controversies. When these protests occurred, the chapters typically deferred and ceased using the flag in public. At the request of university officials and of national officers, the Kappa Alpha chapter of Jacksonville (Alabama) State University voted forty-one to three to cease using the flag and wearing Confederate uniforms during its annual Old South parade.[11]

Protest by black students ended the conspicuous use of the flag by the Kappa Alpha chapter at Auburn University. Acceding to these students' demands, Auburn's president asked the Kappa Alphans to remove their twenty-by-forty-foot flag from their fraternity house in 1985; however, he did allow them to replace it with a five-by-seven version. Seven years later, the Black Student Union protested the use of the flag in KA's Old South parade through the streets of Auburn. KA leaders agreed not to use the flag in the 1992 parade. Confederate flags nevertheless proliferated along College Street, as other students and city residents demonstrated their displeasure at the exclusion of the flag. The parade degenerated into an angry confrontation between black students, who burned a Confederate flag, and flag-carrying white fraternity men.[12]

While denying that the parade was intended to celebrate racism and slavery, the Auburn Kappa Alpha chapter in 1993 agreed to cancel the Old South parade altogether. Black students applauded the decision, but others saw in the Kappa Alpha parade a symptom of the times. "The ideas of the South may not be 'politically correct' in today's world of liberal pinko-liberalist minority sympathizers, but the African-American keeps getting their way, forcing whites to give in to their demands or else they say we are racists," wrote one student in disgust.[13]

As the century ended, universities and their communities grew even more sensitive to and less tolerant of Confederate flag use by Kappa Alpha. In early 2001 the fraternity was compelled to close three chapters because of credible complaints about alcohol violations, violations of university codes, and racial insensitivity. Kappa Alpha's national leadership escalated its own long-standing effort to wean its members from the battle flag, appealing to Kappa Alphans not to tether the order and its symbolism to such a controversial emblem. At its 2001 annual convention, Kappa Alpha voted unequivocally to prohibit display of the Confederate battle flag by its chapters.[14]

The institution most closely associated with the flag, the University of Mississippi, has endured the longest-running and most divisive debate over its quasi-official symbolism. The association between the school and the flag began in 1948 and flourished during the school's football glory years as well as its nadir—the 1962 riots in resistance to the admission of James Meredith and the mean-spirited newsletters of the Rebel Underground. And while artist G. Ray Kerciu drew the clear link between the flag and rabid racism, the flag survived as Ole Miss's unofficial symbol.[15] Generations of Ole Miss students clung tenaciously to the Confederate flag tradition—if the fifteen years before 1963 were enough time to establish a tradition—in the face of racial integration, intense scrutiny and pressure from the outside world, and escalating pressures from university administrators, coaches, and band directors.

Challenges to the flag began as black students established a presence on campus. In early 1970, as part of a larger protest against the lack of black professors, courses, and athletes, black students burned a Confederate flag in the cafeteria and demanded "the immediate curtailment [sic] of the uses of the Confederate flag as a booster symbol of the campus."[16] Although the flag proved a transient issue in 1970, it was rarely out of the university headlines during the 1982–1983 term.

The events of 1982–1983 escalated from an act of conscience by an African-American, John Hawkins. When he became the first black student elected to the varsity cheerleading team, Hawkins declared his election a symbol of a "new age" for the university. He also stated that he would not follow tradition and carry the Confederate flag onto the football field. Hawkins asserted that the flag did not represent him and many other students and should not be used as an official school symbol. A few white cheerleaders expressed resentment at Hawkins's refusal to carry the flag and saw it as part of a purge of the school's Confederate symbols. "They've taken away the Rebel uniform and they've taken away Traveller; what are they going to take away next?" complained one cheerleader. "When are we going to cease to be the Rebels anymore?"[17]

The flag controversy coincided with the twentieth anniversary observation of the episode that university officials continued to refer to as "The Crisis"—the riots against the admission of James Meredith in 1962. The anniversary occasioned statements of optimism about the university's progress. The student editor of the *Daily Mississippian* observed that "we must have come a long way in race relations in Mississippi if the biggest problem we have to address these days is who waves what flag at a football game."[18] James Meredith, however, dissented from that optimistic interpretation of the flag issue. On the eve of his anniversary visit, Meredith threatened to enlist the assistance of the NAACP Legal Defense Fund and bring suit against the university if it did not abandon the Confederate flag, "Dixie," and Colonel Rebel by the 1983–84 school year. Those symbols, he wrote, were "no different from the segregation symbols of the '60s like 'White Only' and 'Move to the Back of the Bus.'" He reiterated his threat in an address to a Black Alumni Reunion. Blacks cheered and whites booed; thirty to fifty of the latter walked out.[19]

As if determined to reprise every facet of the 1962 crisis, local Ku Klux Klansmen came to the defense of the Confederate battle flag. The students were not doing enough to defend the flag, asserted Klansman Gordon Galle, so the Klan would. Over the objections of university officials, twenty-nine Klansmen marched through the streets of Oxford, carrying Confederate flags. "The Rebel flag is more sacred than anything else in the world," Galle said during the march. "Destroy it and the American flag will soon go." Galle also said that black Americans should go back to Africa.[20]

University of Mississippi chancellor Porter Fortune said that the administration would announce its official policy on the Confederate flag in

May. Student leaders, not wanting to have a policy dictated to them, acted first. On April 12, the Associated Student Body Senate passed by voice vote "A Resolution to Retain Ole Miss Tradition." With rhetoric often more poetic than analytical, the resolution argued that the Confederate flag, "Dixie," and Colonel Rebel did not carry racist meaning as they were used by Ole Miss students, that the student body condemned the usurpation of the symbols by racist groups, but that those groups had also usurped such symbols as the U.S. flag. If the retention of Confederate symbols was responsible for "lags in recruitment of students and student athletes," then people who judge a university by such symbols "are very shallow people indeed." The senate resolved that "The Confederate flag, Colonel Rebel and 'Dixie' remain our endeared tradition until the stones crumble from the buildings and Ole Miss is a mere whisper in history." Belligerently asserting that the voice of students "will not be disregarded on this issue," the senate submitted "that a University which betrays its traditions is a University not worth the respect of its students, prospective students, or former students." Black Student Union President Lydia E. Spragin ridiculed the senate's emphasis on defending tradition, reminding students that slavery and "Jim Crow" had also been "traditions."[21]

A week after the passage of the senate resolution, the editor of the university yearbook decided to include photographs of the October Klan march through Oxford. The purpose of the photographs, he explained, was to illustrate graphically why black students like John Hawkins found the flag offensive. BSU president Spragin denounced this decision. The BSU also presented a slate of demands to the state college board president, four of which asked for the banning of the school's "racist" symbols. The demands elicited a predictable response. "Ms. Spragin, the racial atmosphere of Ole Miss was a blissful one until someone decided that a piece of cloth stood for an attitude that prevailed 20 years ago," wrote a student in response to her guest column in the student paper.[22]

An unconfirmed rumor circulated that black students were planning to stage a protest march against the yearbook—or even to seize and burn the yearbooks—which brought the campus to the brink of riot. At dusk on Monday, April 18, 1,500 students, mostly fraternity men carrying Confederate flags, gathered at the center of campus. Chanting "We want Hawkins" and "We want Porter [Fortune]," the students imitated their predecessors of 1962 and raised a Confederate flag on the pole outside the Lyceum building. The mob marched to the building where the BSU meeting was to occur and chanted "We want Lydia" and "We want Hawkins." Confronted by university police, the crowd dispersed after an hour and a half.[23]

The mob scene frightened many students. An editor of the student paper issued a "call to reason. Has everyone forgotten that [the riot of 1962] ended with 30,000 federal troops being called in because of something similar to what took place last night?" she asked. Unconsciously echoing the points made by the 1963 paintings by Kerciu, assistant sports editor Alan Schmidt concluded that "the racial epithets the 'save the flag' group yelled last Monday night have succeeded in associating the Rebel flag and the university with racism, no matter what the case may have been before." Describing the turmoil as "dangerously reminiscent of 1962," a group of "concerned student leaders" counseled "self-control" and recommended that the university cease purchasing and distributing Confederate flags at sporting events.[24]

The university administration reached the same conclusion. Chancellor Fortune tried to find a middle ground that neither gave in to the pro-flag pressure nor punished the flag for the excesses of the demonstrators. The Confederate flag, Fortune announced, was not among the seven officially recognized school symbols. Officials were no longer to use the flag as a school symbol, and the university would no longer purchase or hand out flags at university events. The university would not, however, try to prevent students from bringing flags to games, nor would it instruct the bookstore to stop selling flags.[25]

Reaction in the university community was predictably diverse. Alumni and pro-flag students worried that the policy was another step toward the abolition of school traditions. Resenting the ability of seven percent of the student body to "dictate" to the ninety-three percent, they vowed to wave the flag even more. The BSU denounced what it considered to be a minor restriction on flag use, as well as the university's failure to ban "Dixie" and Colonel Rebel. The faculty senate passed a resolution endorsing the chancellor's policy and urged him to "take all other actions necessary to foster the spirit and substance of racial harmony" at Ole Miss.[26]

As hardcore flag defenders had warned, subsequent years saw the university administration further dissociate the school from Confederate symbols. In December 1989 the university officially adopted a new school flag designed by the senior class. The "Battle M Flag" was essentially the Confederate battle flag but with a star-studded blue M replacing the St. Andrew's cross. The Black Student Union endorsed the new flag, and in 1991 the faculty senate endorsed unanimously an alumni association resolution asking that fans not bring Confederate flags to sporting events. But the new symbols failed to win the support of the students, who waved the Confederate flag with more passion than before. The officially sanctioned Battle M flag was, remarked an Ole Miss professor, "a brilliant, Madison Avenue repackaging of the 'look' of the Confederate flag . . . yet emptied of all content, historical, regional and personal." Little wonder then that the Battle M drowned in a sea of Confederate battle flags at football games.[27]

Flare-ups over the flag continued to bring the university unwanted publicity throughout the 1990s. "Somehow we need to ferret out things that are southern from those that are Confederate," Chancellor R. Gerald Turner explained. The school's image and its ability to recruit black athletes prompted renewed pressure to purge the flag in 1997. A new chancellor, Robert C. Khayat, commissioned a study of the school's image, which stimulated a "divisive discussion about symbols and mascots." Khayat, an Ole Miss football hero from the school's late 1950s championship team, supported the effort of football coach Tommy Tuberville to mute the flag's presence at sporting events. Tuberville asked students not to bring flags to the September 27, 1997, home game against Vanderbilt. Predictably, the student section was flooded with flags. When the team went on the road to play the University of Tennessee, members of the SCV in Knoxville handed out eight hundred Confederate flags to Ole Miss and UT fans alike, making for an impressive show of white support for the embattled banner. The administration's "Plan B" was to impose a "stick ban," prohibiting flags on sticks from the stadium—a rule ostensibly intended as a safety measure (similar to an extant rule forbidding umbrellas). Already in place was a regulation forbidding flags larger than twelve-by-fourteen inches. Federal courts subsequently upheld the stick ban.[28]

A month later, after the Vanderbilt game, the Ole Miss student government followed the lead of the administration and the alumni association and formally dissociated the school from the Confederate flag. After a probing debate, the student senate adopted by a 97–17 vote a resolution asking students to "do what will be the most beneficial for the advancement of the University of Mississippi and refrain from waving the Confederate flag at Ole Miss athletic events." Few flags have appeared at football games in the years since.[29]

The slow death of officially sanctioned Confederate symbols at Ole Miss dramatized the demographic and ideological forces that made college campuses hostile environments for the Confederate flag. The continuing Ole Miss drama also revealed a truism about flag controversies: the fastest way to rally people behind a symbol is to attack it. Even without university support, Ole Miss students waved the flag and proclaimed with all sincerity that their motives were school spirit and "heritage"— southern and school. At Ole Miss, as elsewhere around the country, the Confederate flag became ultimately an issue of individual rights and free speech. In the late 1980s and 1990s that issue again became a contentious one at America's colleges and universities.

Free speech of course had been a major issue on American campuses—and in relation to the Confederate flag—in the 1960s and 1970s. But by the late 1980s, a resurgence of racist attacks and overt racial slurs on American campuses, coupled with a stronger black presence, convinced many in academia that codes restricting and punishing "hate speech" were necessary. A major component of the "political correctness" debate, the hate speech issue convulsed higher education in America. By 1990 at least a dozen colleges and universities had adopted codes proscribing hate speech.[30]

The case for restricting some forms of speech rested on the assumption that unrestrained free speech made traditionally white campuses un-friendly environments for blacks, minorities, and women. Merely deny-ing racist intent did not lessen the racism of acts or forms of speech which blacks perceived as racist. "If we understand the necessity of elimi-nating the signs and symbols that signal the inferiority of African-Ameri-cans," one legal scholar reasoned, "then we should hesitate before pro-claiming that all racist speech which stops short of physical violence must be defended."[31]

Such reasoning made the Confederate battle flag an obvious potential target for campus hate speech codes. Declared by a federal judge to be a virtual symbol of the white resistance to school desegregation, the battle flag was widely regarded as signaling the bearer's belief in the inferiority of blacks. Polls taken in the 1990s suggested that the most highly edu-cated Americans are more likely than others to perceive the flag as a ra-cial symbol.[32]

Campus speech codes did not mention the Confederate flag by name; but given the common assumption in academic circles that the flag is an inherently racist symbol, the flag was clearly among the intended targets of hate speech restrictions. The University of Michigan implemented a policy in 1988 which regarded flags as forms of prohibited harassment. The university issued a guidebook to students interpreting its code on flag use. The guidebook told students that they would be in violation of the code if "you display a confederate flag on the door of your room in the residence hall." Faced with a lawsuit challenging its speech code, the university contended that the guidebook had been withdrawn and should not be considered in the case. The district court disagreed. The Michigan code was one of the first to be challenged and invalidated for being overbroad in language.[33]

Hate speech codes, like affirmative action in employment and sensitiv-ity to black concerns in the wider society, engendered a kind of backlash on campus. The codes were explicitly intended to make members of the university community more aware of the unintended effects of their ac-tions—the way others perceived them as well as the way they intended them. As a consequence, the codes punished acts that the actors did not consider racist or sexist. Inevitably, many people resented and rejected this exercise in "re-education" and lashed out at what one scholar denounced as the new "thought police" of the 1990s.[34]

The typical battleground for campus controversies over display of the Confederate flag was the residence hall, where the line between individual expression and community symbols became blurred. In the fall of 1993 a senior at North Carolina State University displayed a battle flag inside his dormitory room, but students complained to residence hall officials that the flag was visible from the hall when his door was open. Administrators recognized the student's right to display the flag anywhere in his room but "encouraged" him to move it out of public view. After initially complying with the request to move the flag, he eventually exercised his right and moved it back to its original location. Administrators at Hampden-Sydney College, an elite private men's school in Virginia, ordered a Confederate flag removed from the porch of a dormitory. While the school administration insisted that the action was merely an enforcement of a long-standing rule against flag displays, some students detected hostility to the Confederate flag.[35]

In response to an uproar over a student's display of the Confederate flag in 1988, officials at Cornell University in upstate New York prohibited the display of all flags from dormitory windows. The ban was lifted during the 1991 Persian Gulf War after a student faced prosecution for hanging a U.S. flag and yellow ribbon from his window. Students at a Gettysburg College dormitory hung a Confederate flag from a window "in order to improve the bleak facade of our house." The administration asked the students to remove the flag; they did so and issued a somewhat bitter written apology in the student newspaper. Predictably, in the subsequent weeks, the incident provoked denunciations of "censorship" and dark warnings about racism, as well as incredulity that a college steeped in Civil War history would run away from the Confederate flag.[36]

Individuals and groups emerged on campuses (as in the wider society) to combat political correctness and, more specifically, to promote the use and reputation of the Confederate battle flag. Criticism of the flag sent flag sales skyrocketing at local stores in Auburn, Alabama, in 1985 and provoked a pro-flag march at Ole Miss in 1992. At the University of Georgia in Athens, a small group of students in 1986 formed the cunningly named Culture of the South Association (CSA). Echoing explicitly the ideas of the southern agrarians, the CSA dedicated itself to defending and restoring southern symbols and increasing understanding of a traditional southern culture based on values, kinship, and natural and organic community ties.[37]

The most celebrated campus stand in defense of the Confederate flag occurred not in the South but at the institution considered the very soul of Yankeedom and the polar opposite of Ole Miss: Harvard University. The flap was provoked by a self-declared militant southerner who said she wanted to expose the limits of Harvard's liberality as well as stimulate constructive dialogue over the meaning of the Confederacy and its symbols. Although Harvard endured unwanted publicity for the alleged intolerance of its students and for political correctness run rampant, the university administration stood firmly for unrestricted free speech, and the university community engaged in an exhaustive dialogue about the Confederate flag. Free speech and display of the flag won the day, but the long debate made clear that for many people outside the South, the flag unquestionably was a symbol of racism and division.[38]

On February 18, 1991, Bridget Kerrigan, a student from suburban Washington, D.C., hung a Confederate flag outside her window in Kirkland House. When she first transferred to Harvard from the University of Virginia in 1989, she had similarly draped a Confederate flag from her window at Peabody Terrace apartments. Apartment regulations compelled her to remove the flag. This time she was determined not to remove the flag, despite community pressures to do so. Though born in the Chicago area, Kerrigan was raised in the South in a household that honored Robert E. Lee and Thomas Jefferson. Asked months later why she hung the flag out of her window at Harvard, Kerrigan responded: "Just to remind me of home. That's all." Displaying the flag was not a simple tribute to her southern roots; it was also a gauntlet thrown down to challenge Harvard's celebrated liberal tradition. "If they talk about diversity, they're gonna get it," Kerrigan said in a widely quoted statement. "If they talk about tolerance, they better be ready to have it."[39]

True to her word, Kerrigan kept the flag in her window for the re-
mainder of the academic year, ignoring demands and numerous demonstrations. The pressure to remove the flag escalated from a meeting of
house residents to a meeting of campus house masters to "eat-ins" at the
Kirkland and Cabot House cafeterias to a silent protest march. Kerrigan
participated in a forum at the Kennedy School of Government, and the
Confederate flag issue dominated the discussions at Harvard University
for a month.[40]

Days after Kerrigan hung her flag, Harvard's dormitory windows became a veritable forum for testing the limits of symbolic free speech. In
sympathy with Kerrigan, a white student from Maine hung a Confederate flag, along with a sign "Racism No," from his window in Cabot
House. He pledged to leave the flag until there was further campus discussion on the rights of white southerners and blacks. More controversial was the decision of Jacinda T. Townsend, a black junior from Kentucky, to hang from her window in Cabot House a sheet painted with a
swastika and the words "Racism No?" Townsend said she wanted to
dramatize that both the swastika and the Confederate flag represented
"genocide" and that neither should be allowed to be displayed publicly on
campus. The Harvard-Radcliffe Black Students Association created a
poster bearing the Confederate flag and taking issue with Kerrigan's interpretation of its meaning: "This is a signifier of white supremacy," the
poster said. "The official flag of a defeated nation born of treason and
financed by inhumanity." Townsend intended her swastika to shock, and
she succeeded. The campus Jewish organization convinced her to remove
the flag but expressed sympathy with Townsend and pledged support in
the effort to remove Kerrigan's flag.[41]

The administration, student government, and the editors of the campus newspaper all remained committed to the principle of free speech
while agreeing with Townsend that the Confederate flag was a reprehen-
sible form of speech. Hanging the Confederate flag outside the dormitory was "insensitive and unwise," wrote University President Derek Bok
in an official statement issued March 12, but it was a form of protected
symbolic speech. Though Harvard, as a private institution, might be able
to restrict speech more than public institutions could, Bok believed that

testing the limits of free speech would prove a distraction from the business of the university. Instead of forcing students to take down flags and banners, Bok urged students "to take more account of the feelings and sensibilities of others." The *Harvard Crimson,* a student-run daily newspaper, urged "censure, not censor," and the undergraduate council voted down a resolution to ask the students to remove flags from their windows.[42]

The official confirmation of free speech was hardly an endorsement of the Confederate flag. In fact, the discussion at Harvard revealed a predilection to believe that the flag was indeed a symbol of racism and hatred not unfairly linked with the swastika. President Bok's statement treated the Confederate flag and the swastika as comparable "offensive" symbols. Students declared the flag the symbol of "a disgraceful and profoundly ugly chapter in American history, the era of slavery" and of "an illegal, immoral cause." A southern-born student sympathized with Kerrigan's regional pride but urged her to find another symbol that was not the symbol of "the South of David Duke, Bull Connor and Jesse Helms."[43]

Resentful of the censure from administration and students, Kerrigan later remarked that Bok "congratulated himself in an open letter for having upheld freedom of speech by tolerating someone like me at Harvard." The experience left her convinced that "the real bigots are the intellectuals—the overeducated, Ivy-league left who tolerate only the ideas that serve their agenda."[44]

At Harvard, where the majority apparently viewed the Confederate flag with hostility, and at the University of Mississippi, where an apparent majority of students revered or defended the flag, the respective flag controversies were related to larger social, political, and ideological issues. Both universities faced criticism that they were unfriendly to African Americans, and the prominent presence of a Confederate battle flag complicated the problems. Both university administrations made clear their disdain for the flag, but both declined to prohibit it altogether. These decisions reflected well upon the tolerance of the two schools, but the decisions were almost inevitable. On college campuses, unlike in public schools, administrators do not have much latitude for trampling free speech. College students are assumed to have the maturity to exercise free speech without causing disruption that undermines the educational mission of their school. Furthermore, colleges and universities cultivate reputations as centers for free expression and exchange of ideas.

In an era marked by so-called political correctness, the Confederate flag emerged as one of the most politically incorrect of symbols. The pressure put upon students who display the flag suggests the limits of free speech and the enforcement of orthodoxy. The ability of self-conscious rebels to defy this orthodoxy tests and ultimately vindicates the value of free speech.

The most vexing campus problems and most contentious issues occur at the intersection of free speech and school symbolism. Thousands of football fans waving Confederate flags are obviously a collective expression of individual free speech, but they also make a statement about the school. In a thinly veiled effort to change the school's image, the University of Mississippi succeeded in limiting individual free speech with regulations couched in the language of safety and comfort. Colleges and universities dare not regulate students' T-shirts or what students display *in* their rooms, but what students display *outside* their rooms is another matter. The proscriptions of Confederate flags at Gettysburg College, Hampden-Sydney College, and Cornell University—as well as the window wars at Harvard—all resulted from flags displayed *outside* buildings in public view. Were those flags exercises in free speech or did they assume the status of corporate symbols? A fellow Kirkland House resident of Bridget Kerrigan stated the dilemma succinctly when he complained: "If [the flag] were inside her room, it would be different. But it's not. It's on my house, and I do not want it representing me."[45]

A similar desire not to be represented by Confederate flags provoked the most high profile and contentious flag wars of recent decades. The campaigns to change the state flags of Mississippi and Georgia and take down Confederate flags from the state capitols of Alabama and South Carolina grabbed national headlines for more than a dozen years and helped shape national perception of the battle flag and its defenders.

Chapter 12

"What We Stood For, Will Stand For, and Will Fight For"

In March 1987 the National Association for the Advancement of Colored People (NAACP) concentrated its resources and the nation's attention on four former Confederate states that flew the Confederate battle flag over their capitol buildings or incorporated it into their state flags. The NAACP's Southeast Regional Conference passed a resolution requesting the states of South Carolina and Alabama to remove the Confederate battle flag from their capitol domes and the states of Georgia and Mississippi to remove the battle flag emblem from their state flags. The delegates assembled considered the battle flag "to be a symbol of divisiveness, racial animosity, and an insult to black people throughout the Region" and asserted that in 1865 and again in 1915 the Ku Klux Klan brandished the flag, "thereby establishing the battle flag as a symbol of divisiveness." The NAACP's national office called upon branches throughout the region and nation to circulate petitions, speak out, and "dramatize the NAACP's resolve to remove the Confederate Battle Flags from official use." Although the resolution was based on popular misconceptions about early Klan flag use, it took aim at the most visible and vulnerable examples of publicly sponsored display of the Confederate flag.[1] The resolution established the agenda for more than a decade of sustained efforts—efforts that systematically employed legal, political, and economic tactics to accomplish their objectives.

The motives of each state for embracing the St. Andrew's cross battle flag as part of its official symbolism are murky and open to debate. Georgia, Alabama, and South Carolina did so during the eventful 1950s and 1960s. The coincidence of the Civil War Centennial and the civil rights movement makes it difficult to discern whether the states intended the battle flag as an historical war memorial or as a gesture of defiance to federally mandated integration. With no apparent provocation and no fanfare, Mississippi incorporated the battle flag into the state flag in 1894. The flag change attracted so little attention that officials failed to carry it over into the revised 1906 state code—an oversight that led to the state's brief but intense showdown over the flag ninety-five years later.

The NAACP's campaign to end official use of the flag built upon state legislative initiatives already under way. The ensuing controversies polarized the people of each state into readily identifiable camps: African-American and civil rights groups allied with business leaders and "progressive" political leaders and newspaper editors concerned for their state's image, in opposition to southern heritage organizations and powerful pro-flag political leaders who collectively galvanized the white majority in support of the Confederate flag, aided and embarrassed by right-wing hate groups whose presence fulfilled flag opponents' stereotypes of flag supporters. The controversies invariably featured large demonstrations and angry confrontations at public forums. The tactics that the anti-flag forces employed varied among the states, but in every case straightforward constitutional challenges failed, while legal loopholes and economic pressure pushed open the doors to change. The Confederate flag flying over Alabama's state house was the first of the officially sponsored flags that the NAACP campaign targeted, and it was the first flag to be removed.

The Alabama capitol building was the symbolic center of Alabama's public life and history even after the legislature ceased meeting there in 1985. Built in 1851, a decade later it was the site of Jefferson Davis's inauguration as provisional president of the Confederacy. One hundred years later, Montgomery, the "cradle of the Confederacy," was the cradle of the civil rights movement. Just down the hill and within sight of the capitol building stands the Dexter Avenue Baptist Church, the command center for the 1955–1956 bus boycott that launched the Reverend Martin Luther King, Jr., to national prominence. In 1976 the state began an extensive, $28 million restoration of the capitol building—a project that state officials believed would "usher in a new era for Alabama."[2]

Instead, the capitol became the focus of a rancorous debate over the state's past and future. A Confederate battle flag had flown on the dome since the first term of Governor George Wallace in 1963. Conflicting memories and statements created confusion over when and why the battle flag was placed on the dome, but research by the Alabama Department of Archives & History—including a close examination of photographic evidence—confirmed that the battle flag went up on April 25, 1963, coincident with the visit of U.S. Attorney General Robert F. Kennedy, and remained there afterward. As part of the Civil War Centennial observation, the state had raised a seven-star Stars and Bars on March 4, 1961, one hundred years after Letitia Tyler had raised the prototype on a pole outside the Alabama state (and Confederate) capitol. But according to newspaper accounts and other testimony, that flag remained only a few days.[3]

Although Wallace later claimed to have raised the battle flag as a "tourist gimmick," it was interpreted as a gesture of defiance to the federal government. Wallace's former campaign manager and finance director, Seymore Trammell, later corroborated this interpretation. In a November 1992 letter to the *Montgomery Advertiser,* Trammell denied that the battle flag had flown on the capitol before April 1963 and took full responsibility for raising it when Kennedy visited. "The decision that Gov. Wallace and I made to fly the battle flag that day can only be described as an act of defiance," Trammell wrote. "As finance director I was responsible for the capitol building and grounds and personally gave the order to hoist the battle flag."[4]

The first protests against the battle flag's presence over the capitol arose from its implied assertion of Confederate and state supremacy over federal authority. Before 1961, the Alabama state flag—a red St. Andrew's cross on a white field—flew alone over the capitol while the Assembly was in session. The U.S. flag often flew over the dome between Assembly sessions. After 1963, the state flag and the Confederate battle flag flew together over the dome (with the state flag on top), while the Stars and Stripes was relegated to a pole on the south capitol grounds.[5]

Alvin Holmes, a black Alabama representative, began his eighteen-year crusade against the Confederate battle flag with the initial objective of ending that flag's symbolic ascendancy over the Stars and Stripes. A judge rejected Holmes's 1975 lawsuit contending that the presence of the Confederate flag violated the 1924 United States Flag Code. George Wallace (elected for a non-consecutive fourth term following his 1972 presidential bid and the assassination attempt that left him a paraplegic) soon removed the provocation by ordering that the U.S. flag be raised over the state and Confederate flags. Holmes was satisfied. "We never asked that they remove the Confederate flag," he said, "just place it lower than the American flag."[6]

In 1987, when the NAACP took aim at the battle flag on the state capitol, Holmes's legislative colleague, Thomas L. Reed (D-Tuskegee), took up the cause. One of the first two black Alabama representatives since Reconstruction, Reed had represented Tuskegee since 1970 and was serving his second stint as president of the NAACP Alabama State Conference. On December 29, 1987, Reed issued an ultimatum to Republican Governor Guy Hunt that if he did not remove the flag by the beginning of the legislative session on February 2, 1988, he would scale the construction fence surrounding the capitol building and tear down the flag. The battle flag, Reed argued, was linked too inextricably with historical and contemporary racism to be anything but offensive to blacks. "Atop this citadel of freedom and democracy," Reed wrote about the capitol dome, "it is appropriate to fly only those symbols which are universally accepted by the citizens of our state and our nation." Flaunting his credentials as a southerner, Reed expressed pride in the "ethos or value system which makes southerners special," but asserted that the Confederate flag was not an expression of those values. All those arguments aside, however, the bottom line was that there was no constitutional authority for the battle flag's presence over the capitol.[7]

Reed's ultimatum precipitated a month of brinkmanship that riveted attention on the state and divided Alabamians into pro- and anti-flag factions. One poll showed that a majority of Alabamians (sixty-three percent) supported retaining the flag at the capitol. Not surprisingly, Alabamians were divided along racial lines: seventy-five percent of whites polled supported the flag, while fifty-three percent of blacks opposed it. The *Montgomery Advertiser* received a "remarkable" number of replies to a reader poll published only once. Nearly three-quarters of the 912 respondents favored flying a Confederate flag on the capitol or somewhere on the grounds. The governor's office announced that 267 of 285 telephone calls received supported the flag. Buoyed by popular support, Governor Hunt refused to concede that the Confederate flag was inappropriate as a symbol atop the state capitol. "If I had my druthers," Hunt commented, "I would say, Let's let tolerance go both ways, and let's celebrate Martin Luther King's birthday, and let's let the Confederate flag fly, because those are the two things Alabama is known for, the Confederacy and the civil rights movement." Unless the legislature decided explicitly to remove the flag, Hunt said, he would not remove it himself or allow Reed to remove it.[8]

High noon on February 2 brought a carefully choreographed exhibition of civil disobedience. An estimated two thousand people gathered around the construction site surrounding the capitol building while security forces kept them at bay and a police helicopter hovered overhead. Riot police were on hand in case the much-anticipated event took a violent turn, and indeed the atmosphere was rife with confrontation. A group of flag supporters, the Sons and Daughters of the South, carried signs reading "Save Our Flag," while black college students protesting the flag sang "We Shall Overcome." A group of flag-waving Ku Klux Klansmen tried to drown them out with rebel yells. After a brief address, Reed marched to the chain-link fence and was arrested when he tried to scale it. "We will not rest until that Confederate flag is removed from the top of this dome here in Montgomery, Alabama," Reed declared

defiantly. Thirteen other black legislators and NAACP officials were arrested with him for criminal trespass, charged, and released. Later in the
day, the House of Representatives voted 66–21 to banish to the rules
committee Alvin Holmes's resolution to move the Confederate flag from
the capitol to the nearby First White House of the Confederacy, where
symbols of the Confederacy "would be proper and fitting."[9]

The battle moved back to the courts, where in May 1988 the NAACP
had filed a suit alleging that display of the flag violated the rights of Alabama blacks under the First, Thirteenth, and Fourteenth Amendments
to the Constitution. A federal judge dismissed the suit in February
1989.[10] The Alabama NAACP appealed the case.

When NAACP lawyers made their arguments before a panel of the
U.S. Eleventh Circuit Court of Appeals in October 1989, it was clear
that the judges were skeptical. Judge Frank M. Johnson, the jurist whose
controversial decisions two decades earlier had smoothed the process of
integration in Alabama, asked why the Confederate flag had become offensive in the 1980s when it was not considered so offensive at the height
of the civil rights struggle. "I don't understand why you're here asking
the federal court [to remove the flag] when you could have done it on
your own" by making its removal a precondition for giving Governor
Wallace a fourth term. Johnson also questioned the logic of trying to remove everything that was a "vestige of slavery," as the NAACP deemed
the Confederate flag. "Under that argument, the Capitol itself would be a
vestige of slavery. It's where Jeff Davis was sworn in . . . where the secession resolution was passed." In response to the NAACP's argument that
the Confederate flag is "the Klan flag," another judge asked: "Can Alabama be held accountable for the fact that the Confederate flag was ap-
propriated by a group?" The appeals court in January 1990 upheld the
lower court ruling. Unlike Confederate flags in public schools, the flag
over the capitol was not a direct source of racial tension. "It is unfortunate," the judges concluded, "that the State of Alabama chooses to utilize
its property in a manner that offends a large proportion of its population, but that is a political matter which is not within our province to
decide."[11]

In 1991, when all flags were removed from the capitol dome as it underwent restoration, pressure mounted in favor of a historically ironic compromise. A diversity of groups and individuals, including the Montgomery Chamber of Commerce, Alvin Holmes, and influential members of the United Daughters of the Confederacy and the Sons of Confederate Veterans, urged the state to substitute the historically correct flag—the Stars and Bars—for the battle flag. The president of the (First) White House Association of Alabama claimed that she had been telling state officials since 1973 that the battle flag was historically inaccurate.[12]

A poll commissioned by the Montgomery Chamber of Commerce found strong white support for the flying of a Confederate flag over the capitol (seventy-one percent of whites, twenty-one percent of blacks) but also yielded results which advocates of compromise claimed supported their position. By a margin of two to one, respondents to the poll favored the first national flag over the battle flag. The poll question was, however, rather disingenuous, since it asked respondents whether they preferred the "Naval version of the Confederate Battle Flag which was only flown on warships" or the "historically correct" national flag known as the Stars and Bars. Since most Americans mistakenly call the battle flag the "Stars and Bars" and assumed it was the historically correct flag, this poll seemed calculated to take advantage of popular ignorance of Confederate flags. Rather than indicating support for compromise, the poll really revealed the polarization between white and black Alabamians over the flag issue.[13]

Armed with results of his own poll, which emphasized strong support for the battle flag among white (80 percent) and black (50 percent) Alabamians, Hunt rejected calls for compromise. He also discounted arguments that the flag represented racism. "What some of you in the news media have never understood," Hunt argued, "is that slavery was under the Stars and Stripes many years before you ever had a Confederate flag."[14]

As the political struggle reached a climax, a state court unexpectedly altered the entire calculus. Assisted by the Montgomery-based Southern Poverty Law Center (but without his former ally, Thomas Reed, who had been convicted of bribery and lost his seat in the legislature), Alvin

Holmes shifted his effort from federal courts to state courts and seized upon what the NAACP had noted years earlier to be the "dubious legal reasons and foundations" for the display of the Confederate flag. On January 4, 1993, Alabama Circuit Court Judge William Gordon found for the plaintiff in the case of *Holmes v. Hunt* and permanently enjoined Governor Hunt "from ordering or allowing the hoisting and flying of any flag, other than the state and national flags, over the Capitol dome." The decision was based on the state's 1895 flag law which provided only for the flying of the state and national flags over the dome. Gordon reasoned that, thirty years after the Civil War, if the legislature had wanted to fly an emblem of the Confederacy over the capitol, it would have so specified.[15] By adopting a new state flag that was obviously inspired by the Confederate battle flag in 1895, the Assembly undercut the efforts of the flag's partisans a century later.

The issue was not settled, however. Governor Hunt, the defendant in the case, favored retaining the flag and believed that the majority of Alabamians would rally around it. Hunt hinted at an appeal but wanted to give the legislature an opportunity first to pass a bill putting the flag issue up for statewide referendum. Pro-flag groups rallied in support, and the Sons of Confederate Veterans launched a petition drive to get the issue on the ballot.[16]

The Ku Klux Klan—the group most calculated to undermine the SCV's campaign and to substantiate the worst suspicions about the flag—staged a rally at the capitol a few weeks after the court decision. While a tape player blared "Dixie," Klan leaders hailed the flag as "a racial symbol." "The browning of America is going to completely wipe out the white race," warned the Grand Titan of Florida Klans. "Somewhere we have failed to educate our young and to teach them what this banner really means." They urged the small crowd of onlookers and larger number of reporters and photographers to write their representatives and encourage them to reverse the court decision.[17]

Defenders of the Confederate flag lost their most influential champion on April 22, 1993, when a jury convicted Hunt of violating ethics laws by misusing $200,000 from his inaugural fund. Hunt was forced to resign. As expected, Hunt appealed the state court decision concerning the flag, but he did not remain governor long enough to see the appeal through to its conclusion.

Within days of assuming office, Hunt's replacement, James Folsom, Jr., stated that he would not raise the Confederate flag. Instead, he favored relegating the flag to a pole outside the First White House of the Confederacy, adjacent to the capitol grounds. "This has been a divisive issue in our state, and I believe it is time we put it behind us and move our state forward." On May 11 the governor's office announced that Folsom was dropping Hunt's appeal of the *Holmes* case.[18]

Governor Folsom "made good" on his promise to give Confederate flags a "place of honor" at the state capitol. A committee of private citizens and representatives from several state history agencies decided to erect four poles in a circle around the century-old Confederate monument on the capitol grounds. Three of the poles were for the three Confederate national flags; the fourth pole was to fly one of the patterns of battle flags carried by Alabama regiments. The first of the battle flags to be featured was the Army of Northern Virginia pattern. Associated with the state's continuing efforts to preserve Alabama battle flags, the display was educational as well as memorial. On Confederate Memorial Day (April 26 in Alabama), 250 people (including only one African American, a capitol janitor) gathered to dedicate the flag display. "We honor the men who died in what they saw then as the defense of their homeland," declared Governor Folsom in a carefully measured statement.[19]

Many Alabamians disagreed with Folsom's decision, and more than a decade later diehards continued their campaign to restore the flag to the capitol. A month after Folsom succeeded to the governorship, a poll found that his handling of the flag issue was the only source of popular disapproval. Pro-flag groups started a Confederate Heritage Fund and claimed to have punished Folsom and other "scalawags" at the polls.[20]

The same pattern of Confederate battle flag that flew over Alabama's state house also flew over the South Carolina state house in Columbia. The effort to bring down South Carolina's flag was fought not primarily in the courts but in the legislature and on the streets of Columbia, Charleston, and Myrtle Beach. Appropriately for the state that was the seedbed of southern secessionism, the flag battle in South Carolina was the loudest of them all.

A battle flag officially went up on the dome of the South Carolina state house when the legislature passed a concurrent resolution in March 1962. The previous April, during the Fort Sumter centennial proceedings, Representative John A. "Mr. Confederate" May, who was then serving as chairman of the state's Confederate War Centennial Commission, had arranged for a Confederate flag to be placed with the national and state flags on another part of the state house roof. While the resolution did not mention the Civil War Centennial, it was assumed widely that the centennial was the impetus for the resolution and that the flag would come down upon the commemoration's close in 1965. The flag over the state house joined those displayed in the House and Senate chambers at the instigation of John D. Long in 1938 and 1956.[21]

Whatever the reason for raising the flag in 1962, it did not come down in 1965 and became a political issue within a decade. Grass roots demands for the flag's removal began in 1972, and in 1977 the state legislature's Black Caucus took up the cause. Representative Kay Patterson, an African-American Democrat from Richland County (Columbia), played the role in South Carolina that Alvin Holmes played in Alabama. Patterson sponsored a resolution by which the Confederate flag would be retired to the state's Confederate Relic Room. The flag issue became in South Carolina, as it was in Alabama, a periodic exercise in futility. In response to Patterson's pressure, a powerful pro-flag faction emerged in the South Carolina legislature. Its leader, Representative John Bradley (R-Charleston) charged that black legislators were complaining about the flag "for the sole purpose of trying to show white people how far they can push them." Far from being a symbol of racism, the Confederate flag represented a proud period of the state's history, "the only time when the state made a total commitment to anything."[22]

In the wake of the NAACP Southeast Regional Conference's 1987 resolution opposing official use of the Confederate battle flag, Patterson suggested compromises to lower the flag in South Carolina. At various times, Patterson said that he would agree to relegate the battle flag from the capitol dome to the Confederate soldiers statue on the capitol grounds and to substitute the Stars and Bars for the battle flag. Negotiations toward the former solution broke down when the executive council of the state division of the Sons of Confederate Veterans voted unanimously against it. "South Carolina was the first state to secede from the union," explained an SCV member. "That was a very noble thing. On the grounds is not the proper place for that flag."[23]

Inheriting Bradley's flag-guardian mantle were Republican Senators Glenn F. McConnell of North Charleston and John E. Courson of Columbia. In the late 1980s and 1990s they not only defended the Confederate flag passionately in the legislature but also served as honorary co-chairmen of the Save the Flag Initiative. "We must never allow a small group of misguided people to make us ashamed of our past," appealed one of the initiative's advertisements placed in South Carolina newspapers. "No one should ask us to deny our past or to repudiate the memory of our ancestors." The ad's response form ruled out any possibility of compromise, specifically a compromise based on the popular alternative of using the Stars and Bars. Respondents were to urge their legislators "to save the Battle Flag, to keep it flying and not to substitute a less recognizable banner."[24]

Despite such uncompromising rhetoric and despite public demonstrations and confrontations, the prospects for compromise dominated the 1994 legislative session. The legislature considered a broad range of possible compromises: replace the battle flag with the Stars and Bars; fly the flag only during April, which would become Confederate History Month; establish a circle of historical flags on the capitol grounds; add the tri-colored Black Liberation Flag to the dome; submit the flag question to a binding referendum in November. The referendum and the addition of the Black Liberation flag emerged as the most popular solutions among the pro- and anti-flag factions, respectively. Lobbying for the Stars and Bars solution, Senator Robert Ford, a black Democrat from Charleston, reportedly told McConnell: "Nobody could put this flag with lynchings, hate, raping of black women and things like that." McConnell sounded a note of compromise, urging whites "to understand the peaceful struggle for civil rights" and blacks "to understand not everyone fought the Civil War to keep somebody enslaved."[25]

The most immediate stimuli for compromise were several pending lawsuits that challenged the legitimacy of the flag over the capitol and threatened to accomplish what Alvin Holmes's suit had in Alabama. "We came to the conclusion that as hard as we may fight on this issue, the flag will come down from the dome," Courson admitted.[26] The senators fashioned an intricately balanced Heritage Act, the crux of which would move the battle flag from the dome to the capitol grounds. But there were other components of it, which collectively placed "certain symbols" at the capitol and saluted "the contributions and sacrifices to our constitutional history."

Specifically, the bill mandated the display of a battle flag (designated explicitly as the square Army of Northern Virginia battle flag) at the Confederate Soldier's monument; a Confederate First National flag at the Women's monument to the Confederacy; and an "appropriate flag" at a civil rights monument, to be built with private funds but overseen by a state-appointed commission. The bill also prohibited the removal or re-naming of any monument honoring Confederate servicemen, women of the Confederacy, or the civil rights movement or its participants without a two-thirds vote by both branches of the legislature.

An integral part of the measure was a statement to be placed in the journals of both houses of the legislature. The statement, approved by the Senate, read in part:

> The Confederate flags are not racist emblems *per se*. It depends on how they are utilized. The misuse of these emblems for racial purposes is deplored and condemned. These emblems have been misused. These are battle flags which should not be used for political purposes.
>
> The State is displaying the Confederate flags as symbols of our heritage. They are not flown in defiance of any gov-

ernment or as a statement regarding any civil rights, constitutional, or racial issues. These flags represent the valor
which was displayed by the men and women of this state in
another time. That heritage of honor, courage, and independence is worthy of remembering.[27]

This remarkable statement allowed McConnell to tell flag supporters
that the compromise was a significant victory that gave official state recognition to the flag as a symbol of heritage.

Ultimately, the compromise failed. Opposition within the Black Legislative Caucus nearly killed it in the Senate. The compromise bill passed
at the eleventh hour, only to die in the House. Although pundits attributed the failure to political bad blood between House and Senate leaders, southern heritage activists claimed credit for killing the compromise.[28]

The spirit of compromise dissipated quickly in the following months
and years. The NAACP threatened a boycott of the state's tourism industry if the flag did not come down immediately. Myrtle Beach and other
tourism centers braced themselves for a boycott, while business and local government officials begged the politicians to move the flag from the
dome to the capitol grounds. Senator McConnell interpreted the boycott
threat and objections to a one-day historical flag display in Newberry,
South Carolina, as a "slap in the face" of compromise. He began the 1995
session with the mantra that any compromise must be "a mile deep and a
mile wide"—that it must be respected by the citizens and not merely its
legislative architects.[29]

The new session also began with a transformed state political landscape. In the 1994 election—in which the flag issue played a prominent
role—Republicans won the governor's mansion and, for the first time
since Reconstruction, control of the House. More important, the lawsuits that had compelled compromise in 1994 fizzled. The Republicans
exercised their new political muscle by passing a law that would require
legislative approval to remove flags from the capitol.[30]

Officially sanctioned by a friendly legislature and supported by a majority of citizens, the capitol flag seemed untouchable when a new chal-

lenge came from an unexpected direction. In a televised address on November 26, 1996, Governor David Beasley asked South Carolinians whether they wanted their children to be debating the Confederate flag in ten years. At once upholding the honor of the flag and conceding that it had been misused as a "racist tool," Beasley urged the adoption of a compromise measure resembling the 1994 Heritage Act. Senator McConnell and Attorney General Charles Condon spoke politely, but firmly, against Beasley's suggestion. Although polls showed popular support for Beasley's compromise proposal, it found no favor and no sponsor in the legislature. The state House of Representatives instead voted to put the flag question up for a popular referendum (a proposal that died in the state Senate).[31] Chastened by this defeat, Beasley promised during his reelection campaign in 1998 not to campaign again for the flag's removal. He lost the election to Democrat Jim Hodges.

The decisive defeats of the legislative campaign prompted the NAACP to turn to economic action. The state conference in July 1999 recommended a boycott of the state, and the national NAACP approved the strategy in September. The threatened boycott of 1994 became reality on January 1, 2000. The resolution approving the boycott called for "the removal and relocation of the Confederate battle flag to a place of historical rather than sovereign context." Many African-American organizations canceled conventions in South Carolina, and the boycott brought the state unwanted negative publicity; but it did not cripple the state economically.[32] Nevertheless, the boycott strengthened the hand of business leaders and politicians, notably long-time Charleston Mayor Joseph Riley, campaigning to take down the flag.

Flag supporters and critics took to the streets again in January 2000. Several thousand flag defenders participated in a three-day rally organized by the Heritage Coalition. State Senator Arthur Ravenel delivered a stem-winder speech in which he denounced the pressure brought by the "National Association of Retarded People." A week later, nearly 50,000 marchers, dwarfing the size of the Heritage Coalition rally, descended on the state capitol to demand that the flag come down. The rallies, the boycott, and an erosion of public support for keeping the flag on the dome prompted Governor Hodges to declare that the flag should

come down from the capitol. The flag issue became a web that even ensnared presidential candidates during the state's March primaries.[33]

Under intense outside scrutiny and opposition to the flag by the governor, the state legislature worked toward a compromise. By mid-May,
both houses approved a variation of the Heritage Act compromise that
had been on the table for six years. On May 23 Governor Hodges signed
the bill into law. The compromise removed the naval jack from the
capitol dome and replaced it with a square battle flag (specifically a Department of South Carolina, Georgia, and Florida variation on the Army
of Northern Virginia flag) on a new pole erected beside the Confederate
monument on the capitol grounds. The act also removed the flags from
inside the Senate and House chambers. The act did not include the formal statement of the Confederate flag's true meaning, but it did prevent
the removal or alteration of historical monuments on public property
and preserved the historic names of streets and bridges. Legislation
passed concurrently recognized officially for the first time the Martin Luther King, Jr., birthday holiday and Confederate Memorial Day. Flag supporters accused Hodges and the legislature of selling out. The NAACP
vowed to continue its boycott because the compromise relocated the
Confederate flag from the capitol dome to the most prominent location
on the capitol grounds—a spot that an African-American columnist observed was "Columbia's equivalent to New York's Times Square."[34]

July 1, 2000—the day the flag came down—brought expressions of
satisfaction from the architects of the compromise. Senator Kay Patterson, the politician who had been lobbying longest for the flag's removal,
declared it "a proud day. A happy, happy day of jubilee," though he also
confessed that the corner of Main and Gervais streets was "the last place"
he wanted to see the new flag. Glenn McConnell, who, along with his
Senate Republican colleagues John Courson and Arthur Ravenel, had
weathered a storm of criticism and threats to shepherd the compromise
to its conclusion, was philosophical. "The three of us had to make a judgment along the way [about] how to protect the heritage," McConnell told
a reporter. "Their memory's safe now," he observed, gesturing to the
Confederate monument. Governor Hodges stood stoically inside the

state house as he received the flag that had been lowered from the dome by two Citadel cadets—one white, one black. As the naval jack came down, Confederate reenactors raised a fifty-two-inch square battle flag on a thirty-foot flag pole beside the Confederate monument.[35]

The protagonists in the long debate were far from satisfied. July 1 began with a silent march led by the NAACP to protest the retention of the battle flag on the capitol grounds. Black activists were determined to "write the headlines" and let the world know that not all South Carolinians celebrated a compromise that effectively raised a new Confederate flag. At one point along the twelve-block route, the 750 marchers encountered a group of a hundred jeering flag supporters chanting "Dixie Forever." "If you don't like our state, why don't you go back to your own continent?" shouted one. Flag supporters booed and jeered as the flag came down from the dome shortly after noon, then let out cheers and rebel yells as the new flag went up on the new bronze flag pole. As the formal ritual ended, opposing groups communicated their messages. Flag opponents dressed in yellow carried yellow signs reading "Shame." Flag supporters waved large and small battle flags while some chanted "Off the dome and in your face!"[36]

"Off the dome and in your face" was an appropriate metaphor for the compromise. The flag no longer flew in a place that implied sovereignty over or official approval by the people of South Carolina. Flying high over the capitol dome may have been a symbolically significant place for the flag, but it was barely visible to the naked eye. In contrast, flying alone on a pole at the main entrance to the capitol grounds (and across from the city's main commercial artery) made the flag more visible than ever. Few people entering the capitol grounds from the city could miss the flag and the implied approval of the state's Confederate past.

Context was the key. Did the flag's proximity to the Confederate soldier monument (erected in 1879) justify it as an apolitical tribute to the Confederate soldier and not an endorsement of the Confederate cause? Unlike the flags raised around the Confederate monument in Alabama in 1993, South Carolina's was not a historical or educational display but more a gesture and a statement. The flag's prominent location testified that the state's lawmakers were not willing to renounce or dishonor South Carolina's Confederate past.

The NAACP denounced "the Confederacy-of-the-mind mentality of South Carolina's legislators" and vowed to continue the boycott until the flag was "stripped of any sovereignty and placed into a historical context." The NAACP set up checkpoints at rest stops near the state's borders and urged travelers not to spend money in South Carolina. Predictably, flag supporters responded to this "blockade" by arranging "blockade runners" to cross the border and spend more money in the state.[37]

The unwillingness of the legislature to remove the flag from a place of honor should not have been a surprise to the NAACP and other flag critics, since honoring the Confederate flag had been one of the pillars of compromise proposals since 1994. Public opinion polls in 1999–2000 showed growing support for compromise and impatience with those who insisted on keeping the flag over the capitol dome. The NAACP and business leaders against the flag benefited from this impatience. With the issue apparently settled by the dramatic and highly publicized events of July 2000, flag opponents stood to lose public support by continuing their protests. Despite the angry rhetoric, the compromise of 2000 has held.

In February 1956, the Georgia legislature voted to adopt a new state flag featuring a square Confederate battle flag over the (right) two-thirds of its surface and the state seal emblazoned on a blue field on the other (left) third. Ironically, the flag it replaced also featured a modified Confederate flag—the Stars and Bars—along with the state seal. Just as it did in 1863, the St. Andrew's cross replaced the Stars and Bars on the flag of a people seeking to express its devotion to principles in stronger symbolic terms. The adoption of the flag in 1956 occurred as office holders in Georgia and throughout the South mounted a counterattack against the federal government's push to desegregate schools. The same legislators who adopted a new flag bearing a Confederate battle flag emblem devised a strategy to evade compliance with the U.S. Supreme Court's orders to desegregate schools "with all deliberate speed." No absolute proof exists that there was a connection between the flag change and resistance to integration, but, as one newspaper columnist observed: "While there is no smoking gun, the air is thick with the smell of gunpowder."[38]

The author of the flag change was John Sammons Bell, Georgia's Democratic Party chairman. Bell explained in 1992 that he conceived the flag while attending a Confederate veterans reunion in 1924. "This flag was presented and adopted for one reason only," Bell told a reporter. "The motivation was to create a living memorial to a brave and valiant people who gave so much and suffered so much during the War Between the States." According to the official 1956 handbook of Georgia flags, the motive of Bell and his legislative sponsors was "to create a living memorial to the Confederacy and at the same time to give Georgia a distinctive and historically significant flag." Touting the prominence of the Confederate battle flag in the new state flag, the handbook continued: "Embracing the beloved Battle Flag of the Confederacy within our own State emblem, portrays in part the unbounded love, admiration, and respect which we of today have for them of yesterday. Thus in an active and lawful flag, truly a living memorial to the Confederacy takes place."[39]

Bell served also on the Georgia Commission on Education and was a staunch defender of what he called "traditional policies of segregation" in the schools, but he insisted later that "integration and the Supreme Court decision had absolutely nothing to do with adoption of the flag." The organization through which Bell pushed the new flag was the powerful Association of County Commissioners (ACC), for which he served as attorney. At its June 1955 convention, the ACC adopted resolutions declaring that "the flag of a state or nation is a symbol of loyalty and devotion of a people to that government" and that "such a flag should be distinctive and beautiful yet symbolic of the traditions it represents." Other resolutions passed by the Assembly pledged "full support in each and every way or means required . . . to protect and maintain the segregation of the races in our schools."[40]

The only legislator from the 1956 session still serving in 1993 similarly denied that maintaining segregation had anything to do with the flag change. Denmark Groover of Macon emphasized that the flag was intended as a memorial to the Confederate veteran. "Anything we in Georgia can do to preserve the memory of the Confederacy is a step forward," Groover told his colleagues. In contrast to this observation decades after the fact, Groover remarked in 1956 that the new flag "will show that we in Georgia intend to uphold what we stood for, will stand for and will fight for." Disparaging the existing Stars and Bars flag, Groover observed that Georgia's new flag "will replace those meaningless stripes with something that has deep meaning in the true heart of all southerners."[41] Only the St. Andrew's cross, it seemed, held meaning for (white) southerners and showed what they stood for.

During the intense controversy of the 1990s, defenders of the flag made the most of the absence of a smoking gun and dismissed the proximity argument—the coincidence of the flag's adoption and resistance to school integration. The more important coincidence, flag defenders emphasized, was between the adoption of the flag and the initial planning for the Civil War Centennial celebration. "It must be remembered that Confederate patriotism was running high in 1956," argued the "Georgia Flag Facts" brochure.[42]

If there was no smoking gun to link the flag change with resistance to integration, the linkage with the Civil War Centennial was no stronger. The announcement of plans for a national commission was made on January 20, 1956—several months *after* the introduction of the flag bill in the Georgia legislature. The brief discussion about the flag change in the Senate reportedly did refer to the upcoming centennial and to honoring Confederate veterans. However, the individuals and groups that seemed most likely to champion a flag change on behalf of Confederate heritage were silent, uninterested, or even hostile to the change. Speeches and writings about the state's Civil War Centennial preparations never mentioned the 1956 flag change.[43]

While the flag bill was still pending in late 1955, the United Daughters of the Confederacy's general convention passed a resolution against the new flag, which it declared an "incorrect use of the Confederate Flag." According to the Correct Use of the Confederate Flag Committee, which proposed the resolution, "The Battle Flag of the Confederacy is a

Flag of history of sacred and cherished remembrance and it belongs to all thirteen states of the Confederacy . . . No one state can claim it for its own." The John B. Gordon Camp, SCV, and the Children of the Confederacy endorsed the UDC's "disapproval." Unlike the SCV, which rallied behind the 1956 flag thirty-five years later, the UDC leadership never wavered from this position. The divergence became clear in January 1991 when the UDC's Georgia Division resolved that the UDC "believe the Battle Flag of the Confederacy to be a flag of history, and we wish to protect the Battle Flag from misuse."[44]

For completely different reasons, Georgia's African-American leaders also opposed the 1956 flag change. They had no doubt that the legislature that acted to defy the Supreme Court's desegregation order also adopted a new flag as a gesture of defiance. "Out of a spirit of eternal gratitude and native pride one should be constrained to wave or salute a flag," opined the *Atlanta Daily World* in February 1956. The editors were incredulous that lawmakers expected Georgia's black population to salute and stand at attention for or feel devotion to a symbol "that stood for the enslavement of its people and which revives and enlivens a cause that claimed once upon a time so much that it had to be subdued by the federal government as a rebellion and put down at the cost of thousands of lives on both sides."[45]

The first efforts to change the 1956 flag were made in 1969 by Jane Merritt, a white state representative from Americus and a former state regent of the Daughters of the American Revolution. "Regardless of all the rationalizing to memorialize the Confederacy," she told her colleagues, "the time has come to settle down and realize that a Confederate battle flag has no place occupying two-thirds of the flag of forward-moving Georgia." The flag, she said, "was a statement that 'Hell, no, we're not going to have any blacks in our schools.'" Although she garnered some support outside the Assembly, her proposals died.[46]

A highly publicized event in a North Georgia town reinvigorated the campaign to change the flag. In mid-January 1987 a small civil rights march succeeded in drawing national attention to the history of all-white Forsyth County. The county's one thousand blacks had fled in 1912 after the lynching of a black man accused of raping a young white woman. Seventy-five years later, an angry crowd of three hundred whites surrounded the civil rights marchers in the county seat of Cumming. Two weeks later, an estimated twenty thousand marchers, proclaiming a "new generation" of activists, marched through the town, protected by seventeen hundred National Guardsmen. Reminiscent of scenes from a quarter-century before, the crowds taunting the marchers featured white-robed Klansmen shouting "Go, home, niggers!" and adolescents in baseball caps waving Confederate battle flags.[47]

Governor Joe Frank Harris appointed a special committee to investigate the incident. The committee reported that the presence of the Confederate battle flag on the state flag contributed to the violent confrontations and recommended changing the flag. Also as a result of the Forsyth County incident, the NAACP's Southeast Regional Conference passed its March 1987 flag resolution, and Georgia state representative Frank Redding, a black Democrat from Decatur, introduced a bill to change Georgia's flag back to the pre-1956 pattern. That bill failed, as did bills Redding introduced in each subsequent session of the legislature.[48]

Governor Zell Miller, a popular Democrat, made the flag a major political issue in 1992–1993. He had as allies not only the state's African-American and civil rights leadership but also the business leadership of cosmopolitan Atlanta. The "city too busy to hate" had positioned itself as a window onto the South for the national and international media. The campaign to change the flag picked up steam as Atlanta prepared to host the 1996 Summer Olympic Games. "When we are in the international press, it's going to be dreadfully embarrassing to have that flag flying there," remarked the director of Georgia Common Cause, a member of the Civil Rights Network. "It's going to destroy all the work that's been done to promote a progressive image of Atlanta."[49]

Miller's bruising and ultimately futile battle revealed that outside of Atlanta, many Georgians valued tradition more than a progressive image and that the battle flag was central to white southern identity. Atlanta, editorialized North Georgia's *Rome News-Tribune,* "is desperate to be at the head of the world-class cities." Instead of being ashamed of its history and of its symbols, the editors wrote, Atlanta should be proud to exhibit a past symbolized by a Confederate flag and a monument to Martin Luther King. Far from being offended by the flag, international visitors to Atlanta "need to come to Georgia to see how diverse, opinionated peoples can live together under a single democracy, albeit imperfectly."[50]

An unscientific newspaper poll taken in early 1992 revealed that seventy-five percent of the 43,000 respondents favored retaining the existing flag. The overwhelming response was nearly ten times higher than the response to any other poll the newspaper had conducted. A scientific poll conducted a few months earlier revealed that seventy-six percent of white Georgians believed the state flag to be a symbol of southern pride, while fifty percent of blacks perceived it as a symbol of racism. Yet another poll revealed that nearly sixty percent of all Georgians were opposed to changing the flag; fifty-four percent of blacks polled, but only twenty-seven percent of the whites, supported the flag change.[51]

The Georgia Committee to Save the State Flag, its offshoot the Heritage Preservation Association (HPA), and the Sons of Confederate Veterans were able to exploit those attitudes to build a wall of resistance against the flag change. Pro-flag spokesmen portrayed Confederate descendants as a persecuted majority. "If a small minority gets their feelings hurt and goes clamoring to the General Assembly to remove the Martin Luther King, Jr. holiday, would that be right?" P. Charles Lunsford asked rhetorically at a November 1992 forum. "Of course it wouldn't. You must remember this is a double-edged sword."[52]

Governor Miller threw down the gauntlet to the pro-flag forces in his January 12, 1993, state of the state address. After reciting his own family's Confederate credentials and pledging that Georgia would never forget the bravery of its Confederate ancestors, the former college history professor reminded the legislators of the historical context in which the 1956 flag was adopted. With or without a "smoking gun," the flag's adoption was tainted with a "defiance" that had since been repudiated. He then appealed to the legislators to look beyond the polls and consider their own places in history as they debate the proposed flag bill. "If you're truly proud of the South," Miller concluded his remarks on the flag, "if you're truly proud of this state, and all its 260 years, if you look forward and want to play a significant part in what Georgia can become, then help me now to give bigotry no sanction and persecution no assistance."[53]

The legislature registered its disapproval of Miller's message loudly and immediately. Several members booed the governor's speech. Republican Representative Max Davis pronounced the speech "bull." House Speaker Tom Murphy scorned Miller's plea to ignore public opinion and declared that he would follow the will of the ninety-five percent of his constituents who did not want the flag changed.[54]

For flag backers, devotion to Confederate symbols was the litmus test for being southern. Their arguments were tautological: "true Georgians" honored Confederate symbols; those who did not honor or want Confederate symbols to represent their state were not true Georgians. To be a Georgian in the 1990s, a person must accept an ideologically loaded heritage and must embrace the symbols of that ideology. "It's entirely appropriate for any subjugated region to fly the flag of its once independent nation," explained Charles Lunsford. "If there are whites and blacks that are offended by the flag, then either they're northern-born or they don't understand their ancestry." Carrying the burden of defending the existing flag at the governor's January 1993 flag forum, the HPA's R. Lee Collins told a black Georgia legislator: "I don't expect everybody to have the same connection to southern heritage that southerners do." Ed Fields, the still-active founder of the National States' Rights Party, went further and argued that blacks were by definition not "southerners" because they did not share the same cultural background as whites and did not defend the cultural traditions of the Confederate flag. After declaring his opposition to the existing flag, columnist Colin Campbell received letters telling him that he was not a "true" Georgian. Are whites born in the state the only "true" Georgians? Campbell retorted. "There are all kinds of people in Georgia, and there always have been and it is no exercise in 'multicultural' ideology to insist on the fact."[55]

The flag debate also revealed anew just how central the St. Andrew's cross battle flag was to white southern identity. The proposal to revert to

Georgia's pre-1956 flag would still leave Georgia with a state emblem based on a Confederate flag. The Georgia flag from 1879 to 1956 included the Stars and Bars. Changing the flag, therefore, would not "purge" the Confederacy from the state's symbolism but only substitute one Confederate flag for another. Flag opponents were willing to return to a state flag still bearing a Confederate emblem in part because they perceived the Stars and Bars as a less Confederate flag and, more important, because the Stars and Bars has no twentieth-century history as a symbol of hate. The *Atlanta Journal & Constitution* asked rhetorically whether the old flag wasn't "just as objectionable as the battle flag." No, the paper answered. "The battle flag carries a lot more emotional baggage, which is the reason some cling to it." Earl T. Shinhoster, director of the NAACP's southeast regional office and that organization's chief spokesman on the flag issue, agreed that the old flag "takes some of the venom and sting out of it."[56]

Whether flag opponents would accept a Stars and Bars alternative was a moot point, however, since flag supporters refused to consider it. In part this reluctance was based on an unwillingness to concede the argument that the battle flag was a dishonored symbol of racism. For the most vocal flag defenders, a state flag bearing merely the suggestion of a Confederate emblem was not sufficient because they wanted the state's symbols actively and unmistakably to testify to pride in Georgia's Confederate past. In 1992 as in 1956, only the battle flag served that purpose. Lee Collins, of the Heritage Preservation Association, noted approvingly that legislators in 1956 sought "to replace a little-known Confederate symbol with a symbol that is universally recognized as being a proud symbol of southern heritage."[57]

In the midst of public demonstrations for and against the 1956 flag, Miller supporters submitted flag bills to the Georgia House and Senate. A so-called two-flag bill—which would designate the pre-1956 flag the official state flag and the 1956 flag a purely ceremonial memorial flag—passed the Senate. While Governor Miller declared the compromise "a step in the right direction," Southern Christian Leadership Conference Chairman Joseph Lowery articulated a viewpoint that pervaded the civil rights camp: "The state ought to have one flag and it ought not to be the rebel flag." Facing insurmountable opposition in the House, Governor Miller withdrew the flag bill and urged the Assembly to get on with more pressing matters. "It looks as if we have taught a lasting lesson to those who would attack the beloved icons of the South," Charles Lunsford gloated. "That lesson is that we will fight with unending gallantry, against all odds, to achieve victory."[58]

Although Miller backed away from the flag fight, it remained a disruptive public issue. Local officials in Atlanta and surrounding counties took matters into their own hands and replaced the 1956 flag with the old flag. Flag opponents tried to exploit the national and international attention that came with the 1994 Super Bowl and the 1996 Olympics.[59] The Olympics failed to produce any significant pressure toward changing the flag. More prominent than complaints from non-Georgians about the flag was the ridicule of Atlanta for abandoning its Old South history in favor of a soulless, computer-generated mascot called a Whatzit.

Having failed in the realms of politics and public relations, flag opponents tried the courts. A lawsuit contended that the state flag violated the equal protection and due process clauses of the Fourteenth Amendment and free speech rights under the First Amendment. District Court Judge Orinda D. Evans (an African-American woman) agreed that the flag's adoption had a "discriminatory purpose" (among other purposes) but concluded that the plaintiff could not "show a sufficiently concrete, present-day discriminatory impact on African-Americans." Echoing its earlier opinion in the Alabama flag case, the Eleventh U.S. Circuit Court of Appeals in July 1997 upheld the district court decision. The judges offered the blunt opinion that the battle flag "has no place in the official state flag" and regretted "that the Georgia legislature has chosen, and continues to display, as an official symbol a battle flag emblem that divides rather than unifies the citizens of Georgia."[60]

Miller's successor in the governor's mansion, Democrat Roy Barnes, learned lessons from his predecessor's debacle and from the political blood-letting that occurred in South Carolina. Determined to avoid another divisive and politically bruising confrontation over the flag, yet equally determined to avoid an NAACP-orchestrated economic boycott of his state, Barnes worked behind the scenes to build a legislative majority willing to change the flag. Unlike Miller, Barnes courted support and counted votes.

The result of Barnes's work was breathtaking. Within a week in late January 2001, a bill to change Georgia's flag passed through the House and Senate by close but comfortable margins and landed on the governor's desk, and the new flag went up over the state capitol. Unlike its predecessors, the bill did not revive the pre-1956 state flag. Instead, it offered an entirely new flag, the design and origins of which received virtually no attention. The flag emblazoned an enlarged state seal on a blue field and added underneath a ribbon banner with five United States and Georgia state flags—including the 1956 state flag—labeled collectively as "Georgia's History." This unconventional design sought to allay the usual charge that changing the state flag would erase history. To those who claimed that changing the flag "would dishonor our heritage," Barnes told the Senate on the day of its vote, "I say that nothing could be further from the truth. This new flag does not, however, value one Georgian's heritage over another." Even though the new flag retained the St. Andrew's cross, African-American legislators pronounced it a fair compromise.[61]

Critical to the passage of the flag bill was the support of 79-year-old Representative Denmark Groover. Months before his death, the veteran of the 1955–1956 Assembly admitted that defiance was part of his motivation for voting for the St. Andrew's cross in 1956. "I am certain in my own mind that there were some members of the General Assembly who voted for the change in the flag as a complete reaction and aversion to the Supreme Court decision relative to segregation," Groover told the *Macon Telegraph.*[62]

Defenders of the 1956 flag cried foul as the bill passed through the legislature with surprising speed. Flag defenders in the state Assembly tried unsuccessfully to force a popular referendum on the flag. "Our flag will always remain our flag," declared a member of the southern Heritage League. "We will never accept the new flag." "They got what they wanted," observed HPA president Charles Lunsford. "What's going on here is an effort to eradicate any vestiges of the South." The new flag, of course, still included a token "vestige of the South" with the reduced-size 1956 flag. In addition, the flag compromise package included restoration of a seven-foot postwar portrait of General Robert E. Lee to the state capitol.[63]

Two months after the flag change, the Georgia Senate passed a resolution encouraging Georgians to fly the old flag during the officially declared Confederate History and Heritage Month (April). Charles Lunsford reportedly helped draft the resolution. "I don't have a problem with it," remarked prominent African-American Representative Tyrone Brooks. "Because I know that the official symbol of the state, the one that represents all the people of Georgia, will be flying over all of our state facilities very soon."[64]

Regardless of the new flag's official status, diehards determined that what they called the real state flag would not disappear from the Georgia landscape. Within months, heritage activists led by Elijah Coleman of Mableton, launched Project Wave. Underwritten by private donors, Coleman's group erected hundreds of twenty-four-foot poles with four-by-six-foot 1956 Georgia flags on private property visible along highways throughout the state—especially, Coleman declared, along "Scalawag Alley" from the Atlanta suburbs to the Alabama border. Coleman and his allies also mobilized to defeat "King Roy" Barnes and key legislators responsible for the flag change.[65]

Indeed, the Boot Barnes campaign scored a stunning victory in the November 2002 elections. Resentment over the way the flag was changed, along with opposition to Barnes's positions on roads and schools and a nationwide GOP resurgence, swept Sonny Perdue, Georgia's first Republican chief executive since Reconstruction, into the Governor's Mansion. Perdue had voted against the flag change in the legislature and his campaign pledged to seek a referendum on the state flag. He fulfilled this pledge, but in a way that dismayed supporters of the 1956 flag and quite possibly killed their hopes once and for all. In its 2003 session the legislature adopted yet another new flag—one that closely resembled the pre-1956 blend of the state seal and the Confederate Stars and Bars. Perdue approved the change and a nonbinding referendum that gave Georgia voters a choice between only two flags: the new one and Barnes's 2001 flag. Supporters of the 1956 flag renewed their "flaggings" and unleashed their wrath against the "turncoat" Perdue but were unable to restore the St. Andrew's cross to the state flag.[66]

In the March 2004 referendum, Georgians voted for the 2003 flag by a three to one margin. The new flag won a majority in every county. The hardcore supporters of the 1956 flag mounted a last-minute "vote blue" campaign, believing a victory for the detested Barnes flag would repudiate the Perdue flag and compel the legislature to hold a second referendum with the 1956 flag on the ballot. Voters apparently did not share the desire to keep the issue alive.[67]

Even supporters of the 1956 flag came to the conclusion that a state flag based on a Confederate flag—the Stars and Bars—was good enough. Although "flaggers" rallied outside the capitol and vowed to continue the fight for the 1956 flag, an officer of the Heritage Preservation Association noted that the state now had "truly a Confederate flag" and predicted that Georgians would be happy with it. A spokesman for the NAACP similarly declared that the state's African Americans could live with the new flag, despite its Confederate origins.[68] After twelve years of almost continuous controversy, exhausted Georgians—like their neighbors in South Carolina—embraced a compromise that had been on the table all along.

The state that first incorporated the Confederate battle flag into its official symbolism was the last to see it challenged. Virtually absent from the headlines during the 1980s and 1990s flag flaps, Mississippi's state flag did not become a visible issue until the State Supreme Court discovered that the flag had no legal standing. What followed was a relatively brief battle that opened old wounds and revealed the deep cleavages among Mississippians over their state's Confederate heritage.

In April 1993 the state NAACP filed suit in state chancery court contending that the state flag violated equal protection clauses in the state constitution, particularly a prohibition against "symbols or vestiges of slavery" on the state flag. In the years before the suit was filed, African-American state legislators had introduced bills to change the state flag, but the bills never made it to the floor.[69]

The NAACP suit, too, seemed destined to founder on the same rocks that wrecked the similar lawsuits in Alabama and Georgia. The state allowed the Mississippi Division of the Sons of Confederate Veterans to intervene as a defendant in the case. After repeated dismissals and amendments, the case wended a circuitous route to the State Supreme Court. In April 2000 the high court ruled that the state flag did not demonstrably violate the plaintiffs' constitutional rights to free speech and expression, due process, and equal protection as guaranteed by the Mississippi Constitution.

A second part of the court's decision traced the history of the state flag and seal and noted that the laws creating them had not been brought forward into the Code of 1906 and were, therefore, repealed. "Whether the flag currently in use continues as the State Flag by use and custom is a political decision," the court concluded. "Mississippi has no State Flag created, described or adopted by law . . . The decision to adopt or not adopt a flag for Mississippi is wholly within the power of the Mississippi legislature and the executive branch of government."[70]

With the ultimate hot potato dumped suddenly into the state's political lap, Mississippi's Democratic Governor Ronnie Musgrove wasted no time in deflecting the issue to an ostensibly nonpolitical body. On the day after the decision, Musgrove announced the formation of a seventeen-member advisory commission that would report its recommendations to the next legislative session. Flag defenders smelled a rat when Musgrove appointed former governor William Winter, a progressive Democrat and flag opponent, to chair the commission. From the beginning of the state's unexpected flag crisis, supporters of the existing flag insisted on a popular vote, while advocates of a flag change feared the divisiveness—as well as the outcome—of such a vote.[71]

A series of five public hearings held around the state in October and November 2000 underscored the controversy. White flag supporters, many wearing Confederate flag T-shirts and stickers, dominated the hearings. "I want to honor my ancestors while the scalawags want to spit on the grave of my ancestors," explained a flag supporter in Meridian. "My suggestion to those who don't want the flag is there are 49 other states in the nation you can move to." Until the last forum, the commission heard opinion that was divided almost exclusively along racial lines—whites in favor of the old flag, blacks urging the adoption of a new one. A high school teacher in Moorhead was one of the few whites to publicly favor a new flag. Other whites in the audience yelled, "Boy, where you from?" Flag defenders in Meridian warned that attacks on southern culture would not stop with the state flag—guns, the Bible, and the sovereignty of the United States were also in danger. Members of the commission were shocked at the raw hatred they witnessed. "We've attracted too many people on the fringes of each side," noted a state senator serving on the commission. It's been hell," agreed a state representative. "It's the worst thing I've ever dealt with. I've been cussed. One fellow called and said he was going to have me knocked off. We saw a dark side of personalities on both extremes."[72]

Within a month of the hearings, the commission unveiled a proposed new flag and announced that the voters of Mississippi would have the opportunity to decide between it and the 1894 flag. Although widely suspected of anti-flag leanings, the commission recommended proposals that appealed to the acknowledged pro-flag white majority. Voters would go to the polls and decide between the old flag and a proposed new one. The new flag retained the 1894 flag's Stars and Bars appearance but substituted for the St. Andrew's cross a circle of twenty stars: thirteen on the outside representing the original thirteen states, six representing the sovereign entities (including the Confederacy) that have ruled over Mississippi, and one on the inside of the circle representing Mississippi itself. A vote for the new flag would also approve two pieces of legislation that were intended to assuage fears of a wholesale assault on Confederate heritage. One act would prohibit the removal of any monument or memorial on public property and would protect the historical names of streets, bridges, parks, and other structures. A second act would designate the 1894 flag as a "historical flag" that "shall be honored, protected and flown wherever historical flags are flown" and which could be displayed by historical or heritage groups, citizens, and businesses.[73] The only thing that the proposals asked supporters of the 1894 flag to surrender was the St. Andrew's cross in the canton.

Not unexpectedly, this sacrifice proved too much to ask. As in the other states, polls revealed that a majority of Mississippians favored the existing flag. Architects of change or compromise in Alabama, South Carolina, and Georgia successfully avoided putting the flag question to a popular vote. The Mississippi legislature's insistence on doing so virtually doomed the proposed new flag. Mississippians who saw the Supreme Court ruling as a welcome opportunity to change the flag and the state's backward image accused the governor of abdicating leadership.[74]

On April 17, 2001, Mississippians voted by a two-to-one margin for the old flag over the proposed new one. The voting was primarily, but not exclusively, along racial lines. African-American leaders were mortified to find that some majority-black counties voted to retain the old flag, and complained that black voters simply did not appreciate the importance of the flag change.[75]

The flag referendum became in effect a referendum on the larger issue of Mississippi's image. As in the other southern states facing flag issues, Mississippi's business leaders and major media urged adoption of the new flag not only as a gesture of respect to the state's black minority but also as a way of "improving the negative image the state has outside our boundaries." "By adopting a new state flag," editorialized the Biloxi *Sun Herald,* "Mississippians will confirm that a brighter future is more important to them than a darker past." Predictably, national and international media dredged up Mississippi's past racial troubles and the statistics on education which measured the state's stereotypical backwardness. Inexplicably (according to "progressives"), Mississippians voted perversely to reinforce, not eradicate, their state's reputation for backwardness.[76]

The pressure on Mississippians to change the flag in order to improve the state's image backfired, as white citizens reacted against the implication that the state was undereducated and uncivil. White Mississippians resisted demands that they perceived as apologies for or renunciations of the state's Confederate heritage. At a rally in Jackson days before the vote, the leader of a pro-flag organization FreeMississippi.org called supporters of the new flag "agitators" bent on destroying the state's cultural heritage. Conservative ministers also rallied at the capitol, urging Mississippians to retain the flag and resist unwanted change. "We do not need a new image, a new morality, a new gospel or a new flag for the 21st century," insisted a retired Baptist minister at a state capitol rally. "That which is at stake and which hangs in the balance is nothing less than our Christian, southern heritage," remarked another. "God's people have for too long allowed the liberals and the heathens to determine the course and direction of our state and our nation." While the pro-flag position had a deep ideological dimension, it was also rooted in the straightforward human trait of contrariness; people simply did not appreciate being told what they should believe about their own heritage and symbols, out of concern for how other people regard them. "It's about the public being sick of being treated like dirt," concluded Greg Stewart, a lawyer and SCV activist who led the fight to save the flag.[77]

While the vote was decisive, the referendum was not the final chapter in the state flag battle. Officials in the majority-black capital city of Jackson declared that they would not fly the flag but would continue a policy adopted a year earlier to "condemn" state flags bearing the St. Andrew's cross. The NAACP threatened a South Carolina–style boycott of the state but instead passed a resolution opposing the validation of the referendum result and reaffirming its earlier resolutions calling for an end to all public displays of the flag. Pro-flag groups gathered signatures to have the 1894 flag incorporated into the state constitution. The state's "indirect initiative" law would allow citizens to compel a popular vote on the issue. Opponents of the 1894 flag meanwhile filed suit to block the initiative.[78]

The referendum in Mississippi confirmed the hopes and fears of the opposing sides in the flag debates throughout the South. Depending on the perspective, the referendum was either a healthy exercise in democracy or a politically expedient abdication of governmental responsibility to choose a flag that represents all the people of the state. If state symbols were simply questions of majority rule and opinions about symbols were divided primarily along racial lines, African-American citizens would have little control over the symbols that represent them, since they constitute no more than thirty-eight percent of the population of any state. Ironically, southern heritage activists—worshipful admirers of men who developed constitutional theories to protect the rights of minorities, especially John C. Calhoun's "concurrent majority"—found themselves employing the same kind of majority-rule arguments that had prompted the South to secede in 1860–1861. The sociologist John Shelton Reed chastised conservatives for willfully offending black southerners and even denying them their southern identity. "Symbols of the South (a fortiori, a state flag) should enlist the loyalty and affection of as many southerners (citizens of the state) as practicable," Reed wrote. "(In other words, if anything should require a concurrent majority, this is it.)"[79]

Critical of the majority-rule argument, the editors of the *Atlanta Journal & Constitution* asked, "How can it possibly be unimportant that 30 percent of Georgians are forced to live under a flag that honors the brutal enslavement and degradation of their ancestors and that celebrates a time and society in which people of their race were deemed less than human?"[80] In Georgia, unlike in Mississippi, activist governors flouted the will of what polls showed to be the majority and took the initiative to change the flag.

The controversies in Mississippi, Georgia, South Carolina, and Alabama turned on the same basic questions, one explicit and one implicit. Is the Confederate battle flag an appropriate symbol to represent the people of a modern state? What is the proper means of determining the answer to that question? Only in Mississippi was the answer decided by an election. In all four states the will of elected officials kept the battle flag flying for decades and defeated attempts to remove it. Legal challenges contending that the battle flag violated fundamental constitutional rights failed without exception. Judges routinely expressed regret that states chose symbols offensive to large numbers of their citizens but ruled in effect that insensitivity was not unconstitutional. The courts came to the rescue of flag opponents only when they found that the Confederate flag symbols had no legal standing in the state and threw the issue back into the political arena.

In all four states, the battle flag raised (and continues to raise) a fundamentally political question. Neither constitutional law, ethics, nor history suggests unambiguous answers to the question of what *should* be done. The flag issue was unwelcome and disruptive to the executive and legislative branches of the state governments, but the political struggles occurred largely outside elected governments. The contending parties in the state flag wars employed persuasion, propaganda, and coercion. Defenders of the flag accused the NAACP of politicizing it and derided the economic boycotts, but heritage groups used coercion, threats of boycotts, and electoral punishment against those accused of "heritage violations." Boycotts are part of the political process and are especially effective for minorities whose interests would never triumph if politics were simply a matter of counting heads and votes. Ultimately, the legislatures of South Carolina and Georgia agreed to remove battle flag symbols when economic threats and public relations problems made the costs of retaining them outweigh the political costs of change.

Politics, according to the familiar cliché, is the art of compromise. Despite the often shocking rhetoric and apparent extremism that reigned during the flag debates, it is impressive that the legislatures of all four states fashioned creditable compromises. In each case, the compromise removed the St. Andrew's cross battle flag from the state's official symbolism but retained or established the battle flag as an officially recognized—and even honored—historical flag. Considered objectively, the concessions were quite stunning. States that had left the Union, only to be returned forcibly and compelled to renounce the doctrine that justified secession and to surrender the institution that made secession desirable, were allowed to retain and honor the most powerful symbol of their failed secession. The states agreed to give official preeminence to the partisan symbol of a divisive four-year period in their centuries-long histories. And yet flag defenders considered these concessions intolerable.

Reacting to the NAACP's 1987 initiative, the editor of *Confederate Vet-*

eran explained why flag supporters believed compromise was unacceptable: "If the Confederate Battle Flag is removed from the capitol buildings in South Carolina and Alabama we will lose a little bit of ourselves. If the southern Cross design is removed from the state flags in Georgia and Mississippi, then the constant reminder of those states' glorious contributions in lives and property to the lost cause of self determiniation [sic] will forever be gone from all public buildings. We just cannot let it happen."[81] Uncompromising flag supporters insisted upon retaining the St. Andrew's cross for the very reasons that flag opponents wanted it removed: because it was a public testimonial of respect, honor, and approval of Confederate soldiers and the cause (defined as national self-determination) for which they believed they fought. The Stars and Bars would not achieve this end, nor would transferring the battle flag from a highly visible official place with a "sovereign context" to mere historical contexts.

This widely held absolutist position offered testimony to the symbolic importance of the St. Andrew's cross and to the persistence of the late nineteenth-century Lost Cause ideology. Flag defenders a century later held faithfully to the obligation not to let their Confederate ancestors be forgotten or their cause diminished or distorted. The intervening century in fact had added another layer of loyalty—loyalty to the history and tradition that the flag had achieved as a public symbol. Defending the flag was for many white citizens of the four states largely an exercise in preserving the public symbolism with which they were raised.

It is tempting to interpret this dedication to a century-old ideology as a rearguard action of people losing control of their society and their regional identity—much as historians view the late nineteenth-century reform movements that tilted at the windmills of industrialism. While this interpretation is not without merit, it does a disservice to the situation and to the people involved. Granted, white southerners of Confederate ancestry are facing demographic and cultural change, and the dedication to the battle flag is symptomatic of a traditionalist response to change. And polls throughout the region show growing opposition to Confederate flags among wealthier and more educated white southerners. But millions of Americans, not all of them in the Deep South, trace their ancestry to the Confederacy, and millions more share the still-strong Confederate *chic* or the conservative ideology associated with it. For decades, pundits have alternately speculated about the disappearance of the traditional South and marveled at the "southernization of America." The flag wars in four states revealed that proponents of a narrowly defined traditional southern heritage could still flex considerable political muscle and served notice to friends and foes alike that the traditional South is not disappearing any time soon.[82]

Chapter 13

"You Can't Erase History"

African Americans who lobbied unsuccessfully to remove the St. Andrew's cross from the Mississippi state flag tried to assure flag defenders that their agenda was limited. The president of the state NAACP testified that his organization wanted to change the state flag but was not out to erase other reminders of the Civil War. "There is no desire on the NAACP's part to go through the South tearing down Confederate monuments." On the other hand, he argued, the state flag "flies over all Mississippi. It should represent everyone." Justice Fred Banks, Jr., the only African American on the Mississippi State Supreme Court, dissented from a 1998 decision allowing the battle flag to fly in displays along the state's Gulf Coast beaches. "I have no qualms with preserving history," he stated in his opinion. "Such symbols as the Confederate flag and the Nazi swastika are appropriate in museums, exhibits and the like. I do not believe, however, that it is appropriate public policy to continue to fly the Confederate battle flag at government facilities. To continue to do so under the shibboleth of 'preserving tradition' readily lends itself to connotations that, with good reason, offend a large number of Mississippi citizens—sending a message that their feelings do not matter."[1]

Justice Banks's distinction between flags flying at government facilities and flags displayed in museums is a common argument in the flag debates. Flags flying at government facilities imply sovereignty and communicate symbolic messages of inclusion and exclusion that may have real consequences. Flags exhibited in museums are in an unambiguously historical context. These distinctions are often the basis of compromise, as many people honor the Confederate flag yet concede that state flags and state capitols are not the proper place for it.

Many flag flaps, however, occur on middle ground where battle flags exist on public property and on public symbols but in historical contexts that ostensibly make them less than assertions of sovereignty. Symptomatic of this contested middle ground is the compromise that brought down the battle flag from the South Carolina state house. The NAACP's 1999 resolution called for transfer "to a place of historical context rather than sovereignty context." Although the new flag was placed beside a monument honoring Confederate soldiers, the NAACP believed this was still a sovereignty context. A subsequent statement rephrased the demand to emphasize that "if people want to fly the Confederate flag, they should fly it on private property and not public grounds."[2]

Beyond their presence on state flags and state capitols, Confederate flags have adorned public symbols and public property throughout the South. Confederate flags have been on city and county seals, in city halls and court houses, and in public spaces of all kinds. Unlike the flags raised over the state houses of South Carolina and Alabama, few of the flags dotting the South's public landscape appeared in the 1960s in the midst of the civil rights struggles, carrying at least a whisper of a segregationist message. Some appeared during the flag fad of the late 1940s and 1950s when whites rediscovered the flag and felt free to adopt Confederate symbolism without consulting the wishes or feelings of African Americans. Others have appeared in more recent decades, when African Americans have been actors on the political stage. Most of the public flag symbols ostensibly commemorate the Confederate past, and their historical message is louder and clearer than those of Confederate flags on state flags and capitols.

African-American activists tended to define broadly the flag's sovereignty context. "The NAACP will forever fight to remove any remnants of the Confederacy which exist and are displayed as a matter of public policy," declared board chairman Earl T. Shinhoster in 1994. The effect of this posture was to cast African Americans in the role of aggressors, disturbers of the peace and the status quo. Not surprisingly, Confederate heritage advocates blamed the NAACP for making "the battle flag a 'political' issue."[3] The NAACP and Southern Christian Leadership Conference (SCLC) activists who pursued the agenda do so because they contend that the battle flag and other Confederate symbols were "offensive" and "reminders of slavery." More tangibly, activists regarded flags displayed on public property as symptomatic of attitudes and policies that are potentially threatening to the rights and well-being of African-American citizens.

Defenders of Confederate flags displayed on public property contended that the flags represented history and that removing them would be tantamount to erasing history. Indeed, many of the public flags that became the objects of protest seemed to be inoffensive symbols of historical facts. Pondering the prospect of removing the Confederate flag from the Six Flags over Texas theme park (one of several southern theme parks celebrating the sovereign entities to which the state or region has belonged), *Houston Post* editor Lynn Ashby concluded: "Taking down a flag, in this instance, is rather like rewriting history, pretending something didn't happen when we all know it did." For Ashby, flags represented "history"—objective facts about the past that did not necessarily dictate how people should regard the past. The Six Flags displays in Texas also include those of Mexico and Spain. Does that mean, Ashby asked, that Texans are proud of Santa Anna's corrupt rule, the Goliad massacre, or the Spanish Inquisition?[4]

Many of the recent flag flaps turn on the question of whether flags acknowledge objective historical fact or celebrate the Confederacy. Is it possible to accept the public presence of Confederate flags as recognition of history without promoting or celebrating the Confederacy? Conversely, are the demands of flag advocates for the retention of publicly displayed flags preservation of history or are they tacit demands that governments honor and celebrate Confederate soldiers and, more controversial, the Confederate cause for which they fought?

Confederate symbols in public places—often vestiges of the flag fad era—can exist unnoticed for decades. They are tangible reminders of the former prominence of Confederate veterans and their progeny in southern life—and, not coincidentally, of the exclusion of African Americans from mainstream public life during the Jim Crow era. Two incidents in Virginia in 1992 reveal the consequences when old Confederate flags are rediscovered.

In 1914 the former Confederate capital adopted a city flag that incorporated the battle flag. The flag testified to the official pride in the city's Confederate heritage that reigned supreme before racial integration. The flag was the brainchild of Mayor Carlton McCarthy, a prominent Confederate veteran and author of the popular book *Detailed Minutiae of Soldier Life in the Army of Northern Virginia*. One side of the blue silk flag featured a shield bearing the Confederate battle flag and the Confederate motto "Deo Vindice" (usually translated "With God as Our Defender"). "In the eloquent words of Mayor McCarthy," resolved the Confederate Museum in support of the 1907 proposal, the flag would thus "'accept and proclaim to the world the brief period of the War and the gallant part of our proud city as the crowning glory and highest excellence of the past,' this shield expressing 'the historic fact that Richmond was the Capital of the Great Southern Confederacy, and the leading city of the South.'" By the 1990s Richmond's population was more than fifty percent black, and city officials (including many black officials) hardly considered the Confederate period the "crowning glory" of Richmond's past. But the city flag never enjoyed a high public profile and consequently did not become a target of black resentment in the 1970s when activists forced the lowering of other Confederate flags. Its existence did come to public attention in 1992; and a year later the city adopted a new city flag.[5]

The 1992 controversy grew out of another much noisier flag flap that unfolded a month earlier. The *Richmond Free Press* published a story about a complaint from a black member of the 149th Fighter Squadron, 192nd

Fighter Group, Virginia Air National Guard, about his unit's insignia, which featured a screaming eagle holding a bomb in one talon emblazoned against a battle flag motif. Prompted by the story, Virginia Governor L. Douglas Wilder, Jr., a decorated Korean War veteran who was the nation's first elected black governor, ordered the insignia changed. Removed immediately from uniforms and planes, vestiges of the insignia remained—on coffee mugs, on a cartoon figure on the gate, and in the pilot's lounge—until they were removed voluntarily several months later.[6]

The squadron's insignia had originated in the midst of the flag fad that seized American military forces in the early 1950s. Three pilots conceived the idea in early 1951 when they went on active duty in the Korean War. Some of the men in the Richmond-based 149th—an all-white unit until the early 1960s (and still overwhelmingly white in 1992)— called themselves informally the Rebel Squadron. After years of revising the insignia and navigating through government red tape, the airmen won official recognition of the symbol in 1957. Members of the unit had the insignia copyrighted just a few years before Governor Wilder ordered its removal. The squadron commander told the *Free Press* that some of the airmen were disappointed at the order and denied that it carried any racist meaning. It was, insisted another officer, an expression of "the warrior spirit of the militia" from which the squadron descends.[7] Whatever disappointment the commander and his men felt, they obeyed the order without public complaint.

The apparent equanimity with which the controversy was settled masked strong feelings and bitterness. Staff Sergeant Leon D. Brooks, the African-American airman whose complaint triggered the controversy, had voiced his feelings periodically since entering the service in 1971. A month after the governor's order, the Guard dismissed Brooks, reportedly as part of a routine "culling" of veterans. Brooks challenged his nonretention and was reinstated by order of the governor, though a report insisted that the insignia had nothing to do with the dismissal. Not restrained by military protocol, veterans of the unit expressed outrage at the implication that the insignia or the flag was a symbol of slavery or racism and warned that outlawing the insignia heralded a wider attack on history and heritage. "Now that the emblem is gone, what will be next?" asked a retired air force lieutenant colonel. "The statues on Monument Avenue?" If we must eliminate all "reminders of slavery," wrote another retired officer, why not raze the James River plantations, delete all references to slavery in the history books, or ban *Uncle Tom's Cabin?*[8]

The battle flag is part of the official symbolism of cities and counties throughout the South. While sometimes a vestige of earlier generations' fascination with or veneration of the Confederacy, official display of the flag can often be traced to a symbolic recognition of local history. Officials have had to grapple with the hazy distinctions between recognizing the fact of the Confederacy's existence and symbolically approving of the Confederacy.

In 1993 officials in Winchester, Virginia, a small city in the Shenandoah Valley with a rich Civil War history, were contemplating a new city flag to replace one that critics complained resembled the logo of the Food Lion grocery store chain. One suggestion was to replace the Norman lion with the city seal. The seal, however, consisted of four flags that have flown over Winchester: the Union Jack, the Stars and Stripes, the Virginia state flag, and the Confederate battle flag. Faced with "rumblings about a lawsuit" and complaints from the Southern Christian Leadership Conference, the city dropped all talk of a flag change. A decade later, the city seal remained unchanged. In contrast, officials in Hillsborough County (Tampa), Florida, in 1993–1994 removed the Confederate battle flag from the city seal. The Sons of Confederate Veterans declared the change a "heritage violation" and tried unsuccessfully to reverse it.[9]

The NAACP in 2000–2001 mobilized against the logo of Lake City, Florida. Adopted in the 1980s to commemorate the nearby Battle of Olustee, the seal features a battle flag, a white soldier on horseback, and a black foot soldier with a rifle. On the weekend of the annual Olustee reenactment—which was a major source of revenue for the inland Florida city—the NAACP staged a one-day boycott and rally. The event backfired when pro-flag counter-demonstrators outnumbered those in the rally.[10]

In August 2000 the city of Mobile, Alabama, replaced the battle flag on the city seal, which features the flags of the six nations that have governed Mobile since 1702. Instead of a battle flag, the first national flag (Stars and Bars) would represent the Confederacy as it did in other city logos; a compromise solution substituted the Confederate third national flag. Even though the third national flag includes the St. Andrew's cross and was the flag of the Confederacy at the time of Mobile's April 1865 surrender, Confederate heritage organizations protested vehemently and lobbied for restoration of the battle flag. The protest cooled when the city's mayor announced a policy of respect for all cultures, including "Confederate American," and appointed a panel to study heritage issues.[11]

Displays of historical flags on public property have also sparked controversies over the difference between merely acknowledging and celebrating Confederate history. In 1978, outside its newly renovated capitol building, the state of Florida established a display of four historical flags (French, Spanish, British, and Confederate) representing other empires or unions to which the state once belonged. The Confederate flag was initially the third national pattern, replaced in the 1980s with the second national flag—both of which feature a square battle flag in the canton. Two African-American lawmakers in 1996 introduced legislation to cut off funding for the Confederate flags. A state senator maintained that the Confederate flag was "offensive" and that "we ought not be putting up symbols that are offensive." Democratic Governor Lawton Chiles disagreed. The Confederate flag was simply "part of our history" and did not signal a return to "the old days." "You can't erase history," Chiles concluded. Chiles deferred to the secretary of state, who defended the historical integrity of the flag's presence. "There are a lot of people out there who believe very strongly that we need to continue with our historical perspective," she observed.[12]

Five years later, Governor Jeb Bush, brother of the newly elected U.S. president, announced that he would not replace the flag display, which had been removed temporarily as part of a remodeling project. Instead, the flags would be moved to a display at the nearby Florida Museum of History. The governor's office explained that Bush "believes that most

Floridians would agree that the symbols of Florida's past should not be displayed in a manner that may divide Floridians today." A representative of the Florida Division of the SCV expressed a sense of betrayal over the unanticipated decision.[13]

During the Civil War, Oklahoma was part of Indian Territory, home to the so-called Five Civilized Tribes that allied formally with the Confederacy in 1861. Since 1966 the Confederate battle flag had been part of a display on a plaza outside the state capitol building of fourteen flags (including those of Indian nations) that have flown over what is now Oklahoma since 1541. Not unlike the situation in Florida, renovation of the plaza led to the removal of the flags in 1987. State officials declared that the Confederate flag would not be restored. In response, the legislature in 1988 passed a bill requiring the reinstallation of the Confederate flag, and the governor signed it. The governor stipulated, however, that the flag would not be replaced until the legislature directed which Confederate flag should fly. For ten years the pole remained empty. The Claremore Camp of the SCV filed a lawsuit contending that the state violated the 1988 law. A county district judge threw out the suit, agreeing with the state attorney general that the act was "void and unenforceable" because it was ambiguous about which flag should fly (stating only that "the Confederate States of America flag of 1861 to 1865" should fly) and that it was omitted from the state's 1991 Code.[14]

The response to a compromise proposal offered in 1998 by a state legislator revealed where the battle lines were drawn. Representative Wayne Pettigrew proposed to substitute the Stars and Bars in place of the battle flag that had formerly represented the Confederacy in the flag display. African-American legislators rejected the proposal and pledged to prevent the return of any Confederate flag. A spokesman for the SCV also rejected the proposal because most people did not recognize the Stars and Bars as a Confederate flag. Years later, flag supporters were still trying to restore the flag.[15]

In Oklahoma and in other places, the spats over public displays of historical flags reveal several ironies. No one ever complains about the customary display of the Union Jack—the standard of the foreign nation against which the United States fought a war of liberation—while the Confederate flag almost always elicits complaint. The reasons for this apparent inconsistency are easy to see. The Union Jack is the flag of a sovereign state that has been America's closest ally for nearly a century; furthermore, British rule is no longer a threat to the American populace. In contrast, African Americans (primarily) perceive the Confederacy and its prospective resurrection as tangible threats to their security and rights.

The flag display disputes also underscore the continuing ironic relationship between the St. Andrew's cross flag and the Stars and Bars. Displays of flags representing one-time sovereign authorities—whether they are at state capitols or at private theme parks—derive their historical integrity from the use of flags that represent nations. Use of the rectangular or square battle flag in such displays is erroneous; it is a non sequitur to have a battle flag grouped with national flags of other former sovereigns that have ruled territory in the American South.

The erroneous use of the battle flag (or, more accurately, the naval jack) illustrates the continuing widespread popular belief that the battle flag is *the* Confederate flag. It also reveals the desire to use a flag familiar to most people as a Confederate symbol. That the Stars and Bars is a Confederate flag is immaterial; just as Confederates rejected it in 1863 because it was not distinct enough from the Stars and Stripes, Confederate partisans today reject it because it is not a sufficiently Confederate symbol.[16] Defenders of the public display of Confederate flags complain about the effort to erase or revise history. The insistence on using battle flags instead of historically correct national flags reveals a double standard on the issue of revising history.

Insistence on symbolic familiarity over historical accuracy was apparent in a controversy in Pensacola, Florida. In 1949—coincident with the national flag fad—Pensacola boosters promoted the Gulf Coast port and tourist mecca as the City of Five Flags and erected poles for the Spanish, French, British, Confederate, and American flags near the waterfront. At the same time, a committee of citizens inaugurated an annual festival, The Fiesta of Five Flags, to define the city's image. Held variously between April and early June, the fiesta included pageants, parades, balls, auto and boat races, fishing tournaments, and children's treasure hunts. The fiesta was primarily a celebration of the city's founding by Spanish nobleman Tristan De Luna. The Confederate flag was not prominent in the fiesta or the Five Flags tradition. From the beginning of this civic celebration, however, civic boosters chose to use the familiar and popular battle flag, without much thought to either historical accuracy or racial innuendo.[17]

In January 2000 Pensacola City Manager Tom Bonfield announced his decision that the Stars and Bars would replace the battle flag in the city's flag display. Apparently prompted by an impending demand by a local civil rights organization, Movement for Change, to remove the Confederate flag, Bonfield defended the decision as historically correct. Bonfield consulted several historians, including a local historian and newspaper editor who had been arguing since the 1960s that the Stars and Bars should replace the battle flag in the city's official and unofficial iconography. Pensacola was under Confederate control only until the spring of 1862; the Stars and Bars was the only Confederate flag ever to fly over the city. Nevertheless, a stream of local SCV members and other flag supporters publicly accused Bonfield of dishonoring Confederate veterans, erasing history, and "rewriting history" (likening it to the Nazis). Decrying the change for completely different reasons, the Movement for Change president observed sarcastically to Bonfield, "It's supposed to make me feel happier because it's historically correct? You've been insensitive to us." Pensacola's City Council approved the flag change by a seven-to-two vote, but neighboring Escambia County's governing board voted unanimously to retain the battle flag for its version of the Five Flags observances. The organizers of the fiesta quietly began using the Stars and Bars.[18] The pro-flag bitterness in Pensacola was unfounded. The five flags were intended to acknowledge historical fact, not to honor soldiers.

Not unfounded, however, are suspicions that public officials are reluctant to display Confederate flags. One flag pole in Oklahoma City stands bare. Officials in Tallahassee moved the state's flag display to a museum rather than allow a Confederate flag to be part of it. The same fate befell a display of historical flags in Cumberland, Maryland, in August 1994. Officials removed Confederate, British, and French flags from the City Hall rotunda after complaints from the Allegheny County Chapter of the NAACP. Located in a part of western Maryland that was strongly Unionist in the Civil War, Cumberland was occupied briefly by Confederate cavalry in June 1863—thus justifying the Confederate flag, which a citizen had donated to the county history museum thirty years earlier.[19]

Why are historical flag displays objectionable, and why are public officials responsive to complaints against them? Unlike the state flags of Georgia and Mississippi or the flags over the capitols of Alabama and South Carolina, historical flag displays do not imply sovereignty or compel the allegiance of unwilling citizens. They are merely symbolic statements of historical facts. The complaints *could be,* but rarely are, about historical accuracy. It is, for example, open to question whether a Confederate flag of any kind belongs in Oklahoma's flag display; the alliance of five (deeply divided) Indian tribes with the Confederacy hardly made the unorganized Indian Territory part of the Confederacy. Similarly, if the brief Confederate occupation of Cumberland is enough to warrant a flag, why don't Confederate flags fly from poles in every town that Confederate forces entered in Maryland, Pennsylvania, Ohio, and Indiana?

Confederate flags in historical flag displays or on official seals are contextual; they derive their meaning from the other flags. For the same reason, they are ostensibly neutral and make historical rather than political statements. Critics claim, however, that flags still convey political and ideological messages. In part this is because African Americans did not participate in the creation of flag displays. The displays are in a sense testaments of black powerlessness in earlier eras. Similarly, while historical flags can be neutral, they can also be an implicit approval or celebration of history. Complaints that removal of Confederate flags "dishonor" Confederate ancestors imply conversely that the flags' presence is intended to honor Confederates. This, of course, is one of the central sources of contention regarding public displays of Confederate symbols. Flag advocates want governments to honor Confederate soldiers or even to proclaim public approval of the Confederacy itself. Flag critics oppose public display of Confederate symbols because it implies approval of the Confederate cause for which the soldiers fought. They commonly insist that they acknowledge people's rights to display flags on their own property and person and oppose only state-sanctioned use of the flag.

The line between individual expression and state approval is not always clear. Beginning in the mid-1990s, several state governments resisted the efforts of the SCV to obtain state-issued specialty license plates bearing the organization's logo featuring a square Confederate battle flag. Maryland had already issued such plates to seventy-eight motorists when complaints from African-American political leaders prompted a recall. Delegate Clarence Mitchell IV (D-Baltimore) said bluntly: "The Black Caucus will not allow the state to do this." "We don't want to see those tags anywhere in Maryland—not one of them. If the group wants to put a flag sticker on a plain Maryland tag, that is their business, but we are not about to allow state money to be used for that purpose." Black lawmakers objected not only to the battle flag logo but to the word "Confederate." "Their name itself is offensive to us," Mitchell remarked. "It would be just like seeing the words 'Brothers of the Nazi Party.'" The SCV's commander-in-chief, Patrick J. Griffin III, of Maryland, noted incredulously: "If they can block us from even using our name, where have we come as a society?" The Virginia-based conservative Rutherford Institute filed suit on behalf of the SCV, and a judge quickly ruled that the recall was unconstitutional. The SCV allied with the American Civil Liberties Union to compel the North Carolina Department of Motor Vehicles to issue SCV specialty plates. A federal appeals court decided that the SCV qualified as a "nationally recognized civic organization" entitled to have specialty plates.[20]

Virginia legislators attempted to finesse the constitutional problem by allowing plates to be issued without the battle flag logo. The African-American state legislator who persuaded his colleagues to prohibit the flag logo recounted his own childhood experiences. "We were not only told, 'Nigger stay out, nigger go home,' because we would dare to integrate their schools, but we were greeted with waving Confederate flags."

He asked his fellow delegates "to remove my pain and your pain that you will feel every time that flag is flown on this official emblem—a license plate—up and down the highways of Virginia."

Following the precedent in Maryland, the Rutherford Institute represented the SCV in a lawsuit filed in Federal District Court. The outcome was the same as it had been in Maryland and North Carolina. A federal judge ruled that prohibiting the logo was a restriction of free speech. He noted that Virginia had approved almost three hundred specialty plates, many of them for "politically engaged" organizations such as the National Rifle Association and the AFL-CIO. Virginia appealed the ruling, and a federal appeals court upheld it.[21]

The license plate controversies and the court victories gave the SCV an ideal pulpit from which to broadcast its warnings about prejudice against the Confederate flag. Even when associated explicitly and strictly with the organization that claims ownership of it, the battle flag was objectionable to some African-American activists. Apparently, in their view, the perceptions and feelings of people who objected to the flag should take precedence over the intentions and the desires of those who revered it. That state governments issued the plates raised legitimate public concern, but it is far-fetched to conclude that the plates represent state sponsorship of the flag. Unlike the 1961 incident when Spotsylvania County, Virginia, issued plates bearing the Confederate battle flag, state governments were not compelling citizens to display a symbol that offended them. State governments were merely allowing those who want to display the flag in this way to do so. As the several court opinions unanimously agreed, the restrictions on SCV plates amount to the silencing of one voice among the cacophony of voices already being expressed on state-issued license plates. If the SCV tags represent state endorsement of the Confederacy, then the hundreds of other approved plates represent state endorsement of groups ranging from political activists to single-sex private colleges.

Several other controversies demonstrated that hostility to the flag extended to circumstances in which the historical context of the flag display was seemingly clear and appropriate. Regarded by Confederate heritage organizations primarily as a war memorial to Confederate soldiers, the battle flag would seem indisputably appropriate at Confederate cemeteries. Although most Confederate soldiers are buried in private cemeteries in the South, tens of thousands of men who died in federal prison camps lie in national cemeteries in the North, administered by the U.S. Department of Veterans Affairs (VA). One of the largest is the Point Lookout National Cemetery in southern Maryland, which is the burial site of 3,300 Confederate POWs who died in the Civil War's largest prison. A 1998 VA policy limited the flying of Confederate flags to Memorial Day and, where applicable, Confederate Memorial Day.

Patrick J. Griffin III, the SCV's commander-in-chief and a descendant of a soldier buried at the Point Lookout National Cemetery, at his own expense sought to erect a flag pole and fly a Confederate flag at the cemetery permanently. When the department refused, Griffin filed suit in U.S. District Court. "I would submit to you, if there's a legitimate place to fly the Confederate flag, it is a Confederate cemetery," Griffin told reporters. Joining Griffin and the SCV in the suit was the Point Lookout POW Descendants Organization. The NAACP was not party to the dispute, but a spokesman for the local chapter observed that "any time we can limit [the flag's] exposure on public property, it's worthwhile."[22]

Federal courts split on the validity of Griffin's suit. In January 2001 federal judge William N. Nickerson found for Griffin and the SCV. Quoting liberally from the precedents of the Georgia state flag and the Maryland SCV license plate cases, Nickerson agreed that the flag restriction at Point Lookout did amount to restriction of free speech. He rejected the government's contention that the restriction was neutral in viewpoint and was based solely on a desire to prevent disruption at national cemeteries. The government's "continual reference to the Confederate flag as a symbol of racial intolerance and divisiveness," Nickerson argued, "clearly demonstrates that Defendants are choosing, and advancing, the viewpoint of those offended by the flag over the viewpoint of those proud of the flag. This preference is not viewpoint neutral and is, therefore, impermissible." Griffin would be allowed to erect and maintain a flag pole and fly a Confederate flag as long as it is three feet lower than the U.S. flag and erected near the monuments on the site.[23]

A year later, the Fourth Circuit Court of Appeals reversed the District

Court ruling. According to the appeals court, the "pivotal point" of the case was whether the men at Point Lookout were to be honored as Confederates or Americans. Without clear factual evidence on this, the court deferred to the VA and held "that the purpose of Point Lookout is to honor the soldiers buried there as Americans." If the VA believed that the Confederate flag contradicted its fundamental message, it was within its constitutional rights to prohibit the flag. In reality, the judges ruled, far from being discriminated against, "groups who wish to fly the Confederate flag actually enjoy an advantage over other groups" because they were able to fly their flag two days a year "without seeking special permission."[24]

If the Confederate flag could not fly at a Confederate cemetery, could it fly on public property that was also a Confederate shrine? The home of a prominent citizen of Danville, Virginia, William T. Sutherlin, became enshrined as the "Last Capitol of the Confederacy" because Jefferson Davis and his cabinet stayed there for a week after the evacuation of Richmond in April 1865. Saved from destruction in 1912 by the Danville Confederate Memorial Association, the mansion became city property when the association, unable to pay the mortgage and the remaining purchase price, sold it to the city to be used as a Confederate memorial and cultural center. From 1928 until 1971 the building served primarily as the public library for Danville's white population. With the construction of a new library in 1971, the mansion was leased to the Danville Chapter of the Virginia Museum of Fine Arts, which used part of the building for exhibition galleries and restored a few rooms to their 1865 appearance.[25]

The city erected flag poles in front of the building in 1949 and flew U.S. and Confederate flags. During the 1950s and 1960s, according to local lore, a battle flag and a Stars and Bars occupied the two poles. The Danville Museum replaced the battle flag with the Stars and Stripes in the 1970s. In 1985 a local SCV camp provided the museum with the Confederacy's third national flag, which was the historically correct flag at the time of the building's week of fame in 1865.[26]

The presence of the flag on city property did not become a political issue until the early 1990s. During a march in honor of Martin Luther

King, Jr., the local SCLC branch stopped at the museum and ceremoniously lowered the Confederate flag. Eager to dispel its image as "a club for wealthy white people," the museum held a roundtable conference to discuss the museum's continuing outreach programs to the black community; black leaders cited the flag as one barrier to black involvement.[27]

Opponents of flying the flag had political leverage because the city owned and maintained the building. At a city council meeting in June 1993, Joyce Glaise, one of two African-American council members, linked the flag with plans to spend more than $100,000 for modernizing the building. "I have a real problem paying the kind of money we are paying for a building with a Confederate flag," Glaise remarked. Three days later, the museum's governing body voted unanimously to strike the colors. As a gesture to flag defenders, the board voted simultaneously to create inside the museum an educational gallery interpreting the flags of the Confederacy. "We've tried to make everybody a little less happy," explained the museum board chairman. Councilwoman Glaise and the SCLC's leader, the Reverend William Avon Keen, accepted the arrangement.[28] Local Confederate heritage organizations did not.

"We Southern Americans are a little pissed off," remarked one member of the local SCV. Public response was overwhelmingly against the decision to take down the flag. Glaise received more calls on this than she had on any other issue. The local paper made the flag controversy the subject of its weekly poll and received a record number of responses—more than seven thousand, compared with the previous high of three thousand. Ninety-five percent (6,803 of the 7,000) believed that the Confederate flag ought to continue flying at the museum.[29]

Confederate partisans also dramatized their indignation with public demonstrations. Approximately 150 flag supporters rallied outside the museum on a Sunday in late June 1993. Two weeks after the rally, a group calling itself the Confederate American Heritage Association organized the first of a series of controversial "heritage runs." Meeting in a parking lot on the outskirts of town, flag defenders attached flags to their car antennas and drove through the city to, and around, the museum.[30]

In an effort to end the strife, the museum board offered an olive branch in the form of a compromise proposal. With the consultation and the blessing of the city council—including Joyce Glaise—the board offered to raise the Confederate flag on an unspecified number of holidays each year. (Eventually, the board arrived at twenty-three unspecified appropriate Confederate "holidays" to fly the flag.) On some, but not all, of the designated days, the museum would also sponsor educational programs about Confederate flags. "The only way we can deal with the issue of the flag is on an educational basis," declared museum officials. The compromise pleased some but not all. The SCLC leaders opposed it, as did Confederate heritage activists who insisted that the flag must fly at the museum—"A Confederate Memorial"—every day.[31]

A new organization, the Danville Chapter of the Heritage Preservation Association (HPA), committed itself to unrestricted display of the Confederate flag at the museum. The HPA circulated petitions and made the flag an issue in the May 1994 city council elections. The HPA also offered to erect and maintain a new flag pole in front of the museum and raise and lower a Confederate flag. The city attorney drafted an ordinance with fifteen preconditions that in effect required the Danville HPA chapter to become strictly a local historical organization and no longer act as a southern heritage pressure group. One precondition was that the HPA declare its corporate purpose to be the promotion and encouragement of interest in the "Last Capitol" and the commemoration of Danville's Civil War history. The HPA was to pledge that display of the flag was "for historical purposes only and for no political purposes whatsoever."[32]

The HPA changed tactics and offered the city a "gift": a privately funded monument on museum grounds to commemorate the Sutherlin mansion's history as the "last capitol of the Confederacy." Permanently displayed on a fifteen-foot pole atop the marble obelisk would be a third Confederate national flag. "We wanted this to make it clear that this was a historical statement and not a political statement," explained HPA branch lawyer Robert Beard. The transparent underlying reason for the HPA's change was that a monument might give greater assurance to continual display of the flag.[33]

Danville civil rights leaders were distressed at the council's apparent willingness to consider giving the HPA authority to fly the flag at the museum. The SCLC's Avon Keen called the April draft law "city-supported racism." In July a coalition of civil rights groups, black and white, registered their opinion on the proposed monument before the council.[34]

Despite such protest, in September 1994, Danville city council voted seven-to-two along strictly racial lines to authorize the Heritage Preservation Association to erect a monument on museum property. Within six months, the HPA raised seven thousand dollars for a seven-foot-tall granite obelisk topped by a fifteen-foot-tall pole flying a third national flag. Approximately 150 people attended the dedication on March 26, 1995, an event which featured speeches by the state Republican Party chairman, national HPA officers R. Lee Collins and Charles Lunsford, and two black scholars who emphasized the unity of the races in the Old South and the need for racial harmony. "Now [the flag] will fly 365 days, 24 hours a day, and the city nor the museum will never take it down," remarked HPA chapter president R. Wayne Byrd.[35]

The tenor of the speeches at the monument dedication testified to the blurry line between commemoration of Confederate history and the promotion of conservative politics. Dressed in the uniform of a Confederate officer, the local HPA member who had the honor of raising the flag over the monument was the same man who had waved a battle flag at the state Republican convention the previous June and told reporters that the flag "is all about states' rights and limiting the federal government." The keynote speaker was state Republican Party chairman Patrick McSweeney, a conservative who had publicly defended flying the Confederate flag. "The mindless reaction of those who condemn any public expression of sympathy for the Confederacy or Confederate leaders or soldiers cannot go unchallenged," McSweeney intoned at the monument dedication. He excoriated the "political correctness" that would have Virginians ignore or distort their traditions. The Confederacy could not be expunged from the state's history books, he argued, "because Virginia's participation in the Confederate cause was not an aberration." In a letter read aloud at the dedication ceremony, conservative Republican Governor (subsequently U.S. senator) George F. Allen declared that the monument "will help our community and our nation to honor and preserve states' rights."[36]

Governor Allen's remarks and the conservative political activism of flag defenders crossed a line that supposedly exists between merely acknowledging the facts of history and endorsing a point of view about history. Suspecting or knowing that a Confederate battle flag on public property stands as an endorsement of "states' rights" (and the racist purposes that this doctrine has often served) makes black opposition to supposed historical displays understandable. The insistence that acknowledging history does not constitute endorsement belies the truism that historical monuments, markers, and symbols erected on a modern landscape invariably reflect the initiative and the agenda of people removed in time from the period commemorated. Interpreting a monument at a historic site requires a viewer to consider as many as three contexts: the event or period commemorated; the period in which the monument was erected; and the viewer's own time.[37] The same reasoning applies to the interpretation of Confederate flags in historical contexts. Whether or not a flag really symbolizes history in an essentially neutral way depends on the occasion and motives that put it there.

The Confederacy was an undeniably important part of southern and American history and warrants study and remembrance. The South's public landscape should and must carry visible reminders that for four years the South effectively existed apart from the United States. Those who condemn the Confederacy have as much of a stake in remembering those four years as those who celebrate it. But the erection and maintenance of Confederate memorials on public property is necessarily a balancing act and requires diplomacy and compromise. Those who insist on public flag displays scorn the notion that flags should be relegated to museums. South Carolina Senator Glenn McConnell rejected a compromise proposal that would remove the Confederate flag from the state capitol dome and instead display three actual 1860s flags in sealed cases on the capitol grounds. "Encasement represents entombment," McConnell reasoned, and he wanted "no part in symbolically burying the Confederate banner."[38] It is curious that relegating historical symbols of a defunct nation to history museums or to historical displays should elicit such scorn. The Confederate battle flag as a historical symbol would not be erased from history if it were to be relegated to historical displays. Those who insist that the Confederate flag is history and that it should not be erased either have little faith in history museums or they are really insisting the flag be something more than just history. In effect, they insist that the public must accept the flag not merely as a historical symbol but also as a *living* symbol.

The flag is history, but for many people it is also a symbol with a potent ideological meaning to be preserved and perpetuated; its display does not merely acknowledge a *fact* of history but implies a favorable judgment on that history. What is at stake is not so much history as *heritage*. Although the terms are often used interchangeably, they are in many ways opposites of each other. The discipline of history strives to present the past objectively, but acknowledges that historical interpretation is inevitably subjective and must evolve as new evidence and new perspectives emerge. Heritage is more akin to religion than history. It is a presentation of the past based not on critical evaluation of evidence but on faith and the acceptance of dogma. Heritage seeks to define and propagate *Truth* and often does so with the selective use of evidence. Heritage affirms the historical myths essential for national, cultural, or subcultural identity.[39] The southern-heritage insistence that the Confederate battle flag must have a prominent public presence could be, but rarely is, an insistence that people must explore the history of the Confederacy in all its complexity. Instead, it is usually an insistence on the presentation of history that portrays the Confederacy and Confederates in a favorable light. The purging of Confederate flags from the public landscape *can* be tantamount to erasing history. But the casualty of removing flags is usually not history but heritage. Governments have an obligation not to demean the heritage of racial and cultural groups that comprise their public, but they are not obligated to promote them at the expense of others.

Epilogue

The Second American Flag

During the dramatic collapse of communism in Eastern Europe in 1989–1991, the people of the former Soviet bloc countries poured into city streets to celebrate their new freedom. American observers noted with interest that among the flags and banners appearing in the crowds was an occasional Confederate battle flag. The battle flag, explained Sons of Confederate Veterans Commander-in-Chief Robert L. Hawkins III in 1993, "is not just a southern symbol. It is an American symbol and an international symbol." The SCV, he noted, had "received numerous requests from the former Eastern Bloc countries for receipt of Confederate flags, which they viewed as an appropriate symbol of their struggle for independence against totalitarian control." The flag reappeared in the mid-1990s amid student pro-democracy protests in Yugoslavia.[1]

No doubt some East Europeans embraced the flag as a symbol of national liberation, but the battle flag had other meanings in modern Europe. On a three-week trip through Western Europe in 1992, I continually encountered the battle flag—in Trier, Germany, on cloth patches bearing the word "Rebel" over the saltire; in Würzburg, on a triangular pennant hanging on the rearview mirror of a BMW; in Vienna, on a leather-jacket patch that also featured a profile of the young Elvis Presley; and in Florence and Venice, on T-shirts with a motorcycle-riding skeleton emblazoned over the saltire.

Upon my return, I asked a German correspondent what all this meant. While acknowledging that skinheads, Ku Klux Klansmen, and "tougher type" motorcyclists used the flag, the director of the Confederate & Civil War Research Center attributed flag use to the association between the flag, Elvis, the American South, and individual rebellion. An American newspaper correspondent traveling in post-Communist Krakow, Poland, similarly found a Confederate flag hanging outside the Biker and Rebel Shop, located in the same neighborhood as the Dixie Chicken and the Cotton Club. A mail-order catalogue out of Hamburg, Germany, advertised a wide variety of Confederate flag clothing. Calling itself the Western Store, the company sold the flag-adorned shirts and belts along with Stetsons, boots, and other cowboy wear.[2]

Whether as a symbol of national liberation or of individual expression and rebelliousness, in Europe the Confederate battle flag is associated typically with American values and American culture. From a vantage point beyond our shores, the Confederate flag is an American symbol. While Americans naturally have a greater understanding of the Confederate flag's more specific and divisive connotations, the Europeans have grasped something that Americans take for granted: the Confederate flag is fundamentally an American flag.

Realizing and accepting that the battle flag is an American symbol born of and nurtured by American impulses is essential for anyone hoping to understand the flag and the loyalty it commands. Even though the battle flag was the banner of a people striving to break away from the Union and protect the institution of slavery, those people were Americans and the aspirations they expressed were arguably constitutional in 1861.

The Confederate flag is not an alien symbol grafted onto the American tradition and is not therefore simply going to disappear. The people who fly or revere the flag will not become extinct, and they will resist efforts to reeducate them to view it as offensive. On the contrary, they will pass on reverence for the flag from generation to generation and strive to re-educate others to accept their understanding of its meaning. For them, the flag will always be a war memorial and summon heroic visions of soldiers fighting for southern independence, not slavery or racism. If precedent serves as a guide to the future, insults hurled at the flag and demands for its removal will prompt more people to rally to its defense.

Flag scholar Rosalind Urbach Moss has insightfully dubbed the Confederate flag "a second American flag." Like the Stars and Stripes, the battle flag is rooted in American tradition, ever-present and available to express a variety of opinions and viewpoints. Often, the "second American flag" expresses feelings of American patriotism—most notably in the hands of U.S. servicemen during World War II and Korea and in the modern military forces. When a southern heritage fringe group protested the presence of a U.S. flag near a Confederate monument in Luray, Virginia, a Sons of Confederate Veterans officer registered his group's disagreement. "Southerners have a unique heritage in the South as well as a United States heritage—and we're very proud of [both]," explained Henry Kidd. "Many of us gave our lives defending Old Glory."[3] Kidd's statement echoed the "dual loyalty" ideal that Randolph McKim articulated in 1904. Indeed, most SCV camps pledge allegiance to the U.S. flag before they salute the Confederate battle flag at their meetings.

The second American flag has also stood in symbolic opposition to the Stars and Stripes and against those who carry the national standard. This was especially true during the Civil War and again during the civil rights era when white southerners with Confederate flags confronted protesters bearing the Stars and Stripes across a new kind of battle line. The Confederate flag's meaning in the 1960s was logically and historically consistent with its meaning in the 1860s—as a symbol of opposition to the employment of federal authority to change the South's racial status quo. There could be no more fitting symbol for this opposition than the Confederate battle flag. Although segregationists lost their battle and their cause was discredited, attitudes of white supremacy live on. So, too, does the campaign for states' rights, which is endemic to the American political tradition and enshrined in the Ninth and Tenth Amendments to the U.S. Constitution. And when the banners of white supremacy or of states' rights have been raised, the Confederate battle flag is raised along with them.

The capacity of the battle flag to express both American patriotism and often strident opposition to mainstream American ideals is further confirmation of its status as the second American flag. It shares this ambidextrous quality with the Stars and Stripes, which has stood both in symbolic opposition to and unity with the battle flag. The Ku Klux Klan has used the Stars and Stripes far longer and far more often than it has the St. Andrew's cross. Right-wing organizations in general, even those with southern origins and southern principles, have tended to similarly employ the national standard instead of the flag of the Confederacy.[4] In other words, the Stars and Stripes has proven perfectly capable of expressing the thoughts and values that critics of the Confederate flag fear and loathe. While the Stars and Stripes was the standard of the armies that defeated the Confederacy and of the civil rights activists who defeated Jim Crow, it was also the beloved standard of slaveholders in the antebellum South and of patriotic American segregationists in the 1950s and 1960s. They did not require a Confederate flag to express their visions of what they believed America was and should be.

The Citizens' Councils and other segregationist organizations and Confederate heritage groups have used the Stars and Stripes and the Confederate battle flag in tandem. While some may see the symbols as mutually exclusive, members of those groups regard them as complementary. The Confederate flag modifies the U.S. flag, defiantly symbolizing constitutional ideals and, for an untold number of people, social and cultural values they believe that modern America has rejected. The Confederate flag gives this defiance a specific reference point in time and place—the South in the 1860s. Responding to the charge that it was unpatriotic not to fly the Stars and Stripes on the Alabama capitol dome above the Confederate flag, Governor George Wallace denied that the Confederate flag was un-American. "The Confederate flag not only belongs to the people of the South but it belongs to the Nation—it is part of American history and American heritage."[5] The Confederate flag—

specifically the St. Andrew's cross—represented George Wallace's attitude toward the contentious issues of race and states' rights, but so too did the Stars and Stripes, which Wallace made a major part of his iconography.

Modern writers have documented the "southernization" of America, but it is no revelation that "southern" attitudes toward states' rights and race are not just southern but are in fact American attitudes. Historians acknowledge that "anti-slavery" impulses in the antebellum era were based on antipathy toward blacks and that the nation's willingness to allow the South to handle the "Negro problem" in its own way at the beginning of the twentieth century revealed common racial attitudes. "The way of the South," declared pioneering southern sociologist Howard Odum in 1947, "is first of all American and then southern." This was true especially in what Odum called "the supreme task" of race relations and opportunities. History, Odum wrote, taught that when faced with demographic circumstances resembling those of the South, white people of other regions turn against blacks as quickly and ferociously as white southerners.[6] The national electoral appeal of George Wallace and upheavals in the North over school busing vindicated Odum's observations.

The second American flag represents accurately the place of the South in the United States since 1865—as simultaneously an integral, even fiercely patriotic, part of the country and a distinct, sometimes alienated region that carries the unique burden of having fought and lost a war against the rest of the nation. This ambiguity figures prominently in the many musings over southern distinctiveness that have preoccupied pundits for the last half-century. What makes the South and southerners "southern" and what makes the South distinctive? Vanderbilt University sociologist Larry Griffin has argued that the South's distinctiveness and identity were "forged and honed" by a tradition of "political, legal, cultural, and even military contestation" with the rest of America. But, he hastened to add, the South has always been "American," even in its opposition.[7]

In the last decade, southern heritage activists have revived the oppositional tradition—replete with quasi-scientific racism and secession—

and have made the Confederate battle flag the sacred symbol of their cause. A congress of southern heritage organizations at New Albany, Mississippi, in October 1996 adopted a declaration based on the "historical regard for the integrity of distinct peoples" and the necessity of resisting the subversion of this "in a multicultural 'melting pot.'" Defining "southerners" as "a Christian people of Northwest European descent, with predominantly Anglo-Celtic institutions, traditions, culture, and heritage" (wherever they "may abide"), the New Albany Congress observed that "the European-derived peoples who constitute the American South" are the most threatened of all "distinct peoples." The Civil War had been a campaign to subjugate and obliterate the southern people, as were Reconstruction, the subsequent three-quarters of a century of continued "economic exploitation," and the "second, more terrible reconstruction" in the civil rights era. Civil rights "was thrust on us through propaganda, deceit, and force of arms by adherents of the Marxist, universalist ideology known as liberalism, an ideology alien to the southern people, contrary to God's laws, and destructive of all who are deceived by it." The attack continues today in a "relentless campaign of slander and abasement against our institutions, traditions, symbols, and history through destructive laws, biased reporting, and teaching of false universalist doctrines."

In response to these destructive tendencies, the New Albany Declaration offered a seven-point "Southern Creed" and a five-point "Resolve for Southern Self-Determination." The first two points of the resolve declared that "we shall never accept the defeat of the Confederacy, the subjugation of our people, nor the eradication of our symbols as the final judgment of history" and that "no honorable retreat or compromise is possible" in the "defense and preservation of southern symbols, monuments, relics, and history." The third point resolved "that the Confederate Battle flag is the banner of the southern people and stands preeminent as the most powerful symbol of liberty and southern nationhood in a constellation of venerable southern symbols."[8]

Since the New Albany Declaration, several southern heritage writers have published manuals for mobilizing grassroots efforts not only to protect Confederate symbols but to effect secession. Beyond displaying Confederate flags, the manifestoes recommend other gestures such as using "southron" language, playing "Dixie" and other southern anthems, and signaling rejection of the modern federal government by referring to their states as "occupied" and to zip codes as "occupation zones."[9]

Some southern heritage organizations combine reverence for Confederate symbols with explicit political and cultural agendas that descend logically from the states' rights, white supremacy, and religious conservatism of preceding generations. The League of the South and its offspring, the Southern Party, espouse symbolic and actual secession from the Union as a viable means of escaping a mainstream American culture they denounce as "violent and profane, coarse and rude, cynical and deviant, and repugnant to the southern people and to every people with Christian sensibilities."[10]

Unsettling as these statements and gestures are to those who do not subscribe to them, they represent an enduring voice in the American political and cultural dialogue. The increasingly bellicose southern heritage movement resonates mostly among white Americans who are on the conservative side of today's culture wars. While no opinion polls or surveys exist to prove the association, anecdotal evidence suggests that defenders of the Confederate flag overwhelmingly support the conservative position on hot-button issues such as abortion, gun control, welfare reform, and affirmative action.[11] It is, of course, perfectly logical and consistent to associate Confederate symbols with states' rights, opposition to the federal government, and resistance to measures imposed by the federal government. Opposition to a strong federal government is a viewpoint that was born with the American republic and continues to be valid and compelling today for many citizens. It is a viewpoint that—in relation to the burning questions about slavery—precipitated civil war in 1861. Slavery was eradicated, but suspicion of the federal government survived the war and has emerged repeatedly in the years since. That the Confederate battle flag so effectively symbolizes this endemic political tradition is further testimony to its role as a second American flag.

The flag's oppositional meaning finds a parallel in the ambiguous position of traditional white southerners in post-1865 America. Despite the image of victimhood that modern southern heritage activists have cultivated, the identity and symbols of the separatist South have not been suppressed for most of the years since the Civil War. Quite the opposite is true. Herein lies the origins of the continuing feuds over Confederate heritage and symbols. Successful white southern resistance to Reconstruction and the subsequent counterrevolution allowed ex-Confederates to win a "victory in defeat"—to recover political control of their region, impose a new form of institutionalized white supremacy, achieve leadership roles in the U.S. Senate, and celebrate Confederate heroes and symbols without outside interference. The figures, faces, and names of Confederate heroes blanket the southern landscape—evidence of national acquiescence as well as white southern devotion. The national consensus for most of the past century has been not only to tolerate but to join in the celebration of Confederate heroes. Confederates and their descendants were not forced to choose between their identities as Confederates and as Americans. The reunited states accepted the Confederate flag as an American flag. Indeed, the United States welcomed former Confederates back into the fabric of American life without first sending them to "reeducation camps" or even requiring that they renounce everything associated with their "lost cause." As the historian Charles Dew has written insightfully, the United States appointed no "truth and reconciliation commission" to promote understanding of the war, its causes, and its consequences.[12]

But circumstances, power relationships, and perceptions have changed. The consensus among nonsouthern white Americans to accept and honor the "dual loyalty" of Confederates and their descendants has eroded; and not coincidentally, the once-oppressed people who feel the greatest stake in the Confederacy's defeat and repudiation are now empowered. In such radically altered circumstances, how should modern America regard and treat descendants of Confederates who wish to honor their ancestors and vindicate the cause for which they believe they fought? More germane is the question of how modern America should regard and treat the preeminent symbol of this group.

Historians now recognize the injustices heaped upon African Americans in the name of (white) national reconciliation, but this belated recognition does not erase the legacy of a century in which white southerners were not asked to dishonor or feel ashamed of their ancestors and in which black southerners had no voice in determining the heroes and symbols of their region. During a recent dispute over the renaming of Confederate Memorial Hall at Vanderbilt University in Nashville, Tennessee, a black math professor asserted bluntly that "the race problems that wrack America to this day are due largely to the fact that the Confederacy was not thoroughly destroyed, its leaders and soldiers executed and their lands given to the landless free slaves."[13] Shocking as this statement was, it verbalized the frustration that some people feel toward the moderate settlement of America's Civil War. It also suggested what *could* have happened to the losers of this conflict but didn't. It underscored the challenges facing a society that reincorporated a defeated people, their beliefs, and their symbols.

The passage of generations has complicated the answer to the question of how America should treat self-styled Confederate Americans. For many people today, the Confederacy and the flag are part of their personal and familial heritage, effectively devoid of ideological content. Allegiance to the Confederacy and the battle flag arise from a desire to honor their ancestors and from an innate sense that "it's always been this way." Anything that forces change—even in the name of righting past wrongs—is resisted in principle. A recent survey of how Americans learn their history and what history they regard as most trustworthy reveals the importance of family history and personal heritage. By honoring their ancestors, vindicating their cause, and revering their symbols, Confederate descendants are engaging with history in the same way that other Americans do. Confederate heritage activists decry what they perceive as a double standard at work: that white southerners are the only Americans not allowed to celebrate their ancestry openly.[14]

If precedent and fairness suggest that Americans should allow "Confederate Americans" to retain their dual loyalty, the association of Confederate heritage and symbols with extremist political movements suggests vigilance. Flag defenders claim that "liberals" fear the flag because it stands for freedom. The rhetoric of the New Albany Declaration provides a more cogent explanation of why liberals fear the flag: because it so often serves as the symbol of the darker side of the American oppositional tradition, a reminder of how close to the surface are beliefs and attitudes that most Americans think are relics of the past. Just as the 1990s taught us that ethnic groups are still capable of slaughtering one another in so-called civilized countries, the New Albany Declaration reveals the survival of atavistic tendencies in our own country. New rules of civility have banished "nigger" from the speech of white Americans, and laws and custom have evolved to make lynching a rarity. But the ideas and prejudices that gave rise to slurs and ritualized murder live on, and there is no reason to believe that Americans are not capable of reviving them should the rules and customs change.

The flag's effectiveness as an expression of an ideological tradition subverts its legitimacy as a publicly sanctioned or sponsored symbol. If even a minority of vocal flag loyalists regards the flag not merely as a memorial to Confederate dead but as a living testament to the power of anti-federal ideology or the symbol of a still-living Confederacy, it is difficult to defend the flag as a neutral, apolitical symbol that everyone should learn to respect. Why should people who have gained by the defeat of the Confederacy and the expansion of federal power be compelled to recognize a symbol that proponents tout as representing the values of states' rights and opposition to the federal government? Because the battle flag is associated so closely with the Confederacy and with a states' rights agenda, it symbolizes hostility to the rights and well-being of those who benefited from the defeat of states' rights in the 1860s and again in the 1960s.

One careful student of the subject has concluded that "the Confederate flag has become one of the last means of expressing racial attitudes no longer acceptable to verbalize."[15] Consequently, accepting the flag as an honorable or a benign symbol may help mask its past and present significance as an exclusive and even threatening symbol. Many people insist that virtually everyone who rallies behind the Confederate flag harbors

racist feelings somewhere in his soul and that it is naive to accept dis-
avowals of racism at face value. Short of taking polls and subjecting respondents to psychological exams, there is no way to validate or invali-
date this assumption. Constant vigilance against racism is prudent, but
even the vigilant can afford to demonstrate charitable attitudes toward
their fellow citizens.

Opinion polls, particularly those taken during the flag wars in Alabama, Georgia, and South Carolina, suggest that Americans may be able
to find a middle ground on the battle flag. As the flag wars dragged on
and as pollsters began asking more nuanced questions, more people answered that they believed the flag to be a symbol of honor but that they
did not believe it should fly on state flags or over state capitols. As on
other fronts in America's culture wars, the debates and media coverage
tend to magnify the extreme positions and obscure the moderate positions to which most people adhere.[16]

A suitably moderate position would recognize the Confederate flag as
an American symbol with an inevitable place on the American landscape—without, however, allowing it to be displayed as a symbol of sovereignty. Descendants of Confederate veterans who wish to display the
flag to honor their ancestors should favor a return to the practice, prior
to World War II, of displaying the flag only as an unambiguously historical or memorial symbol. They should resurrect an older, intellectually
consistent understanding of protecting the flag from desecration. This
does not mean banishing the flag from public view. Confederate heritage
groups should be free to use the flag in their functions, including Memorial Day observances, parades, and ceremonies commemorating important anniversaries—knowing, of course, that it still may be the target of
protest from people who believe that it is wrong to honor anyone or anything associated with the Confederacy. But instead of urging everyone to
keep it flying everywhere, flag advocates should censure any use of the
flag that is not unambiguously memorial or historical in nature. Those
who truly regard the battle flag as a sacred war memorial for Confederate ancestors should oppose its use on T-shirts, baseball caps, and other
popular culture items that trivialize its meaning. Such use of the flag may

be consistent with contemporary culture and protected by current interpretations of free speech rights, but Confederate heritage groups should
use their free speech to curb such use, not to encourage it.

Similarly, flag defenders should seek to remove battle flags displayed
on state flags or in any sovereignty context, since this use blurs the distinction between the flag as a memorial and the flag as a symbol of sovereignty. If the flag is displayed as a public symbol representing or commanding the fealty of people who do not honor it, it becomes a
legitimate target of protest. It also undermines the case for tolerating the
flag as an apolitical memorial or historical symbol. Flag activists are loath
to restrict any use of the flag because they view it as surrender to their
critics, but they must redefine surrender and victory to emphasize the
flag's role as a war memorial, not as a slap at the NAACP or a strike
against political correctness.

Flag critics in turn must be more tolerant of the flag's presence as a
war memorial and historical symbol. Because of the flag's association
with the Confederacy and its use by modern groups intent on reviving
the Confederacy, critics will remain suspicious of anyone who displays
the flag, even if it is not publicly sponsored or political in nature. But in a
culture that is willing to tolerate so much that offends so many people in
the name of free speech and free expression, the offensiveness of the
Confederate flag is not sufficient reason to censor it. Elected officials,
community leaders, and intellectuals must cease encouraging the untenable belief that there is an inherent American right not to be offended.
Flag critics must (for practical as well as ethical reasons) become more
willing to distinguish between a Ku Klux Klan rally and a Memorial Day
parade. Confederate national flags belong in publicly sponsored displays
of historical flags, just as they do not belong on contemporary symbols of
sovereignty. Americans must learn to accept displays of the flag that
merely acknowledge the Confederacy's existence. The Confederacy is an
important part of American history, and it behooves everyone to study it
and understand it in all its complexity. Flag displays that remind people
of this complex history nourish rather than poison the public dialogue.

Historical reasoning and ethical principles dictate such a compromise and also provide a test for arbitrating the many controversies that defy easy solution. In order to understand the history of the flag, we must study the *whole* history of the flag—not just 1861 to 1865—and accept that uses of the flag since the end of the Civil War have created real meanings and perceptions. Although the most obvious implication of this reasoning is to undercut those who believe that the flag's only true meaning is its honorable association with the Confederate soldier, it also undercuts those who want to tar all flag wavers with a racist brush. Anyone who argues that the Ku Klux Klan's use of the flag in the last half-century has transformed the flag's meaning must also concede that its use, for example, as a symbol for high schools and colleges has made it an object of affection for many people, without regard to its association with slavery, racism, or an idealized Confederacy.

It is a fundamental mistake to believe—as Carol Moseley-Braun suggested in her 1993 speech in the U.S. Senate—that one's own perception of a flag's meaning is the flag's *only* legitimate meaning. Many people believe that the flag is an honorable symbol of heritage, but this does not make the flag an honorable symbol of heritage to everyone. Others have just cause to regard the flag as a symbol of racism, but this does not mean that the flag is a symbol of racism to everyone. People must not impose their interpretation of the flag on others nor project their interpretation of the flag's meaning onto others' motives for displaying it. Just because someone views the flag as a symbol of racism does not give him the ethical right to assume that someone who displays it is a racist. To make such a judgment is an exercise in prejudice.

American Civil Liberties Union attorney William Simpson, who helped broker a settlement in a North Carolina school T-shirt case, explained the fundamental ethical principle to the students: "If your need to express pride in your southern heritage is worth hurting those who are offended by the flag, then do what you must," Simpson said. "But at least try to see why the message you intend to send is not always the one that is received." On the other hand, Simpson asked those offended by the flag "to see that the Confederate flag means many different things to many different people. Recognize that the flag has significance beyond racism. Try to understand that the message you receive when you see the flag may not be the message the person displaying it intends to send."[17] The ethical clarity and simplicity of Simpson's message provide guidelines and ground rules for mutual tolerance and even mutual understanding.

Any realistic and practical solution to the flag wars must accept the inevitability of the Confederate flag as part of America's cultural landscape. Not only does the flag have persistent and determined advocates, but it also has an innate visual appeal and graphic familiarity. With its bold colors and simple design, the battle flag is striking and memorable. Confronted with the flag's omnipresence as a symbol of things southern, pundits, scholars, and activists have sought to replace it with a new symbol or to transform it into a more inclusive and unifying emblem. Rather than accept its fixed meaning as a symbol of the Confederacy, states' rights, or racism, some people have embraced it as a logo of "southern," and made it represent their own vision of the South. In 1964 the Southern Student Organizing Committee (SSOC), a white student civil rights group, considered adopting as its official logo clasped white and black hands (the symbol of the Student Non-Violent Coordinating Committee) emblazoned on a Confederate battle flag. Proposed for SSOC by a black Harvard University student, the design nearly caused a rift within the organization and was ultimately rejected. Nevertheless, more than thirty years later, veterans of the short-lived organization still used the powerful and controversial logo. A professor at the University of Mississippi decried the school's effort to purge its symbolism and suggested as an alternative a Confederate flag "made funky"—using the colors of the African liberation flag. "Against a field of green—a fateful confederation— the white and black 'stars and bars' of the funky flag mark an intersection of races whose cultural collaboration has only begun."[18]

Two Charleston, South Carolina, African-American men parlayed the same notion into a successful clothing line. For the cover of an album by a local rap group they designed a T-shirt with a black and green cross against a bloodred field. When a school suspended a student for wearing the T-shirt, the northern-born transplant and the Cuban immigrant decided to mass market the provocative shirt and started NuSouth Apparel. "NuSouth offers an opportunity for dialogue. That's the real solution to race relations: dialogue," insisted partner Sherman Evans. "It's like our new ad campaign says, 'For the sons and daughters of former slaves. For the sons and daughters of former slave owners. Threads that connect us. Words that free us.'"[19]

Charles Nixon, an African-American man living in the former Confederate capital, endeavored to transform the Confederate flag, "a symbol of division," into "a tool of progress." He designed a "ballot" on which he superimposed the words "Vote Next Election" onto a naval jack, incorporating the St. Andrew's cross into the word "Next." Nixon still remembered his first encounter with the Confederate flag: as a teenager in the late 1950s, he and a few friends were walking down a street in Greensboro, North Carolina, when a car of whites drove by, held out a Confederate flag, and shouted "Niggers!" He envisaged the ballot as a "creative" way for African Americans to claim the symbol. It says to white flag wavers: "It doesn't matter if you wave a Confederate flag at me. Now I know I have my own." Nixon brought a Confederate flag to the October 1995 Million Man March in Washington, D.C. "The flag is part of the history of the black man in the United States," he told a reporter. "We have to fight to overcome this as much as anything else."[20]

Overcoming the Confederate flag, seeking to understand why people revere it, or simply making peace with it are more constructive and realistic ways of dealing with the flag than campaigning to banish it. The Confederate battle flag is an American flag, and some Americans will continue to revere and defend it, especially as others attack it. Above all, the Confederate battle flag represents the most contested chapter in American history, and it is destined to remain a contested symbol. Continuing controversy over the battle flag could be healthy for America's public dialogue. The flag is an accurate barometer of disagreement over the meaning and the proper place of the Confederacy in American history and memory. If the public dialogue about the flag were intelligent and free of dogma and unrestrained emotion, it might generate genuine insights into the complex issues of race and states' rights in the American past, present, and future. Arguments over the "second American flag" remind us how vital these issues still are, and help to keep them out in the open—as visible on today's ideological battlefields as the battle flag was amid the smoke and chaos of actual battlefields more than a century ago.

Abbreviations

AC	*Atlanta Constitution* (Georgia)
ADAH	Alabama Department of Archives & History, Montgomery
AJC	*Atlanta Journal-Constitution* (Georgia)
AU	Ralph Draughton Library, Auburn University, Alabama
BN	*Birmingham News*
BP	*Birmingham Post*
BPL	Birmingham Public Library
CMLS	Confederate Memorial Literary Society [The Museum of the Confederacy]
CN	*Chattanooga News*
CPL	Chattanooga Bicentennial Public Library, Tennessee
CR	*Congressional Record*
CV	*Confederate Veteran*
CWCC	Civil War Centennial Commission
DM	*Daily Mississippian,* University of Mississippi
DRB	*Danville Register & Bee*
ESBL, MOC	Eleanor S. Brockenbrough Library, The Museum of the Confederacy, Richmond, Virginia
Hargrett, UGA	Hargrett Rare Book and Manuscript Library, The University of Georgia, Athens
HC	*Harvard Crimson,* Harvard University

LC	Library of Congress Manuscripts Division, Washington, DC
LOV	Library of Virginia, Richmond
MA	*Montgomery Advertiser*
Miss.	*The Mississippian,* University of Mississippi
NAACP	National Association for the Advancement of Colored People
NARA	National Archives and Records Administration, Washington, DC
NYT	*New York Times*
OR	*Official Records* [War of the Rebellion: Official Records of the Union and Confederate Armies]
PC	*Pittsburgh Courier*
PISF	Public Information Subject Files (ADAH)
RFP	*Richmond Free Press*
RG	Record Group (National Archives)
RNL	*Richmond News-Leader*
RTD	*Richmond Times-Dispatch*
Russell, UGA	Richard B. Russell Library for Political Research & Studies, The University of Georgia, Athens
SC	Special Collections, South Caroliniana Library, University of South Carolina, Columbia
SCV	Sons of Confederate Veterans
SH	Biloxi, MS, *Sun Herald*
SHC, UNC	Southern Historical Collection, University of North Carolina, Chapel Hill
SHSP	Southern Historical Society Papers
Smithsonian	Archives Center, National Museum of American History, Smithsonian Institution
SN	Myrtle Beach, SC, *Sun News*
SP	*Southern Partisan*
SPLC	Southern Poverty Law Center, Montgomery, Alabama
State	Columbia, SC, *The State*

UA William S. Hoole Special Collections, University of
Alabama, Tuscaloosa, Alabama

UCV United Confederate Veterans

UDC *United Daughters of the Confederacy*

UDC Mag. The United Daughters of the Confederacy Magazine

UF P. K. Yonge Library of Florida History, George D.
Smathers Library, University of Florida, Gainesville

UM Archives and Special Collections, J. D. Williams
Library, University of Mississippi, University,
Mississippi

VHS Virginia Historical Society, Richmond

VP Norfolk *Virginian-Pilot*

WFRL West Florida Regional Library, Pensacola

WP *Washington Post*

WSJ *Wall Street Journal*

Notes

Preface

1. *CR* 139 (July 22, 1993): S-9253–9254; letters to the editor, *RTD*, August 2, 1993, and August 13, 1993.
2. Dan Balz, "Dean Is Criticized over Remark on Confederate Flag," *WP*, November 2, 2003; Charles Krauthammer, "Can Dean Sell His Liberalism to Southern Guys in Silverados?" *RTD*, November 10, 2003; Paul Greenberg, "Dean Remark Raised Red Flags for Dems," *RTD*, November 12, 2003.
3. This book does not explicitly employ semiotics—the theory and study of symbols—or anthropological theory in its analysis. For explicit discussions of semiotics and the flag, see Patrick M. McElroy, "The Confederate Battle Flag: Social History and Cultural Contestation" (M.A. thesis, University of Alabama, 1995); and especially Jack Hiatt, "Confederate Semiotics," *Nation*, April 28, 1997, 11–17.

1. "Emblem of a Separate and Independent Nation"

1. Devereaux D. Cannon, Jr., *The Flags of the Confederacy: An Illustrated History* (Memphis: St. Luke Press, 1988); Robert E. Bonner, *Colors and Blood: Flag Passions of the Confederate South* (Princeton: Princeton University Press, 2002).
2. Cannon, *Flags*, 32–33.
3. *Journal of the Congress of the Confederate States of America*, 7 vols. (Washington, DC: Government Printing Office, 1904–05), 1:40, 101; Raphael P. Thian, comp., *Documentary History of the Flag and Seal of the Confederate States of America, 1861–1865* (Washington, 1880), is a convenient sum-

mary of official proceedings and unofficial commentaries regarding the committee's work. *Journal* 1:101; William Porcher Miles to the Reverend R. S. Trapin, August 12, 1861, transcript in ESBL, MOC; R. S. Trapin to William Porcher Miles, April 22, 1862, William Porcher Miles Papers, SHC, UNC, file 51; J. D. P. to Miles, February 21, 1861, in Thian, *Documentary History,* 43; M. E. Huger to William Porcher Miles, February 7, 1861, Miles Papers, SHC, UNC, file 36.

4. Charleston *Mercury,* May 6, 1863; *Journal* 1:102.

5. *Journal* 1:102.

6. Harry Macarthy, "Our Flag and Its Origin" (New Orleans: A. E. Blackmar, 1862). Bonner, *Colors,* offers an insightful analysis of the Stars and Bars and Confederate patriotic culture.

7. Throughout the chapters that follow, many quotations use "Stars and Bars" when, as the context makes clear, the writer or speaker was referring to the Confederate battle flag. Peleg D. Harrison, *The Stars and Stripes and Other American Flags* (Boston: Little, Brown, 1906), 312–313; Moise quoted in Bonner, *Colors,* 101–102.

8. William Porcher Miles to P. G. T. Beauregard, August 27, 1861, ESBL, MOC. Miles to Beauregard, August 27, 1861, ESBL, MOC.

9. Cannon, *Flags,* 27–28.

10. Bonner, *Colors,* 52, 97–98; Charleston *Mercury,* May 6, 1863.

11. For descriptions and images of company flags, see Rebecca Ansell Rose, *Colours of the Gray: An Illustrated Index of Wartime Flags from The Museum of the Confederacy's Collection* (Richmond: Museum of the Confederacy, 1998).

12. *War of the Rebellion: Official Records of the Union and Confederate Armies,* 128 vols. (Washington, DC: Government Printing Office, 1880–1900), ser. I, 2:538; Richmond *Daily Dispatch,* November 27, 1861.

13. Beauregard to Captain George H. Preble, January 24, 1872, ESBL, MOC; Carlton McCarthy, "Origin of the Confederate Battle Flag," *SHSP,* 8 (1880), 497–499; Miles to Beauregard, August 27, 1861, ESBL, MOC.

14. Beauregard to Joseph E. Johnston, September 5, 1861, ESBL, MOC.

15. Beauregard to Preble, January 24, 1872, ESBL, MOC.

16. J. B. Walton to Beauregard, January 30, 1872, ESBL, MOC; E. H. Hancock to Beauregard, February 21, 1872, ESBL, MOC; Miles to Beauregard, May 14, 1872, quoted in Harrison, *Stars and Stripes,* 342–

343; Alfred Roman, *The Military Operations of General Beauregard,* 2 vols. (New York: Harper, 1884), 1:171–172. According to another story, credit for designing the flag belongs to Lieutenant Roswell Morse Shurtleff, 99th New York Infantry. Alfred L. Donaldson, *A History of the Adirondacks* (1921; rpt. Harrison, NY: Harbor Hill, 1977), 39–40.

17. W. L. Cabell, "Vivid History of Our Battle Flag," *CV* 8 (May 1900): 238–239. Greg Biggs to author, October 24, 1997, and March 31, 2004, clarifies details about production of first flags; Constance Cary Harrison to Peleg Harrison, March 25, 1905, in Harrison, *Stars and Stripes,* 347–348; Constance Cary Harrison, *Recollections Grave and Gay* (New York: Scribner's, 1916), 61–64; "Our Flag and Seal," *Southern Illustrated News,* March 21, 1863, 2; Diary of John B. Richardson, entry of October 28, 1861, ESBL, MOC; Beauregard's order is in *OR* I, 5:969.

18. Brigadier General G. Moxley Sorrel, C. S. A., *Recollections of a Staff Officer* (New York: Neale Publishing, 1905), 34–35; Roman, *Military Operations,* 1:481.

19. J. W. Reid, *History of the Fourth Regiment of S. C. Volunteers* (rpt. Dayton, OH: Morningside, 1975), 60; Sam Payne to Cousin [Mollie], December 1, 1861, "To Molly" Letters, ESBL, MOC.

20. William J. Reese to Margaret Elizabeth Walker, November 26, 1861, UA. See also Richardson Diary, entry for November 28, 1861, ESBL, MOC.

21. Henry Woodhead, ed., *Echoes of Glory: Arms and Equipment of the Confederacy* (Alexandria, VA: Time-Life, 1991), 232, 246–252, gives a summary of research on successive issues of government-produced flags.

22. Beauregard to Preble, January 21, 1872, ESBL, MOC; Howard Madaus and Robert D. Needham, *The Battle Flags of the Confederate Army of Tennessee* (Milwaukee: Milwaukee Public Museum, 1976), 11–15, 23–24; *OR* I, 8:748–749; Rose, *Colours,* 14, 26.

23. Madaus and Needham, *Battle Flags,* 24, 32–35; Cannon, *Flags,* 56.

24. Beauregard to Preble, January 24, 1872, ESBL, MOC.

25. General Orders No. 38, March 11, 1864, General Orders and Circulars, Hood's/Lee's Corps, Army of Tennessee, 1864–1865, ESBL, MOC; Circular from Headquarters Hardee's Corps, April 21, 1864, William J. Hardee files, Confederate Military Leaders Collection, ESBL, MOC; Madaus and Needham, *Battle Flags,* 63.

26. Madaus and Needham, *Battle Flags,* 92–93; Greg Biggs and Richard

Rollins, "Ragged Rags of Rebellion: The Flags of the Confederacy," unpub. slide lecture script, 1993, courtesy of the authors; Rose, *Colours*, 40 (War Department capture #144).

27. Cannon, *Flags*, 66–69; H. Michael Madaus, "Rebel Flags Afloat: A Survey of the Surviving Flags of the Confederate States Navy, Revenue Service, and Merchant Marine," *Flag Bulletin*, January–April 1986.

28. Gary W. Gallagher, *The Confederate War: How Popular Will, Nationalism, and Military Strategy Could Not Stave Off Defeat* (Cambridge: Harvard University Press, 1997), 72, and chap. 2.

29. Richmond *Daily Dispatch*, November 14, 1861; *New Orleans Delta*, December 21, 1861, quoted in Bonner, *Colors*, 103; Matthew Fontaine Maury to Franklin Minor, August 21, 1861, Letterbook #14, Matthew Fontaine Maury Papers, LC; Memorial of the Ladies of Fredericksburg to the Congress of the Confederate States of America, n.d. [ca. August 1861], ESBL, MOC; Bonner, *Colors*, 119–121.

30. *Examiner* quoted in Thian, *Documentary History*, 33.

31. *Journal* 5:272; *Mercury* quoted in Thian, *Documentary History*, 22 (original emphasis).

32. Cannon, *Flags*, 16–19; "Our Flag and Seal," 2.

33. Charleston *Mercury*, May 6, 1863.

34. Ibid.

35. James M. Matthews, ed., *The Statutes at Large of the Confederate States of America . . . 1863* (Richmond: R. M. Smith, 1863), 163; Rose, *Colours*, 19.

36. "Flag of the Sunny South," lyrics by E. V. Sharp and melody by J. H. Hewitt (Augusta, GA: J. H. Hewitt, ca. 1863); Richmond *Daily Dispatch*, May 16, 1863; *Daily South Carolinian*, May 5, 1863, quoting the *Richmond Sentinel*.

37. Savannah *Daily Morning News*, April 23, 28, 1863.

38. Madaus and Needham, *Battle Flags*, 103.

39. Charleston *Mercury*, May 6, 1863; Major Arthur L. Rogers to Edward Sparrow, January 2, 1865, transcript in ESBL, MOC.

40. See www.confederateflags.com for details and analysis by vexillologists.

41. Carlton McCarthy, *Detailed Minutiae of Soldier Life in the Army of Northern Virginia* (Richmond: Carlton McCarthy, 1882), 220.

42. George Schedler, *Racist Symbols and Reparations: Philosophical Reflections on Vestiges of the American Civil War* (Lanham, MD: Rowman & Littlefield, 1998).

43. See especially Don Hinkle, *Embattled Banner: A Reasonable Defense of the Confederate Battle Flag* (Paducah, KY: Turner, 1997); James R. Kennedy and Walter D. Kennedy, *The South Was Right* (Baton Rouge: Land and Land, 1991); James M. McPherson, *For Cause and Comrades: Why Men Fought in the Civil War* (New York: Oxford University Press, 1997). Bell I. Wiley, *The Life of Johnny Reb: The Common Soldier of the Confederacy* (Indianapolis: Bobbs-Merrill, 1943), 18–20, emphasized the hatred for Yankees, desire for adventure, and social pressures as the major reasons for fighting.

44. See for example Charles Adams, *When in the Course of Human Events: Arguing the Case for Southern Secession* (Lanham, MD: Rowman & Littlefield, 2000); R. Gordon Thornton, *The Southern Nation: The New Rise of the Old South* (Gretna, LA: Pelican Press, 2000); Jeffrey Hummell, *Emancipating Slaves and Enslaving Free Men: A History of the American Civil War* (Chicago: Open Court, 1996); Thomas DiLorenzo, *The Real Lincoln: A New Look at Abraham Lincoln, His Agenda, and an Unnecessary War* (Roseville, CA: Prima Publishing, 2002).

45. Dunbar S. Rowland, *Jefferson Davis Constitutionalist* (Jackson: Mississippi Department of Archives and History, 1923), 5:24–26.

46. [Robert Barnwell Rhett], *The Address of the People of South Carolina, Assembled in Convention, to the People of the Slaveholding States of the United States* (Charleston: Evans & Cogswell, 1860), 4–7.

47. Rowland, *Jefferson Davis Constitutionalist*, 5:29–30; Rhett, *Address*, 8–14; George C. Rable, *The Confederate Republic: A Revolution against Politics* (Chapel Hill: University of North Carolina Press, 1994), 50–53.

48. "Declaration of the Immediate Causes Which Indure and Justify the Secession of South Caroline from the Federal Union," in *Ordinances and Constitution of the State of South Carolina . . .* (Charleston: Evans & Cogswell, 1861), 330–331; Charles B. Dew, *Apostles of Disunion: Southern Secession Commissioners and the Causes of the Civil War* (Charlottesville: University Press of Virginia, 2001); see also Jon Wakelyn, ed., *Pamphlets of Secession* (Chapel Hill: University of North Carolina Press, 1996); Paul D. Escott, *After Secession: Jefferson Davis and the Failure of Confederate Nationalism* (Baton Rouge: Louisiana State University Press, 1978).

49. Wakelyn, ed., *Pamphlets*, 405–406; Drew Gilpin Faust, *The Creation of Confederate Nationalism: Ideology and Identity in the Civil War South* (Baton Rouge: Louisiana State University Press, 1988), 58–61; Dew, *Apostles,*

15–17. Adams, *When in the Course of Human Events,* 4–5, argues that the rhetoric about slavery was intended to rally people behind a popular emotional cause (slavery) and masked the true cause for action: the high tariffs passed by the northern-dominated Congress.

50. For the number of slaveholders, see *Agriculture of the United States in 1860; Compiled from the Original Returns of the Eighth Census* (Washington: GPO, 1864), 247; Emory M. Thomas, *The Confederate Nation: 1861–1865* (New York: Harper, 1979), 6, lays out the calculation that modern historians commonly understand as the extent of slaveholding in the southern and border states. De Bow quoted in Otto Olsen, "Historians and the Extent of Slave Ownership in the Southern United States," *Civil War History* 18 (June 1972): 104.

51. Rowland, *Jefferson Davis Constitutionalist,* 2:74.

52. "The New Heresy," *Southern Punch,* September 19, 1864, 2 (original emphasis).

53. Address of Captain Ed Baxter, *Second Annual Reunion of the Association of Confederate Soldiers, Tennessee Division,* Nashville, October 3, 1889 (Nashville: Foster & Webb, 1889), 23.

54. Cornelia Branch Stone, *U.D.C. Catechism for Children* (Galveston, TX: Veuve Jefferson Davis Chapter, UDC, 1904), 3; John S. Mosby to Aristides Monteiro, June 9, 1894, ESBL, MOC.

2. "The War-Torn Cross"

1. Ellen Glasgow, *The Battle-Ground* (New York: Doubleday, Page, 1902), 472–473, 478.

2. Ellen Glasgow, *A Certain Measure: An Interpretation of Prose Fiction* (New York: Harcourt Brace, 1943), 24–25.

3. Richard A. Sauers, *Advance the Colors! Pennsylvania Civil War Battle Flags,* 2 vols. (Harrisburg, PA: Capitol Preservation Committee, 1987); *OR* I, 51(1):632.

4. Flag Staff Collection file, flag curator's records, The Museum of the Confederacy; Madaus and Needham, *Battle Flags,* 11–12; Henry Woodhead, ed., *Echoes of Glory: Arms and Equipment of the Confederacy* (Alexandria, VA: Time-Life, 1991), 233.

5. William Gilham, *Manual of Instruction for the Volunteers and Militia of the Confederate States* (Richmond: West & Johnston, 1861), 32; Madaus and

Needham, *Battle Flags,* 13–14; Richard Rollins, *"The Damned Red Flags of Rebellion": The Confederate Battle Flag at Gettysburg* (Redondo Beach, CA: Rank and File, 1997), 77.

6. William J. Hardee, *Rifle and Light Infantry Tactics for Exercise and Maneuvres* (1855; Richmond: J. W. Randolph, 1861), 9–10.

7. Edward Payson Reeve, "Civil War Narrative of Captain Edward Payson Reeve, 1861–1865," in Reeve Papers, SHC, UNC (emphasis added).

8. "Roll of Honour," ESBL, MOC, vol. 125, entry 199; Robert H. Moore II, *The Charlottesville, Lee Lynchburg and Johnson's Bedford Artillery* (Lynchburg: H. E. Howard, 1990), 45–48.

9. "The Standard Bearer," words by Major T. N. P., music by H. S. Coleman (Richmond: George Dunn, 1864).

10. *OR* IV, 3:190. A year later, Congress abolished the position of ensign but retained the temporary promotion in pay only for a private or noncommissioned officer chosen to carry the colors. See *OR* IV, 3:1167; William S. Woods to mother, March 20, 1864, and for sister, March 17, 1864, William S. Woods Letters, ESBL, MOC; Mary S. Collins to [husband], February 12, 1865, South Carolina Women file, "Soldier Letters" collection, ESBL, MOC.

11. Rollins, *Red Flags,* 1–47, offers a detailed interpretation of the soldier's "world view" associated with the battle flag. Alexander Robert Chisholm, "The Confederate Battle Flag," *CV* 11 (January 1903): 22; Mauriel Phillips Joslyn, ed., *Charlotte's Boys: Civil War Letters of the Branch Family of Savannah* (Berryville, VA: Rockbridge Publishing, 1996), 107.

12. Rose, *Colours,* 18; "South Carolina Daughters: They Pay Tribute to Four Color Bearers," *CV* 5 (January 1897): 14–15.

13. Greg Biggs to author, April 14, 2004; Woodhead, ed., *Echoes,* 232–234; Charleston *Mercury,* May 22, 1862; *OR* IV, 2:14.

14. Whitfield Kisling to Dear Cousin, August 26, 1863, Kisling Letters, ESBL, MOC.

15. *CV* 5 (December 1897): 93–94. Biggs to author, April 14, 2004, clarifies some inconsistencies in the story of this flag.

16. Craig L. Symonds, *Stonewall of the West: Patrick Cleburne and the Civil War* (Lawrence: University Press of Kansas, 1997), 135; "Sketch of Major General P. R. Cleburne," *Land We Love* 1 (April 1866): 462–463; Mauriel Phillips Joslyn, "Comrades of the Southern Cross," *North & South* 3 (November 2000): 27–31.

17. *OR* III, 2:270; III, 4:810; I, 45(1):140; I, 45(1):410.

18. Gregg S. Clemmer, *Valor in Gray: The Recipients of the Confederate Medal of Honor* (Staunton, VA: Hearthside, 1996). None of the men on the Confederacy's Roll of Honor who were subsequently cited as recipients of the Sons of Confederate Veterans Medal of Honor captured enemy flags.

19. Sam R. Watkins, *Co. Aytch: A Side Show of the Big Show* (Nashville: Cumberland Presbyterian Publishing House, 1882), 171–172.

20. *OR* I, 19(1):875.

21. *OR* I, 45(2):690; Madaus and Needham, *Battle Flags,* 133–137, analyze the evidence and conclude that at least 17–22 were captured. Featherston's report in *OR* I, 45(1):714.

22. J. T. Carter, "Flag of the 53rd Virginia," *CV* 10 (June 1902): 263; Rollins, *Red Flags,* 168–169, 160.

23. Rod Gragg, *Covered with Glory: The 26th North Carolina Infantry at the Battle of Gettysburg* (New York: HarperCollins, 2000), 111–135 (esp. 129–131), 188–200, 209–210; Clemmer, 232–240.

24. *OR* I, 45(1):348.

25. Rollins, *Red Flags,* 191–193.

26. "Gave His Life for His Flag," *CV* 12 (February 1904): 70–71; notes on Morton and Woodram in Terry Lowry, *26th Battalion Virginia Infantry* (Lynchburg: H. E. Howard, 1991), 140, 161. When Morton, the narrator of this story, died in 1907, he was, according to an obituary, "buried in his Confederate uniform with Confederate flag on bier."

27. "The Way the Color-Bearer of the Nineteenth Virginia Gave Up His Flag," *Southern Bivouac,* August 1886, 194–195.

28. N. B. Bowyer to Cunningham, June 25, 1899, Sumner A. Cunningham Papers, SHC, UNC, file 1; Rose, *Colours,* 11.

29. N. Edwards, *Shelby and His Men: or The War in the West* (Cincinnati: Miami Printing & Publishing Co., 1867), 547–549.

30. Charleston *Mercury,* January 12, 1864.

31. Joshua L. Chamberlain, *The Passing of the Armies* (New York: G. P. Putnam, 1915), 261–262, 270–271. William Marvel, *A Place Called Appomattox* (Chapel Hill: University of North Carolina Press, 2000), 258–259, notes that some Confederate units stacked their colors two days before the parade that Chamberlain described.

32. Watkins, *Co. Aytch,* 231–232. Watkins exaggerated the service of the flag

surrendered, which was at least the third the regiment carried during the war.

33. *CV* 5 (December 1897): 94.

34. For information on existing collections of Confederate flags, see Rose, *Colours;* Paul Ellingson, comp., *Confederate Flags in the Georgia State Capitol Collection* (Atlanta: Office of the Secretary of State, 1994); Glenn Dedmondt, *The Flags of Civil War South Carolina* (Gretna, LA: Pelican, 2000); Glenn Dedmondt, *The Flags of Civil War Alabama* (Gretna, LA: Pelican, 2001); Robert Maberry, Jr., *Texas Flags* (College Station: Texas A&M University Press, 2001).

3. "Unfurl the Old Flag"

1. Abram J. Ryan, *Poems: Patriotic, Religious, Miscellaneous* (New York: P. J. Kennedy, 1904), 232–234. The illustrated cover for a musical version of "The Conquered Banner" (New Orleans: A. E. Blackmar, 1866) featured the "Stainless Banner" flag with its prominent St. Andrew's cross. The April 1893 issue of *Confederate Veteran* illustrated the poem with a St. Andrew's cross battle flag.

2. *CV* 2 (November 1894): 333.

3. Milton H. Lee, "Unfurl the Old Banner," in *CV* 37 (May 1929): 166; also Albert Sidney Morton, "To a Confederate Battle Flag," *CV* 1 (June 1893): 175; S. A. Steel, "The Folded Banner," *CV* 31 (July 1923): 245; Fred A. Campbell, "Let It Wave!" and "The Confederate Flag," in Rutherford Scrapbook, vol. 10, ESBL, MOC.

4. Michael Grissom, *Southern by the Grace of God* (Nashville: Rebel Press, 1988), 62; Mrs. M. L. Shipp, "Women of North Carolina," *CV* 6 (May 1898): 227; Special Order #30, in "Letter from the Secretary of War . . . " *House Executive Document 342,* 40th Congress, 2nd Session, 1868, 88; Walter L. Fleming, ed., *Documentary History of Reconstruction* (1907; rpt. New York: McGraw-Hill, 1966), 1:66–67, 204; General Orders No. 83, 86, and 110, U.S. Army Middle Department and General Orders No. 18, Army of the Potomac, in U.S. Army Orders, vols. 615A and 955, RG 94, NARA; Thomas and Debra Goodrich, *The Day Dixie Died: Southern Occupation, 1865–1866* (Mechanicsburg, PA: Stackpole Books, 2001), 143–144.

5. De la Mesa to Major General Davis Tillson, December 17, 1866, and

January 3, 1867, NARA, RG 393, Department of Tennessee, 1862–1866: Letters Received, 1863–1866, Box 5. I am indebted to Michael Musick for bringing this incident to my attention.

6. Mayor Charles H. Smith to General Tillson, January 15, 1867, and "The Arrest on Friday Last," Rome *Weekly Commercial*, January 31, 1867, NARA. "Perilous Tableaux," unidentified Macon newspaper; also "That Awful Tableaux," Rome *Courier*, January 29, 1867, both enclosed in Captain William Mills to General William D. Whipple, January 31, 1867, NARA.

7. Whipple's letter, February 9, 1867, rpt. in unidentified newspaper, in clippings related to "The Rome Prisoners," in Letters Received, Department of Tennessee, 1867, NARA, RG 393, Part I, entry 4720.

8. Clipping from unidentified New York paper, ca. February 1867, "The Rome Prisoners" file, NARA; for absence of U.S. flags, see United States Congress, *Report of the Joint Committee on Reconstruction* (Washington, DC: GPO, 1866), part 4:127, xvi-xvii; part 3:11, 18–19; Woodruff quoted in Gallagher, *The Confederate War*, 167.

9. C. Irvine Walker (vice president, 1869–1873; president 1875–1879), *Carolina Rifle Club Charleston, S. C., July 30th, 1869* (n.p., n.d.), 45–48, quote on 46; on mission, see 21, 43, 76.

10. Behan, *History*, 93; Mary H. Mitchell, *Hollywood Cemetery: The History of a Southern Shrine* (Richmond: Virginia State Library, 1985), 88, 94.

11. Gaines M. Foster, *Ghosts of the Confederacy: Defeat, the Lost Cause, and the Emergence of the New South, 1865 to 1913* (New York: Oxford University Press, 1987); Rollin G. Osterweis, *The Myth of the Lost Cause, 1865–1900* (Hamden, CT: Archon, 1973); Thomas L. Connelly and Barbara Bellows, *God and General Longstreet: The Lost Cause and the Southern Mind* (Baton Rouge: Louisiana State University Press, 1982).

12. William W. White, *The Confederate Veteran* (Tuscaloosa: Confederate Publishing, 1962), 12–22.

13. "Monuments and Cemeteries in Virginia," *CV* 11 (February 1903): 70; "Work of the Daughters at Camden, Ark.," *CV* 13 (September 1905): 40; "Monthly Programs," rpt. in *CV* 24 (March 1916): 110; letter to *Columbus Enquirer* quoted in Scott Marsden, "The Damned Confederate Flag: The Development of an American Symbol, 1865–1995" (M.A. thesis, University of Alberta, Canada, 1996), 34.

14. Mrs. E. D. Taylor to Ladies Hollywood Memorial Association (LHMA),

June 14, 1912, in LHMA minute book, 1907–1914, ESBL, MOC; Kate S. Winn, report of June 7, 1910, LHMA minute book, 1907–1914, ESBL, MOC (original emphasis).

15. J. William Jones, history of the statue, in John Esten Cooke, *Stonewall Jackson: A Military Biography* (New York: D. Appleton, 1876), 540.

16. Proceedings of monument dedication in *SHSP* 17 (1889 [sic]): 292.

17. Account of monument dedications in *CV* 15 (July 1907): 293–295.

18. F. H. James to Mrs. J. Taylor Ellyson, March 16, 1896, and notes on history of the 46th North Carolina flag, 1897, MOC.

19. *Minutes of the Thirteenth Annual Convention and Reunion, UCV, 1903,* 14.

20. *Minutes of the Sixteenth Annual Convention and Reunion, UCV, 1906,* 11; *Minutes of the Seventeenth Annual Meeting and Reunion, UCV, 1907,* 40; Katharine Du Pre Lumpkin, *The Making of a Southerner* (New York: Knopf, 1947), 116.

21. *Charter, Articles of Organization and Rules and Regulations of the Association of the Army of Tennessee Louisiana Division* (New Orleans: Lightning Printing, 1883), 5–6; "The Flag of the South," *Lost Cause* (March 1904), 115.

22. Wallace Evan Davies, *Patriotism on Parade* (Cambridge: Harvard University Press, 1955), 218–222 and chap. 10, passim; Rosalind Urbach Moss, "'Tangled in the Stars and Covered with the Stripes': Symbolic Struggles over Flag Use and National Direction in the 1960s" (unpub. conference paper, 1990), 3–5; Stuart McConnell, *Glorious Contentment: The Grand Army of the Republic, 1865–1900* (Chapel Hill: University of North Carolina Press, 1992), 228–230; Cecelia E. O'Leary, *To Die For: The Paradox of American Patriotism* (Princeton: Princeton University Press, 1999).

23. *CV* 11 (October 1903): 445.

24. Samuel E. Lewis, "Explanatory Matter," typescript p. 6 in Samuel E. Lewis Papers, VHS, folder 8.

25. William H. Pope to Lewis, November 6, 1893, and Alexander Robert Chisholm to Lewis, December 8, 1903, Lewis Papers, VHS, Box 18, folder 1.

26. John H. Hill to Lewis, January 3, 1905, and May 7, 1905, Lewis Papers, VHS, Box 18, file 3; Lewis, draft of "Report," Lewis Papers, VHS, Box 20, file 8; Walker to Lewis, July 1, 1904, Lewis Papers, VHS, Box 18, folder 2; Lewis to Mrs. Lily McDowell, September 1, 1906, Lewis Papers, VHS, Box 18, folder 4; also Lewis, "Explanatory Matter," typescript p. 38, Lewis Papers, VHS, Box 20, folder 8.

27. *The Flags of the Confederate States of America* (United Confederate Veterans, 1907); *Minutes of the Fourteenth Annual Meeting and Reunion, UCV, 1904,* 33.

28. "Flags of America," catalog of American Flag Manufacturing Co., 1895; Annin & Co. catalogs, 1912, 1924, 1931, in Warshaw Collection of Business Americana, Smithsonian, Flags, Box 1; Janet Randolph to Annin, September 21, 1925, and Annin to Janet W. Randolph, February 17, 1926, UDC Collection (Janet Randolph Papers), ESBL, MOC, Box 16; *Minutes of the General Convention, UDC,* 1932, 195–197.

29. U.S. Flag and Signal Co. to Mrs. N. V. Randolph, March 15, 1926, UDC Collection (Janet Randolph Papers), ESBL, MOC, Box 16.

30. Edward A. Pollard, *The Lost Cause* (New York: E. B. Treat, 1866), 752 (original emphasis).

31. Charles Reagan Wilson, *Baptized in Blood: The Religion of the Lost Cause, 1865–1920* (Athens: University of Georgia Press, 1980).

32. *Minutes of the Fifth Annual Meeting of the United Daughters of the Confederacy, 1898,* 58; *U.D.C. Catechism for Children* (Galveston, TX: Veuve Jefferson Davis Chapter, UDC, 1904), 8–9; E. Merton Coulter, "A Name for the American War of 1861–1865," *Georgia Historical Quarterly* 36 (June 1952): 123–124, 129.

33. *Minutes of the Fifth Annual Meeting and Reunion, UCV, 1895,* 175.

34. *Minutes of the Eighth Annual Meeting and Reunion, UCV, 1898,* 47; *Minutes of the Seventeenth Annual Meeting and Reunion, UCV, 1907,* 70–71.

35. *Minutes of the Thirty-Fourth Annual Meeting and Reunion, UCV, 1924,* 19; Mrs. C. G. Bierbower, "The Cause Triumphant," *CV* 26 (March 1918): 131.

36. "Why You Should Join the S.C.V." in *Hand Book of the Virginia Division Sons of Confederate Veterans* (Richmond, ca. 1923).

37. *Minutes of the Fortieth Annual Meeting and Reunion, UCV, 1930,* 23–24.

38. *Minutes of the Forty-Second Annual Meeting and Reunion, UCV, 1932,* 19.

39. Irvine Walker to Samuel E. Lewis, April 26, 1912, Lewis Papers, VHS, Box 19, file 7.

40. Lewis, "Explanatory Matter," typescript pp. 4–5.

41. Randolph H. McKim, *A Soldier's Recollections: Leaves from the Diary of a Young Confederate* (London: Longmans, Green, 1911), 289.

42. David W. Blight, *Race and Reunion: The Civil War in American Memory* (Cambridge: Harvard University Press, 2001), 397 and passim.

43. J. William Jones in Cooke, *Stonewall Jackson,* 540, 573, 576; *Harper's Weekly* quoted in Maurice Duke and Daniel P. Jordan, eds., *A Richmond Reader, 1733–1983* (Chapel Hill: University of North Carolina Press,

1983), 166; *SHSP,* 265; *The Forrest Monument: Its History and Dedication* (Forrest Monument Association, 1905), 19. (It is not clear whether the Confederate flag was the first national flag or the battle flag.) Richmond newspaper quoted in *Minutes, UCV,* 1907, 10.

44. "The Lee Monument Unveiling," Richmond Planet, May 31, 1890; GAR quoted in Paul Buck, *The Road to Reunion, 1865–1900* (Boston: Little, Brown, 1937), 237.

45. Quoted in Huber Winton Ellingsworth, "Southern Reconciliation Orators in the North, 1868–1899" (Ph.D. diss., Florida State University, 1955), 163, 173.

46. Mary R. Dearing, *Patriotism on Parade: The Story of the G.A.R.* (Baton Rouge: Louisiana State University Press, 1952), 410; Palmer quoted in Davies, 265; McConnell, 192; "The Confederate Flag," *NYT,* February 9, 1892.

47. October 1, 1881, quoted in McConnell, *Glorious Commitment,* 191.

48. "Captured Battle Flags," *House Executive Document* 163, 50th Congress, 2d session, 1888.

49. William Allen White, *The Autobiography of William Allen White* (New York: Macmillan, 1946), 155–156; "Captured Battle Flags," *House Miscellaneous Document* 74, 50th Congress, 1st session, 1888, *House Executive Document* 163.

50. Robert McElroy, *Grover Cleveland, the Man and the Statesman: An Authorized Biography* (New York: Harper, 1923), 208, 211–212; for a good overview see John M. Taylor, "Grover Cleveland and the Rebel Banners," in *Civil War Times Illustrated,* September–October 1993, 22–24.

51. *Official Programme 1888 Reunion of the Army of the Potomac and the Army of Northern Virginia at Gettysburg,* section 16; "The Battle Flag Flurry," *Nation,* June 23, 1887, 524.

52. "The Confederate Flag," *CV* 3 (December 1895): 353–354.

53. *CV* 4 (September 1896): 313.

54. "Unidentified Confederate Battle Flags," *House Report* 1114, 59th Congress, 1st session, 1905; *The Returned Battle Flags Presented to the Confederate Veterans at Their Re-Union, Louisville, Ky., June 14, 1905* (St. Louis: Buxton & Skinner, 1905).

55. C. Vann Woodward, *The Strange Career of Jim Crow,* 3rd ed. (New York: Oxford University Press, 1974); Rayford W. Logan, *The Negro in American*

Life and Thought: The Nadir, 1877–1901 (New York: Dial Press, 1954); Leon Littwack, *Trouble in Mind: Black Southerners in the Age of Jim Crow* (New York: Alfred A. Knopf, 1998).

56. *Minutes of Annual Meeting and Reunion, UCV, 1898,* 26–27.

57. W. C. Dodson, ed., *Campaigns of Wheeler and His Cavalry 1862–1865/The Santiago Campaign of 1898* (Atlanta: Hudgins, 1899), 2–5; *CV* 14 (July 1906): 300.

58. *Minutes of the Eighth Annual Meeting and Reunion, UCV, 1898,* 55–56, 57.

59. *CV* 6 (June 1898): 252, 252–255.

60. *CV* 17 (October 1909): 514; *CR* 45(2):1538–1539 (vote on 1540), 61st Congress, 2nd session; "Heyburn Bitter against Loaning Tents for Reunion," *MA,* February 8, 1910.

61. *Fiftieth Anniversary of the Battle of Gettysburg: Report of the Pennsylvania Commission* (Harrisburg: State Printer, 1914), 17–18.

62. Ibid., 168. The presentation flag is now in the collections of The Museum of the Confederacy.

63. The Reverend James H. McNeilly, in *CV* 21 (November 1913): 556.

64. "Reunion of Confederate Veterans," Senate Document No. 5, 65th Congress, 1st session, 1918, 30–31.

65. Ibid., 13, 14, 58–59, 73.

66. *CV* 25 (April 1917): 185.

67. "Reunion of Confederate Veterans," 79.

68. *RTD,* April 15, 1936, CMLS scrapbooks.

69. *RTD,* September 4, 1935; *Minutes of the Forty-Fifth Annual Meeting and Reunion, UCV, 1935,* 43; Virginius Dabney, *Below the Potomac: A Book about the New South* (New York: D. Appleton-Century, 1942), 265–268.

70. Douglas Southall Freeman, *The South to Posterity: An Introduction to the Writing of Confederate History* (New York: Scribner's, 1939), ix–x.

71. "Future of the Confederate Flag," *CV* 14 (June 1906): 267, original emphasis.

72. Milton H. Lee, "Unfurl the Old Banner: To the Vanishing Army of the Gray," *CV* 37 (May 1929): 166.

4. "A Harmless and Rather Amusing Gesture"

1. *CV* 15 (June 1907): 283.

2. Robert M. Jarvis, "The History of Florida's State Flag," *Nova Law Review* 18 (1994): 1058–1059.

3. Mrs. L. M. Bashinksy, "Alabama State Flag," in "Historical Records of the United Daughters of the Confederacy," Mildred Lewis Rutherford, comp., 1911–1916 [Rutherford Scrapbooks], vol. 11, ESBL, MOC; Marie Bankhead Owen, *Alabama Official and Statistical Register, 1939* (Wetumpka: Wetumpka Printing, 1949), 21.

4. *Journal of the Senate of the State of Mississippi Special Session, January 2, 1894– February 10, 1894* (Jackson: Clarion-Ledger, 1894), 158, 175, 238. The Jackson *Clarion-Ledger* noted only the introduction and passage of the flag bill.

5. Dunbar Rowland, *History of Mississippi: The Heart of the South* (Chicago-Jackson: S. J. Clarke, 1925), 246–248, 251–252; Albert D. Kirwan, *Revolt of the Rednecks: Mississippi Politics: 1876–1925* (Lexington: University Press of Kentucky, 1951), chap. 7. *Daniels v. Harrison County Board of Supervisors,* No. 96-CA-01129-SCT on www.mssc.state.ms.us. The chairman of the joint committee that reported the flag change bill to the legislature was a former Confederate officer and a member of the 1890 convention committee that drafted the Mississippi Plan.

6. "Bill to Prevent Flag Desecration Introduced," *Jackson Daily News,* March 16, 1916; "Mississippi Has Fallen in Line," *Daughters of the American Revolution Magazine* 48 (July 1916): 410; "Committee to Prevent Desecration of the Flag," *Daughters of the American Revolution Magazine* 49 (December 1916): 379–381; *Jackson Daily News,* April 7, 1916; *Journal of the House of Representatives of the State of Mississippi, January 4, 1916–April 8, 1916* (Memphis: Dixon-Paul, 1916), 2279–2280; *Journal of the Senate of the State of Mississippi, January 4, 1916–April 8, 1916* (Memphis: Dixon-Paul, 1916), 843, 1786–1787, 1819; *Code of Mississippi* 1972, vol. 20, sect. 97-7-39.

7. Emily Bellinger and Joan Reynold Faunt, comps., *Biographical Dictionary of the Senate of South Carolina, 1776–1964* (Columbia: South Carolina Archives Department, 1964), 259; Allan D. Charles, *The Narrative History of Union County South Carolina* (Spartanburg: Reprint Company, 1987), 222–223, 230–231; Owen, *Alabama Official and Statistical Register, 1939,* 20.

8. Ellison Durant Smith, "'Cotton Ed' Smith," in Allan A. Michie and Frank Ryhlick, *Dixie Demagogues* (New York: Vanguard Press, 1939), 265, 285; Turner Catledge, "Set Pace for South, Carolina Believes," *NYT,* September 1, 1938. These conclusions are based on "negative evidence" and thus subject to contradiction. I failed to find evidence of political uses of the

flag in newspaper accounts of political campaigns or in the extensive political memorabilia collection of the McKissick Museum of the University of South Carolina. The conclusions are necessarily tentative without a systematic investigation of all sources.

9. The Nicholls broadside is in the collections of the Louisiana State Museum in New Orleans. Ted Tunnell, *The Crucible of Reconstruction: War, Radicalism and Race in Louisiana, 1862–1877* (Baton Rouge: Louisiana State University Press, 1984), 129–130; John Purifoy campaign poster in Political Campaign Ephemera Collection, ADAH, Box 1, folder 14; Thomas McAdory Owen, *History of Alabama and Dictionary of Alabama Biography* (1928; Spartanburg, SC: Reprint Company, 1978), 4:1399–1400. Purifoy's poster is the only pre-1948 Confederate flag in a four-box collection of political campaign ephemera at the ADAH.

10. Sally Archer Anderson to Mr. Hotchkiss, August 28, 1940, in Sally Archer Anderson Papers, ESBL, MOC. Contemporary newspapers contain no articles or photos of the poster and its "senseless slogan."

11. Marjorie Spruill Wheeler, "Divided Legacy: The Civil War, Tradition, and 'The Woman Question,' 1870–1920," in Edward D. C. Campbell, Jr., and Kym S. Rice, *A Woman's War: Southern Women, Civil War, and the Confederate Legacy* (Charlottesville: University Press of Virginia, 1996), 187, 165–191.

12. Lee Photograph Gallery *cartes-de-visite* in collections of MOC and VHS; J. W. Reed to Isabel Maury, July 29, 1907, ESBL, MOC.

13. James Forman, *The Making of Black Revolutionaries: A Personal Account* (New York: Macmillan, 1972), 112–113; "A Brutal Lynching in Arkansas," *Richmond Planet*, May 7, 1927; "With Officers Making No Attempt at Restraint, Mob Burns Negro's Body, and Creates a Reign of Terror," *Arkansas Gazette*, May 5, 1927; Theodore Holmes, "Cops Direct Traffic as Arkansas Stages 'Bon-Fire' Lynch Orgy," *PC*, May 14, 1927.

14. See, for example, Mrs. S. E. F. Rose, *The Ku Klux Klan or Invisible Empire* (New Orleans: L. Graham, 1914); Mildred Rutherford, *The Truths of History* (Atlanta: Southern Lion Books, 1998), 127–131; Stetson Kennedy, *After Appomattox* (Gainesville: University Press of Florida, 1995).

15. Wyn Craig Wade, *The Fiery Cross: The Ku Klux Klan in America* (London: Simon & Schuster, 1987), 31–37, 58, 86, 105; Allen W. Trelease, *White Terror: The Ku Klux Klan Conspiracy and Southern Reconstruction* (New York: Harper, 1971).

16. Rose, *Ku Klux Klan,* 39.

17. *CV* 21 (May 1913): 240; James Van Eldik, *From the Flame of Battle to the Fiery Cross: The 3rd Tennessee Infantry* (Las Cruces, NM: Yucca Tree Press, 2001), 281–283; Mrs. Grace Meredith Newbill, "Birthplace of the Ku Klux Klan," *CV* 25 (July 1917): 335.

18. David M. Chalmers, *Hooded Americanism: The History of the Ku Klux Klan* (Chicago: Quadrangle Books, 1965); Nancy MacLean, *Behind the Mask of Chivalry: The Making of the Second Ku Klux Klan* (New York: Oxford University Press, 1994); Ku Klux Klan Revival file, UDC Collection (Janet Randolph Papers), ESBL, MOC, Box 15; testimony of Simmons in U.S. Congress, House of Representatives Committee on Rules, 67th Congress, 1st session, *The Ku Klux Klan* (Washington: Government Printing Office, 1921), 90–91.

19. David Freeman, *Carved in Stone: The History of Stone Mountain* (Macon, GA: Mercer University Press, 1997), 43, 52, 61, 78–80.

20. Ibid., 94, 125; "300 Women in Masks Parade in Atlanta," *NYT,* November 23, 1922; Nancy MacLean to author, March 3, 1995. Five boxes of materials generated by the Athens, Georgia, Chapter No. 5 of the Klan in the 1920s (Hargrett, UGA) and a collection of 1910s–1920s illustrated sheet music (DeVincent Collection, Smithsonian, Series 5, Box 16) contain no items bearing the battle flag.

21. U.S. Information Agency (NYT, Paris Bureau), NARA, RG 306, Box 650; accounts of parade in Willard Cope, "75,000 See Colorful Parade in Tribute to Heroes in Gray," and Ralph McGill, "One More Word," *AC,* April 27, 1939.

22. William Blanchard, "Racial Nationalism: Principles and Purposes" (Live Oak, FL: White Front Publishing Co., 1938), in Stetson Kennedy Collection, Schomburg, NYPL, Box 2, folder 4; notes on United Sons of Dixie, ca. 1944, in ibid., Box 5, folder 11; Stetson Kennedy, *Southern Exposure* (Garden City, NY: Doubleday, 1946), 223.

23. Stetson Kennedy, *I Rode with the Ku Klux Klan* (London: Arco, 1954), 59, 96, 98; "The Ku Klux Klan Tries a Comeback," *Life* 20 (May 27, 1946), 42–43.

24. Kennedy, *I Rode,* 120–121.

25. "College Boys and the Confederate Flag," *National Tribune,* April 21, 1904; President Patrick Hues Mell to Adjutant General, War Department, March 23, 1904, and "A Tall Clemson Tale Improves with Age," clipping

from *Greenville News,* June 21, 1959, both from University Archives, Clemson University Libraries, Clemson, South Carolina.

26. Paul Murrill, comp., *Catalogue of the Kappa Alpha Fraternity 1865–1906* (Charlotte, NC: Kappa Alpha, 1906), 3; Reynolds S. Cheney, "The Old South Ball . . . Its 53rd Anniversary," *Kappa Alpha Journal,* Winter 1973–1974; R. Vinson Lackey, *Our First Fifty Years . . .* (1955).

27. The [University of Florida] *Seminole, 1942,* Kappa Alpha pages and social page (photographs); *1946,* Kappa Alpha pages; *Florida Alligator,* April 6, 1951; *Pandora* [University of Georgia], 1946, KA snapshots page (no page numbers); 1949, 314.

28. "Stars to Parade Peachtree Today; City to Relive 60's at Gay Ball," *AC,* December 14, 1939; Willard Cope, "Cheering 300,000 Hail Clark Gable in Wild Welcome," *AC,* December 15, 1939; "U.D.C.'s Complete Plans for G.W.T.W. Ball Friday," *RTD,* January 31, 1940, and "Gone with the Wind," *RTD,* February 3, 1940.

29. "Camp Lee Service Club—1917 Fashion," *Camp Lee Traveller,* February 25, 1942 (photograph of a postcard); "Confederate Flag Waves over La Haye," *RTD,* July 10, 1944.

30. "Confederate Flag on Shuri," Charleston *Post & Courier,* May 31, 1945; John T. Smith, Jr. (USMC photographer on Okinawa) to author, July 9, 2001; article in Florence, SC, *Morning News,* July 24, 1945, in Julian Delano Dusenbury scrapbooks, private collection; interviews with Martha Rollins Dusenbury, April 28, 1994, and June 23, 1995; Ogburn quoted in *UDC Magazine* 10 (February 1947): 12; Walter Wood, "A Heroic Memorial Day Flag Raising," *Washington Times,* May 26, 1986; Mason Brunson, Jr., "Palmetto Profiles: Julian D. Dusenbury," *South Carolina Magazine,* October 1948, 9; Terry Joyce, "Medal Paperwork Gathering Dust?" Charleston *Post and Courier,* May 2, 1999.

31. The flag is now in the possession of Dusenbury's widow; photograph by Pfc. Sam J. Bushemi, U.S. Marine Corps Archives, copy courtesy of John T. Smith, Jr.; "Local Store Sells CSA Flags for World-Wide Display," *RTD,* August 13, 1945.

32. "Flags of the Confederacy," rpt. in *RTD,* July 3, 1944.

33. J. Bryan III, *Sword over the Mantel: The Civil War and I* (New York: McGraw-Hill, 1960), 1–20; "Confederate Flag Waves in Solomons," *RNL,* February 18, 1944.

34. Brunson, "Palmetto Profiles," 9. The UDC's president-general reported

in November 1944 and November 1945 about the demand for Confederate flags by soldiers and the "amusing letters" received about the establishment of "Confederate forces" on foreign soil. *Minutes of the Fifty-First Annual Convention of the General Division, United Daughters of the Confederacy, November 1944,* 69; *Minutes of the Fifty-Second Annual Convention of the General Division, United Daughters of the Confederacy, November 1945,* 69; "'Marines' Professional Rebels, Inc.' To Receive Confederate Battle Flag," *RNL,* July 4, 1945.

35. Clark G. Reynolds, *The Fighting Lady: New Yorktown in the Pacific War* (Missoula, MT: Pictorial Histories, 1986), 61, 114, 225; "Confederate Flag Banned as Emblem," *RNL,* August 13, 1941.

36. Program in pamphlet collection, ESBL, MOC; Grover C. Hall quoted in Edward T. Folliard, "How Comes the Unfurling of the Confederate Flag?" *WP,* rpt. in *MA,* November 20, 1951.

37. Andrew Doyle, "Turning the Tide: College Football and Southern Progressivism," *Southern Cultures,* 3 (Fall 1997): 42 and 29–32; Andrew Doyle, "Causes Won, Not Lost: College Football and the Modernization of the American South," *International Journal of the History of Sport,* 11 (August 1994): 242. The *Tuscaloosa News* (January 5, 1926) noted that "flags today cover the entire downtown business section of the city in honor of the team," but did not clarify which flags were flown.

38. On the school's symbolism, see David G. Sansing, *The University of Mississippi: A Sesquicentennial History* (University: University of Mississippi, 1999), 168–169, 269–70; and Kevin Pierce Thornton, "Symbolism at Ole Miss and the Crisis of Southern Identity" (M.A. thesis, University of Virginia, 1983), 19–20; Billy Gates, "'Rebels' Battle Flag Historic at Ole Miss," *Alumni Review* (October 1951), 12; "Some of Your Profs," *Ole Miss* 53 (1947); *Miss.,* November 21, 1947.

39. Photo with caption "Miss Confederacy 1941" in *Corks & Curls 1941; College Topics* [University of Virginia], October 6, 1941; Chris Springer, "The Troubled Resurgence of the Confederate Flag," *History Today* 43 (June 1993): 7; Chris Springer, "The Rebel Flag: The Confederate Flag and Its Image in America from 1865 to the Present" (B.A. thesis, Brown University, 1990), 18.

40. *Time* 50 (October 20, 1947); "Virginia Victory," rpt. in *RTD,* October 16, 1947.

41. "Committee Bans 'Stars and Bars' from Penn Game," *College Topics,* No-

vember 4, 1947; Christopher C. Nehls, "Flag-Waving Wahoos: Confederate Symbols at the University of Virginia, 1941–1951," *Virginia Magazine
of History and Biography* 110 (2002): 472–478; "Flag Sales Soar as Wahoos
Plan Large Scale Invasion of Philly," *College Topics,* November 6, 1947;
"Stars, Bars Fly, Wahoos Invade Quaker Heaven," and "Crowd James Hall,
Gives Team Biggest Send-Off of Season," in *College Topics,* November 8,
1947.

II. Rebel Flag

1. Visitors to The Museum of the Confederacy's 1993–1995 exhibition,
   "Embattled Emblem," responded to an open-ended survey question,
   "What does the Confederate battle flag mean to you?" By far the most
   prevalent answer (appearing on one-quarter of the surveys) was some
   variation of "history."

5. "The Shadow of States' Rights"

1. "Hats Go Off for Stars and Bars," *BP,* July 17, 1948; Associated Press wire
   photos in *BN,* July 17, 1948; July 18, 1948.
2. Robert A. Garson, *The Democratic Party and the Politics of Sectionalism,
   1941–1948* (Baton Rouge: Louisiana State University Press, 1974), 258–
   259; J. Barton Starr, "Birmingham and the 'Dixiecrat' Convention of
   1948," *Alabama Historical Quarterly* 32 (Spring–Summer 1970): 30–31.
3. Arthur M. Schlesinger, Jr., ed., *History of American Presidential Elections
   1789–1968* (New York: Chelsea House, 1971), 4:3182; photograph caption, "Alabamians Fly Confederate Flag," *BP,* July 15, 1948.
4. "Civil Rights Tension Explodes into Drama," *Christian Science Monitor,* July
   15, 1948.
5. V. O. Key, *Southern Politics* (New York: Random House/Vintage, 1949),
   331; Springer, "The Rebel Flag," 19.
6. "Governor Wright Bids Negroes Be Quiet," *NYT,* May 10, 1948; Starr,
   "Birmingham," 26–27.
7. Schlesinger, *History,* 4:3169–3172.
8. Roland Dopson, "Thurmond and Wright Head Dixie Rights Ticket," *AC,*
   July 18, 1948; speech quoted in Nadine Cohodas, *Strom Thurmond and the
   Politics of Southern Change* (New York: Simon & Schuster, 1993), 177.
9. Gene Wortman, "There's an Auditorium Full of Suspense before Opening," *BP,* July 17, 1948; Anniston *Star* quoted in Starr, "Birmingham," 47.

10. Dean DuBois, "Fifty-Five Ole Miss Students Attend States' Rights Meeting," *Miss.*, July 22, 1948; "Ole Miss Boys Cut Up," *BN*, July 18, 1948; "Hats Go Off," photograph and caption in *BN*, July 18, 1948.

11. Ole Miss student quoted in DuBois, "Fifty-Five Ole Miss Students"; Alabama student quoted in Wortman, "Auditorium Full."

12. "Dixie 'Rebs' Say U.S. Can't Stop South's Segregation," *Pittsburgh Courier*, July 24, 1948 (ellipsis in original); "Dixiecrats Defy 'Rights' Plans," *Birmingham World*, July 20, 1948; Charley Cherokee, "National Grapevine," in *Chicago Defender*, July 24, 1948; "The Southern Revolt—Our Shame," Tuscaloosa *Alabama Citizen*, July 24, 1948.

13. William D. Workman, Jr., "Birmingham Brings Out Fighting Spirit," July 18, 1948, in William D. Workman clippings scrapbooks, 2:162, William D. Workman Papers, Modern Political Collection, SC; [Dabney,] "Claghornesque Antics," *RTD*, July 18, 1948.

14. Graves, "This Afternoon," *BP*, July 24, 1948; McGill, "Just Like Silver Fox Furs," *AC*, July 30, 1948.

15. Campaign materials in Workman Papers, Box 2, files 1 and 2; *States' Rights Information and Speakers Handbook* (Jackson: National States' Rights Democrats Campaign Committee [1948]); *Alexandria Gazette*, August 23, 1948.

16. "Help Dixie's Cause," Alabama Democratic States' Rights Committee advertisement in Political Campaign Ephemera Collection, ADAH, Box 1, folder 3; Gessner T. McCorvey to Frank Dixon, December 14, 1948, Frank Dixon Papers, ADAH, Box 2, folder 5; Gessner T. McCorvey, text of interview given to reporter, August 25, 1949, State Democratic Executive Committee Records (Gessner T. McCorvey administration), ADAH, Box 84, folder 13.

17. Margaret Lee Davis to "Dixiecrats," Dixon Papers, Box 2, folder 2; Everett Collier, "Dixiecrat Chiefs Here for Kickoff," *Houston Chronicle*, August 11, 1948; photographs in *Houston Chronicle*, August 12, 29, 1948.

18. Charles Parmer, "Thurmond Challenges Truman to Debate 'Rights,'" *Alexandria Gazette*, October 9, 1948; "Supporters of Thurmond Encouraged," *RNL*, October 9, 1948; "The Fifth Freedom," *Alexandria Gazette*, July 19, 1948.

19. Sylvia Costen, "Dixiecrat's Banner," *RNL*, August 10, 1948; Betty Sessler, "Confederate Flag Sales Show No 'Dixiecrat' Boom in City," *RTD*, August

10, 1948; Frances Boushall, "Dixie's Flag Still Waves (and Sells)," *RTD*, May 30, 1948.

20. "'Young' General J. W. Moore, 97, Is New Commander of 'Rebels,'" *MA*, October 7, 1948; and "Confederate Veterans Honored with Luncheon," *MA*, October 8, 1948; *Minutes of the Fifty-Sixth Annual Convention of the General Division, United Daughters of the Confederacy, 1948*, 185–187.

21. Election results in Schlesinger, *History*, 4:3140–3141, 3211.

22. *Miss.*, October 15, 1948, and November 26, 1948; Sansing, *University of Mississippi*, 269–270; Thornton, "Symbolism" (1983) 21.

23. "Newly Formed University Greys," *Miss.*, October 8, 1948.

24. *"M" Book, 1948*, quoted in Kevin Pierce Thornton, "Symbolism at Ole Miss and the Crisis of Southern Identity," in *South Atlantic Quarterly* 86 (Summer 1987): 258.

25. 1949 yearbook quoted in Thornton, "Symbolism at Ole Miss," 258–259; *Ole Miss 1951*, foreword.

26. Jim Harland, "Confederate Flags Fly Again on Capstone Fraternity Houses," *Crimson-White*, July 20, 1948; "Rise up . . . " quoted in Springer, "Rebel Flag," 21; "Old South to Live Again at KA Rebel Weekend," *Crimson-White*, April 26, 1949; *Corolla, 1949*, 296; George R. Jackson to Confederate Museum, October 14, 1948, Correspondence Files of India W. Thomas, ESBL, MOC.

27. See letters from Holt Rast to Mayor Cooper Green, February 16, 1948, and October 30, 1948, Cooper Green Papers, BPL, file 7:2.

6. "Keep Your Eyes on Those Confederate Flags"

1. "Stars and Bars Fly Again: Oh, Happy Student Days," *NYT*, May 31, 1950; Edward T. Folliard, "How Comes the Unfurling of the Confederate Flag?" *WP* rpt. in *MA*, November 20, 1951; "Autos Flying Confederate Flags Barred from Parking at Capitol," *NYT*, November 9, 1951; Arnold Snow, "Confederate Flag Mailed Here to Boy Scouts in Lincoln's Home Town of Springfield, Ill.," *MA*, February 10, 1952.

2. "The Flags Are Flying in Dixie," *Business Week* (November 25, 1950), 48; "Those Rebel Flags," *Newsweek* 38 (September 24, 1951), 24; "The Flag, Suh!" *Life* 31 (October 15, 1951), 66; Herbert R. Sass, Jr., "Confederate Flag Sales Skyrocket," in Charleston *News & Courier*, August 22, 1950; "Flag Boom of the Week," *Jet* (December 27, 1951), 15; Ruth Danehower Wilson, "Confederate Flag-Wavers," *Crisis* 59 (April 1952), 240;

Georgiana M. Root, "Stars and Bars Flying from Korea to Boston in Furious Flag Fad," *WSJ,* September 1, 1951, cites figures more modestly at 100,000 to date, up from 50,000 in 1950; Report of India W. Thomas, House Regent, for 1950, ESBL, MOC.

3. "Those Rebel Flags," 24; John Long, "Conquest by Bunting," *NYT Magazine,* October 14, 1951, 52.

4. Bem Price, "South Will Win That War Yet," *Mobile Press,* September 25, 1951; Edward T. Folliard, "How Comes the Unfurling of the Confederate Flag?" *WP,* rpt. in *MA,* November 20, 1951; Long, "Conquest," 52 (original emphasis).

5. "The Flags of the Confederacy," *UDC Magazine* 15 (May 1952): 20; Wilson, "Confederate Flag-Wavers," 242; Vulcan, "From Where I Stand," *BN,* August 27, 1951.

6. *Operation Pacific,* Warner Brothers, 1951.

7. "Even U.S. Army Trucks Fly the Confederate Flag," *RTD,* September 3, 1951; "Fad Spreads to the Union Army," *NYT,* August 31, 1951.

8. Report of House Regent India W. Thomas, September 1949 in CMLS Minutes, ESBL, MOC.

9. History of Dixie Division in printed brochure, ca. 1941, State Government Public Information Files—Alabamians at War, ADAH, Box SG17125, folder 17; *Presenting the 31st Division* [yearbook, 1951], multiple (unnumbered) pages; "A Year in Columbia with the Dixie Division," *State Magazine,* December 30, 1951, 7–9, in Fort Jackson Museum research files–units; photograph of "Mascot of the 31st Infantry Division," in *Mobile Register,* March 24, 1952; *Dixie* [division newspaper], 1941 in ADAH; *History of the 31st Division in Training and Combat, 1940–1945* (1946; rpt. Nashville: Battery Press, 1994).

10. Quoted in *PC: Army & Navy Register,* December 16, 1944, 12; Army Regulations [AR] 260-210, October 25, 1944, paragraphs 1d and 2a; SR 840–10–1, October 28, 1952, paragraph 67, reproduced in Leslie D. Jensen, "Notes on Flags, Colors, Standards, and Guidons" (unpub. report, Planning and Development Branch, Museum Division, U.S. Army Center of Military History, 1991).

11. Senate Report 684, 78th Congress, 2nd session, February 7, 1944; House Report 1423, 80th Congress, 2nd session, February 25, 1948; "Confederate Flags Legalized," *NYT,* March 10, 1948. *UDC Magazine* 11 (May 1948): 8–9, specified the units authorized to carry Confederate battle

streamers. Standards for the streamers are specified in AR 840-10, section 9-12, October 1979, reproduced in Jensen, "Notes."

12. "Southern Airmen Forced to Lower Stars and Bars," *RTD,* November 11, 1951.

13. "World to See Flag of Dixie," *Mobile Press,* March 5, 1952; "4 U.S. Destroyers Won't Fly Confederate Flags Any More," *RTD,* April 4, 1952; "U.S. Ships Told to Stop Flying Confederate Flag," *NYT,* April 4, 1952; *Jet,* March 26, 1952, 18.

14. Universal Newsreels, 6625x (reel 1), Division of Motion Pictures, Sound and Video, NARA; letter of Donald Massey to author, January 16, 1999; "Confederate Banner Sent to Soldiers on Korean Front," *UDC Magazine* 15 (May 1952): 9; "Confederate Flags in Korea," *UDC Mag.* 15 (August 1952): 19; *Minutes of the Fifty-Eighth Annual Convention of the General Division, United Daughters of the Confederacy, November 1951,* 124; Mary Poppenheim et al., eds., *History of the United Daughters of the Confederacy* (Raleigh: Edwards & Broughton, 1956), 262.

15. Telephone interview with Richard Athey, November 16, 1998; letters from Melvin L. Bailey, January 11, 1999; George J. Ellis, October 27 and November 2, 11, 1998; Eddie "Gene" Garner, November 17, 1998; D. E. "Dave" Newman, November 13 and 25, 1998; George N. Iseri, June 21, 1999; Harold Brouphy, November 1998; William T. Dunn, February 24, 1999; Kenneth "Shep" Eldridge, October 27, 1998, and January 21, 1999; Arthur G. Keene, January 21 and February 1, 1999; Lawrence C. Lander, November 23, 1998; Graham L. Sisson, January 27, 1999; Wayne E. Smith, October 20, 1998. These interviews and letters were in response to a query placed in the September–October 1998 issue of *Graybeards.*

16. Scott Blomeley to *NYT Magazine,* November 4, 1951.

17. "Marine 100th New Yorker in Korea to Fly a City Flag," *NYT,* March 23, 1952; Henry H. Sampson to author, December 1, 1998.

18. Telephone interview with Athey; Ellis letters.

19. Letters from Brouphy, Eldridge, Ellis, and Newman; telephone interviews with Ben Alexander, November 2, 1998, and L. Douglas Wilder, Jr., November 19, 1998; Charles C. Diggs, Jr., *The Diggs Report: Investigation of Alleged Discriminatory Practices in the Armed Forces* in *Blacks in the United States Armed Forces: Basic Documents,* ed. Morris J. MacGregor and

Bernard C. Nalty (Wilmington, DE: Scholarly Resources, 1977), 12:345–346.

20. *UDC Mag.* 12 (October 1949): 14; *American Legion Magazine,* November 1951, 34; "Confederate Flags To Stay Despite Yankee's Protest," *NYT,* August 30, 1951; "VFW Claims First Use," *RTD,* November 11, 1951.

21. "The Flag, Suh!" 65; Long, "Conquest," 52; "The Flags of the Confederacy," *UDC Mag.* 15 (May 1952): 20.

22. Quoted in Betty Sessler, "Dixie's Unflagging Banner," *RTD,* August 19, 1951; also Price, "South Will Win That War Yet"; Josephine Connerat, "Confederate Flag Sales Boom; Yankees the Best Customers," *Savannah Morning News,* August 3, 1951; Roy V. Harris, "Strictly Personal," *Augusta Courier,* September 17, 1951; *Augusta Courier,* September 24, 1951.

23. Quoted in "Dixie Flags Up North Held Sign of Confederate Revival," *RNL,* August 29, 1951; Hatley Norton Mason, Jr., "The Official Flags of the Confederate States," *Commonwealth: The Magazine of Virginia* 18 (December 1951): 80; SCV commander-in-chief messages in *UDC Mag.* 13 (November 1950): 20, 25, 26; 13 (October 1950), 21; 14 (January 1951), 26.

24. "Fighting Alderman Halts 'Rebel Day' at Chicago High School," American Negro Press release dated October 10, 1951, in Claude A. Barnett Papers, Part I: ANP News Releases, 1928–1964, series B, reel 46, frame 01128; "No 'Rebel Day' at Hyde Park," *Chicago Defender,* October 13, 1951; "Rebel Flags and Rebel Views," *Chicago Defender,* October 13, 1951.

25. "It Was a Rebellion," *Richmond Afro-American,* January 12, 1952; "Confederate Flag Revives Issues of Civil War: Historian Says Dixie on Political Offensive," *Richmond Afro-American,* January 12, 1952.

26. "Awake America!," *Richmond Afro-American,* April 19, 1952.

27. *PC,* September 29, 1951.

28. Stanley Roberts, "Top Brass Silent as Alarm Spreads," *PC,* September 29, 1951.

29. E. B. Henderson, "American Flags on Cars Suggested from Writer," *Norfolk Journal and Guide,* November 3, 1951; "Confederate Flag 'Craze' Opposed," *Norfolk Journal and Guide,* November 24, 1951.

30. "Confederate Flag Fad Passes; Few Rebel Items Are Now Sold," *MA,* November 8, 1953.

31. "Life Goes to the Old South Ball," *Life* 28 (May 22, 1950), 162–168. The Auburn University yearbook suggests that the Old South event and secession ritual had begun by 1947 but that the flag did not become part of the ritual until 1950. *Glomerata*, 1947, KA page (no page numbers); 1948, KA page (no page numbers); 1949, 299; 1950, 260; 1951, 255; 1952, [82]; 1953, 150; 1954, snapshots pages (caption: "It Happens Every Spring"); *Corolla* [University of Alabama], *1951*, guidebooks photo section and "Dixie Doin's" page; *1954*, 254; also *1959*, 46, 292; *Pandora* [University of Georgia], *1953*, 69; *The 1952 Southern Accent* [Birmingham-Southern College], Kappa Alpha page; *Garnet and Black* [University of South Carolina], *1952*, 68. The yearbooks for 1952–1959 show similar activities. For details and analysis of the Old South rituals and the use of the flag, see Anthony W. James, "The Defenders of Tradition: College Social Fraternities, Race and Gender, 1945–1980" (Ph.D. diss., University of Mississippi, 1998), 206–216.

32. *Ole Miss*, 1955, 192; 1957, 26–27; 1958, 149; 1962, 238; 1950, 16–17; 1953, cover, Homecoming and football section, 138; 1955, title page, 1957, 31, 122–123; 1958, 28; 1959, cover, 27, 161, 183; 1962, 148–149, 1963, 15.

33. "University to Have Official School Flag," *Florida Alligator*, undated clipping; "Fernandez Named Winner in University Flag Contest," *Florida Alligator*, May 9, 1952; Don Adams, "Official UF Flag Is Revised," *Florida Alligator*, September 20, 1957; *Florida Alligator*, September 25, 1953; *Seminole* [University of Florida] 1953, 43; 1952, 84, 95; 1955, 181; 1962, 27; *Gator History: A Pictorial History of the University of Florida* (Gainesville: South Star, 1986); "Florida under Five Flags—One Will Win," *Florida Alligator*, December 1, 1961; September 27, 1962.

34. William Neely, *Daytona U.S.A.: The Official History of Daytona and Ormond Beach Racing from 1902 to Today's NASCAR* (Tucson, AZ: AZTEX, 1979); telephone interview with Bob Latford, June 14, 1994; undated program for Dixie Speedway and 1960 program for Dixie 500 in International Motor Sports Hall of Fame Library, Talladega Speedway, Talladega, Alabama.

35. Lyle Kenyon Engel, *The Complete Book of NASCAR Stock Car Racing* (New York: Four Winds Press, 1968), 97–98; Jim Hunter, *A History of the Darlington Raceway and the Joe Weatherly Stock Car Museum* (Darlington: Dar-

lington Raceway, ca. 1969), 4, 6, 22, 28, 36, 79; Latford interview; Darlington race covers in International Motor Sports Hall of Fame Library, Talladega Speedway, Talladega, Alabama, and Vertical Files (Darlington Speedway), SC; Tom Priddy, "More than Just a Stock Car Race," *Anderson Independent,* September 9, 1973; Blanche Boyd McCrary, *The Redneck Way of Knowledge: Down-Home Tales* (New York: Alfred A. Knopf, 1982), 21–22.

36. Telephone interviews with Dr. Frederick Moore, December 27, 1999, and February 24, 2000; C. R. Chandler, "World War II as Southern Entertainment: The Confederate Air Force and Warfare Re-enactment Ritual," in Ray B. Browne, ed., *Rituals and Ceremonies in Popular Culture* (Bowling Green, OH: Bowling Green Popular Press, 1980): 264–266; www.confederateairforce.org. CAF leaders solicited suggestions for a new name and, amid predictable protests, selected the name "Commemorative Air Force" in 2001.

37. Program of 30th Cotton Ball, 1962, Clippings files ("Cotton Ball"), CPL; typescript notes/memoranda for 1956 program and other programs in Cotton Ball Collection, Box 1, file 2, CPL.

38. Charles H. Wesley, "The Civil War and the Negro-American," *Journal of Negro History* 47 (April 1962): 80–81; also paraphrase of CWCC Executive Director Karl Betts in "The South Will Rise Again," *Newsweek* 56 (December 12, 1960), 64; Minutes of Virginia CWCC, August 4, 1958, in minute book, 1958–1965, Records of the Virginia CWCC, LOV, Record Group 71; Barnett's speech, November 3, 1961, CWCC Subject Files, NARA, RG 79, entry 32, Box 107; David W. Bledsoe, "'South Won Centennial," May Sums Up Centennial, *State,* July 10, 1965.

39. *Mississippi's Greatest Hour: A Manual for Local Observances of the Centennial of the War between the States, 1961–1965* (Jackson: Mississippi Commission [1960]), 38. CWCC Subject Files, NARA, RG 79, entry 32, Boxes 45, 117, 125; George M. Street to Lester Wren, March 15, 1961, in Mississippi CWCC Collection, UM, file 3; *Virginia CWCC Newsletter* 2, no. 11 (February 1961).

40. Draft legislation, ca. April 21, 1961, in CWCC Subject Files, NARA, RG 79, entry 32, Box 73; *Tallahassee Democrat,* March 6, 1963, courtesy of Bruce Graetz; Myra P. McQuain to Major General U.S. Grant III, December 24, 1960, and January 16, 1961, and Edmund C. Gass to Myra P.

McQuain, December 30, 1960, in CWCC Subject Files, NARA, RG 79, entry 32, Box 73.

41. "The Civil War Marketing Marches In," *Sales Management* 86 (March 17, 1961), 38; "Centennial of the Civil War . . . Business Booms Like the Gettysburg Cannon," *Newsweek* (March 27, 1961), 78; John Bodnar, *Remaking America: Public Memory, Commemoration, and Patriotism in the Twentieth Century* (Princeton: Princeton University Press, 1992), 213–215.

42. U.S. CWCC, *The Civil War Centennial: A Report to the Congress* (Washington, DC: U.S. Government Printing Office, 1968), 3; "Aids to Advertisers," Committee on Advertising, CWCC, 1961, in CWCC Subject Files, NARA, RG 79, entry 32, Box 45; "Civil War Marketing," 41.

43. Harry Golden, "Let's End the Civil War," *Saturday Evening Post* 235 (August 22, 1962), 10; John Hope Franklin, "A Century of Civil War Observance," *Journal of Negro History* 47 (April 1962): 104; Howard N. Meyer, "Rally Round What Flag?" *Commonweal* 74 (June 1961): 271.

44. C. Vann Woodward, *The Burden of Southern History* (Baton Rouge: LSU Press, 1960), 86–87; Charles G. Sellers, *The Southerner as American* (Chapel Hill: UNC Press, 1960), v; also C. Vann Woodward, "Reflections on a Centennial: The American Civil War," *Yale Review* 50 (Summer 1961): 484–485.

7. "Symbol of the White Race and White Supremacy"

1. U.S. Civil War Centennial Commission, *The Civil War Commission: A Report to the Congress* (Washington: GPO, 1968), 6–7, 11–12; "S.C. Hotel Holds to Bias; JFK Urges Meeting," *Jet,* March 30, 1961, 4; "N.Y. Quits S.C. Civil War Meet, Plans Own Fete" and "Civil War Commission Heeds Integration Edict," *Jet,* April 6, 1961, 4, 5; Congressman William M. Tuck, chairman of the executive committee of the CWCC, statement, March 21, 1961, CWCC Subject Files, NARA, RG 79, entry 32, Box 52.

2. Address of Mr. Ashley Halsey, April 11, 1961, CWCC Subject Files, NARA, RG 79, entry 32, Box 52.

3. Dan T. Carter, *The Politics of Rage: George Wallace, the Origins of the New Conservatism, and the Transformation of American Politics,* 2nd ed. (Baton Rouge: LSU Press, 2000), 11; Stephen Lesher, *George Wallace: American Populist* (Reading, MA: Addison Wesley, 1994), 174. The "official" full text of the address is available on the ADAH website.

4. Virginius Dabney, "The Perverted Banner," *RTD,* March 23, 1965; Charles E. Fager, *Selma 1965* (New York: Charles Scribner, 1974), 150, and photograph between 178–179; photograph (#1673615) by Matt Herron/ Take Stock; "The Various Shady Lives of the Ku Klux Klan," *Time* 85 (April 9, 1965): 25.

5. Interview with James Farmer, Fredericksburg, Virginia, May 18, 1994; interview with Oliver Hill, Richmond, Virginia, May 3, 1994.

6. Interview with Julian Bond, Charlottesville, Virginia, April 12, 1995.

7. "The Ku Klux Klan Tries a Comeback," *Life* 20 (May 27, 1946), 42–43.

8. Harold Martin, "The Truth about the Klan Today," *Saturday Evening Post* 222 (October 22, 1949), 17–18, 122; photograph in *MA,* August 24, 1949; *Christian Science Monitor,* August 24, 1949; Wade, *Fiery Cross,* 278–291.

9. Fred Taylor, "Alabama Ku Klux Weighing Merger with Georgians after Pep Show Here," *Birmingham News,* April 25, 1949.

10. See especially John Egerton's *Speak Now against the Day: The Generation before the Civil Rights Movement in the South* (New York: Alfred A. Knopf, 1995); Roy V. Harris, "Strictly Personal" column, *Augusta Courier,* September 17, 1951.

11. Larry Weekley, "Confederate Flags Waved as House Begins Session," *RTD,* August 28, 1956; for details on Georgia flag, see Chapter 12.

12. Rosalind Urbach Moss, "'Yes, There's a Reason I Salute the Flag': Flag Use and the Civil Rights Movement," *Raven* [a journal of vexillology] 5 (1998); "Chicago 'Bombed' by Rebel Garbed Dixie Pilot," *Atlanta Daily World,* March 3, 1956.

13. See Neill R. McMillen, *The Citizens' Council: Organized Resistance to the Second Reconstruction, 1954–1964* (Urbana, IL: University of Illinois Press, 1971), 153; "Manual for Southerners," quoted in Hodding Carter III, *The South Strikes Back* (Garden City, NY: Doubleday, 1959), 174–175.

14. See "Articles of Incorporation of the Association of Citizens' Councils of Louisiana" and "The Platform of the Citizens' Councils," in *Hearings before the United States Commission on Civil Rights* (Washington, DC: Government Printing Office, 1961), 526–533.

15. McMillen, 124; Birmingham *Dixie American,* March 1, 1956; Association of Citizens' Council of Mississippi, *2nd Annual Report, August 1956,* 4; Citizens' Council Collection, UM, Box 1, folder 29; *The Citizens' Council,*

from July 1957 to October 1959, Citizens' Council Collection, UM, Box 3, folder 2; Roy Vincent Harris Papers, Russell, UGA, photographs 70374-10 and 70374-12.

16. *Virginian,* January, March, May, and June 1956 issues in Hatley Norton Mason Papers, LOV, Box 7; *Virginian;* photograph in *Southern School News* 2 (December 1956): 5.

17. *UDC Magazine* 14 (January 1951): 11; Mason to R. Carter Pittman, February 26, 1963; Mason to Judge Walter B. Jones, September 23, 1957, and October 9, 1957, in H. Norton Mason Papers, LOV, Boxes 1, 3.

18. "Confederate Flag," text of address, unidentified clipping, March 11, 1957, in Vertical Files (Confederate, general), SC; quoted in K. Michael Prince, *Rally 'Round the Flag, Boys: South Carolina and the Confederate Flag* (Columbia: University of South Carolina Press, 2004), 30, 45.

19. "Klan Parades Here," and "200 Robed Klansmen Burn 3 Crosses at Birmingham," in Tuscaloosa-Northport newspaper, April 21, 1956, and August 25, 1956, resp.; Bob Cohn, "Robed Klansmen in 68–Car Cavalcade Roll through City to Summit Parley," *MA,* November 20, 1960; Fletcher Knebel and Clark Mollenhoff, "Eight Klans Bring to the South," *Look,* April 30, 1957, 29f.

20. Drew Pearson column in unidentified newspaper, March 31, 196[5], in Schomburg Center Clipping File, 1925–1974, microfiche edition, fiche 002–695–4; Margaret Long, "The Imperial Wizard Explains the Klan," *NYT Magazine,* July 5, 1964, 8; "The Various Shady Lives of the Ku Klux Klan," *Time,* April 9, 1965, 25; telephone interview with Calvin L. Neighbors, "Great Titan/State Leader of the Realm of Virginia, Imperial Order, Knights of the Ku Klux Klan," July 28, 1993; telephone interview with Horace King, "Grand Dragon," Christian Knights of the Ku Klux Klan, June 22, 1995.

21. Melissa Fay Greene, *The Temple Bombing* (Reading, MA: Addison Wesley, 1996), 1–2, 9, 225, 227, 246, 256–257, 297–298.

22. Greene, *The Temple Bombing,* 158–161; "Stoner Always a White Supremacist, Didn't Let Anyone Affect His Thinking," *Chattanooga Times,* June 3, 1983; "73, 443 Georgians Vote for Stoner," *Thunderbolt* 177 (October 1974): 6–7; see, for example, election literature ("J. B. Stoner/Candidate for Lieutenant Governor . . . " and "J. B. Stoner/The White Racist/For United States Senator from Georgia . . . ") in *Thunderbolt* 146 (February 1972): 13.

23. Greene, 156–161; "Brief History of N.S.R.P.," *Thunderbolt* 50 (April 1963); photograph in *Thunderbolt*, 51 (May 1963): 6.

24. "Atty. Stoner and Dr. Fields Lead School Demonstrations," *Thunderbolt* 61 (September 1964): 9; "Raise That Confederate Banner," *Thunderbolt* 46 (October 1962): 11; "God Bless Mississppi [sic] Students [sic] Courage & Valor," *Thunderbolt* 46 (October 1962): 1–2; "Lynch and Stoner—Leaders of the White Masses," *Thunderbolt* 70 (September 1965); *Thunderbolt* 67 (February 1965): 12.

25. "Confederate Flag Banned," *Thunderbolt* 166 (November 1973): 5; "Blacks Seek to Ban Confederate Flag," *Thunderbolt* 143 (November 1971): 11; "New Orleans Students Demand Their Rights," *Thunderbolt* 135 (March 1971): 8; "Louisville—Pensacola Schools Do Not Punish Blacks Who Assault Whites," *Thunderbolt* 203 (March 1976): 2.

26. "Those Confederate Flags," *RTD,* May 14, 1967.

27. Bob Kyle, "1,200 UA Students Stage Midnight Demonstration," *Tuscaloosa News,* February 4, 1956; profile on Wilson from E. Culpepper Clark, *The Schoolhouse Door: Segregation's Last Stand at the University of Alabama* (New York: Oxford University Press, 1993), 62–65.

28. "Photographer Catches Scenes of Bama's 'Involved' Week," *Crimson-White,* February 7, 1956; photograph in *BN,* February 6, 1956, and February 7, 1956; "Flag Wavers," photograph in *Birmingham Post-Herald,* February 8, 1956; photographs in *Life* 30 (February 6, 1956): 23, and 30 (February 20, 1956): 28–29; and photographs in *Alabama Citizen*, February 11, 1956; "UA Expels Leonard Wilson," *Tuscaloosa News,* March 12, 1956, 1. Lucy returned to the university thirty years later to earn a master's in education.

29. Pete Daniel, *Lost Revolutions: The South in the 1950s* (Chapel Hill: University of North Carolina Press, 2000), chap. 12; Virgil Blossom, *It Has Happened Here* (New York: Harper, 1959).

30. Blossom, 81, 136, 140, 144; Elizabeth Huckaby, *Crisis at Central High: Little Rock, 1957–58* (Baton Rouge: Louisiana State University Press, 1980), 61; photograph of youth in leather jackets by Bern Keating in Daniel, *Lost Revolutions,* 177, 269, and *RTD,* September 11, 1957; "Opening Day of Integrated Schools at Little Rock," *U.S. News & World Report,* August 24, 1959, 39. The memoirs by the leader of the Little Rock NAACP and one of the nine students do not mention the presence of Confederate flags. See Daisy Bates, *The Long Shadow of Little Rock: A Memoir* (New York: Da-

vid McKay, 1962); Melba Patillo Beals, *Warriors Don't Cry: A Searing Memoir of the Battle to Integrate Little Rock's Central High* (New York: Pocket Books, 1994).

31. Photographic source for Atlanta and New Orleans flag use in *Southern School News* 9 (September 1962): 5; "Jeers, Violence Mark March," *New Orleans Picayune*, November 17, 1960.

32. "Birmingham Has Uneasy Peace," *RTD*, September 11, 1957; photographs in *Birmingham Post-Herald*, September 4, 5, 1963; "4 States Righters Fined, Sentenced," *Birmingham Post-Herald*, September 13, 1963; Tom Lankford, "Yelling Whites Set Off Melee at Graymont," *BN*, September 4, 1963. Ted Bryant, "Students Protest at West End High," *BN*, September 11, 1963; Joe Campbell, "1,000 Skip Classes, Nine Adults Arrested," *BN*, September 10, 1963; Paul Sims, "Private Schools' Group Holds Rally," *BN*, September 12, 1963; "Birmingham's Students: A Message," *BN*, September 11, 1963.

33. These photographs appear in Nadine Cohodas, *The Band Played Dixie: Race and the Liberal Conscience at Ole Miss* (New York: Free Press, 1997), and James Meredith, *Three Years in Mississippi* (Bloomington: Indiana University Press, 1966), dust jacket photograph; Russell H. Barrett, *Integration at Ole Miss* (Chicago: Quadrangle, 1965), 106, 121 (Barnett quote); Walter Lord, *The Past That Would Not Die* (New York: Harper & Row, 1965), 153, 167.

34. Barrett, *Integration,* 139; Jan Humber, "Chancellor Issues Plea," *Miss.,* October 1, 1962; Lord, *Past,* 202; Sidna Brower, "Troops Surround Ole Miss," *Miss.,* October 2, 1962.

35. "Rebel Underground," 1, no. 1 (October 1962) and no. 4 (January 1963), in Race Relations Collection, UM, Box 1 (Ole Miss Silver Collection), folder 12; Conservative Students' Association brochure, ca. December 1964, Race Relations Collection, UM, Box 1 (Ole Miss Silver Collection), folder 12.

36. "Confederate Uniforms, Flag Won't Be Used," *BN*, May 8, 1963; Thornton, "Symbolism," 262–263.

37. Ed Williams, "Artist Paints 'Reality,'" *Miss.,* April 9, 1963; "Removal of Paintings Stirs Student Protest," *Miss.,* April 9, 1963; "Editor's Comments," *Miss.,* April 9, 1963; Meredith, *Three Years in Mississippi,* 279; James W. Silver, *Mississippi: The Closed Society* (New York: Harcourt, Brace

and World, 1963), 108; Barrett, *Integration at Ole Miss,* 217–218. Kerciu later showed his works at a Los Angeles gallery. See review (and photograph) in *ArtForum,* March 1964, 13–15.

38. On "Ace" Carter, see Glenn T. Eskew, *But for Birmingham: The Local and National Movements in the Civil Rights Struggle* (Chapel Hill: UNC Press, 1997), 114–116.

39. George C. Wallace Collection, ADAH, Box 144, folders 33–38; S. Ernest Vandiver Photograph Collection, Russell, UGA, photographs PF010 and PF013; "Stars and Bars," *BN,* April 28, 1963; Carter, *The Politics of Rage,* photographs following 320; Charles Morgan, Jr., *A Time to Speak* (New York: Harper, 1964), 7, 52; Wallace to Mrs. Edwin Durham, March 23, 1965, Governors Papers, ADAH, Box 22387, folder 16.

40. Wallace to Mrs. Edwin Durham, March 23, 1965, Governors Papers, ADAH, Box SG22387, folder 16; Wallace to the Reverend Raymond T. DeArmond, January 31, 1964, Governors Papers, ADAH, Box SG22387, folder 16.

41. Wallace to Larry Kreh, December 15, 1966, Governors Papers, ADAH, Box SG22425, folder 14; Wallace to Mickey Griffin, July 15, 1964, Governors Papers, ADAH, Box SG22387, folder 16; Wallace to Reverend Raymond T. DeArmond, January 31, 1964, Governors Papers, ADAH, Box SG22387, folder 16; Wallace to Mrs. William Owen Whitten, February 8, 1965, Governors Papers, ADAH, Box SG22387, folder 16; Wallace to Miss Mary M. Hyland, January 9, 1965, and Wallace to Mr. Herbert B. Kirkpatrick, May 3, 1965, Governors Papers, ADAH, Box 22387, folder 16.

42. Wallace to Mrs. Edwin Durham, March 23, 1965, Governors Papers, ADAH, Box SG22387, folder 16.

43. Wallace to Miss Donna Heins, March 27, 1964, Governors Papers, ADAH, Box SG22387, folder 16; Wallace to L. F. Ryan, Jr., February 29, 1964, Governors Papers, ADAH, Box SG22387, folder 16; Samuel J. Pierce to Wallace, July 15, 1966, Wallace to Pierce, July 20, 1966, and Pierce to Wallace, July 25, 1966, Governors Papers, ADAH, Box SG22405, folder 22.

44. *Speaking Out: The Autobiography of Lester Garfield Maddox* (Garden City: Doubleday, 1975), photos between 136–137; Bruce Galphin, *The Riddle of Lester Maddox* (Atlanta: Camelot, 1968), photos between 106–107.

45. Martin Oppenheimer, *The Sit-In Movement of 1960* (Brooklyn, NY: Carlson, 1989), 143; William H. Chafe, *Civilities and Civil Rights: Greensboro, North Carolina and the Black Struggle for Freedom* (New York: Oxford, 1980), 119; *RTD*, February 21, 1960; "34 Are Arrested in Sitdowns Here," *RTD*, February 23, 1960; "40 Cheered to Jail: Students Picketing the Stores," Richmond *Afro-American*, February 27, 1960; Edward W. Kallal, Jr., "St. Augustine and the Ku Klux Klan: 1963 and 1964," in *St. Augustine, Florida, 1963–1964: Mass Protest and Racial Violence*, ed. David J. Garrow (Brooklyn, NY: Carlson Publishing, 1989), 139, 146, 148; Trevor Armbrister, "Portrait of an Extremist," *Saturday Evening Post* 237 (August 22, 1964), 80–83.

46. Photograph P71.37.4, Richmond History Center [Valentine Museum]; photographs in *Louisville Courier-Journal*, September 6, 1975, and on cover of *Citizen*, January 1976.

47. "Confederate Flag Protested," *State*, June 24, 1959; Donald Evans, "Liberal Proposes to Ban Confederate Flag in NY," *State*, August 9, 1963; *NYT*, July 27, 1963.

48. *San Francisco Chronicle*, June 17, 1964, July 25, 1964, April 16, 1984, June 6, 1984.

49. "The Diggs Report: Investigation of Alleged Discriminatory Practices in the Armed Forces," in *Blacks in the United States Armed Forces: Basic Documents*, ed. Morris J. MacGregor and Bernard C. Nalty (Wilmington, DE: Scholarly Resources, 1977), 12:345–346.

50. Jack Stillman, "Georgia Flag an Issue in Vietnam," *Macon Telegraph*, May 2, 1968, and Keith Coulbourn, "Should Georgia Change Its State Flag?" *AJC Magazine*, May 4, 1969, 69. "Protest against an Absurd Order," extension of remarks by the Honorable W. S. "Bill" Stuckey, U.S. Congress, *CR* 114 (May 1, 1968): part 9, 11628–11629; "Pentagon Settles State Flag Rift," *RNL*, May 16, 1968.

51. Quoted in William W. Starr, "Foote Defends Confederate Flag's Place," *State*, July 2, 1995.

52. Richmond Flowers, "Southern Plain Talk about the Ku Klux Klan," *Look* 30 (May 3, 1966): 36.

53. Dabney, "The Perverted Banner," *RTD*, March 23, 1965; Dabney, "An Insult to the Confederacy," *RTD*, July 3, 1964.

54. Ralph McGill, *The South and the Southerner* (Boston: Little, Brown, 1963), 236; "The Ever-Ever Land," in *The South Today: 100 Years after Appomattox,* ed. Willie Morris (New York: Harper & Row, 1965), 124; "The Blame—And Beyond," *NYT,* September 17, 1963.

8. "The Perverted Banner"

1. The quote about the "silly" flags "brandished" by football fans is from "'Silly' Confederate Flags," *RTD,* November 20, 1949. The other quotations were cited in previous chapters.

2. *Minutes of the Fifty-Fifth Annual Convention, 1948,* 68–69.

3. *Minutes of the Fifty-Sixth Annual Convention, 1949,* 186–187.

4. *Minutes of the Fifty-Seventh Annual Convention of the General Division, United Daughters of the Confederacy, 1950,* 195–196.

5. "Rules for Flag Display," *Minutes of the Fifty-First Annual Convention of the Alabama Division, United Daughters of the Confederacy, 1947,* 5–6; *Minutes of the Fifty-Sixth Annual Convention of the Virginia Division, United Daughters of the Confederacy, 1951,* 172–173.

6. United Daughters of the Confederacy, *Our Confederate Flag: Traditions and Code for the Correct Use of the Confederate Flags,* ca. 1994.

7. "Richmond Chapter UDC Joins Condemnation," *RNL,* September 13, 1951; *Minutes of the Fifty-Eighth Annual Convention of the General Division, United Daughters of the Confederacy, 1951,* 124–125.

8. *Minutes of the Sixty-First Annual Convention of the General Division, United Daughters of the Confederacy, 1954,* 176–177.

9. *Minutes of the Sixty-Fourth Annual Convention of the General Division, United Daughters of the Confederacy, 1957,* 202–203.

10. "Statement of Policy of the Advisory Council of the Kappa Alpha Order," December 7–8, 1951, in *Kappa Alpha Journal,* May 1966, 1–2.

11. Ibid., 203; "Correct Use of Confederate Flags," *Seventy-First Annual Convention of the General Division, United Daughters of the Confederacy, 1964,* 158–159.

12. William M. Beard, letter to *Washington Star,* 1952, rpt. in *UDC Magazine* 15 (October 1952): 32–33.

13. "Those Confederate Beach Towels," *RTD,* March 3, 1958; *Journal of the*

Senate of the State of South Carolina, Regular Session, 1958 (Columbia: State Budget and Control Board, 1958), 434–435.

14. William D. Workman, Jr., "Opposition to 'Dixie Towel' Growing," February 27, 1958, in clipping book 8, Workman Papers, SC; T. W. Crigler, Jr., commander-in-chief, Sons of Confederate Veterans, to the Honorable Richard K. Jackson, March 2, 1958, and Richard K. Jackson to William D. Workman, Jr., March 6, 1958, in Vertical Files (Flags, Confederate), SC; William D. Workman, Jr., "Group Seeking Ban on 'Dixie' Towels," February 26, 1958, clipping book 8, Workman Papers, SC.

15. Crigler to Jackson; Jackson to Workman; *Acts and Joint Resolutions of the General Assembly of the State of South Carolina Regular Session, 1958* (Columbia: State Budget and Control Board, 1958), 1676–1677.

16. *Code of South Carolina, 1976,* vol. 8, section 16-17-220; K. Michael Prince, *Rally 'Round the Flag, Boys! South Carolina and the Confederate Flag* (Columbia: University of South Carolina Press, 2004), 38.

17. William E. Mahoney, "Pickens County's Sen. Morris Deplores 'Cheapening' Abuse of Confederate Flag," *State,* December 2, 1965; *Journal of the Senate of the Second Session of the 96th General Assembly of the State of South Carolina, 1966* (Columbia: State Budget & Control Board, 1966), 1004–1005; *Journal of the House of Representatives of the Second Session of the 96th General Assembly of the State of South Carolina, 1966* (Columbia: State Budget & Control Board, 1966), 1224–1225; Earle E. Morris to author, July 24, 1995.

18. Undated typescript (ca. December 1965) of column, probably by William D. Workman, Jr., in Vertical Files (Flags, Confederate), SC.

19. *General Acts and Resolutions Adopted by the Legislature of Florida Regular Session, 1961,* 1, part 1, 181–182, 697–698; telephone interview with Mack Cleveland, April 12, 1999; *Journal of the House of Representatives State of Florida Thirty-Seventh Regular Session,* 143, 497, 617, 838, 913, 1316, 1361; *Journal of the Senate State of Florida Thirty-Seventh Regular Session,* 921, 985; *Florida Division United Daughters of the Confederacy Minutes of the Sixty-Fourth Annual Convention,* October 13–15, 1959, 31; *Journal of the House of Representatives State of Florida Thirty-Eighth Regular Session,* 722, 1086, 1156, 1308, 1737, 1760, 1770, 1771, 1978, 2653; *Journal of the Senate State of Florida Thirty-Eighth Regular Session,* 28, 347, 540, 1155, 1174, 1192, 1324, 1607–1608, 1839; *Florida Division United Daughters of*

the *Confederacy Minutes of the Sixty-Sixth Annual Convention*, October 3–6, 1961, 30; "NAACP Scoffs at Bill Lauding Stars and Bars," Jacksonville *Florida Times-Union*, May 13, 1961; and "Flag Defiling Ban Is Passed," *Florida Times-Union*, May 23, 1959.

20. *Statutes . . . Louisiana*, section 116, 270–271; *Code of Georgia*, 1990 ed., vol. 38, sections 50-3-8, 50-3-9, and 50-3-10.

21. Christopher Crittenden to Various Leaders Interested in the Proper Display of the Confederate Flags and Other Confederate Mememtoes, April 21, 1861, CWCC Subject Files, NARA, RG 79, entry 32, Box 73.

22. *Code of Alabama 1975* (Charlottesville, VA: Michie Company, 1994), 12:712; House Joint Resolution 50, *Alabama Laws (and Joint Resolutions) of the Legislature of Alabama Passed at the Organizational Session, 1967 . . .* (Montgomery: Legislative Reference Service, 1967), 1:541; Don F. Wasson, "Stand, Sing, Sit, Stand, Sing, Etc.," *MA*, August 4, 1967.

23. William M. Beard to Major General U.S. Grant III, June 25, 1959; William M. Beard to Karl S. Betts, August 12, 1959; Karl S. Betts to William M. Beard, June 30, 1959, Karl S. Betts to Wint Smith, August 20, 1959; Wint Smith to Karl S. Betts, August 21, 1959, CWCC Subject Files, NARA, RG 79, entry 32, Box 73.

24. Opinion 67-323 (unofficial), September 7, 1967, *Opinions of the Attorney General*, 444; copy courtesy of the Georgia State Law Library.

25. "Artist Arrested, Released by J. P.," *Miss.*, April 10, 1963, 1; "Removal of Paintings Stirs Students Protest" and "Blackwell Files 'Flag' Complaint against Artist," *Miss.*, April 9, 1963, 1, 2; Russell H. Barrett, *Integration at Ole Miss.* (Chicago: Quadrangle Books, 1965), 217–218.; *Southern School News* 10 (May 1963): 9.

26. *State*, February 18, 1969; Attorney General Daniel R. McLeod to Mrs. Trippett [sic] L. Boineau, February 17, 1969, opinions of the South Carolina attorney general, Attorney General's Office, Columbia; interview with Brett A. Bursey, Columbia, South Carolina, June 20, 1995; Prince, *Rally*, 129; Brett Bursey, "My Stars & Bars: A Look at Dixie with Her Flag Down," *Point*, June 1991.

27. "Confederate Flag Is Torn Up by Protesters against Police," *Alexandria Journal-Standard*, November 27, 1969; Maurine McLaughlin, "Alexandria Demonstrators Trample Confederate Flag," *WP*, November 23, 1969; House Joint Resolution 69, *Journal of the Senate of the Commonwealth of Vir-*

ginia Regular Session, 1970 (Richmond: Department of Purchase and Supply, 1970), 507.

28. Keith Coulbourn, "Should Georgia Change Its State Flag?" *AJC Magazine* (May 4, 1969), 20.

29. Charles Reagan Wilson and William Ferris, *Encyclopedia of Southern Culture* (Chapel Hill: UNC Press, 1989), 705; Sarah Rice, "Confederate Flags Symbolize Rebellion," *Kansas State Collegian,* July 3, 2002 (http://kstatecollegian.com); Springer, "Rebel Flag," 67.

30. See Francis N. Boney, *Southerners All,* rev. ed. (Mercersburg, GA: Mercer University Press, 1990), chap. 2; and John Shelton Reed, *Southern Folk, Plain & Fancy: Native White Southern Types* (Athens: University of Georgia Press, 1986), and Florence King, *Southern Ladies and Gentlemen* (New York: St. Martin's Press, 1975); Lynyrd Skynyrd, "Sweet Home Alabama" and "One More from the Road," *Legend* (1987), "Southern by the Grace of God" (1988), "Southern Knights" (1995), and "Freebird the Movie" (1996); Alabama, "My Home's in Alabama" (1980), "Mountain Music" (1981), "Roll On" (1984); Randy Arnold, "Bad Boys Make Good," *Chattanooga Times,* September 29, 1993. For scholarly analysis of southern rock and Confederate symbols, see Jim Cullen, *The Civil War and Popular Culture: A Reusable Past* (Washington, DC: Smithsonian Institution Press, 1995), chap. 4, and George Schedler, "Southern Minorities, Popular Culture, and the Old South," in *Confederate Symbols in the Contemporary South,* ed. J. Michael Martinez, William D. Richardson, and Ron McNinch-Su (Gainesville: University Press of Florida, 2000), 57–62.

31. *Warner Brothers, Inc.* v. *Gay Toys, Inc.,* 724 F. 2d. 327 (1983), 331–332; *Processed Plastic Co.* v. *Warner Communications* 675 F. 2d 852 (1982), 854; Tony Schwarz, "The Attraction of Hazzard," *NYT,* April 25, 1981, 48.

32. Rebecca Bailey, "Race Car Officials Ban SCV Logo," *Civil War News,* December 1994, 9; letter of Jim Zeirke in *Civil War News,* October 1994, 3, and in *Bugle Call* [monthly newsletter of the Lieutenant General Leonidas Polk Camp 1446, SCV], October 1994; letter of Jim Zeirke to *Civil War News,* January 1995, 4.

33. Hinkle, *Embattled Banner,* 59, 75, 80–81, 160.

34. Ibid., 56–57; *CV,* n.s., 38 (March–April 1990): 3; Edwin W. Carpenter, "Legacy of Confederates Is Not Racist," *RTD,* August 9, 1992; *WSJ,* October 2, 1990.

NOTES TO PAGES 177–188

349

35. The decisions are excerpted in Robert Justin Goldstein, ed., *Desecrating the American Flag: Key Documents of the Controversy from the Civil War to 1995* (Syracuse: Syracuse University Press, 1996), 168–174, 262–265.

36. McGill, read by Rep. Daniel Flood of Pennsylvania into *CR* 107 (February 13, 1961): A-874.

37. The Cavalier Shoppe mail order catalogue, ca. 1995; Craig W. Turner, "In the Heart of Dixie—Rex and Janice Jarrett of the Cavalier Shoppe," *Civil War Courier,* July 1998, 1.

38. See website www.dixieoutfitter.com.

9. "Vindication of the Cause"

1. "Symbolism Turns Deadly When a Flag Is Misread," *NYT,* January 22, 1995; M. David Goodwin, "Seven from Guthrie Indicted in Slaying on Tennessee Highway," Louisville *Courier-Journal*, February 7, 1995; Tony Horwitz, "A Death for Dixie," *New Yorker,* March 18, 1996, 64.

2. *Truth at Last,* 379:1; Devereaux D. Cannon, "To Live and Die for Dixie," *SP,* 4th Quarter 1994, 17; "Forward the Colors," *CV,* n.s., 43, vol. 2 (1995): 6; Hinkle, *Embattled Banner,* 179.

3. Warren Duzak, "Hundreds Honor 'Fallen Patriot,'" *Tennesseean,* March 5, 1995; M. David Goodwin and Joseph Gerth, "Memorial to Victim Turns into Flag Rally," Louisville *Courier-Journal,* March 5, 1995; Hill quoted in Horwitz, "A Death for Dixie," 73.

4. M. David Goodwin and James Malone, "Flag Controversy Divides Todd County," Louisville *Courier-Journal,* January 29, 1995.

5. Lori D. Roberts, "Columbia Scout Took on Confederate Flag and Won," *State,* August 22, 1991; "The Boy Scouts Lower the Battle Flag," *AJC,* August 28, 1991; "Boy Scouts Abandon Confederate Regalia," *NYT,* August 25, 1991.

6. John Reid Blackwell, "DuPont Workers Staging Protests," *RTD,* November 3, 2000; Melissa Scott Sinclair, "The Flag Bearers," Richmond *Style Weekly* (March 26, 2002), 17–23.

7. "South Carolina Utility Bans Confederate Flag," www.cnn.com, August 17, 2002; John Monk, "Sen. Glenn McConnell Wants Legislature to Punish the Company," *State,* August 17, 2002.

8. "Students' Petition Brings Citywide Comment, Action," *Alexandria Journal-Standard,* May 23, 1968, 8; "Readers: Keep Flag," *MA,* February 1,

1988; Charles Hunt, "Flag Flap Draws Flurry of Opinions," *DRB* , June 12, 1993.

9. P. Charles Lunsford, "Attacks on the Colors: Arguments against Confederate Symbols," *CV*, n.s., 42 (January–February 1994), 5; Hinkle, *Embattled Banner,* 75, 63, 64.

10. Quoted in John F. Cummings III, "Heritage, Not Hate," *Southern Heritage Magazine* 2 (January–February 1994): 41. "Resolutions submitted under Article X, Section 2 of the Constitution of the NAACP 1991" courtesy of the NAACP; Julian Bond to author, September 19, 2002. "NAACP Convention Delegates Pass Mississippi Confederate Flag Resolution," *NAACP News* [press release], July 10, 2001 (www.naacp.org).

11. "Confederate Flag 'Mystery' Arouses County Drivers' Ire," *Richmond Afro-American,* April 22, 1961; "Confederate Flag Controversy," *Richmond Afro-American,* April 29, 1961, 9; "Dixie Flag Hassle Spurs Voter Drive," *Richmond Afro-American,* May 6, 1961, 3; Harriet Allen, "Flag Removal Set in '62," Fredericksburg *Free Lance-Star,* April 17, 1961. W. Lester Banks to Dr. John A. Morsell, April 18, 1961, NAACP Papers, LC, Group III, Sect. C, Box 160; "Of Flags and Songs," *Crisis* 79 (March 1972), 77.

12. Interview with James Farmer, May 18, 1994; Denise Crittendon, "Dr. Gibson Keeps NAACP on Course with Change," *Crisis* 101 (January 1994), 23–24; Eric L. Clarke, "Dr. Chavis Draws Support and Charts New Frontier," *Crisis* 101 (August/September 1994), 2–6; Sylvester Monroe, "After the Revolution," *Time* 144 (August 29, 1994), 40; "NAACP Votes Gibson Out as Chairman," *RTD,* February 19, 1995; "An Embattled Emblem," *Southern Cultures* 1 (1995): 396–397.

13. Earl T. Shinhoster, audiotaped comment for "Embattled Emblem" exhibition, The Museum of the Confederacy, May 1993, and statements on "Talk of the Nation," National Public Radio News, January 31, 1994. For background on Shinhoster, see Alan Sverdlik, "For Earl Shinhoster, Keeping a Low Profile Just Doesn't Come Easily," *AJC,* March 22, 1990.

14. "General S. D. Lee's Address at New Orleans," *CV* 14 (June 1906): 255. The charge appears on the masthead of the new *Confederate Veteran* and on the SCV homepage. The SCV's membership was not unified behind its most vocal public spokesmen. In 2002, a major schism opened within the organization, primarily over how politically active it should be in vindicating the Confederate cause.

15. The SCV claimed to have gained 5,000 new members (a 50 percent in-

crease) between 1989 and 1993. By the end of the century, the SCV claimed more than 30,000 members nationwide. Jim Auchmutey, "Keepers of the Confederacy," *AJC,* January 19, 1993.

16. Peter W. Orlebeke and E. Murfee Gewin, "Attacks on the Colors," *CV,* n.s., 39 (May–June 1991): 4; resolution adopted August 19, 1989 in *CV,* n.s., 38 (March–April 1990): 3; Robert Stacy McCain, "Southern Pride Fuels 1,300-Mile March," *Washington Times,* October 13, 2002, http://asp.washtimes.com/asp; on Dr. Leonard Haynes see Stacie Mackenzie, "Confederate Flag Waves Again," *DRB,* March 27, 1995; on Black Confederates see P. Charles Lunsford, "The Forgotten Confederates," *CV,* n.s., 40 (November 1992): 12–15; Charles Kelly Barrow, ed., *Forgotten Confederates: An Anthology about Black Southerners* (Atlanta: Southern Heritage Press, 1995); Tony Horwitz, "Shades of Grey: Did Blacks Fight Freely for the Confederacy?" *WSJ,* May 8, 1997.

17. Lunsford, "Attacks on the Colors: Arguments against Confederate Symbols." For background on Lunsford, see "Profile of a Patriot: P. Charles Lunsford," *Front Line* [Newsletter of the Heritage Preservation Association] 1 (March–April 1994): 10. Tony Horwitz, *Confederates in the Attic: Dispatches from the Unfinished Civil War* (New York: Random House, 1998), provides an insightful portrait of "neo-Confederates," including a sketch of HPA founder R. Lee Collins.

18. Cummings, "Heritage, Not Hate," 37, 41; David Martin, "What Is the Confederate Society of America?" *CSA News* ["Voice of the Confederacy"] 3, no. 5 (August–September 1993): 1.

19. Maria D. Martirano, "Group Wants Banner Back," Cumberland *Times-News,* December 19, 1994; P. Charles Lunsford, "Why I Resigned," ca. June 1994; "Profile of a Patriot," 10.

20. Lunsford, "Arguments," 4.

21. Statement of Carol Moseley-Braun on the United Daughters of the Confederacy, Judiciary Committee Executive Business Meeting, May 12, 1993; Joe Davidson, "Daughters of the Confederacy Lose Battle over Insignia in Panel Vote," *WSJ,* May 7, 1993.

22. *CR,* 103d Congress, 1st Session, Thursday, July 22, 1993, S-9251–9252, S-9253, 9257–9258, S-9258–9263.

23. See *Blue & Gray Magazine,* October 1993, 40; Speeches of Sen. Jesse Helms and Sen. Robert Byrd, *CR,* S-9268, 9270–9271; Jonathan Yardley,

"This Senator Grants UDC No Lee-way," *RTD,* August 1, 1993; Samuel Francis, "Slurring Symbols, Cultural Clashes," *Washington Times,* April 20, 1993; Richard Quinn, "Fed Up Yet?" *SP,* 2nd Quarter 1993, 5; Nat Hentoff, "Trumping History with the Race Card," *Liberal Opinion Week,* August 23, 1993.

24. For summary of the controversy over the Richmond floodwall banner, see Gordon Hickey and Carrie Johnson, "Council Supports Mural of Lee," *RTD,* July 27, 2000.

25. See Edward L. Linenthal and Tom Englehardt, eds., *History Wars: The Enola Gay and Other Battles for the American Past* (New York: Holt, 1995); Gary B. Nash et al., *History on Trial: Culture Wars and the Teaching of the Past* (New York: Knopf, 1998); David Goldfield, *Still Fighting the Civil War: The American South* (Baton Rouge: Louisiana State University Press, 2002), 317.

26. Grady McWhiney, *Cracker Culture: Celtic Ways in the Old South* (Tuscaloosa: University Press of Alabama, 1988); Allen G. Breed, "Gone with the Wind, Secession's Back," *RTD,* July 5, 1999; "Southern Party's Win May Be Hollow One," *RTD,* September 10, 2000; www.southernparty.org.

27. James R. and Walter D. Kennedy, *The South Was Right* (Baton Rouge: Land and Land, 1991), iv, 113, 115, 142.

28. See Peter Applebome, *Dixie Rising: How the South Is Shaping American Values, Politics, and Culture* (New York: Times Books, 1996); "The Williamsburg Resolve" of the December 1994 Republican Governors Conference (copy in possession of author courtesy of the office of the Governor of Virginia).

29. "Police Arrest 3 after Men Attack Home, Shout Slurs," *Orlando Sentinel,* September 19, 1998; Alan Cooper, "Teen Sentenced to 22 Years in Slaying," *RTD,* March 16, 1993; Jeanene Harlick, "Violence Erupts over Confederate Flag," *Santa Cruz Sentinel,* August 4, 2002; Hinkle, *Embattled Banner,* 180–181; list of "Hate Crimes against Confederate Heritage," contributed to *CV,* n.s., 49, vol. 3 (2001): 48.

10. "The Bitterest Battleground"

1. Bonnie Miller Ruben, "Thornton Raises New Flag, but Not All Salute," *Chicago Tribune,* February 11, 1994; Donna Kiesling, "Confederate Flag Flap Still Flying at School," *Chicago Tribune,* August 18, 1993.

2. Jerry Shmay, "Feelings Unfurled about School's Confederate Flag," *Chicago Tribune,* April 12, 1993.

3. Kiesling, "Confederate Flag"; Robert Becker, "Lansing Accused of Racism," *Chicago Tribune,* January 25, 1994.

4. Anthony DePalma, "Free Speech and a Flag, but This Time It's the Stars and Bars," *NYT,* March 13, 1991.

5. "'Rebels' Protest School Flag Policy," Columbia *State,* March 8, 1991; Mark Wood (of *Spartanburg Herald-Journal*), "School Suspends Students Who Protested Flag Ban," in *State,* March 9, 1991.

6. Summons in a Civil Action, *Vikki Parham et al. v. Ed Austin et al.*, May 18, 1991, filed in United States District Court, District of South Carolina.

7. Order of Settlement, *Parham et al. v. Austin et al.*, United States District Court, District of South Carolina, April 29, 1991.

8. David Martin, "Justice Prevails! A Great Confederate Victory!" *CSA News,* March–April 1991.

9. *Southern School News* 5 (October 1958): 13; 10 (October 1963): 11.

10. John Egerton, *Shades of Gray: Dispatches from the Modern South* (Baton Rouge: Louisiana State University Press, 1991), 237, 239; Jim Leeson, "Private Schools for Whites Face Some Hurdles," *Southern Education Report,* October 1967, 13.

11. *The South and Her Children: School Desegregation, 1970–1971* (Atlanta: Southern Regional Council, Inc., 1971), 12–13.

12. *Smith v. St. Tammany Parish School Board,* 316 F. Supp. 1176–1177; *Banks v. Muncie Community Schools,* 433 F. 2d 296–297, 299; *Augustus v. School Board of Escambia County,* 361 F. Supp. 383 (1973), 385–389; *Augustus v. School Board,* 507 F. 2d 152 (1975), 156; Bodie McCrory, "'All over a Silly Name,'" *Pensacola Journal,* February 6, 1976.

13. *Melton v. Young,* 328 F. Supp. 91–92 (1971); "400 Students Walk Out at Brainerd High School," *CT,* October 19, 1969, and Clarence Scaife, "Bond Says Brainerd High Unrest Is Due to Lack of Communication," *CT,* October 19, 1969; *Heritage* [Brainerd Senior High School], 4 (1966): 2, 109; 5 (1967): 142.

14. Scaife, "Bond," and "400 Students"; Springer Gibson, "Dr. Hoover Arrested on Campus of Brainerd High," *CT,* October 10, 1969; Springer Gibson, "Crowd of 9,000 Peaceful as Brainerd, Central Play," *CT,* October 12, 1969.

15. Bill Carbine, "Mayor Appeals for Restraint in School Furor," *CT,* October 13, 1969.

16. Bill Casteel, "Racial Scuffle at Brainerd High Draws Police; Nine Are Arrested," *CT,* April 15, 1970; "Brainerd High Is Closed Today after More Strife Wednesday," *CT,* April 16, 1970; *Melton v. Young,* 92–93.

17. "Brainerd Forms Advisory Group," *CT,* May 17, 1970; text of Brainerd High Report," *CT,* July 7, 1970; "Education Board Accepts Changes at Brainerd High," *CT,* July 9, 1970; *Melton v. Young,* 93–94.

18. *Melton v. Young,* 94–95; "Rebels Congregate in Area of School," *CT,* September 17. 1970.

19. *Melton v. Young,* 98.

20. *Melton v. Young,* 98–99. One of the appellate judges rejected this logic, contending that the clear and present danger had passed before Melton was suspended. *Melton v. Young,* 465 F. 2d, 1337–1338 (1972).

21. *Melton v. Young,* 95; George Short, "Brainerd Pupil to Return without His Rebel Patch," *CT,* September 24, 1970; *Melton v. Young* (Appellate), 1334.

22. Miller, "Thornton Raises New Flag," Egerton, *Shades,* 240; "Winds of Change Blow Away Confederate Flag," *CT,* February 25, 1993; *McCallie News,* Spring 1993.

23. *Virginia High School League Directory,* 1965–1966, 1971–1972, 1983–1984; *Crosby v. Holsinger,* 852 F. 2d 801–802; Thomas Heath, "Flag Foments School Unrest," *WP,* December 1, 1990.

24. For summaries of recent cases, see Del Stover, "To Ban or Not to Ban: Confederate Flag Stirs Conflicts for Schools," *School Board News,* February 8, 2000, online edition; and David L. Hudson, Jr., "Stars and Bars Wars," *ABA Network* (November 1, 2000); *Phillips v. Anderson County School District Five,* 987 F. Supp. 488 (D.S.C. 1997), 492; quoted in *West v. Derby Unified School District,* 1231, 1233; "Court Upholds Ban on T-Shirts," *RTD,* March 20, 2001; "Disagreeing over Dress," *American School Board Journal,* January 2001.

25. Hudson, "Stars and Bars Wars." The accounts of the Wichita case are based primarily on the District Court opinion, *West v. Derby Unified School District 260,* 23 F. Supp. 2d 1220 (D. Kan. 1998), 1224, 1228, 1236, and the Appellate Court opinion, *West v. Derby Unified School District No. 260,* 206 F. 3d 1358 (10th Cir. 2000); *Denno v. School Board of Volusia County, Florida,* 218 F. 3d 1267 (11th Cir. 2000).

26. Jack Holmes, "Confederate Flag Incident Rocks Chewning School," *Durham Morning Herald,* March 12, 1988; coverage also in Warren P. Mass, "The Confederate Battle Flag," *New American,* June 6, 1988, 9. Research into this incident benefited from Michael Ferguson, "The Confederate Flag," a video documentary produced for sociology class, University of North Carolina, Chapel Hill, 1989; Exhibit B of "Mutual Release and Settlement Agreement," August 17, 1989, for *Pruitt v. Cartwright et al.,* copy courtesy of ACLU of North Carolina. "Mutual Release and Settlement Agreement," point 4.

27. Rhea R. Boria, "Henrico Expunges Flag Suspensions," *RTD,* January 7, 2001; Paige Akin, "Wearing Flag Is Issue," *RTD,* March 14, 2001; Carol Farrington, "Schools Winning Fights on Student Rights," *State,* April 21, 1995; John Barnette, "7 Students File Lawsuit, Say Rights Violated," Barnwell, SC, *People-Sentinel,* ca. October 1995; "Blackville T-shirt Lawsuit Settled," *People-Sentinel,* January 31, 1996; *Castorina v. Madison County School Board,* United States Court of Appeals for the Sixth Circuit, electronic citation: 2001 FED App. 0064P (6th Cir.); *SP,* September–October 2002, 13.

28. Jamie C. Ruff, "African Attire Causes Dispute," *RTD,* February 28, 1995; "Amelia Students Hold Sit-in Protest," *RTD,* March 1, 1995; "SCV 'Condemns' Klan Activities in County; Student Boycott Fizzles," *Amelia Bulletin,* April 6, 1995.

29. Lisa Greene, "Students Sue to Wear Confederate Flag T-Shirts," *State,* April 19, 1995; Carol Farrington, "'It Doesn't Have Anything to Do with Race,' *State,* April 21, 1995; Mickie Anderson, "Volusia School Banning the Rebel Flag," *Orlando Sentinel,* December 5, 1995; Mickie Anderson, "More Suspensions in Flag Flap," *Orlando Sentinel,* December 6, 1995; Robin Farmer, "Confederate Flag-Waving Led to Action on X, Official Says," *RTD,* May 13, 1992; Robin Farmer, "Stonewall Jackson Pupils Discuss Dispute over Attire," *RTD,* May 16, 1992; "Confederate Flags and 'X' Were Not Welcome in Hanover County School," *Black Issues in Higher Education* 9 (June 4, 1992): 6.

30. Tony Horwitz, in *Confederates in the Attic,* 105–106, 368, similarly found this slogan to be a metaphor for the chasm between the races regarding the Civil War.

31. SCV Heritage Defense Fund brochure, ca. February 2001, SCV Collection, ESBL, MOC.

32. See *Phillips v. Anderson County School Dist. Five,* 987 F. Supp. 492 (D.S.C. 1997); "Alabama a Disaster in Federal Court," *CV,* n.s., 43 (1995): 8.

11. "If They Talk about Diversity, They're Gonna Get It"

1. *Stars and Bars* [Walker College], *1956–1957.*

2. *Corolla* [University of Alabama], *1959,* 292, 46; *1960,* 294; also *1961,* 272; see Anthony W. James, "The Defenders of Tradition: College Social Fraternities, Race and Gender, 1945–1980" (Ph.D. diss., University of Mississippi, 1998), 210–216.

3. "Rebel Flag Lowered after War between States of Mind," *Jet,* November 27, 1969, 18–21; Jim Wannamaker, "Playing of 'Dixie' under Study Here," *Gamecock,* February 11, 1969; Mike Krochnalny, "Confederate Flag Burned on Campus," *Gamecock,* February 14, 1969; Carl Stepp, "Tension Sparks 'Dixie' Incidents," *Gamecock,* February 18, 1969; "Dixie Land," *Gamecock,* February 14, 1969; "In Da Land . . . " *Tiger,* October 24, 1969; Bob Thompson, "Senate Backs 'Dixie' and Confederate Flag," *Tiger,* November 13, 1969.

4. Letter from Jack Gravely to author, June 27, 1994; "Right or Slur," *RTD/ RNL,* October 17, 1971.

5. Gravely to author, June 27, 1994; Jean Myking, "Confederate Flag May Join Dixie," Charlottesville *Daily Progress,* September 29, 1971.

6. "UVA Confirms Banning Confederate Flag Use," *Daily Progress,* September 30, 1971; "Flag Suit Filed," *Daily Progress,* October 9, 1971; Jean Myking, "ACLU May Challenge Confederate Flag Policy," *Daily Progress,* October 1, 1971; "UVA Rescinds Flag Ruling," *Daily Progress,* October 20, 1971; Jean Myking, "Flag Suit Dropped; 5 Cleared," *Daily Progress,* October 21, 1971; "His Ghost Relieved," *RNL/RTD,* October 21, 1971.

7. Telephone interview with Christopher Lewis, June 28, 1995.

8. "Cadet Protests Confederate Flag," *State,* November 1, 1991; "Citadel Should Retire 'Dixie' Flag, Panel Says," *State,* March 6, 1992; "Citadel Won't Ban 'Dixie,' Confederate Flag," *State,* September 12, 1992.

9. Charles Slack, "VMI to Cadets: Leave Confederate Flag off Ring," *RTD,* April 26, 1992.

10. Executive Council Regulation R16–113, copy courtesy of the Kappa Alpha Order; "Old South, Battle Flags & Multiculturalism," *Talisman,* February 1991.

11. "Confederate Bastion Lowers the Flag," *NYT,* March 3, 1992.

12. Rick Bragg, "Old Wounds Fester as Confederate-Flag Issue Surfaces at AU," *BN,* February 24, 1985; Jay Evans, "Old South Parade Sparks Student Demonstrations," *Auburn Plainsman,* April 30, 1992; Tom Gordon, "Confederate Flag Fires Up Parade," *BN,* April 25, 1992; "Fraternity's 'Old South' Parade Riles Students at Auburn U," *Chronicle of Higher Education,* May 6, 1992.

13. *Chronicle of Higher Education,* February 17, 1993; letters in *Auburn Plainsman,* February 11, 1993.

14. "Early 2001 Plagued with Chapter Closings," *Kappa Alpha Journal* 118 (Spring 2001): 7; press release from Kappa Alpha Order, January 31, 2001, courtesy of Kappa Alpha Order; *Kappa Alpha Journal* 118 (Spring 2001): 4, 5, 7, 16–21; Kappa Alpha Law 9-264, *Kappa Alpha Laws,* 11th ed. (Lexington, VA: Kappa Alpha Order, 2002), 30.

15. Kevin Pierce Thornton, "Symbolism at Ole Miss and the Crisis of Southern Identity," *South Atlantic Quarterly* 86 (Summer 1987): 254–268.

16. Thornton, 264.

17. "UM Elects Black Cheerleader," *DM,* April 23, 1982. The first black Ole Miss cheerleader, Greg Thompson, a member of the junior varsity squad, noted after the 1982 strife began that while he, too, resented the flag, he did not believe that the issue was worth the controversy. Lauren Lexa, "Former Cheerleader Objects to Race Issue," *DM,* October 1, 1982; John Hawkins, "A Flag Should Not Divide Us," *DM,* October 7, 1982; Kate McGandy, "Hawkins Carries His Own Flag at Game," *DM,* September 21, 1982.

18. Charles T. Farrell, "Ole Miss, Now Part of the New South, Still Feels the Stigma of Its Past," *Chronicle of Higher Education* 25 (October 6, 1982): 9–10; Paul Crutcher, "Twenty Years in Retrospect," *DM,* September 30, 1982.

19. Stephanie Hall and Peggy Hodges, "On Meredith: Comments on Suit Bring UM Reaction," *DM,* September 24, 1982; Stephanie Hall, "Meredith Talk Sparks Praise and Criticism," *DM,* October 1, 1982.

20. Lee Freeland, "Leader Says Flag Key Issue," *DM,* October 19, 1982, 1; Patti Patterson, "Klan Demonstration Calm," *DM,* October 25, 1982.

21. Lee Freeland, "May Flag Decision," *DM,* March 9, 1983; "ASB Flag Bill," *DM,* April 12, 1983; Jimmy Henderson, "Rebel Flag," *DM,* April 6, 1983; Lydia Evelyn Spragin, "Flag: Dare Tradition," *DM,* April 12, 1983.

22. Lynda Tullos, "Reflecting . . . 1982–3 Events: Racial Struggles," *DM,*

April 29, 1983; Dan Turner and Mary Nettleton, "Blacks May Protest Klan Pics," *DM,* April 14, 1983; "BSU Has 13 Specific Demands," *DM,* April 18, 1983; letter of David Powell, *DM,* April 18, 1983.

23. "Rumors Stir Protest," *DM,* April 19, 1983.

24. Sallie Read, "Call to Reason," *DM,* April 12, 1983; Alan Schmidt, "Flag Won't Be the Same," *DM,* April 28, 1983; letter in *DM,* April 22, 1983.

25. Dan Turner, "Rebel Flag: Half-Mast," *DM,* April 21, 1983.

26. "Reaction," *DM,* April 21, 1983; Mary Nettleton, "Flag Verdict Rejected," *DM,* April 22, 1983; Clara Bibbs and Terry R. Cassreino, "Spragin Says 'Not Enough,'" *DM,* April 21, 1983; *DM,* April 25, 1983.

27. "U. of Miss. Still Working to Drop Confederate Flag," *Chronicle of Higher Education,* 37 (July 10, 1991): A3; Vernon Chadwick, "Papa's Got a Brand New Flag: Confederate Symbolism and the Funky New South," *Southern Reader* 3 (November/December 1991): 2.

28. Douglas Lederman, "Old Times Not Forgotten," *Chronicle of Higher Education* 40 (October 26, 1993): A51–52; Donald P. Baker, "Confederate Battle Flag Still a Point of Contention on Ole Miss Campus," *WP,* October 5, 1997; Jacques Billeaud, "Rebel Flags Fail to Stir Fans' Ire," *Knoxville News-Sentinel,* October 3, 1997; William Nack, "Look Away, Dixie Land," *Sports Illustrated* 87 (November 3, 1997): 114; *Richard N. Barrett v. Robert C. Khayat et al.,* Memorandum Opinion, U.S. District Court for the Northern District of Mississippi Western Division, November 22, 1999.

29. David G. Sansing, *The University of Mississippi: A Sesquicentennial History* (Jackson: University Press of Mississippi, 1999), 338, 341, 342.

30. Charles R. Lawrence III, "If He Hollers Let Him Go: Regulating Racist Speech on Campus, *Duke Law Journal* 1990: 436; also Dinesh D'Souza, *Illiberal Education: The Politics of Race and Sex on Campus* (New York: Free Press, 1991); Darryl Brown, "Racism and Race Relations in the University," *Virginia Law Review* 76 (March 1990): 295–335.

31. Charles R. Lawrence III, "Speech That Harms: An Exchange Acknowledging the Victim's Cry," *Academe* 76 (December 1990): 15.

32. Data from Southern Focus Polls, Institute for Research in Social Sciences, University of North Carolina, March 1992, March 1993, October 1993, compiled by John Shelton Reed for presentation at "Embattled Emblem" symposium, Richmond, Virginia, March 18, 1994.

33. *John Doe v. University of Michigan,* 721 F. Supp. 852 (2d Mich., 1989), 858;

Robert W. McGee, "Hate Speech, Free Speech, and the University," *Akron Law Review* 24 (Fall 1990): 386.

34. McGee, "Hate Speech," 364.

35. *SP,* 4th Quarter 1993, 11; Spencer Culp, "Stars and Bars Don't Fly at Hampden-Sydney; College Orders Residents to Take Down Flag," *Hampden-Sydney Tiger,* October 4, 1991.

36. "Rule against Flags in Dorm Windows Is Suspended," *NYT,* March 3, 1991; Michael E. Balaguer, "Cornell Removes Flag Ban," *HC,* March 5, 1991; "Lampost Residents Apologize for Hanging Confederate Flag," *Gettysburgian,* November 2, 1995; letters to the editor, *Gettysburgian,* November 9, 16, and 23, 1995.

37. Athens Statement: A Manifesto of Southern Principles by the Culture of the South Association, University of Georgia, March 1989; Gregory Pearson, "Culture of the South," University of Georgia Yearbook, 1993, 231.

38. Statements of Kerrigan's motives quoted in Daniel H. Chomi, "Kirkland Debates Confederate Flag," *HC,* February 20, 1991, and Joshua Shenk, "Confederate Flags Spark Controversy," *HC,* February 28, 1991; Ira E. Stoll, "Who Is Bridget Kerrigan?" *HC,* March 19, 1991.

39. Stoll, "Who Is Bridget Kerrigan?"; "Partisan Conversation with Bridget Kerrigan," *SP,* 3rd Quarter 1991, 35; Kerrigan quoted in Carol Stocker, "The War between the Flags," *Boston Globe,* April 10, 1991.

40. Ira E. Stoll, "Protesters Stage Eat-In at Kirkland," *HC,* March 6, 1991; Douglas M. Kaden, "Second Eat-In Held to Protest Flags," *HC,* March 7, 1991; Sean L. Presant, "Masters Discuss Flags, Speech," *HC,* March 8, 1991; Esme Howard, "Seventy Students March Silently from Kirkland to Cabot to Protest Confederate Flags," *HC,* March 9, 1991; Ira E. Stoll, "Kerrigan: Confederate Flag to Remain," *HC,* March 14, 1991.

41. Shenk, "Confederate Flags"; Sarah Koch and Adrian Walker, "Displays of Confederate Flags, Swastika Stir Harvard Campus," *Boston Globe,* March 7, 1991; Michael E. Balagur, "Swastika Removed by Cabot Resident," *HC,* March 5, 1991.

42. "Bok Issues Free Speech Statement," *Harvard University Gazette,* copy provided by Harvard News Office; excerpted in Derek Bok, "Protecting Freedom of Expression at Harvard," *Boston Globe,* March 25, 1991; "Censure, not Censor," *HC,* March 4, 1991; Joanna M. Weiss, "Council Enters Flag Debate," *HC,* March 12, 1991.

43. Letters to the editor of Ron A. Fein et al., March 8, 1991; Peter Ivan Armstrong, March 11, 1991; also letters of March 21, 1991, and comments of *Crimson* editor Michael Grunwald in Ira E. Stoll, "Kerrigan: Confederate Flag to Remain."

44. "Partisan Conversation," 37.

45. Quoted in Benjamin O. Davis, "Confederate Flag Causes Debate," *HC,* February 22, 1991.

12. "What We Stood For, Will Stand For, and Will Fight For"

1. "Resolution requesting removal of Confederate Battle Flags from State Capitol Buildings in Alabama and South Carolina and from State Flags in Georgia and Mississippi," NAACP Southeast Region, March 1987, copy courtesy of NAACP business office, Baltimore, MD; William H. Penn, Sr., "The NAACP Battlefront," *Crisis* 94 (August–September 1987): 44.

2. Thomas W. McSweeney, "Power of Place," *Historic Preservation News,* January 1993, 16; Suzy Fleming, "Historic Flag Worth Saving, Supporters Say," *MA,* January 15, 1988.

3. "Flags over the Alabama Capitol: A Review of Major Events," unpub. document prepared by the ADAH, 1992. Statements that the flag had been on the dome during the administration of John Patterson (1959–1963) are cited in Joe McFadden, "The Lingering Legacy of a Bit of Bunting," *MA,* January 17, 1988; "Confederate Battle Flag," *BN,* February 26, 1988.

4. "Confederate Flag Was 'Tourist Gimmick,' says Wallace," *BN,* April 20, 1988; Suzy Fleming, "Confederate Flag: History of Honor for Some; History of Racism for Others," *MA,* January 16, 1988; Attachments 8 and 9 of ADAH, "Review."

5. ADAH, "Review"; McFadden, "Lingering Legacy."

6. *Holmes v. Wallace,* 407 F. Supp. 496–498; Holmes quoted in McFadden, "Lingering Legacy."

7. "Reed Vows Removal in Flag Fight," *BN,* December 31, 1988; Emily Bentley, "Reed Has Gone Out on a Limb, Some Opponents Say," *MA,* January 23, 1988; Thomas L. Reed, "No Authority Exists for Flying Confederate Flag," *MA,* January 24, 1988.

8. Tom Lindley, "Confederate Flag Still Flies at Capitol While Battle Brews

Below," *BN*, January 31, 1988; "Hunt May Appoint Flag Commission; Reed Announces Future Plans Today," *MA*, January 28, 1988; "Readers: Keep Flag," *MA*, February 1, 1988; Michael Bruman, "Hunt Says Let Flag Wave over the Capitol," *BN*, January 20, 1988.

9. Ishmael Ahmad, "Reed Arrested; Flag Still Flies," *MA*, February 3, 1988; Tom Lindley, "Flag Still Flies, but Reed Vows Fight 'Has Just Begun,'" *BN*, February 3, 1988; "Authorities Arrest 11 for Trying To Remove the Confederate Flag," *Birmingham World*, February 6, 1988; HJR 29 in *Journal of the House of Representatives of the State of Alabama Regular Session of 1988* (Montgomery: Brown Printing, 1988), 1:93–94.

10. Tom Lindley, "NAACP Loses U.S. Suit To Get Flag off Capitol," *BN*, March 1, 1989.

11. *BN*, October 18, 1989; on Johnson see Jack Bass, *Taming the Storm: The Life and Times of Judge Frank M. Johnson, Jr., and the South's Fight over Civil Rights* (New York: Doubleday, 1993), 422–423 and passim; *NAACP v. Hunt*, 891 F. 2d. 1555 (11th Cir. 1990), 1562–1566; James Forman, Jr., "Driving Dixie Down: Removing the Confederate Flag from Southern State Capitols," *Yale Law Journal* 101 (November 1991): 505–526.

12. "Flag Flap Revisited," *BN*, October 16, 1991; "It's the Wrong Flag," *BN*, April 22, 1992; "Historian Backs Chamber Chairman's Bid to Remove Rebel Flag from Capitol," *BN*, July 28, 1992; David White, "Hunt Refuses To Back Down in Flag Flap," *BN*, July 30, 1992. This proposed compromise had come up before in 1988. "Won't Be Flag Confrontation, Clark Reports Reed as Saying," *BN*, January 30, 1988.

13. Tom Lindley, "Alabamians Want Other Rebel Flag," *MA*, December 3, 1992.

14. White, "Hunt Refuses"; "Chamber Wants Battle Flag Hauled Down," *BN*, July 31, 1992.

15. Tom Lindley, "Reed Eyes Legal Effort To Yank Flag," *BN*, February 15, 1988; Frank Sikora, "State Law Says Only That Alabama or U.S. Flag Will Fly over Capitol," *BN*, February 21, 1988; *Holmes v. Hunt;* also Dan Morse, "Judge: Remove Flag," *MA*, January 5, 1993; "Biracial Effort Brings Flag Victory," *MA*, January 6, 1993.

16. Dan Morse, "Hunt Wants Voters To End Flag Dispute," *MA*, January 9, 1993; "Battle over Flag Continues with Drive for Vote on Issues," *MA*, January 7, 1993.

17. Stan Bailey, "Onlookers Outnumber Klan at Capitol Rally," *BN*, January 17, 1993.

18. Folsom quoted in *RTD*, May 13, 1993; "Folsom Drops Flag Appeal," *MA*, May 12, 1993; letter in *MA*, May 13, 1993.

19. Stan Bailey, "Confederate Flag Bill Calls for State Vote," *BN*, January 12, 1994; classified ad in *SP*, 3rd Quarter 1994, 49; *MA*, April 25, 1994; Dan Morse, "250 Attend Confederate Flag Dedication at State Capitol," *MA*, April 26, 1994.

20. "Poll: Folsom Liked Except on Flag Decision," *MA*, May 31, 1993; Bailey, "Confederate Flag Bill."

21. Clark Surrat, "Flag Flap," *State*, February 22, 1987; K. Michael Prince's *Rally 'Round the Flag, Boys! South Carolina and the Confederate Flag* (Columbia: University of South Carolina Press, 2004), 40–47, provides a full narrative and analysis of this controversy.

22. "Confederate Flag Show Criticized," *State*, February 10, 1972; William Stracener, "Confederate Flag Is Involved in Skirmish," *State*, April 10, 1977; Ed Rowland, "Rep. Patterson Hopes Flags To Come Down," *State*, April 17, 1979; David F. Kern, "A White Joins Call for Dixie's Flag To Fall," *State*, May 8, 1983.

23. Clark Surratt, "Flag Plan Nixed," *State*, February 24, 1987; Jan Tuten, "Removal of Flag Predicted," *State*, June 17, 1987; Surratt, "Flag Flap."

24. "Senator Defends Confederate Flag; NAACP Leader Calls It 'Odious Symbol,'" *State*, January 11, 1988; "State House Confederate Flag To Be Issue Again Next Year," *State*, June 9, 1992; Richard Quinn, "The Battle Flag Controversy," *SP*, Spring 1987, 17; "Confidential Briefing for Confederate Flag Supporters," undated letter ca. January 1994, from Glenn F. McConnell and John Courson; advertisement clipped from *State*.

25. Senate Bill 1061, South Carolina General Assembly, 1994; Nina Brook and Cindi Ross Scoppe, "Compromise Simply Couldn't Beat the Clock," *State*, June 5, 1994; Nina Brook, "Marathon Hearing Fuels 2-Flag Compromise," *State*, April 22, 1994.

26. Nina Brook, "Banner Opponent Would Prefer Not To Go to Court," *State*, June 10, 1994; Nina Brook, "NAACP May File Lawsuit over Flag," *State*, April 29, 1994; Courson quoted in Nina Brook, "Flag Compromise Coming Apart," *State*, June 1, 1994.

27. Amendment No. 17 to H 4818, Senate Journal No. 83, Wednesday, June 1, 1994.

28. Lee Bandy, "Rebel Banner Deal Hanging by Thread," *State,* May 31, 1994; Nina Brook et al., "Lawmakers Leave; Battle Flag Stays, *State,* June 3, 1994; Brook and Scoppe, "Compromise"; interview with Glenn McConnell, North Charleston, SC, June 21, 1995; Charles Lunsford, "Why I Resigned," open letter, [August] 1994, 10–11.

29. Nina Brook, "Battle Flag's Friends, Foes Eye Boycotts," *State,* June 29, 1994; Mike Soraghan, "Boycott Would Put Strain on Strand," *Sun News,* June 29, 1994; interview with Sen. Glenn F. McConnell, North Charleston, SC, June 21, 1995.

30. Nina Brook, "Justice May Kick Flag Issue to Legislature," Myrtle Beach *Sun News,* November 16, 1994; Nina Brook, "Battle Flag Wins House Protection," *State,* March 31, 1995; Nina Brook, "Bill Keeps Flag Issue from Court," *State,* March 30, 1995.

31. Text of speeches in *Sun News,* November 27, 1996; "The Flag and the Fury," *US News & World Report,* March 10, 1997; Prince, *Rally,* 187–191.

32. "Boycott of S.C. OK'd," *RFP,* October 21–23, 1999; "NAACP Challenges South Carolina Confederate Flag," NAACP news release, January 12, 2001 (www.naacp.org); Kathleen Dayton, "Officials: Tourism Surviving Boycott," *Sun News,* July 1, 2000.

33. "Confederate Flag Supporters Rally," *RTD,* January 8, 2000; "46,000 protest in S.C. over Confederate flag," *RTD,* January 18, 2000; "S.C. Governor Says Flag Should Be Removed," *RTD,* January 20, 2000; "Southern Heritage Celebration 2000," Omnivideo Productions, Minneapolis, 2001; Jim Davenport [AP], "McCain Supports Removing Confederate flag," *VP,* April 20, 2000.

34. Flag act on www.scstatehouse.net/sess113_1999–2000/bills/1266.doc; E. Gail Anderson Holness, "Don't Put That Flag in Our Face!" *Black News,* June 29–July 5, 2000.

35. Joseph Stroud and Kenneth A. Harris, "Flag Comes Down from the Dome," *State,* July 2, 2000; Kenneth A. Harris, "Patterson's Tenacity Finally Pays Off Today," *State,* July 1, 2000.

36. Bernard Legette, "March/Rally, Civil Disobedience Planned July 1," *Black News,* June 29–July 5, 2000; Lyn Riddle, "Tempers Fly as Flag Brought Down," *Greenville News,* July 2, 2000.

37. NAACP news release, January 12, 2001 (www.naacp.org).

38. See Alexander J. Azarian and Eden Feshazion, "The State Flag of Georgia: The 1956 Change in Its Historical Context," report of the Georgia Senate

Research Office, August 2000; Tom Opdyke, "History Unfurled," *AJC*,
August 2, 1992.

39. *Marietta Daily News,* July 5, 1992; Ben Fortson, Secretary of State, *Georgia
Flags 1956* (Atlanta: State Capitol, 1956).

40. ACC quoted in John Walker Davis, "An Air of Defiance: Georgia's State
Flag Change of 1956," *Georgia Historical Quarterly* 82 (Summer 1998):
317.

41. Groover quoted in C. Kelly Barrow, "The TRUTH about Georgia's Flag,"
CV, n.s., 40 (September–October 1992): 4–5, and in Cynthia Durcanin,
"Should Georgia Change Its Flag?" *AJC,* March 29, 1992.

42. P. Charles Lunsford, telephone conversation with author, March 10,
1993; also SCV Commander-in-Chief Robert L. Hawkins III, on NPR,
"Talk of the Nation," January 31, 1994; [Charles Kelly Barrow], "Georgia
Flag Facts" (The Flag Facts Committee, 1991); also letter of P. Charles
Lunsford, *AJC,* April 19, 1992.

43. Discussion in Georgia Senate cited in *Coleman v. Miller,* 885 F. Supp. 1566;
Azarian and Fesshazion, 20, conclude that all references to the centennial
were made after the fact. Davis, "An Air of Defiance," 320–322.

44. *Minutes of the Sixty-Second Annual Convention, General Convention, UDC, 1955,*
168; also *Minutes of the Sixty-Third Annual Convention, General Convention,
UDC, 1956,* 169; Davis, "An Air of Defiance," 320; Azarian and
Fesshazion, 22; Georgia Division, UDC, January 11, 1991, resolution in
Vertical Files (Subject files—Georgia Flags), Hargrett, UGA. The chairman of the SCV's heritage protection committee suggested that the
UDC's position arose from parochial self-interest: that the UDC wanted
to retain the pre-1956 flag that featured the Confederate Stars and Bars,
which was the flag adopted by the UDC. *CV,* n.s., 41 (March–April
1991): 3; Jim Auchmutey, "Keepers of the Confederacy," *AJC,* January 19,
1993.

45. "On Changing the State Flag," *Atlanta Daily World,* February 14, 1956.

46. Steve Harvey, "'It Needed To Be Done,'" *AJC,* June 9, 1992; "A Lady's
Special Edge," *Gainesville Daily Times,* February 10, 1969; Keith
Coulbourn, "Should Georgia Change Its State Flag?" *AJC Magazine,* May 4,
1969, 19–20+; David Lawson, "Ga. Flag Re-Adoption Urged," *Athens
Banner-Herald,* February 12, 1969.

47. Otto Friedrich, "Racism on the Rise," *Time* 129 (February 2, 1987): 18.

48. Harvey, "'It Needed to Be Done'"; Ron McNinch-Su, William D. Richardson, and J. Michael Martinez, "Traditionalists versus Reconstructionists: The Case of the Georgia State Flag, Part One," in Martinez et al., eds., *Confederate Symbols,* 306–307.

49. Steve Harvey and Bill Montgomery, "Governor Flags Down a Hot Issue," *AJ,* May 29, 1992. Quoted in Durcanin, "Should Georgia Change?"

50. "Atlanta Is Just Plain Nuts," *Rome News-Tribune,* February 7, 1993; "Flag of Today, Not Yesterday," *Rome News-Tribune,* April 20, 1992; "Ga. Newspapers Praise, Criticize Flag Proposal," *AJC,* February 7, 1993.

51. Cynthia Durcanin, "Emotions, Interest in State-Flag Issue Running High," *AJC,* April 1, 1992; "Poll Shows Georgians Like Flag the Way It Is," *AJC,* June 4, 1992; "Views on the Flag," *AJC,* May 29, 1992; Richard Hyatt, *Zell: The Governor Who Gave Georgia Hope* (Mercersburg: Mercer University Press, 1997), 337 and 324–344, passim.

52. Mark Sherman, "Confederate Sons Post Opposition," *AJC,* February 9, 1993; Mark Sherman, "Flag Supporters Mount Capitol Volley," *AJC,* January 20, 1993; Mark Sherman, "Flag Debate Rages Inside, Outside Capitol," *AJC,* February 10, 1993; *CV,* n.s., 40 (November–December 1992): 48; Kathy Alexander, "Cobb Forum on State Flag Stirs Emotional Response," *AJC,* November 19, 1992.

53. Miller's speech excerpted in *AJC,* January 13, 1993.

54. Ben Smith III, "Flag Speech Both Inspires and Infuriates," *AJC,* January 13, 1993.

55. Durcanin, "Should Georgia Change"; "Flag Changers Are Southerners, Too," January 31, 1993, G4; Ed Fields letter in *AJC,* February 10, 1993; Colin Campbell, "Now What Exactly Is a 'True' Georgian?" *AJC,* January 17, 1993.

56. "Mr. Miller Joins"; John Head, "Common Ground on the Ga. Flag," *AJC,* June 3, 1992; Cynthia Durcanin, "Miller Flag Won't Fly, Say Critics," *AJC,* October 11, 1992.

57. Mark Sherman, "Pledging Allegiances at Flag Forum," *AJC,* January 29, 1993.

58. "Student Protesters Burn State Flag at Capitol," *AJC,* February 16, 1993; "General Miller Retreats," *Rome News-Tribune,* March 11, 1993; "Senate Flag Proposal Draws Mixed Reviews," *AJC,* March 4, 1993; Mark Sherman, "Senate Votes to Put Issue on the Ballot," *AJC,* March 6, 1993;

Mark Sherman, "Miller Calls Halt to Efforts for a New Flag," *AJC*, March 10, 1993; "Attacks on the Colors," *CV*, n.s., 41 (May–June 1993): 3.

59. Douglas A. Blackmon, "Council Wants to Remove City Hall's Only State Flag," *AJC*, January 26, 1993; Ken Foskett and Betsy White, "State Flags Taken Down in 'Growing Movement' in Atlanta," *AJC*, February 7, 1993; Sherman, "Dramatically"; Tom Watson, "Old Fight over Ga. Flag Moves to New Field," *USA Today*, January 26, 1994; Peter Applebome, "Boosterism Isn't Gone with the Wind," *NYT*, January 27, 1994; Susan Laccetti, "Competing Flag Views on Display," *AJC*, January 31, 1994.

60. *Coleman v. Miller*, 885 F. Supp. 1561 (N.D.Ga. 1995), 1568–1571; *Coleman v. Miller*, United States Court of Appeals, Eleventh Circuit, No. 96–8149.

61. "Text of Speech of Gov. Roy Barnes on the Proposed New Flag," *AJC*, January 30, 2001; Rhonda Cook and Jim Galloway, "New Flag Flies over Capitol after Barnes Signs Historic Bill," *AJC*, January 31, 2001; Elliott Brack, "A Smiling Governor Offers Insights into His Flag Victory," *AJC*, February 2, 2001.

62. Quoted in Rick Lavender, "Why This Flag?" Gainesville [Georgia] *Times*, March 16, 2003.

63. SHL quoted in "Georgia Approves New Flag," *RTD*, January 31, 2001; Lunsford quoted in Cook and Galloway, "New Flag."

64. "Senate Resolution Encourages Flying of Former Georgia Flags," *AJC*, March 21, 2001.

65. Jim Galloway, "Unfurled Emotions," *AJC*, July 9, 2002; Elijah S. Coleman to Jim Galloway, posted on "Southern Heritage News & Views" (southernheritage@topica.com), July 10, 2002.

66. James Salzer, "Election 2002: Governor: 'Anti-Roy' Campaign Delivers Sonny Day," *AJC*, November 6, 2002; Richard Whitt, "Confederate Flag Supporters to Next Governor: You Owe Us," *AJC*, November 10, 2002; Hank Rowland, "Flaggers Cheer Barnes' Defeat," *Brunswick News*, November 8, 2002; Michael Hill, "Barnes Booted in Georgia!" *Dixie Daily News* (www.southerncaucus.org/205.htm). Jim Galloway, "Perdue OKs New Ga. Flag; May Fly Soon," *AJC*, April 5, 2003.

67. Ben Smith, "Current Georgia Flag Cruises to Victory in Referendum," *AJC*, March 2, 2004.

68. Ben Smith, "Flag Debate May Be 'History,'" *AJC,* March 3, 2004; Wayne Crenshaw, "Fate of Georgia's Banner in the Air," *Macon Telegraph,* February 29, 2004.

69. Jack Elliott, Jr., "Blacks Ask Judge to Ban State Flag," *DM,* April 20, 1993; Alia Smith, "Black Groups File Lawsuit to Lower Mississippi's State Flag," *Daily Tar Heel,* April 22, 1993.

70. *Mississippi Division of the United Sons of Confederate Veterans v. Mississippi State Conference of NAACP Branches et al.,* Supreme Court of Mississippi, May 4, 2000 (www.mssc.state.ms.us).

71. Mario Rossilli, "Future of Flag on Line," *Clarion-Ledger,* May 6, 2000; David Hampton, "State Flag Hearings Show Just How Divisive the Current Banner Can Be," *Clarion-Ledger,* November 19, 2000.

72. "Public Debate on Flag Grows More Heated," Memphis *Commercial Appeal*, October 28, 2000; Emily Wagster, "Is Public Debate on Flag Helping?" *Clarion-Ledger,* November 13, 2000; Emily Wagster, "New Flag Proposal Expected Today," *Clarion-Ledger,* December 12, 2000.

73. "History of the Advisory Commission on the Mississippi State Flag and the Coat of Arms," *Clarion-Ledger,* December 13, 2000; "House Sets April 17 Vote on State Flag," *Clarion-Ledger,* January 9, 2001.

74. Patrice Sawyer, "Flag Vote Fallout Possible," *Clarion-Ledger,* April 19, 2001; "Leave the Flag in the Past," New Orleans *Times-Picayune*, January 16, 2001.

75. "The Flag Vote," *Clarion-Ledger,* April 18, 2001, online edition; Sherri Williams, "Turnout Troubles Black Mayor," *Clarion-Ledger,* April 19, 2001; Courtland Milloy, "Blacks Helped Keep Old Flag Waving in Mississippi," *WP,* April 22, 2001.

76. "Future of Flag and State Up to Voters," *Natchez Democrat,* April 17, 2001; Biloxi *Sun Herald*, April 17, 2001; David G. Sansing, "Mississippi Needs a Better Symbol," *Starkville Daily News,* April 17, 2001; Steve Mullen, "Media Knock State after Vote on Flag," *Clarion-Ledger,* April 19, 2001; Gregory Kane, "Mississippi Is Deserving of Its Worst Schools Rank," *Baltimore Sun,* April 25, 2001.

77. Jack Elliott, Jr., "Rally 'Round the Flag," Biloxi *Sun Herald*, April 15, 2001; Emily Wagster, "Ministers Hold Rally To Support 1894 Flag," Biloxi *Sun Herald*, March 27, 2001; Patrice Sawyer, "Fight Not Over, State

NAACP President Says," *Clarion-Ledger,* April 18, 2001; John Shelton Reed, "The Banner That Won't Stay Furled," *Southern Cultures* (Spring 2002): 76–100.

78. "Flag Won't Fly Everywhere, Despite Win," *Clarion-Ledger,* April 18, 2001; "NAACP Convention Delegates Pass Mississippi Confederate Flag Resolution," *NAACP News,* July 10, 2001 (www.naacp.org/news/releases/mississippi); Jimmie E. Gates, "Supporters to Push Constitutional Inclusion," *Clarion-Ledger,* April 18, 2001.

79. John Shelton Reed, *Kicking Back: Further Dispatches from the South* (Columbia: University of Missouri Press, 1995), 47.

80. "The Truth about the Flag," *AJC,* January 13, 1993.

81. Jack Tyler, ed., "The Confederate Flag: An NAACP Non-Issue," *CV,* n.s., 36 (January–February 1988): 46.

82. John Egerton, *The Americanization of Dixie: The Southernization of America* (New York: Harper's Magazine Press, 1974); John Shelton Reed, *The Enduring South: Subcultural Persistence in Mass Society* (Lexington, MA: D. C. Heath, 1972); Peter Applebome, *Dixie Rising: How the South Is Shaping American Values, Politics, and Culture* (New York: Times Books, 1996); Clyde N. Wilson, ed., *Why the South Will Survive, by Fifteen Southerners* (Athens: University of Georgia Press, 1981).

13. "You Can't Erase History"

1. Patrice Sawyer, "Closed Meetings on Flag Issue Called Eye-Opening," *Clarion-Ledger,* November 25, 2000; *Daniels v. Harrison County Board of Supervisors,* Mississippi Supreme Court, No. 96-CA-01129-SCT.

2. NAACP News Release, January 12, 2001 (www.naacp.org/news/releases).

3. Shinhoster quoted in Wes Allison, "Protecting the Confederacy," *RTD,* February 14, 1994; Hinkle, *Embattled Banner,* 75.

4. "Six Flags: They're History, Not Halos," rpt. in *CV,* n.s., May–June 1988: 3.

5. "Mayor M'Carthy's Design of Flag for City of Richmond," *RTD,* May 7, 1907; Resolution in CMLS Minutes, June 1907, ESBL, MOC; letter of Gordon P. Luetjen, Jr., *RFP,* August 27–29, 1992; "Another Confederate Flag Removed," *RFP,* August 27–29, 1992; Bill Wasson, "City Official Flag Unfurled," *RTD,* November 25, 1993.

6. Hazel Trice Edney, "Confederate Flags on State Planes," *RFP,* July 23–25, 1992; Hazel Trice Edney, "Governor Wipes Out Rebel Flag," *RFP,* July 30–August 1, 1992; Peter Bacque, "Guard To Remove Insignia Displays," *RTD,* October 9, 1992.

7. Letter of John Stonnell, *RTD,* August 2, 1992; telephone interview with John Stonnell, May 12, 1995; Edney, "Governor."

8. Hazel Trice Edney, "Rebel Flag Protests Linked to Dismissal," *RFP,* September 24–26, 1992; Edney, "Governor Overturns Guard's Order," *RFP,* December 10–12, 1992; Frank Green, "Sergeant Reinstated; Guard Insignia Foe," *RTD,* December 9, 1992; letters of Richard M. Wray, Lieutenant Colonel (ret.), and Jeff Wilkins, Lieutenant Colonel (ret.), in *RTD,* August 2, 1992.

9. Mel Oberg-Olmi, "For City Flag, Confusion Beats the Confederacy," *RTD,* July 4, 1993; David J. Melton, "The Battleflag: Just What Did the Stars & Bars Stand For?" *Winchester Star,* March 18, 1993; P. Charles Lunsford, "Attacks on the Colors," *CV,* n.s., 42 (January–February 1994): 6.

10. A. P. Thompson, "NAACP Requests Removal of Confederate Flag," *Gainesville Sun,* December 15, 2000; A. P. Thompson, "Battle of the Flag," *Gainesville Sun,* February 18, 2001; A. P. Thompson, "Flag a Symbol of Pride, Racism," *Gainesville Sun,* April 9, 2001.

11. Mark Holan, "Dixie Détente," *Mobile Register,* January 19, 2002; Mark Holan, "Protest Set To Keep Flag on City Seal," *Mobile Register,* July 13, 2000; "Great News for All Rebels from Mobile on Lee-Jackson Day," Friends of the Flag News Release, January 20, 2002 (www.shucks.net/shucks/27.htm).

12. Gary Fineout, "Flag Controversy Flutters in the Breeze at Capitol," *Tallahassee Democrat,* April 12, 1996; Brian E. Browley, *Palm Beach Post,* April 16, 1998; Diane Hirth, "Confederate Flag at Capitol Angers Black Lawmakers," *Orlando Sentinel,* April 11, 1996; Brent Kallestad, "Mortham Says Flag Is Worth Keeping," *Tallahassee Democrat,* April 13, 1996.

13. "Confederate Flag at Florida State Capitol Pulled," *Gainesville Sun,* February 11, 2001.

14. "Oklahoma Officials at Odds over Flying Confederate Flag," *NYT,* April 6, 1988; "Confederate Flag Backers Hold Rally," *Daily Oklahoman,* October 19, 1998, p. 3; Ashby, "Six Flags"; Ed Godfrey, "Confederate Flag Lawsuit Thrown Out," *Daily Oklahoman,* October 30, 1998, 1–2; also *CV,* n.s., 46 (1998): 4–5.

15. Mike Hinton, "New Rebel Flag Idea Still Flies in the Face of Controversy," *Daily Oklahoman,* October 21, 1998; Thomas Mullen, "Groups Defend Confederate Culture at State Capitol," Associated Press News Wire Story, November 11, 2000.

16. According to the Southern Heritage Internet News Service, "Aw, Shucks," "Politically-correct individuals were pushing for the first national flag to replace the naval jack on the Mobile city seal. Great news for all rebels."

17. "Pensacola Picture Book" no. 20 published by the T. T. Wentworth, Jr., Museum; and Programs of the Fiesta of the Five Flags, 1967, 1968, 1972, 1974, 1975, 1981, in Local History Vertical Files, WFRL; telephone interview with J. Earle Bowden, May 22, 2001.

18. Telephone interview with J. Earle Bowden, May 22, 2001; Cindy George, "Stars and Bars Now Flies over Pensacola," *Pensacola News Journal,* February 2, 2000; Cindy George and Troy Moon, "Council Votes Stars and Bars Will Fly in City," *Pensacola News Journal,* February 11, 2000.

19. Maria D. Martirano, "Dixie Flag Comes Down," Cumberland *Times-News,* August 17, 1994; Maria D. Martirano, "Group Wants Banner Back," *Times-News,* December 19, 1994; Deb Riechmann, "Removal of Confederate Flag Upsets Activists in Cumberland," *Washington Times,* January 2, 1995; Marsha Rader, "Confederates 'Invade' City Hall, Display Flag in Cumberland, Md.," *Civil War News,* June 1995, 27.

20. Michael Abramowitz, "License Plates Bearing Confederate Flag Stir New Battle," *WP,* December 27, 1996; Linda Wheeler, "Black Leaders Demand Recall of Md. Confederate Tags," *WP,* January 2, 1997; Fern Shen, "Md. To Recall Auto Tags with Confederate Flag," *WP,* January 4, 1997; Paul W. Valentine, "Confederate Tag Recall Must Halt, Judge Rules," *WP,* February 25, 1997; *North Carolina Division of Sons of Confederate Veterans v. Janice Faulkner, Commissioner of Motor Vehicles,* Opinion No. COA97–1563.

21. Jeremy M. Lazarus, "Rebel Flag Off Tag," *RFP,* January 28–30, 1999; undated clippings from *Virginian Pilot:* Linda Mcnatt, "'Sons' Say Flag a Sign of Pride, Not Prejudice," Jennifer Peter, "Confederate Flag Sparks License Plates Debate," Linda Mcnatt, "Rutherford Institute Joins Battle for Confederate Flag License Plate," April 30, 1999, and "Group Sues over License-Plate Decision"; Rex Bowman, "Judge OKs Rebel Flag on Licenses," *RTD,* January 19, 2001; statement by Attorney General Mark Earley, January 19, 2001, on Website of Attorney General's office,

www.vaag.com; Tyler Whitley, "Earley Appeals Licenses," *RTD*, January 20, 2001; *Sons of Confederate Veterans, Inc., etc., et al., v. Commissioner of the Virginia Department of Motor Vehicles, etc.*, U.S. Court of Appeals, 4th Circuit Website (published as 288 F 3d. 610); Tom Campbell, "Court Backs Rebel-Flag Car Tags," *RTD*, April 30, 2002; Jeff E. Schapiro, "State Bows in Battle on Confederate Tags," *RTD*, May 30, 2002; News Release, Office of the Governor, May 2, 2002 (www.governor.state.va.us).

22. Steve Vogel, "New Controversy under Old Banner," *WP*, October 18, 2000.

23. *Patrick J. Griffin III v. Department of Veterans Affairs, et al.*, U.S. District Court, District of Maryland, January 29, 2001, civil action WMN-00–2837, opinion on Website of U.S. District Court, District of Maryland, 23–24; Ed Ballam, "Federal Judge OK's Confederate Flag at Point Lookout," *Civil War News*, February–March 2001, 1, 23.

24. *Patrick G.* [sic] *Griffin III v. Department of Veterans Affairs*, U.S. Fourth Circuit Court of Appeals, Case No. 01-1450, decided December 17, 2001 (Website), 6–7, 10 and passim. The U.S. Supreme Court in October 2002 allowed the Appellate Court's ruling to stand.

25. Letter of Robert Wayne Byrd to *DRB*, April 3, 1994; John H. Brubaker III, *The Last Capital: Danville, Virginia, and the Final Days of the Confederacy* (Danville: Womack Press, 1979), 65–69.

26. Presentation by Executive Director Thomas W. Jones at "Embattled Emblem: A Symposium on the Confederate Battle Flag," The Museum of the Confederacy, March 18, 1994.

27. Presentation by Thomas W. Jones.

28. Sam McDonald, "Flag at Museum Draws Glaise Fire," June 2, 1993; Sam McDonald, "Museum To Strike Flag," *DRB*, June 5, 1993; Charles Hurt, "Flag Flap Draws Flurry of Opinions," *DRB*, June 12, 1993.

29. Quoted in Jim Washington, "Soldiers' Descendants Want Confederate Flag Back Up," *DRB*, June 8, 1993; McDonald, "Flag at Museum"; Charles Hunt, "Flag Flap Draws Flurry of Opinions," *DRB*, June 12, 1993.

30. Stacie Mackenzie, "Confederate Flag 'Belongs Here,' Says Rally-Goer," *DRB*, June 28, 1993; Sam McDonald, "Rebel Flag Wavers Want Parade Permit," *DRB*, August 4, 1993; Sam McDonald, "Police Backed on Parade Permit," *DRB*, August 6, 1993; letter from Brian Barbour and Clayton Barbour to *DRB*, July 31, 1993.

31. Sam McDonald, "Confederate Flag To Fly Again at Museum," July 20,

1993; Hoke, "Museum To Fly."; Sam McDonald, "Flag's Status Still No-Fly at Museum," *DRB,* July 9, 1993; see "Censorship Alerts" in *DRB,* April 3, 1994, April 10, 1994, May 29, 1994, June 5, 1994.

32. "Local Heritage Chapter Endorses Council Candidates," *DRB,* April 6, 1994; Sam McDonald, "Council Gets a New-Old Mix," *DRB,* May 4, 1994; Sam McDonald, "City Council Asks State for Public Hearing on Proposed Mini-Bypass," *DRB,* April 6, 1994; "A Resolution Requesting the Danville Museum of Fine Arts and History To Grant the Heritage Preservation Association a License To Erect a Flagpole and Display the Confederate Flag on Museum Property under Certain Terms and Conditions," City Attorney James R. Saul, April 1994; copy provided by Saul; Sam McDonald, "Flag's Status on Hold for Month," *DRB,* April 20, 1994.

33. Jeff Buchanan, "Monument Replaces Flag as a Gift to City," *DRB,* June 8, 1994; Wes Allison, "Danville Flag Controversy Waves Anew," *RTD,* April 21, 1994.

34. Allison, "Danville Flag Controversy"; Wes Allison, "Danville Rights Groups Oppose Monument," *RTD,* July 7, 1993.

35. Stacie Mackenzie, "Confederate Flag Waves Again," *DRB,* March 27, 1995; Bernard Baker, "Celebration To Mark Coming of Controversial Confederate Marker," *DRB,* March 26, 1995; Wes Allison, "Confederate Flag Waves in Danville," *RTD,* March 27, 1995; Wes Allison, "Following the Flag into Battle," *RTD,* March 28, 1995; Byrd quoted in Greg Schneider, "GOP Chairman Plans To Attend Ceremony Honoring Rebel Flag," *VP,* March 24, 1995.

36. Mike Allen, "Song of the Day: Ollie-Luia," *RTD,* June 5, 1994; letter to the editor, *RTD,* October 22, 1994; text of address rpt. in *RTD,* April 9, 1995; Allison, "Confederate Flag Waves."

37. James Loewen, *Lies across America: What Our Historic Sites Get Wrong* (New York: New Press, 1999), 36.

38. Quoted in Prince, *Rally,* 220.

39. See especially David Lowenthal, *Possessed by the Past: The Heritage Crusade and the Spoils of History* (New York: Free Press, 1996).

Epilogue: The Second American Flag

1. Photograph of Chancellor Helmut addressing crowds in Erfürt, Germany, April 1990, by Robert Wallis, published by SIPA Press; John Shelton

Reed, "Confederate Agents in the Ivy League," in *Kicking Back: Further Dispatches from the South* (Columbia: University of Missouri Press, 1995), 38; Hawkins quoted in John M. Coski, "The Confederate Battle Flag in American History and Culture," *Southern Cultures* 1 (Winter 1996): 211; *SP,* 1st Quarter 1997, cover and 20.

2. John M. Coski, "In Search of . . . the Confederate Flag," *UDC Magazine* 56 (April 1993): 24; Gerhard Lack to author, October 10, 1992; John Hall, "Sweet Freedom Buffers Sour System," *RTD,* May 15, 1993; Paul Hundertmark [Hamburg, Germany] Catalogue, 1993.

3. Rosalind Urbach Moss, "'Yes, There's a Reason I Salute the Flag': Flag Use and the Civil Rights Movement," *Raven* [a journal of vexillology] 5 (1998): 36, 49; Calvin R. Trice, "Group Questions U.S. Flag Challenge," *RTD,* September 5, 2001.

4. This conclusion is based specifically on the printed literature in the Right Wing Collection (MS #2790), Hargrett, UGA.

5. The Reverend Raymond T. Dearmond to Wallace, January 30, 1964, and Wallace to the Reverend Raymond T. Dearmond, January 31, 1964, ADAH, Box SG 22387, folder 16.

6. Peter Applebome, *Dixie Rising: How the South Is Shaping American Values, Politics, and Culture* (New York: Random House, 1996); John Egerton, *The Americanization of Dixie: The Southernization of America* (New York: Harper's Magazine Press, 1974); Howard W. Odum, *The Way of the South: Toward the Regional Balance of America* (New York: Macmillan, 1947), 295, 292, 317-318, 246-247.

7. C. Vann Woodward, *The Burden of Southern History* (Baton Rouge: LSU Press, 1960), 15-21; Larry J. Griffin and Don H. Doyle, eds., *The South as an American Problem* (Athens: University of Georgia Press, 1995), 28, 21; Clyde N. Wilson, ed., *Why the South Will Survive by Fifteen Southerners* (Athens: University of Georgia Press, 1981); John Shelton Reed, *The Enduring South: Subcultural Persistence in Mass Society* (Lexington, MA: D. C. Heath, 1972).

8. New Albany Declaration in R. Gordon Thornton, *The Southern Nation: The New Rise of the Old South* (Gretna, LA: Pelican, 2000), 227-231.

9. Ron Holland, *The Southern Heritage Survival Manual* (Bridgewater, NJ: Traveller Press, 2002).

10. "Declaration of Southern Cultural Independence" created by

www.freemississippi.org and endorsed by League of the South at www.dixienet.org/ls-homepg/declaration.htm; Allen G. Breed, "Gone with the Wind, Secession's Back," *RTD,* July 5, 1999.

11. James Davison Hunter, *Culture Wars: The Struggle To Define America* (New York: Harpercollins/Basic Books, 1991), employs the concepts of "ortho-dox" and "progressive" positions.

12. Charles B. Dew, *Apostles of Disunion: Southern Secession Commissioners and the Causes of the Civil War* (Charlottesville, VA: University Press of Virginia, 2001), 17.

13. Jonathan David Farley, "Remnants of the Confederacy: Glorifying a Time of Tyranny," *Tennessean,* November 20, 2002. A native of Jamaica, Farley may owe to his national origin his willingness to express views that even the harshest African-American critics of the Confederacy seldom articulate.

14. Roy Rosenzweig and David Thelen, *The Presence of the Past: Popular Uses of History in American Life* (New York: Columbia University Press, 1998); John M. Coski, "The Confederate Flag and the Verdict(s) of History" (unpub. paper presented to the Southern Historical Association Annual Meeting, November 2000).

15. Springer, "Rebel Flag," 73.

16. James Davison Hunter, *Before the Shooting Begins: Searching for Democracy in America's Culture Wars* (New York: Free Press, 1994).

17. Address of William P. Simpson to Chewning Junior High, September 21, 1989, copy provided by ACLU of North Carolina.

18. Jim McElhinney, comments at "Embattled Emblem" symposium, The Museum of the Confederacy, March 18, 1994; "Loaded Symbols," *Southern Magazine* 1 (June 1987): 44–49; Charles Reagan Wilson, *Judgment and Grace in Dixie: Southern Faiths from Faulkner to Elvis* (Athens: University of Georgia Press, 1996), 159–163; interview with Ed Hamlett at SSOC Thirtieth Reunion and Conference, Charlottesville, Virginia, April 7, 1994; "We'll Take Our Stand," April 4, 1964, unidentified clipping in Schomburg Center Clipping Files, NYPL, Microfiche 004-687-1 & 2; Vernon Chadwick, "Papa's Got a Brand New Flag: Confederate Symbol-ism and the Funky New South," *Southern Reader* 3 (November–December 1991): 27.

19. John T. Edge, "Living (and Dining) in the Nu South," *Oxford American* (Jan-

uary–February 1999): 76–77; Andy Steiner, "Dixie Rising," *Utne Reader* (July–August 1999): 22–24; "Disruptive Symbols?" *State,* March 5, 1994; Mike Smith, "Banner Combines Confederate Flag, Colors of Black Liberation," *AJC,* April 22, 1994.

20. Telephone interview with Charles Nixon, August 3, 1994; "A BALLOTT: An Original Design by Charles Nixon, 1988," proposal courtesy of Charles Nixon; Michael Hedges, "Confederate Battle Flag Flies at Million Man March," *Salisbury Post,* October 17, 1995.

Acknowledgments

The work on this book has taken so long that many of the people deserving acknowledgment have moved on—some, tragically, forever. I want to recognize by name as many of them as possible. Steve Hoge encouraged me to embark upon what we both thought to be a quick and easy book project. In the early stages of the work, I enjoyed the assistance and friendship of the staff at the Library of Virginia, especially Daisey Goldsborough, Sara Huggins, Tina Miller, Janet Perkins, Jennifer Phillips, Ted Polk, and Gina Woodward. As the work branched out, I benefited from the assistance of Bob Bradley, Rickie Brunner, Norwood Kerr, and Ken Tilley at the Alabama Department of Archives & History; Dwayne Cox at Auburn University Library; Jim Baggett and Don Veasey at the Birmingham Public Library; Guy Hubbs at Birmingham-Southern; Jim Cross at Clemson University; Bruce Graetz at the Florida Museum of History; Bessie Williams at the Fort Jackson Museum; Luther Hanson at the Quartermaster Museum, Fort Lee; Greta Browning, Skip Hulett, and Mary McKay at the University of Georgia Libraries; Betty Carlan at the International Motor Sports Hall of Fame in Talladega, Alabama; Wayne Phillips at the Louisiana State Museum; Jennifer Aronson at the University of Mississippi Library; Fath Davis Ruffins at the Smithsonian; Rebecka Tol and Marian Gianassi at the United Daughters of the Confederacy; Jeanne Pardee at the University of Virginia Libraries; Lynn Myers at the *Birmingham News*; Charles Saunders and Joanne Slough at the *Richmond Times-Dispatch*; and the helpful staffs at the W. Stanley Hoole Special Collections Library at the University of Alabama, the local history and genealogy department of the Chattanooga Public Library, the West Florida Regional Library, Pensacola, Florida, and South Caroliniana Library, University of South Carolina (especially the keeper of the vertical files!). Julie

Golia, of Columbia University, assisted with research at the New York Public Library.

As my research on the subject became known, family, friends, colleagues, and total strangers sent newspaper clippings, photographs, and other sources and ideas about the battle flag. I am indebted to Shirley Anderson, Chad Arrant, Alex Azarian, Jim Balloch, Frances Barnes, Pete Barnes, Keith Bohannon, Matt Bonner, Jim Campbell, Travis Charbeneau, Mel Collins, Cliff Dickinson, George Ewert, William Forrester, Darron Franta, Linda A. Gibson, Walter Griggs, David Hahn, Chris Harvin, Susan Harvin, Jack Keller, Walter J. Kline, Robert E. L. Krick, Lisa Kroll, Beverly Lowry, Tom Lowry, Starke Miller, Kent Morehead, Michael Musick, Charles Nixon, Pierre-Rene Noth, Thomas G. Parramore, Don Pfanz, Kym Rice, Norm Saunders, William Simpson, John T. Smith, Jr., Saul Viener, Chuck Walton, and Elwood Yates as well as my parents, Bernard and Linda Coski, my in-laws, Tom and Ann Spivey, and my aunt, Ruth Anderson. Chris Fullerton not only sent clippings and copies but introduced me to many of the other people acknowledged here and inspired me with his wit and zest for life.

Many fellow scholars have offered their assistance or expertise: David Blight, Gabor Boritt, Fitz Brundage, Andy Doyle, Glenn Eskew, Kari Fredrickson, Gary Freeze, Gary Gallagher, Lloyd Hunter, Harvey Jackson, Les Jensen, Bob Kenzer, Ed Linenthal, Nancy MacLean, Charles Martin, Scott Nelson, Ted Ownby, Michael Parrish, George Schedler, Clarence Walker, Lori Walters, and Charles Wilson. Robert Bonner gave me a sneak preview of his brilliant analysis of Confederate flag culture during the Civil War. Kevin Thornton, Glen Cangelosi, Rich Rollins, and Chris Springer shared with me their own insightful works on the Confederate flag. I am especially grateful for the intellectual camaraderie of Richmond flag scholar Rosalind Urbach Moss. John and Dale Reed have shared with me (and with many others) their extraordinary knowledge, humor, and warmth. Tony Horwitz provided tips and vicarious adventures from his travels across the landscape of the Unfinished Civil War.

Susan Glisson, Tony Iacono, and Pete Hunt arranged speaking engagements that also proved to be invaluable long-distance research trips. Mike Martinez, William D. Richardson, and Keith Poulter gave me the opportunity to publish substantial summaries of my work in progress.

I am deeply grateful to the people from all walks of life and perspectives who shared their memories with me through oral history and telephone interviews. Their names appear in the Notes. I am particularly grateful to those Korean War veterans who responded to my research query in *The Graybeards* and to Martha Rollins Dusenbury, who shared family scrapbooks and memories of her late husband. Peggy Peattie put at my disposal her brilliant portfolio of photographs from South Carolina's 1990s flag wars.

When the research finally became a manuscript, Sam Craghead, Walter D. Tucker, John Reed, and Robert Bonner agreed to read it and offered valuable perspectives and suggestions. Flag historian Greg Biggs gave me the benefit of his exhaustive research on wartime flags and advice about how to make the generalizations in my first two chapters more accurate; David Sansing similarly reviewed the sections about the University of Mississippi. William C. "Jack" Davis took on the role of patron and provided contacts and moral support that have been essential to getting the book into print. The Harvard University Press team of Susan Wallace Boehmer, Tim Jones, Joyce Seltzer, and Rachel Weinstein found the right balance between compliments and cajolery to improve the book in every way. Don Pierce enthusiastically agreed to add "dust jacket author's photographer" to his long résumé, while Norma Pierce expanded her impressive graphic design skills to include flags.

At The Museum of the Confederacy, interns and volunteers Dan Jasman, Lynn Brogis, Stefan Cohn, Pamela Fulghum, and Kendon Light assisted with initial research for the Confederate battle flag exhibit. My colleagues at the Museum have given me their assistance, ideas, criticisms, friendship, indulgence, and darn good parties over the years. I am especially indebted to Eva Ahladas, John Ahladas, Eric App, Trish Balderson, Chris Barnett, Elizabeth Wyatt Bennett, Charlie Bizzell, Malinda Collier, Charity Coman, Sarah Dowdey, David Epstein, Beth Galer, Cara Griggs, Robert Hancock, Doug Harvey, Tucker Hill, Terri Hudgins, Doug Knapp, Sheryl Kingery Mays, Lisa Middleton, Heather Milne, Ida O'Leary, Waite Rawls, May Sherrod Reed, Robin Reed, Rebecca Rose, Kathleen Ryder, Guy Swanson, Bryce Vanstavern, and Vickie Yates. Old times and old friends there will never be forgotten.

Ruth Ann has lived with this project not only at home but also at the Museum, where we have worked together for more years than most happily married couples could and should. Our beloved dogs Dexter, Eleanor, and India have listened patiently to my rambling thoughts about the Confederate flag during our many walks and runs. Ruth Ann and the dogs have helped keep the preoccupying work on this book in proper perspective by constantly reminding me of the value of love and laughter, of belly rubs and good books read aloud, of warm hearts and cold noses.

Illustration Credits

1. Courtesy of The Museum of the Confederacy, Richmond, Virginia

2. Portrait of William Porcher Miles by John Stolle, courtesy of The Museum of the Confederacy, Richmond, Virginia; photograph by Tucker H. Hill

3. Courtesy of The Museum of the Confederacy, Richmond, Virginia

4. Courtesy of The Museum of the Confederacy, Richmond, Virginia; photograph by Katherine Wetzel

5. Courtesy of the Minnesota Historical Society; photograph by Joel E. Whitney

6. "Right of Cashtown Road" by Allen Redwood; courtesy of The Museum of the Confederacy, Richmond, Virginia; photograph by Katherine Wetzel

7. Courtesy of West Point Museum Art Collection, United States Military Academy

8. Cabinet card photograph by Wertz, Abingdon, Virginia, 1897; courtesy of The Museum of the Confederacy, Richmond, Virginia

9. Courtesy of the Valentine Richmond History Center, Richmond, Virginia

10. Courtesy of Dementi Studio, Richmond, Virginia

11. Courtesy of the Alabama Department of Archives & History, Montgomery, Alabama; photograph LPP80

12. Courtesy of the National Archives and Records Administration; photograph 127-GW-549 by Sam J. Bushemi, USMC

13. Courtesy of U.S. Information Agency (New York Times, Paris Bureau), Record Group 306, National Archives and Records Administration, Washington, D.C.; photograph 306-NT-650–18

14. Courtesy of AP/Wide World Photos

15. Courtesy of Special Collections, University of Mississippi Libraries; reprinted from the *Ole Miss, 1956*

16. Bob Brooks Photo, 6 Brierbridge Lane, Chapel Hill, from the *Yackety Yack, 1950;* copy print from the University of North Carolina Archives

17. Courtesy of the Auburn University Libraries; from the *Glomerata,* 1959

18. Courtesy of the Fort Jackson Museum; U.S. Army photograph SC 391991

19. Cartoon by Fred O. Seibel, reprinted with permission from the *Richmond*

Times-Dispatch; copy courtesy of Special Collections, James Branch Cabell Library, Virginia Commonwealth University, Richmond, Virginia

20. Courtesy of Getty Images; photograph by Mark Kaufman, *Life* Magazine © 1951

21. Collections of the Museum of Florida History; courtesy of Lake County Discovery Museum/Curt Teich Postcard Archives, Lake County, Illinois

22. Courtesy of U.S. Information Agency (New York Times, Paris Bureau), Record Group 306, National Archives and Records Administration, Washington, D.C.; photograph 306-NT-650–16

23. Courtesy of the Richard B. Russell Library for Political Research and Studies, The University of Georgia Libraries; photograph by Reeves Studios, Atlanta, from the Roy V. Harris Papers (RVHPF 26.05)

24. Courtesy of the Alabama Department of Archives and History, Montgomery, Alabama

25. Courtesy of Getty Images; photograph by Margaret Bourke-White, *Life* Magazine © 1956

26. Courtesy of the Library of Congress, Washington, D.C.; photograph LC-310663

27. Photo by *The Birmingham News* © 2004. All rights reserved. Reprinted with permission; copy print courtesy of Birmingham Public Library Department of Archives and Manuscripts (1076.1.48)

28. Oliphant © Universal Press Syndicate. Reprinted with permission. All rights reserved

29. Photograph by John M. Coski

30. Courtesy of *Richmond Times-Dispatch;* photograph by Don Pennell

31. Courtesy of Peggy Peattie; photograph by Peggy Peattie

32. Courtesy of Tucker H. Hill; photograph by Tucker H. Hill

33. Courtesy of *The Tennessean* [Nashville, Tennessee]; staff photograph by Kats Barry

34. Courtesy of the Louisville *Courier-Journal* © *The Courier-Journal;* photograph by Melissa Farlow

35. Courtesy of *Richmond Times-Dispatch;* photograph by Clement Britt

36. Courtesy of Special Collections, University of Mississippi Libraries; reprinted from *Ole Miss, 1965*

37, 38, 39. Courtesy of Peggy Peattie; photographs by Peggy Peattie

40. Graphic by Norma Pierce, Page One, Inc.

41. Graphic by Norma Pierce, Page One, Inc.

42. Courtesy of *Richmond Times-Dispatch;* photograph by Bruce Parker

43. SSOC button courtesy of Ervin L. Jordan, Jr.; photograph by Robert F. Hancock

44. Courtesy of Charles Nixon

45. Courtesy of DixiePix; photograph by John Shelton Reed

46. Photograph by John M. Coski

Index